MW01121175

Street Teaching in the Tenderloin

Don Stannard-Friel

Street Teaching in the Tenderloin

Jumpin' Down the Rabbit Hole

palgrave
macmillan

Don Stannard-Friel
Notre Dame de Namur University
Belmont, CA, USA

ISBN 978-1-137-56436-8   ISBN 978-1-137-56437-5   (eBook)
DOI 10.1057/978-1-137-56437-5

Library of Congress Control Number: 2016947042

Cover image © Jake Lyell / Alamy Stock Photo

Printed on acid-free paper

This Palgrave Macmillan imprint is published by Springer Nature
The registered company is Nature America Inc. New York
The registered company address is 1 New York Plaza, New York, NY 10004, U.S.A.

To the Tenderloin community: the secret garden

"Hi, my name is Moon." The man, dressed entirely in blue denim, sweeps his hands through the air, taking in the big, cavernous, concrete room. "This is my home." He seems like a nice guy. Moon reminds me a lot of the late, great folksinger, John Denver, with his neat, straight, long-ish, light-colored hair combed over his forehead. He even wears round wire-rimmed glasses, a silly hat on his head that he crocheted himself, has an easy smile, and is a natural-born storyteller, just like John Denver.

"Why are you here?" Chris, one of my students, asks.

"I killed two people. I take responsibility for my actions. I did it. I snapped one day. They didn't deserve it, and I accept full responsibility." Moon nods his head, affirming his commitment to the truth. He seems very sincere, just like John Denver, except for the murders.

As we walk out of Death Row, heading over to the death chamber—where Moon is sentenced to be strapped to a gurney, have a needle stuck in his arm, and die—our tour guide calls over his shoulder, "He beat his ex-girlfriend and her mother to death, with a fire log and a hammer."

What lessons are to be learned inside the walls of San Quentin State Prison? What new knowledge will we glean from our street teachers today, the men behind bars and those who keep them here? What do I say to Rebecca, a bright-eyed, enthusiastic sociology student and campus leader, when she whispers to me—in the noisy, chaotic South Block, where new prisoners in orange jumpsuits are being processed—"Right there!" She points to a shadow, moving behind bars on the second tier, "That's my brother's cell." Or Bianca, whose brother, now in Monterey County Jail in Salinas, is headed to the state prison in Solano? Or Crystal, whose little sister did time in Chowchilla? What can I say to these three young women, walking with their classmates and me through California's oldest prison? I say to them what I say to those who challenge me with, "What's the point of bringing *privileged* college students into prisons and the inner city?"

"The lessons we learn here will make our own lives more meaningful and purposeful, and the world a better place to be."

CONTENTS

"I wonder if I shall fall right through the earth! How funny it'll seem to come out among the people that walk with their heads downwards! The antipathies, I think – " (she was rather glad there was no one listening, this time, as it didn't sound at all the right word) – "but I shall have to ask them what the name of the country is, you know. Please, Ma'am, is this New Zealand? Or Australia?"

Alice, in Lewis Carroll's
Alice's Adventures in Wonderland[6]

"I remember sittin' *naked* on the back of a bull in a fuckin' rice paddy. Next thing, I'm dealin' dope in The TL. Fuckin' *crazy*, man."

Rey, Cambodian refugee

About the Author

Since 1978, Don Stannard-Friel has been Professor of Sociology and Anthropology at Notre Dame de Namur University (NDNU) in Belmont, California. From 1984 to 1993, he served as the university's Dean of Faculty, before leaving the administrative position to do "street sociology." Over the years, he has also been a lecturer or visiting professor at San Francisco State University, The Presidio (US Army) of San Francisco, University of San Francisco, University of California, Santa Cruz, Santa Rita Jail in Alameda County, and the Federal Correctional Institution for Women in Dublin, California. Before teaching, he worked as a waiter in Malibu, a cabdriver in San Francisco, and, for five years, a mental health worker on psychiatric wards that served the Haight-Ashbury and Fillmore Districts in San Francisco, during the cultural revolution of the late 1960s and early 1970s.

He has also served as California Site Director, Notre Dame-AmeriCorps; Founding Director of the Dorothy Stang Center for Social Justice and Community Engagement at NDNU; and was a Board Member, including Chair, of Indochinese Housing Development Corporation (IHDC) in the Tenderloin.

His recognitions include being selected as a California Campus Compact-Carnegie Foundation Faculty Fellow for Service Learning and Political Engagement, and on campus, The Living Torch Award, for carrying on the social justice mission and values of the Sisters of Notre Dame; the NDNU Mission Values in Action Award for Exemplifying and Promoting Social Justice and Global Peace; the Inner Fire Award, granted by the Center for Student Leadership; and the George M. Keller Teaching Excellence Award.

He was profiled by Julia Moulden (2008) in *We Are the New Radicals?* (as was his son, Sean, for his work promoting Philanthropy 2.0), a book about using one's workplace to contribute to positive social change.

Stannard-Friel has presented at professional conferences and been a keynote speaker on topics related to community engagement and service learning and has two previous books, *City Baby and Star: Addiction, Transcendence, and the Tenderloin* (University Press of America), a study of two female drug addicts in the Tenderloin, and *Harassment Therapy: A Case Study of Psychiatric Violence* (G.K. Hall and Co./Schenkman Publishing Co.), a result of participant-observation research conducted during the five years that he worked on the psychiatric wards.

His PhD is from University of California, Davis. His MA and BA are from San Francisco State University.

LIST OF FIGURES

INTRODUCTION

WHAT WAITS BELOW

GOIN' DOWN THE RABBIT HOLE

© The Author(s) 2017
D. Stannard-Friel, *Street Teaching in the Tenderloin*,
DOI 10.1057/978-1-137-56437-5

...it flashed across her mind that she had never before seen a rabbit with either a waistcoat-pocket, or a watch to take out of it, and burning with curiosity, she ran across the field after it, and fortunately was just in time to see it pop down a large rabbit-hole under the hedge.

In another moment down went Alice after it, never once considering how in the world she was to get out again.

Lewis Carroll
Alice's Adventures in Wonderland

* * *

On the streets, "Jumpin'" is the act of using illicit drugs to change the way the mind perceives reality and "Go down the rabbit hole" means to trip on a psychedelic drug or to enter into an emotional and intellectual state of chaos and confusion. But in concluding *Alice's Adventures in Wonderland*, Lewis Carroll wrote about how her big sister pictured Alice as a grown woman, "in the after-time," and "how she would gather about her other little children, and make *their* eyes bright and eager with many a strange tale, perhaps even with the dream of Wonderland of long ago." It *was*, in the end, a mind-altering experience, but not just a place of distortion or terror, as the street references infer. As the name implies, it was also a place of awe and inspiration, a place of wonder. You never know what waits below, when you jump down the rabbit hole.

* * *

"Beginning next week, we'll spend the rest of the semester in the Tenderloin," I tell my new Streetwise Sociology students. "Directions to Civic Center Parking and Wild Awakenings Coffeehouse are attached to the syllabus. After you park, take the stairs up to the Plaza, not the elevator. I want you to *observe* your surroundings. By 'observe,' I don't mean to just 'see' the Tenderloin. I want you to hear, smell, taste, and touch it, too. I want you to *feel* it. I want it to become a part of you, something you will always remember. A place you will take your friends or kids to and tell them, 'I remember.... I was part of this.' I want you to be able to say, 'I loved being here!'"

In the two-block, six-minute walk from the garage to the coffeehouse, the students will smell a mixture of urine and ammonia in the stairwell of the garage. They will be inundated with the sounds of emergency vehicle sirens or squawking horns, traffic noise, people shouting, and the hum of urban life. They will see the small, twisted, legless man, sitting in a wheelchair on the corner of Larkin and McAllister, selling *STREET SHEET* for a dollar. They may touch his heavily calloused hand as they pay for the newspaper. They'll encounter children, lots of them, many in small clusters, making their way to after-school destinations. They'll see a tall man in a long, dirty trench coat, wearing a bright purple pageboy wig, shaking his fist and shouting at Hastings College of the Law students going to and from their classes at McAllister and Hyde. Then, they'll hang out at Wild Awakenings Coffeehouse for half an hour, eating Middle Eastern wraps or deli sandwiches or baklava or an oatmeal cookie, while I drink my cappuccino and orient them to the neighborhood and what they will be doing for the next few hours and the next several months. We'll walk to the police station, four blocks away, to hear the community-liaison officer tell us about crime in "The TL." On the way, we'll pass by drug deals, streetwalkers, dozens of homeless people, elderly poor, and severely disabled.

Some of the students stay close to me; it's their first time here. Others, who have been in Tenderloin classes before, drift back to get a closer look at a new wall mural or to take an exaggerated sniff at the pungent smell of marijuana in the air. "Come on, come on," I encourage the stragglers. I don't care how cool they are, I don't want anyone falling behind.

Later, we'll reflect on the day, and talk about why things are the way they are.

* * *

Street Teaching in the Tenderloin: Jumpin' Down the Rabbit Hole is the story of what happened when—after 22 years of being a professor and college dean—I returned to San Francisco's high-crime, low-income Tenderloin District, a neighborhood I lived, worked, and played in as a young man, to write a book, *City Baby and Star: Addiction, Transcendence, and the Tenderloin,*[1] and wound up becoming a part of a community that most people abhor. While *City Baby and Star* told the stories of two female drug addicts, *Street Teaching* tells the story of my encounters, usually accompanied by students, with a wide variety of people who became our teachers in the Tenderloin. Many were people who lifted themselves or were lifted—or did the lifting of others—out of dire, often bizarre situations. Others died.

Street Teaching is about my students learning inner-city life by becoming a part of it. It's about our experiences, over a period of 20 years, in community-based learning (CBL) courses, using the Tenderloin as classroom and its people as teachers, as we immersed ourselves in this difficult and sometimes dangerous world, where children who live here normalize sex work, street crime, homelessness, poverty, and the deaths of young friends by suicide or murder, but nonetheless, find hope and inspiration in the good efforts of good people who work and reside here. *Street Teaching* is also about the lives of the college students, themselves, who opened up not only their hearts and minds to the community, but their own stories, as they shared their personal struggles with their fellow students and me, and with the people they learned from on the streets and in youth programs, soup kitchens, jails, service agencies, SRO (single-room occupancy) hotels, advocacy groups, government offices, and other inner-city organizations and other ways of life—people we call "street teachers"—as the stories of the inner city resonated with and reflected their own experiences in ways I never imagined.

* * *

Street Teaching in the Tenderloin is a personal story of teaching on the streets, told within the context of a social movement that has redefined the way many of us in the education community do what we do. Rooted in a century of development, CBL has now matured at all levels of learning. Direct learning, service learning, and community engagement are some of the names it goes by. Some call it "real-life learning."

The person reading this book, or someone close to you, has likely been exposed to this pedagogy when, in elementary school, you helped clean up the beach or a park; in middle school, served in a soup kitchen; in high school, sorted food for The Food Bank; in college, helped build a house with Habitat for Humanity or interned at a program for at-risk youth; in graduate school, maybe you wrote a business plan for an inner-city non-profit organization (NPO) or learned post-catastrophe redevelopment by going to New Orleans, Louisiana, or Joplin, Missouri. In the process, ideally through some kind of facilitated reflection and analysis, you learned something worthwhile about ecology, homelessness, hunger, poverty, politics, and the society that you live in. What began as community service (doing good), morphed into service learning (intentional learning, while doing good), and became community engagement (a broader range of CBL, with clearly identified reciprocal benefits for the student and the community) as the educational value of students participating in meaningful *exchange* (service for knowledge)—*within worlds that they are not usually a part of*—became apparent. As the practice evolved, it was discovered that students were more likely to be engaged in learning when the content has or takes on personal meaning, and they are more likely to retain and transfer knowledge to new situations when given opportunities to apply lessons to real-world issues.[2]

* * *

It is interesting that this "direct learning" movement has been happening at a time when "distance learning" has been seen to be the future of education. As the Internet opened up a vast new world of instant connections and communication, we developed the online ability to access people, places, and information hitherto off-limits to most of us. In schools, students now interact with people and programs in all corners of the globe and explore the universe beyond. Coming the other way, from home, libraries, community centers, workplaces, hospitals, cafés, and on the go, students access their schools. Distance learning has allowed people in isolated environments, or with restricted mobility, or everyday demands that inhibit enrollment in traditional campus-based academic programs, or simply because they prefer this approach, to engage in "remote" education. This is not a totally new concept—the postal system gave rise to correspondence courses in Europe and the USA in the mid-nineteenth century—but this is revolutionary, part of a restructuring of society and its major institutions—family, economy, religion, politics, education, and language—that the introduction of powerful new mega-energy shifting technologies[3] always produce. The Big Three transformations in history gave us the Agricultural Age (domesticating the land, animals, and ourselves), the Industrial Age (machines, standardization, and mass production), and, now, the Age of Information and Communication (electronics, diversity, and accelerated change). The first two were characterized by physically gathering great numbers of people into villages, towns, cities, states, nations, and international unions. The last transformation, propelled by the computer (and integrated miniaturization) revolution, is noted for reducing the practical, but not emotional, need for physical contact. Electronic technologies, while developing an intricate web of universal interrelationships, have also produced a massive disconnect of direct, physical, human-to-human contact. Increasingly, communication and transactions are conducted online between merchants and consumers, politicians and constituents, priests and parishioners, parents and children, teachers and students, colleagues, friends, and strangers. We can see, hear, and learn from each other over the Internet and cell phone communication systems from anywhere in the world. Distance learning is an incredibly powerful and useful method of teaching and learning. But it is not enough. By its very nature, it cannot teach that which can only be learned through human-to-human contact, the knowledge that comes from being in each other's *presence*, engaging in one another's lives as fully and meaningfully as possible. The potential to understand is enhanced by *intimacy*.

Distant and direct learning are not mutually exclusive pedagogies. Each can and does benefit from the other, as the practices are integrated in teaching methodologies. Many classes that promote community engagement use both. Both are outcomes of the paradigm emerging, which emphasizes interconnectivity, transparency, and participation (think of the use of Internet *and* direct interaction in the Arab Spring, Occupy, Black Lives Matter, and Hong Kong's pro-democracy political movements, or even calls for social gatherings, such as flash mobs, or online dating). And as distance learning becomes more widespread, so does CBL. As we leave the classroom to explore the online world of the Internet, progressively separating our physical selves from each other, we are also leaving the classroom, in increasing numbers, to learn from the physical and emotional worlds that surround us. Another revolution is happening—this one in education. Teachers and students are taking to the streets, not in protest, but to learn.

* * *

As *Street Teaching in the Tenderloin* unfolds, the reader, as was the "Tenderloin U" student, is referred to relevant online images, discussions, illustrations, and other Internet resources such as live, or archived, street webcams that pop up occasionally in inner-city locations—archived, because live street webcam broadcasters in the Tenderloin have had their equipment attacked and individuals have been threatened (see, e.g., "Adam's Block"[4]), so live webcams come and go; YouTube videos (e.g., a controversial police drug raid in an SRO hotel,[5] community cultural events, and inside San Quentin State Prison); websites, produced by neighborhood groups, such as The Standing Against Global Exploitation (SAGE) Project ("Working to bring about an end to commercial sexual exploitation"), Faithful Fools Street Ministry ("Discovering on the street our common humanity"), Vietnamese Youth Development Center (VYDC), Tenderloin Neighborhood Development Corporation (TNDC), SF Coalition on Homelessness, The Shooting Gallery (an art gallery), and San Francisco Police Department (SFPD)-Tenderloin Station; blogs and websites by locals (e.g., Mark Ellinger has a fascinating website (upfromthedeep.com) on the culture and history of "Central City"—the Tenderloin, Mid-Market

Street, and the 6th Street corridor—and his personal story of living there as a homeless, bipolar, heroin addict); specific articles on alternative and mainstream newspaper websites (e.g., *San Francisco Chronicle* reporter Kevin Fagan's award-winning "Shame of the City" continuing series on homelessness at SFGate.com); and other Internet sources to facilitate more access to the inner world of the inner city. But nothing—not even this book—can compare with what is actually out there in the streets. That's where the action is, and lessons that can only be learned from *engagement*. Fortunately (or not), there are tenderloins everywhere. Readers are encouraged to jump down their own rabbit holes.

NOTES

1. Stannard-Friel, Don, *City Baby and Star: Addiction, Transcendence, and the Tenderloin*, Lanham, Maryland: University Press of America, 2005.
2. Campus Compact, among the most prominent organizations promoting CBL, has a membership of over 1100 colleges and universities, with a combined enrollment of nearly six million students. In a recent survey, Campus Compact reported that 44 percent of students in member institutions participated in community engagement classes.
3. Mega-energy shifting technology: the widespread passing on human effort from our bodies to complex tools and other animals, to simple machines, to evermore complex machines. The direction, so far, has been to redirect energy consumption away from ourselves to our technologies, and in so doing, changing the nature of our relationships to each other.
4. See the street scene on "Adam's Block," an archived webcam on Taylor near Ellis Street, that went off-line when the broadcaster's life was threatened: sfcitizen.com/.../death-threats-force-san-franciscos-adamsblock-website-to- shut-down/
5. See video on "Henry Hotel Jan 5 2011 - YouTube."
6. For all references to Alice in Wonderland, see Lewis Carroll, *Alice's Adventures in Wonderland*, New York: New American Library (Signet Classic Printing), 2000.
7. Moulden, Julia, *We Are the New Radicals*, Columbus, OH, McGraw Hill Education, 2008.

CHAPTER 1

Wild Awakenings

SACRED SLEEP

© The Author(s) 2017
D. Stannard-Friel, *Street Teaching in the Tenderloin*,
DOI 10.1057/978-1-137-56437-5_1

"I am choosing to understand."

Becky Morrison,
Inner City Studies Student

* * *

A siren screams down Hyde Street hill, cutting through the low roar of street noise. It demands recognition, even from those too distracted by the effort of just staying alive to pay much attention to the flashing lights and big red-and-white box on wheels, screeching its way around Golden Gate Avenue. The wail continues for another block and a half, until the ambulance slams to a halt in front of a mound of rags, a bag of bones, left on the sidewalk by the rest of us. Across the street, inside old St. Boniface Church, lay more bags of bones, a 123 of them, driven in by a late rainy season downpour and chronic exhaustion. Squirming humps of dirty blankets and dark clothing are scattered among the long, intricately carved wooden pews, below the massive grand pipe organ in the upper balcony. A few brown bundles curl up on the red rug near the main altar, under the curving staircase leading up to the elaborately sculpted pulpit, left over from another day when St. Boniface served as the center of the immigrant German Catholic community in San Francisco. Then everything changed, and the Franciscan friars, in their brown, hooded robes and leather sandals, found themselves walking among the almost dead. It's quiet, except for the sacred sounds of sleep.[1]

In the back of the church sit Adam and the two Leslies, Inner City Studies students, bearing witness to what happens when a society throws its most vulnerable citizens into human trash bins.

* * *

Welcome to the Tenderloin—The Dumping Grounds, Drug Store, Tender Loin, Grey Ghetto, The Magnet, The Mental Hospital Without Walls— where 31,565 living bodies and 3000 almost dead are crammed onto less than a third-of-a-square-mile slab of concrete and asphalt, contained by walls of brick, stone, stucco, good intentions, power, arrogance, and ignorance.

The 2010 census says that 2709 of those who live here in San Francisco's high-crime, low-income, most inner-city neighborhood are children, but hundreds more live with too many others in too little space to be reported to the body counters. Families that crowd into studio apartments, stack bunk beds three-high in empty Murphy bed closets, and spread mattresses on the floor, don't tell strangers how many people live there,[2] especially when those people are here illegally or suffered unimaginable horrors at the hands of government officials in their homelands.[3]

Others squeeze into single-room occupancy (SRO), aka "piss-in-the-sink," hotel rooms, eight feet by ten, furnished, maybe, with a bed, a sink, and a chest of drawers, but no toilet, bath, or shower. These shared-with-many amenities are down the hall. No kitchens at all in the SROs. Meals are cooked surreptitiously on hot plates or in microwaves plugged into overloaded extension cords, or taken, with the homeless, at St. Anthony's Dining Hall, Glide Memorial's soup kitchen, or one of the little missions that trade the Word of God for food.

Those who can, when they can, break bread (scoop rice) at one of the many mom 'n' pop restaurants offering familiar food and reminders of homes left behind in Vietnam, Cambodia, Thailand, Laos, China, Latin America, India, Pakistan, Polynesia, Turkey, Ethiopia, Morocco, Russia, the Middle East, the East Coast, the Midwest, New Orleans, and Alabama.

On the streets, disheveled, desperately strung out female loners sell sex on the lower slope of the hill, spilling over onto Market Street and into the 6th Street corridor. For years, groups of transgender prostitutes, some strikingly beautiful, others not so much, trolled Larkin Street; young male hustlers did their thing in Polk Gulch, a few blocks north of City Hall; and animated women, standing in small clusters, wearing leather and heels, smiled, waved, and posed suggestively at commuters driving through Tendernob, the porous boundary where upscale Nob Hill and downtrodden Tenderloin merge. But their numbers dwindled as younger, computer-savvy streetwalkers—or their pimps—moved solicitation off the streets and onto the Internet, and the police corralled working girls into heavily curtained massage parlors, getting as many as they could off the street and out of sight by aggressively arresting pimps and johns. The Paradise Spa, Fuji Massage and Hot Bath, Hong Kong Oriental Massage, Nights of Paris, Sun Spa, The Butterfly, Springtime Parlor, Dragon Spa, and other body shops dot the neighborhood, some offering special deals like "Deluxe Massage," with "extra fees for extra service."[4] Casual sexual encounters, for money or drugs, take place inside strip joints, porn shops, X-rated movie houses, hotel rooms, and in alleys where dope fiends sell whatever they have to feed the monkeys on their backs.

The drug market here is like a Whole Foods produce section, but instead of polished apples and pears in the center bin, organic lettuce and broccoli crowns along the wall, and chopped up mixed fruit and prepared vegetable shish kabob in the cooler, it's heroin on Golden Gate Avenue, oxycodone on Turk and Taylor, crack and coke on Eddy Street, and methamphetamine on Jones. Smoke shops sell bongs, Zig-Zag paper, roach clips, pipes, and "Smelly Proof" baggies. Liquor stores sell mini bottles of hard liquor and fortified "Skid Row wine."

And everywhere are the almost dead: mentally ill zombies who wander the streets screaming, crying, laughing out loud, talking to themselves, or saying absolutely nothing at all; the homeless who make the sidewalks their home, alone or in clusters, many too strung out or drunk to care where (or who) they are; and the elderly poor, with nowhere else to go, but SF General Hospital or Colma, the city of cemeteries, where San Francisco sends its completely dead.

Poverty, prostitution, drugs, crime, violence, homelessness, mental illness, infirmity, death, and despair. Welcome to Tenderloin U.

* * *

"Kids coming!"

The raspy, female voice raises to little more than a whisper, but the message gets through. Hands stained from life in the streets scurry to hide the crack pipe from the little troupe of Southeast Asian children passing by, burdened with backpacks full of all the necessary things that schoolchildren need, or think they need, to do what they do at Tenderloin Community School on Turk Street. An ancient, white-haired lady in gray pajamas, a sleeping baby wrapped to her back, brings up the rear. The four homeless crackheads nod their heads and give little gap-toothed smiles at the beauty of healthy, young life passing by. The schoolkids take no notice of them, at all. A group of young Cambodian men deals dope on one corner; an early-bird transgender streetwalker struts her stuff on another. The sounds of sirens, traffic, hip-hop music, and people shouting fill the air. Becky, a student from Notre Dame de Namur University (NDNU), sitting with the homeless people as part of her class assignment in Exploring the Inner World of the Inner City, takes it all in.

Seven weeks earlier:

We're sitting in Wild Awakenings, a very funky coffeehouse in the Tenderloin. It's home base for our community-based learning (CBL) classes that meet weekly in the neighborhood. The Middle Eastern music on the CD player is loud. Raymundo, the manager, offers to turn it down. It's a nice gesture, but I decline it. The high-pitched music is as much a part of the inner-city world as the fire engine blaring its way up McAllister Street, or the crazy man, sitting at a sidewalk table, engaged in a furious conversation with himself. Victor, the owner, lets us use a rear corner of the coffeehouse, sectioned off from the rest of the large room by low ornamental walls, left over from another day, when this was a hotel lobby and the Tenderloin was a major jazz scene. We stretch yellow plastic "caution" tape across the two narrow entryways to reserve our "classroom," though we're often joined by street people who wander in or are already sitting there. Twenty students are plopped down on the big faux-leather couch, a couple of overstuffed easy chairs, and various kinds of straight-backed wooden chairs that have accumulated over the years. Victor warns the couch-sitters not to stick their hands down the back of the seat cushions. "You never know what you will find," he says with a wicked grin. "And do not put your hands in the wastebasket in the bathroom," he admonishes, serious now. It's not likely that any of us would, but needles, discarded by junkies using the bathroom as a shooting gallery, have stuck more than one unsuspecting hand.

It's Becky Morrison's turn to present her midterm research proposal to her classmates. "Most people believe that homeless people create their own problems. Unfortunately, this is the idea that I was taught, even though I was raised in a caring community. I am not blaming the community that I was raised in for this, because I know that those ideas came from the world they grew up in. These same negative, ignorant outside sources exist today. I honestly believe it is simply a misunderstanding that they have concerning the homeless situation. This misunderstanding of why people are homeless, for some reason, has had the power to maintain itself through generation after generation. I am choosing to understand. This semester, it is my plan to open my eyes and heart to my neighbors on the street, completely."

And she did. Just a few weeks before Becky submitted her proposal, the class attended a presentation by one of our community partners, "street teachers" we call them, on the plight of the homeless in the Tenderloin. Faithful Fools Street Ministry's mission is to help the greater community "discover on the streets our common humanity."[5] When we visited their offices near Turk and Hyde—once known as the "jazz corner of the West," when the world-famous Blackhawk Club was where a parking lot is now[6]—Becky learned about Fools' "Street Retreat" program, a day- to *week*-long experience on the streets, alone, without any money.[7] Fools explains, "There is nothing that anyone must or should do except trust that they will be led to that which is theirs to encounter in the day." Becky was led to Maxine, a homeless woman, who became her guide, her personal street teacher, through a day encountering the lives of homeless people. More than four decades earlier, I was led to the Tenderloin to encounter that which was mine.

* * *

The Tenderloin was my first home away from home, as a 20-year-old, after thumbing my way into San Francisco. Five years later, as a cabbie, I picked up my holdup man there. In 1995, after 22 years of being a professor and college dean, I came back to write a book about the community and met some remarkable people there. When service providers asked if I could provide interns and volunteers for their programs, I asked if they would talk to my students about their lives and the neighborhood. Out of this developed a network of people experienced in the ways of the streets—street teachers—who offer knowledge, expertise, and hands-on opportunities for students to learn lessons about life in the inner city, and in so doing, learn lessons about living life. Homeless folks, like Maxine, became our street teachers, as did drug addicts, inmates, ex-cons, prison guards, former sex workers, cops, service providers, residents, merchants, religious workers, artists, activists, government officials, street people, politicians, and youth. Eventually, I made the transition from being a professor, who teaches in the streets, to being a street teacher, myself, as I found my place in this complex community.

In the years that I have taught in the Tenderloin, I have become a different person, a better person I hope, certainly a better educated person, because of the depth of experience, passion to contribute, openness to our inquiries and involvement, and the diversity of backgrounds of the people we encountered in this challenging community—and because the lessons took place in a hard-core, in-your-face reality. Students report the same powerful, positive, personal outcome, as new insights and paradigms emerge. Milañ, an international student from the Marshall Islands, sent me this email after completing her fourth CBL class:

hello dr. don,

i want to thank you again for allowing me to attend your classes. "thank you" does not even come close to expressing my sincere gratitude for what you have allowed me to be a part of. i really, really needed this. these inner-city classes have helped tremendously in many ways, but most especially in my own personal healing.

i've gone through my lowest point in life these past couple of years feeling pressured, dealing with depression, as well as coping with the loss of a close friend, and it crippled me and left me thoroughly discombobulated. i lost myself in the turmoil. the things that i never had trouble with became daily challenges, and i lost focus. i have been a good student my whole life until then. for a while, i dealt with these problems quietly on my own. it took me a year to finally open up to someone about them and it was scary, but at the same time it brought a sense of relief.

i love community engagement/community-based learning, and i find quiet joy and purpose in taking an active part in your inner-city classes. i connected with the people of the tenderloin and developed a greater understanding and appreciation for the world that i had so scorned during my hard times, and in the process have also come to embrace myself and others. i have been truly humbled. the experiences that i have had in the city have been liberating, and i feel more hopeful than i have ever been. KOMMOL TATA! (thank you very much!)

milañ

* * *

Milañ Loeak is a tiny person, maybe 4′11″ and under a hundred pounds. She has light brown skin, dark brown eyes, and long black hair, usually tied up into a bun. She often wears a serious, contemplative look, but is a fun-loving person, with a great sense of humor, and her smile lights up her whole face. When I first walked the Tenderloin with her, I asked her how she felt being in a community so different from her own. "It *is* very different," she said. "But I like it. It feels … *real*." I was impressed with how easily this island girl adapted to the streets of The TL.

Milañ journeyed to the Tenderloin, outside of class time, with her friends, doing projects for the CBL classes. She spent some time hanging out with her Tongan-New Zealander soul mate, Justina, and her big buddy, 6′5″, 260 pounds. Drew, waiting in food lines, eating at soup kitchens, and wandering the streets together as part of Faithful Fools' Street Retreat program. She became the unofficial Tenderloin U photographer and, as part of her classes, helped organize Halloween in the Tenderloin, helped develop and presented at College Night (including giving a lesson on the Marshall Islands), volunteered with Project Homeless Connect (PHC) (helping more than 800 other volunteers provide services at a one-day event for nearly 3000 homeless people), participated in the Bi-Annual Homeless Count, and resonated with The TL in ways that, at first, were hard for me to understand. It was so different from the world that she came from. On the very first day that we walked the streets together, she looked at all the street people and said, "There are no homeless back home."

"Why not?" I asked.

"We have family." Then, she added, "We *do* have problems."
The Republic of the Marshall Islands is a tropical, Micronesian nation of atolls and islands in the middle of the Pacific Ocean, 4662 miles from the Tenderloin. The entire country has a total population of about 72,000, a little more than twice as much as The TL, the smallest neighborhood in San Francisco. Its embassy in Washington, DC, describes Marshallese culture this way[8]:

> Marshall Islanders are known throughout the Pacific and the world for their friendly and peaceful nature. Sharing with family and friends, a warm welcome for the stranger, and caring consideration for others are values inherent to the Marshallese culture. The people have nurtured these values over the centuries. Cooperation and caring are necessary elements of survival on these small islands, surrounded by the sea.
> The concept of family and community thus remain inextricably intertwined in Marshallese society. People still consider grandparents, aunts, uncles, cousins and far-flung relatives among their closest family. The strong family ties contribute to close-knit communities rooted in the values of caring, kindness and respect.

In a congressional study, the islands were also described as "by far the most contaminated places in the world," a result of massive post-World War II nuclear testing, including "Operation Ivy," the first test of a hydrogen device, which vaporized one island. Its power was estimated to be 10.4 megatons, 750 times larger than the bomb that destroyed Hiroshima. Later, "Castle Bravo," detonated at Bikini Atoll, had an *accidental* yield of 15 megatons (4–6 megatons were expected), more than *1000 times* as powerful as the Hiroshima bomb. The unanticipated yield, combined with an unexpected change in the weather, spread nuclear fallout all over inhabited atolls.[9]

In all, 67 nuclear devices were set off in the Marshall Islands, resulting in breast, lung, skin, and thyroid cancers, leukemia, infertility, and the discovery that the Atomic Energy Commission, through the Brookhaven National Laboratory, used the people as guinea pigs by returning evacuated people to contaminated areas, and then "planned and conducted test after test on these people to study their bodies' reaction to life in that contaminated environment."

A years-long governmental campaign of misinformation led to the intentional exposure of thousands of Marshallese to radiation, resulting illnesses and death. In 1994, Rep. George Miller, in a letter to President Bill Clinton, commented on an ongoing study,[10] "The findings of the thyroid survey are disturbing. The Committee has been informed that even if only 50 percent of the survey results are verified ... the incidence rate is still significantly higher, by a factor of 100, than the rate of thyroid cancer found anywhere else in the world." In February 1995, Marshall Islands officials testified before President Clinton's Advisory Committee on Human Radiation Experiments in Washington, DC, that fallout exposed many more than the four atolls acknowledged by the US government to radiation, and that islanders were purposefully resettled on contaminated islands so the USA could study the long-term effects.

But the long-term effects of such mistreatment were not just physical, and not just the result of radiation exposure. The relatively recent history of the Republic of the Marshall Islands is one of external control. After nearly *4000 years* of being completely off the beaten path, these inhabited islands, with their rich cultures, were "discovered" and later claimed by the Spanish, who sold them to Germany in 1885. Germany then "administered" the islands until its defeat in World War I, when control was handed over to Japan by the League of Nations. Unlike Germany's interest, which was mainly economic, Japan's was to establish a colony. A thousand Japanese immigrated to their new land and introduced, to the indigenous people, Japanese schools, taught the Japanese language, and encouraged Japanese culture. Japan manipulated the political system and tried to switch the traditional Marshallese matriarchy for a Japanese patriarchy, but in this they failed. Then World War II erupted, and Japan lost their colony, but only after raging battles devastated many of the islands and their inhabitants.

After World War II, the islands came under the purview of the Trust Territory of the Pacific, administered by the USA, until the Republic of the Marshall Islands gained independence in 1986. It was during the period of the Trust Treaty that the nuclear assault on the island nation and its people occurred. But the suffering went way beyond the effects of radiation. The Marshallese, in their "island paradise," had endured centuries of imposed dependency, deceit, physical and mental oppression, and societal manipulation. The results were just what should be expected from such political and cultural alienation: poverty, hunger, substance abuse, violence, and suicide.

A while ago, Radio New Zealand International posted this report on the Internet[11]:

Marshall Islands looks to deal with social problems among youth
The Marshall Islands government is considering putting up funding for projects to deal with youth related problems.
A team funded by the Asian Development Bank has spent several months meeting with urban and rural communities to identify the areas of most need.
The main issues to be focused on are teenage pregnancy, substance abuse, suicide, school dropouts, youth unemployment and a loss of identity and culture.

Sounds like the Tenderloin, to me.

When I recall Milañ's talk about the Marshall Islands at College Night and reflect on what, as a result, I later read about the impact of the violence done to the Marshallese people, I think about the comment in her email, "i've gone through my lowest point in life these past couple of years feeling pressured, dealing with depression, as well as coping with the loss of a close friend, and it crippled me and left me thoroughly discombobulated." Her best friend, a Marshallese boy, committed suicide. Even her tiny stature may be a consequence of the testing. "Growth retardation," it's called.

I think of Milañ whenever someone dismisses my CBL students as "naïve rich kids." Ninety-three percent of them, including Milañ, are on financial aid. And I think of her when I hear someone—from academia, The TL, or wherever—question the "appropriateness" of bringing "privileged" college students into the Tenderloin: "How's a four-hour class gonna change their minds?" or "Isn't it disrespectful looking at all the poor people?"

It is if you look at them with disrespect.

And a semester-long, four-hour-a-week class is not likely to *change* anyone's mind. The hope is to *expand* it, by connecting the inner-city lessons to what the student already *intimately* knows.

Substance abuse, being homeless, family violence, family incompetence, prison time served, sibling in jail, parent in jail, sibling on death row, alcoholic parent, drug addicted parent, parent murdered, sibling murdered, sibling suicide, sexually abused, physically abused, emotionally abused, emancipated teen, aged-out foster child, abandoned as a child, trafficked as a child, mentally ill, victim of a crime of violence, poverty stricken, undocumented immigrant, refugee from an oppressive regime, gross learning disability, crippling disease, life-threatening disease, disfigurement: this is not a list of qualities of people I have met in the Tenderloin. This is a list of students' experiences, *from all walks of life*, that I have taken *to* the Tenderloin. Lived experience, of the kind found in the Tenderloin, is no stranger to many (any?) of my students, no matter what their backgrounds are. Helping the student relate intellectually *and* emotionally to the lives of the people of the inner city—as a way of enhancing compassion and understanding (of the self as well as the other)—is a worthwhile challenge for community-based teaching. By appreciating the *social* and *shared* nature of the human experience, individuals can be empowered to engage in meaningful social and personal change.

Because of her own struggles, Milañ approached the Tenderloin with open heart and mind. She came to appreciate the social forces that underlie suffering in The TL and, by extension, in her home islands. She understood that her people's struggles are marginalized people's struggles, everywhere. And because she related to the inner-city community in an intimate way, and was able to contribute to it in meaningful ways, she found "quiet joy and purpose" there.

* * *

It was in August of 1963 that I first entered the Tenderloin. My brother, David, and I had just thumbed up the California coast from Malibu, the last leg of a cross-country journey. Our last ride, a cowboy in an old station wagon, dropped us off at 6th and Mission Streets. We spent the night right there at the Henry Hotel, sharing a shower and bathroom— and the blended smells of urine, mold, and cigarette smoke that permeated the stairwell, halls, and rooms—with quiet, gray, worn-out-looking men. The next day, we wove our way down 6th Street, past pawnshops, prostitutes, and panhandlers, crossed over Market Street, and entered the Tenderloin. We found a nice enough, clean enough, cheap enough room at the Lyric Hotel and paid our first month's rent.

For reasons related to the mild misadventures of young men with lots of energy and no goals, we left New Jersey, becoming a part of, what was just beginning to be, a great migration of young people to the Bay Area. We took off from the East Coast separately, agreeing to meet up in Los Angeles, at the apartment of an old girlfriend of mine. David arranged a ride to Chicago with a truck driver friend, then stuck out his thumb and headed to LA. A few days later, with $40 in my pocket, toiletries, and changes of clothes in a duffle bag, my thumb went out at the George Washington Bridge. Eighty hours later, with absolutely no sleep and only pizza, French fries, donuts, and way too much coffee in my belly, I was on

Route 66, driving the sleeping owner of a fast-moving sports car, convertible top down, through the Mojave Desert, enjoying the endless, starlit sky and the thrill of being a 20-year-old on the road. Years later, as a professor of sociology, I would use this experience in my Deviant Behavior classes at San Francisco State and NDNU in discussions about causes and consequences of hallucinations. As I wound my way through the nighttime desert, more than three days of no sleep and really bad nutrition caught up with me: cows appeared in my path, then turned into tumbleweed (and vice versa); a slow-moving elephant crossed the road (I stopped to let it pass); and, finally, headlights penetrated my consciousness (or absence of) as an automobile coming right at me, on the wrong side of the road, left the pavement and flew over the top of the sports car, at which point I pulled over and went to sleep. The next thing I remember was the voice of the sports car owner, "We're in LA."

Stories about my time in LA—sleeping in a Laundromat, hanging out at MacArthur Park, learning from homeless men there how to sell our blood, and find work, food, and shelter at "Finney's Flop House"—also found their ways into class lectures in various courses, as did other life experiences as my personal and professional lives evolved and intertwined. Storytelling, drawing on real-life experiences, became a fundamental part of my pedagogy, my teaching style. Crossing the country; working as a waiter at an ocean-side Malibu restaurant, which had seen much better times; living in the Tenderloin; driving the cab (and being held up at gunpoint); discouraging a friend, aspiring writer Paul Stine, from taking a job as a cabbie, but he did anyway, and was soon dead, murdered by The Zodiac Killer; participating in the campus strike at San Francisco State; living in the Haight-Ashbury as it blossomed to become the center of the universe and working for five years on the locked wards of the mental hospital that served the hippie neighborhood[12] as the peace-and-love paradigm withered on the vine; learning how to trance from then rookie, now prominent, witch-author Starhawk (trances that produced more material for my hallucination lectures, as did accidentally taking mescaline on the mental ward); teaching men in jail and women in prison; living in the pot-infested Santa Cruz mountains; exploring pubs and stone circles in England and Ireland and coffeehouses in San Francisco: all these experiences–and the stories of others I met along the way—became examples used to illustrate theoretical points and sociological concepts and issues in classes. Then, after more than two decades of teaching, I went back to the Tenderloin to write a book that became *City Baby and Star: Addiction,*

Transcendence, and the Tenderloin, and in so doing, had some of the most extraordinary experiences of my life. But this time, instead of bringing the experiences back to the class, I brought the class to the experiences. Instead of telling the stories, we entered them, becoming a part of the narrative.

NOTES

1. See SFGate.com/Shame of the City for Sacred Sleep program at St. Boniface Church.
2. See YouTube video on "The Battle for Accurate Census in San Francisco," www.youtube.com/
3. Tiffany Torrevillas, a former Inner City Studies student, doing work for the Census Bureau while studying for her master's degree in public policy at UC Berkeley, went back to San Francisco's inner city to knock on the doors of people who didn't return 2010 census questionnaires. She told me that, often, "we could hear muffled sounds, hear the TV on, but no one answered the door." In the 2000 census, 100,000 San Franciscans were overlooked, mostly in poor neighborhoods.
4. Cf., Zhu, Julie Chen, "A Chinese massage parlor: An inside look at an Oriental massage parlor in San Francisco," http://www.logoi.com/logi_notes.html, that "'Madam' in one parlor said, 'Just remember, …we only offer massage, nothing else.' She winks at us, 'Of course, the price is not rigid, and there may be some extra services. I cannot promise. You'll see when you come.'"
5. www.faithfulfools.org/
6. See, for example, www.morrisonhotelgallery.com/photo/black hawk club for an image and text on Miles Davis transforming jazz there in 1961.
7. Cf., http://www.sfgate.com/opinion/article/A-week-on-the-streets-An-odyssey-into-the-world-2677652.php
8. http://www.rmiembassyus.org/Culture.htm
9. See http://www.rmiembassyus.org/Nuclear%20Issues.htm#Chronology for discussion on nuclear issues in RMI
10. See http://www.rmiembassyus.org/Nuclear%20Issues.htm#Chronology for discussion on nuclear issues in RMI
11. http://www.rnzi.com/index.php (June 21, 2005).
12. For a discussion of the experience, see Stannard-Friel, Don, *Harassment Therapy: A Case Study of Psychiatric Violence,* Boston: G.K. Hall & Co./ Schenkman Publishing Co., 1981.

CHAPTER 2

Jumpin' Down the Rabbit Hole

Big D

© The Author(s) 2017
D. Stannard-Friel, *Street Teaching in the Tenderloin*,
DOI 10.1057/978-1-137-56437-5_2

Early in his term, Mayor Newsom made a habit of jogging through the Tenderloin. He didn't like what he saw. Police union boss Gary Delagnes had this response:

"With all due respect, Mr. Mayor, we could put a cop on every corner, and the drug dealers would just deal in between them," Delagnes said. "But if you are really tired of seeing drug dealers, there is one solution I could suggest."

"What's that?" the mayor asked.

"Try jogging somewhere else."

The City Obscure
All things San Francisco

* * *

Sam Soun graduated in sociology from University of Oregon in 2010, at the age of 29. Eighteen years earlier, in sixth grade, he dropped out of school, as, eventually, did his friends Phanna Phay and David Mack, and other Tenderloin children born of refugees from Cambodia, Vietnam, Thailand, Laos, and other war-torn, poverty-stricken countries. Sam is ethnically Cambodian, but he started life in a refugee camp in Thailand and grew up in the Tenderloin. As a little boy, his route to and from school was a walk through a gauntlet of social ills. He passed by homeless people lying in doorways, often passed out in their own vomit or feces; hungry people, waiting in long lines at soup kitchens; strung out streetwalkers selling sex to strangers; drug dealers hawking their wares; addicts shooting up or smoking dope; mentally ill, acting out the chaos of their minds; and predators of many kinds.

Years later, but before Oregon, Sam took four CBL courses with me in the Tenderloin.[1] In one of the classes, he told the story of his walk to and from school.

"What was it like for you, as a little boy?" he was asked, by a fellow student.

"What do you mean?"

"To walk by prostitutes and drug dealers every day."

A big smile spread across Sam's face, a look he comes by easily. "I walked by fire hydrants and streetlights, too."

What happens when the tragedies of the streets become normal to little boys? How is it that a neighborhood so abhorrent to most of us is embraced—even beloved—by many of the young people who live there? Why is it that we think that it is OK to push "misfits" among us into grossly under-resourced, leper colony-like enclaves, contain and maintain their suffering, then scatter disadvantaged children, their families, the elderly poor, and severely handicapped among them? How does one raised here find legitimate success, as many do, when all the cards seem overwhelmingly stacked against that happening? Why are so many insoluble social problems "insoluble"? And how does one go about finding the right questions to ask about inner-city life, let alone the answers?

Jump down the rabbit hole.

* * *

We're walking on Leavenworth Street, the spine of The TL. Fifteen students in Streetwise Sociology follow me up the hill. Across the street, sidewalk sales of CDs, tee shirts, old magazines (ranging from *National Geographic* to *Hustler*), kitchenware, and shoes are going on along the wall that leads up to MOMS Pharmacy, where a long line of patients wait for HIV meds and/or methadone. We skirt a drug sale taking place on this side of the street and a pile of what in any other neighborhood would confidently be called "dog shit." "Count the number of dogs you see today," I say. In two and a half hours, the answer will come back as, "None at all."[2] A guy taking a leak against a brick wall nonchalantly looks over his shoulder at us. We arouse about as much inhibition in him as the pigeons do, excitedly pecking at some dead thing in the gutter. We're headed up to Children's Playground on Ellis Street to help plan the Halloween in the Tenderloin Festival, a celebration that will be attended by several hundred of the kids living here. Diana Chin, the senior playground director, is our street teacher there today. As we walk by an apartment building between Turk and Eddy Streets, a huge figure jumps out of the doorway and blocks our way.

The students in Streetwise Sociology are frozen in their tracks. The giant looking down on them looks carnivorous. He surveys the flock like lambs being led to slaughter. Then he flashes a big Cheshire cat grin, "You students from the college?"

"This is Donal," I tell them. "You got a minute to talk?" I ask him.

"Nah, not today. 'Nother time. Gotta work. Mother-in-law's after school program." He's told me about this new job before. It's hard to believe. Security guard, nightclub bouncer, bodyguard, drug dealer: these are some of his other jobs we've talked about. Childcare worker? I don't get it. "Enjoy The TL," he calls over his shoulder, as he hurries up Leavenworth Street hill, causing other pedestrians to part like the sea, plowed through by an ocean liner.

"*Dude!* What was *that* all about?" a student almost shouts at me.

* * *

November 1, 1996:

The White Ghost cruises up the 200 block of Leavenworth Street and drives by a bunch of Southeast Asian kids throwing hand signs. "That's The Fish Stick Gang," Jimmy tells me. He holds up his hand and makes a "V" with it, two fingers on either side. "They send messages like this." He manipulates his fingers into different configurations. "It looks like fish sticks," he says of the various positions, holding up the thick "V" sign again. Jimmy points to the kids on the street. "We call 'em The Fish Stick Gang." I chuckle and smile at the three other cops in the car. None of them seems to be amused.

For a year now, I've been walking the streets of the Tenderloin, day and night, trying to figure out what's going on, what to write about, and working on feeling at ease in a neighborhood I used to feel comfortable in. When I came back to the Tenderloin, I felt threatened just walking by groups of street people. I was afraid that someone was going to confront me, yell at me, demand something, and/or hurt me in some way. That hasn't happened. Recently, I've been attending community meetings, looking up friends who work in the neighborhood, introducing myself to service providers and talking about developing CBL projects with them, and hanging around the Tenderloin Task Force police station,[3] watching the goings-on and taking ride-alongs with the officers. Jimmy was working hard to show me his world. He chatted with streetwalkers and pimps on Jones Street, while I sat next to him in the police car. He introduced me to a group of Southeast Asian gamblers in a little coffee shop on Hyde Street, startled by the sudden arrival of street cops and a tagalong, bearded professor. I ran the streets with him and his partners to get to the scene of an unfolding crime ("Faster than a squad car, sometimes," in this little, traffic congested neighborhood). And he introduced me to "The Fish Stick Gang."

"Let's go check 'em out, Professor," Jimmy says, as he pulls over to the curb and climbs out of the unmarked police car.

"Get 'em up," Jimmy commands The Fish Stick Gang.

"Shit, wha' did we do?" one of them says. "Damn! We didn' do nothin'! Jus' standin' here." He puts up his arms to let Jimmy frisk him. The arms go way up. The young man is huge.

"No problem," Jimmy says, after he and his partners check for weapons. "Put 'em down. Wan'cha to meet someone. This here's a professor. He's writin' about The TL. Wanna talk to him?"

The giant looks down on me, the cause of his humiliation, and surprises me. "Whadda ya writin' about?" he asks. Jimmy and his partners pull back to The White Ghost, out of earshot.

"The TL," I say. "People who live here, work here. Have you been here long?"

Just then, an Asian woman pushes her way into the crowd, talking in a language I don't understand. She looks worried. I ask one of the kids, an Asian boy with dreadlocks, "What's happening?"

He gives me a funny look, but says, "She wanna know wha's goin' on." He looks sheepish. "Tha's my mom. She wanna know if I do somethin' wrong."

The boy in dreads talks to the woman in what I think is Cambodian. The mother looks at me, points to him, and says in hesitant English, "He do somethin'?"

"No, ma'am. He didn't do anything." I shake my head. She looks over at Jimmy and his crew, hanging out by the big, white Chevy Caprice undercover police car, known on the streets as The White Ghost or The White Whale. "I'm writing about the Tenderloin," I say. "I'm just talking to the guys." She looks at me like I'm completely out of my mind, turns back to her son, and says something in their language.

"Is OK, Mom," he says in English. They exchange words that, again, I don't understand. She looks over at the cops, then at me. Her eyes look like she is in actual physical pain. She is obviously very concerned, but turns away and leaves her son with the crowd.

"You better come back some other time," the young giant says. "This is not a good time."

"That's OK," I say. "I'll be back tomorrow, OK? My name is Don." I reach out to shake his hand. He takes it. "What's your name?" I ask, handing him one of my business cards.

He looks at the card. "You a 'Donald'?" he asks. My card reads "Don."

"Yes," I answer.

"Me too. Donal. D-O-N-A-L. Donald, without the 'd.' It means 'king,' you know?"

"Yes, I do."[4]

Donal laughs and waves my card through the air. "I'm King of Leavenworth Street!" He looks down at me. "They call me Big D." His head is bullet-shaped; his hair is buzz cut. The arms are thick. The body is massive. The face is young.

"Big D," I repeat. "That for Big Donal?"

"No! Tha's for Big Demon." He dismisses me, "I see you tomorrow." The 200 block of Leavenworth Street is in the heart of what's been called "The Kill Zone," although that designation moves around. When I first came back to the Tenderloin, many of the young men who hung out along the middle of the block were Southeast Asian—Vietnamese, Laotian, Thai, and, especially, Cambodian (born in refugee camps to families that fled the horror of the Killing Fields)—but those who clustered near the corners were black (born into families that fled the apartheid of the Old South, winding up in San Francisco's housing projects). The groups didn't mingle much, except when they sold crack cocaine up at Leavenworth and Eddy. Then, color, culture, and competition didn't seem to matter much. There was plenty of drug money to go around on "Crack Corner."

The next day I went back down to Leavenworth Street to interview Donal. It was about 4:00 p.m. He was nowhere to be found. Three Cambodian girls, about 15 or 16 years old, were hanging out across the street. I walked over, gave them my business card, explained that I'm a professor, and told them what I'm doing in the Tenderloin. They looked at the card, then at each other, and turned away, but in a little while, one got curious. "You bring your students here?" she asked.

"I do."

"They think The TL is a dangerous place?"

"The TL *is* a dangerous place," I answered.

The girls giggled at each other and at this funny, bearded white man in Birkenstocks. "Naw," said the spokesgirl. "TL's cool. Ain' anymore dangerous than somewherze else."

"Do you spend much time somewhere else?" I asked.

"We go continuation high, '1950,' out in da Mission," (1950 Mission Street[5]) one of the other girls said, a high school for dropouts, teenage moms, at-risk kids, and teens with discipline problems, in another neighborhood (16th and Mission Streets) known for drug sales, prostitution, and street crime. "Rest a da time, we here. Why go someplace else?" she wondered. "TL's got it all."

The conversation reminds me of a play my daughter, Jessica, and I went to called "Take me to the Tenderloin, now!" put on by Pearl Ubungen's Dancers. For about six months, I shared an office with Pearl, cultural activist and community-based artist,[6] who had a dance studio in the old community building at St. Boniface Church, over on Golden Gate Avenue. She told me that she was inspired to do the play when she took a group of Tenderloin kids to Stern Grove—a wooded park in the Avenues, out near the beach—to hear a free concert by the San Francisco Symphony. On Sundays, in the summer, cold and gray as it often is, people come from all over to set up folding chairs, spread blankets on the grass, pop open bottles of wine or beer or mineral water or soda, eat grapes and cheese and sandwiches and the food of many places, and listen to all kinds of great concerts. Pearl's group was just settling in when one of the girls looked around at all the different kinds of mellow people packed together, the tall eucalyptus trees surrounding the wide meadow, the grass and bushes and the great, big sky, and she was overwhelmed. It was all just too, too much! She got a panicky look in her eyes, turned to Pearl and cried, "Take me to the Tenderloin, *now!*"

Pearl turned the experience into a multimedia production of dance (including neighborhood kids break-dancing); ten-foot-tall slides of Tenderloin street scenes and people, especially young people (a later version included a slide of Donal); music played by a small band; and the tape-recorded voices of children and youth talking about life in The TL.[7]

"Kids feel safe here, you know," Pearl told me one day, while I watched her teach a little kids' dance class at Tenderloin Children's Playground. "This is, after all, their home."

I asked the three Cambodian girls if they know Donal.

"Donal? He Big D. Ev'ybody know D," one said. They looked at me with suspicion now.

"I just met him last night. He said to come back today, but he's not here. I guess I'll catch him some other time. Thanks for talking to me." I smiled at them and began walking down Leavenworth Street, toward McAllister Street and Wild Awakenings Coffeehouse.

"You come back at night," one of the girls called after me. "You find Big D at night."

"Thanks," I said. "See you later."

They all giggled.

I went back to the 200 block of Leavenworth Street at about 10:00 p.m. I could see The Fish Stick Gang hanging out where they were the night before, but I didn't see Donal. I approached the gathering, nodded my head. "Hey, guys. How you doin'? Remember me?" No one responded. Except for sideways glances, I was ignored. Then one said, "Hi, you be the professor. Lookin' for Big D?" It was the kid with the dreadlocks. "He not here. He be back later, maybe."

"How are you doing?" I asked. I reached out to shake his hand. He took it, gave me a little nod, and we made small talk for a while. Most of the guys chatted with each other and just hung out along the wall, looking the other way, occasionally checking me out, but not showing any real interest, one way or the other. A few edged up to the kid with dreadlocks and listened to our conversation. Every now and then, one or another would throw in a comment or an observation. Everyone seemed relaxed and casual. I knew I was an intruder, but my presence didn't seem to bother anyone. I figured I was a novelty and, given my age and appearance, posed no threat of any kind. And even on the streets of the Tenderloin, the Asian community extends respect to the teacher. Nothing was going on around us anyway, not here in the middle of the block. All the action was on the corner, 150 feet away.

The kid with dreadlocks told me that he is Cambodian, his real name is Rey, but in America they call him Kevin, "An American name." His family fled the Killing Fields, just like so many of his friends'. "Like his," Kevin told me, pointing to a short, young man leaning against the wall. "Hey, Rey, come ova here," Kevin said.

The young man sauntered over to us, hands shoved deep in his coat pockets, a dark, flat-brimmed baseball cap pulled down low on his forehead. Kevin introduced us, "His name Rey, jus' like me, but in America, dey call him Rey." Kevin laughed, held out his arms, and shrugged his shoulders in a "Go figure" gesture. Kevin told Rey what I was doing in The TL.

"Will you talk to me?" I asked him.

Rey shot me a worried look, turned around, and looked up and down the block. "Whadda ya wanna know?"

"What's your life like? How did you get here?"

"How I get here?" Rey gave a disgusted kind of laugh. "My father carried me outta da fuckin' jungle on his back." Rey shook his head at the memory. "Da Khmer Rouge was killing everybodies. We was tryin' to escape, but got caught by da motherfuckin' soldiers. We saw 'em ahead, with, ya know, motherfuckin' machine guns, but it was too late to turn around. We figure dey kill us, but we was too weak to run. So, we keep walkin'. When dey saw me hangin' on my father's back, I was all skinny and sick and shit, with bones stickin' out." He spread his fingers out over his rib cage to simulate protruding bones. "We was *all* sick and skinny. Fuckin' soldiers just laughed and pushed us away. One shot his gun in da air to scare us, motherfuckin' asshole, but dey let us go. I guess dey figured we was dead anyways. So, my father carried me on his back till we got to da refugee camp. Then we made it here, to The TL."

"And how's The TL treating you, Rey?"

"Aww, is OK. Is hard. I just got outta motherfuckin' San Quentin. I gotta wife and kid, but I can't get a job. Nobodies wanna hire me outta Q. Sucks. Da wife and me fightin' all da time. She blame me, but *I'm tryin'*!" He looked like he might burst out crying. "I gotta get a mother-fuckin' job! I got a lead at a movin' company. Dis here's my friend Chea," Rey gestured to a young man on the edge of our group. "He workin' dere now. He gonna help."

His friend, another Cambodian, with a round face and short black hair, nodded once at me, but he didn't say anything.

"Ya know," Rey went on, "I remember sittin' *naked* on the back of a bull in a fuckin' rice paddy. Next thing, I'm dealin' dope in The TL. Fuckin' *crazy*, man." Rey shook his head. "I gotta go," he said abruptly. He turned to Kevin and said, "I see ya later." He shook my hand, nodded a goodbye, sauntered off down the street, and disappeared around the Turk Street corner.

I hung out with The Fish Stick Gang for a couple of hours. Every now and then one of the guys would walk up to Crack Corner, but most of the time, they'd just shoot the breeze, maybe take a toke or drink a soda or a beer, and stand around looking at the world go by. At around midnight I figured Donal was still a no-show. I said goodnight and headed for home.

It took three more trips back to the 200 block of Leavenworth Street before I reconnected with Donal. By then, The Fish Stick Gang almost seemed to welcome me. I'd just hang out with them, waiting for Donal. I heard he was in Las Vegas, or maybe Los Angeles. "He be back, anytime." Maybe tonight. Maybe tomorrow. Finally, I walked up Leavenworth Street and saw the big man pacing in front of one of the two apartment buildings that I learned from the gang he'd been hired to protect.

"Protect the dealers," a cop told me.

"Hey, Donal, remember me?"

"No cops tonight?" he replied. His voice was soft and gruff at the same time. Menacing.

"Just me." I said hello to Kevin and the other guys. I asked Donal, "You know Jimmy and his partners?"

"Jimmy? That the undercover cop you was with? Don't know his name. We call him Fish Sticks."

"WHAT?!" Fish Sticks? "*You* call *him* 'Fish Sticks'? That's what he calls you. 'The Fish Sticks Gang.'"

"He's 'Fish Sticks.' When he wants to fuck with you, he pats ya down, fishes around, sticks some shit on you and busts you for it. Sticks it to you. Fish sticks. Asshole."

"Uh, you don't know he calls *you* 'Fish Sticks'?"

Donal just looked at me like I was speaking another language. "Fuckin' cops always fuckin' with ya. Assholes."

We don't talk about fish sticks, anymore.

"Where are you from, Donal?" He looked Samoan or Tongan. I couldn't tell which, and wasn't going to guess.

"LA," he said. "I'm from LA. God's country." Donal's eyes constantly swept the street while he talked to me, as he paced in front of "his" buildings.

"Uh, LA. I mean, what's your ancestry? Where are your people from?"

"Tonga. My people's from Tonga. Tongan kings."

* * *

In 1996, Donal was, depending on whom you asked, a street thug, a drug dealer, a street warrior, a security guard, a gangster, or a community activist. In the years that I came to know him, through interviews, from conversations between Donal and my students, and just hanging out with him and his friends on the street, in his apartment, and the basements and backyards of the buildings on the 200 block of Leavenworth Street, he self-identified as all of the above, with the exception of "street thug." That came from others. Later, before he moved back to "God's country," he became manager of one of the buildings he used to guard on Leavenworth, a nightclub bouncer, and a childcare worker. Donal told me details of his life that I struggle with knowing, stories of violent acts he committed that I find appalling. On the other hand, he told me of acts committed against him, especially when he was a boy, that not only did I find incredibly disturbing, but they created the context for his worldview and the offensive, often vicious behavior that followed. He was highly regarded by some in the neighborhood, vehemently disliked by others. But he knew the inner workings of the community, had a fascinating (if bizarre) life story, enjoyed telling us his version of Tenderloin reality, and introduced me to others. So he became our first street teacher, followed by other young people of the neighborhood, and more than a hundred others, who willingly—sometimes spontaneously as we encountered them in their environments, but most often through prior arrangement as I came to know them—engaged us as we walked the streets and entered their lives. They answered our inquiries, opened up to us, literally opened doors for us to walk through into worlds hidden from passersby, and, in so doing, provoked more questions, leading to more answers, as the streets became our classroom and its people our guides.

What is it about our society that we produce neighborhoods where people shit and piss on the sidewalks? What was our government *thinking* when it relocated poor, war-weary refugees from a largely rural, agricultural, village-based Cambodian community—where more than a million and a half of their brethren were slaughtered by their own government, and many who survived suffered unspeakable horrors in concentration camps—to poverty-stricken urban slums? (What was the government thinking when it radiated then re-inhabited communities in the Marshall Islands, and what do these two *conscious acts* of our government inflicting suffering on already suffering people—Cambodian and Marshallese—have in common?) What impact does life in the inner city have on family life and the minds of children brought up there? What opportunities, in mainstream society, do young people of the neighborhood—born into families beset by poverty, cultural incompetence, and post-traumatic stress disorder (PTSD)—really have? Why have we, *as a culture*, normalized the world of the Tenderloin, and what *is* the normal world of the Tenderloin? And, in grappling with these questions, and engaging this community, what can we learn from the experience that will make our own lives more meaningful and purposeful, and the world a better place to be?

NOTES

1. Residents and workers in the Tenderloin receive scholarships to enroll in the Inner City Studies classes.
2. In the years since this particular walk up Leavenworth Street, dogs *have* become a more prominent part of the neighborhood, even among the homeless folks, but dog feces have not. Apparently, they are, generally, picked up, unlike the humankind.
3. The Tenderloin Task Force was the designation then for what would later become the Tenderloin Police Station. An old auto body shop and garage up on Eddy Street was renovated, and police operations in the neighborhood were moved from the basement of the seismically unsafe, abandoned Hibernia Bank building, to a permanent home across from Boeddeker Park. Drug dealers who hung around the park then moved to the steps of the old Hibernia Bank, a containment zone flow. When control pressure is exerted

in one problematic place, without addressing the root cause, the problem just moves somewhere else.

4. Not quite "king." Donald and Donal are Anglicized versions of the Gaelic names Domnall and Domhnall, meaning World Ruler or Great Chief. They were the names of many ancient and medieval Scottish and Irish kings, for example, Domnall Mór Ua Briain, the king of Limerick.

5. The term "1950" was the colloquial name for Phoenix High School, at 1950 Mission Street, a high school established for at-risk youth who get in trouble with the law, are expelled from their regular schools, are habitual truants, or dropouts, and 1950 has its own neighborhood problems. Near 16th and Mission, the area is notorious for prostitution, drugs, and violence.

6. See Pearl's website (http://pearlubungen.com/pearl/critical-response) for a powerful video illustrating her community-based art. The dance, "Refugee," took place in UN Plaza in the Tenderloin. It tells the horrible story of the Cambodian experience during the Khmer Rouge genocide of its own people.

7. See a review of "Take Me to the Tenderloin, Now!" at http://www.sfgate.com/style/article/Dancing-to-Tenderloin-s-music-3127676.php

CHAPTER 3

Hōküao's Tears

GOODBYE HŌKÜAO

D. Stannard-Friel, *Street Teaching in the Tenderloin*,

DOI 10.1057/978-1-137-56437-5_3

27

The Tenderloin is San Francisco's poorest neighborhood, a high-density, human services ghetto where hundreds of nonprofits and public providers serve a citywide caseload of homeless people in addition to treating the tribulations of the area's 30,000 residents.
Our hood is a mere few dozen square blocks cemented between downtown and Civic Center. Nob Hill is above, Skid Row below. ... [T]his historic, notorious neighborhood and its medley of people [is] absolutely the most diverse community in San Francisco, the heart of the city in more ways than one.

Tom Carter, Marjorie Beggs, and Others,
edited by Geoff Link
Death in the Tenderloin

* * *

Streetwise Sociology is walking down Leavenworth Street to visit the children at Indochinese Housing Development Corporation's (IHDC) after-school program. There is some kind of police action happening near the corner of Eddy, alongside Empire Market, just up from the pink IHDC building. Three police cars, with flashing yellow lights, are parked at the curb. A half-dozen men and women in blue are standing around on the sidewalk, and pedestrians and street people are clustered in small groups, checking out the goings-on.
"What's happening, Dr. Don?"
"I don't know. Let's take a look."
We cross the street and look in the direction that everyone else is. In an open space, between two parked cars, is what appears to be a small, young man, dressed in a light-colored tank-top shirt and faded cutoff jeans, kneeling on the pavement. His shaggy light blond hair and pale white skin contrast with the black asphalt and grime all around him. His body—folded over onto itself, his face buried in his lap, his forearms and hands pressed flat against the roadway—could be admired as being in some kind of remarkable yoga position, if it wasn't so pathetic. He is absolutely still. No movement at all. A white marble statue. But something about the body gives it a fluid appearance, more like a fleshy sack of water than stone. We, and everyone else, stand, stare, and wait for something to happen. Nothing does. He looks like a ball of lifeless flesh, a sad blob of humanity tossed in the gutter. Dead or alive? We can't tell.
"What's happening?" I ask a bystander.
"I dunno? He hasn't moved. It's been a long time. I think he's dead."

A siren breaks the relative silence, coming up Eddy Street. The big red-and-white city ambulance weaves its way in and out of cars trying, some not too hard, to get out of the way. It comes to a halt alongside the body and the EMTs take charge. The blob never moves at all as it is unfolded, examined, laid flat on a stretcher, and slipped into the ambulance. The door closes on another Tenderloin story.

"Let's go," I say.

"What's happening?"

"I dunno."

* * *

When I lived in the Tenderloin, it was a crazy neighborhood, but not this crazy. That was before we "deinstitutionalized" state mental hospital patients, with the stated intention of integrating the mentally ill back into the community. Actually, we abandoned many of them to the streets and SROs of our inner cities.[1] When I waited for a fare in my Yellow Cab at the Hilton Hotel taxi stand on Mason Street (where I met my holdup man) or drove for DeSoto out of their garage on Geary Street, there were homeless people here, but not nearly so many. That was before we cut the Federal government's support for low-income housing by 75 percent,[2] and, in San Francisco alone, eliminated thousands of SRO and other low-income housing units in urban renewal ("slum removal") projects designed to eliminate "blight." There weren't many children, either. Their numbers soared with the arrival of the Southeast Asian refugee families, after we lost the war in Vietnam (what the Vietnamese call "The American War"), and the rise and eventual fall of the murderous Khmer Rouge regime in Cambodia. The first time I remember hearing about children living in the Tenderloin was in the early 1980s when I read an article in *The Chronicle* about a Vietnamese girl's body being found at the bottom of an elevator shaft in a hotel. Pushed, jumped, or fell? No one knew. There were so few children in the neighborhood back then, I remember thinking, "What's a kid doing living in the Tenderloin?" There are more than 3000 of them now.

Other arrivals, since I first left The TL, included the AIDS epidemic, crack cocaine, oxycodone, and poor families from all over the world.

* * *

We're walking the streets, again. The class today is Promise of the Inner City, but the same question has been asked by students walking these same streets in all of my other CBL classes that have used this neighborhood as classroom: Exploring the Inner World of the Inner City; Streetwise

Sociology; Analyzing Social Settings; Sports, Service, and Society; and Tenderloin Immersion:

"Dr. Don, if I can see all these drug deals, why can't the police?"

"They can," I answer.

The Tenderloin is a "containment zone," of the kind found in every big city where certain kinds of "deviant" street behavior—open-air drug use and sales, prostitution, homelessness, and the bizarre behavior resulting from untreated or untreatable mental illness—are, to a greater or lesser degree, tolerated by the general community, but not elsewhere, so the behavior won't spread to those elsewheres. Everybody knows they exist, though an official policy of containment is denied.[3] Locals know where to find them. Tourist guides warn travelers to avoid them,[4] thereby telling out-of-towners where they can buy sex and drugs. They've been called "the red light district" (from red paper lanterns hung outside brothels in ancient China), "tenderloin," "slum," and "skid road" (referring, at first, to corduroy roads used by lumberjacks to skid logs through the woods, before it came to mean the logging camps, themselves, which attracted prostitutes, large-scale alcohol consumption, and general rowdiness. The name evolved to become "skid row" in the cities).[5] In San Jose, it was East Side. In Los Angeles, The Nickel or just Skid Row. In Portland, Old Town; in Seattle, Pioneer Square. In Denver, Colfax. In Honolulu, Chinatown. In San Francisco, it's the Tenderloin, uppercase "T," the official name of the neighborhood. The likely explanation of where the name came from is that it originated in New York's nineteenth-century Midtown entertainment district, where vice, graft, and corruption were so great, even the cop on the beat could bring home the best cut of beef to his family, the least stringy, most tender part, cut from the loin: the tenderloin.

Each of the many Tenderloin monikers—"The Dumping Grounds," "The Drug Store," "Tender Loin," "The Grey Ghetto," "The Mental Hospital Without Walls"—tells a story, but "The Magnet" tells it all. This is not just a zone to contain society's poor castoffs. It is also a neighborhood that is organized to *attract* them. With the city's highest concentrations of soup kitchens, shelters, rehab programs, clinics, and social service agencies (what the authors of *Death in the Tenderloin* refer to as a "human services ghetto"[6]), those in need are *lured* here. Some argue that it's the *services* that are lured here, because this is where the people who need them are. It makes no difference which perspective is right. The outcome is the same. New arrivals continually flow in because individual survival often depends on access to these services. Add to the mix the relatively cheap rooms and supportive housing in some of the SROs, community tolerance for low-level street crime and sidewalk society, intolerance of the street scene in other neighborhoods and the lack of services and "affordable" housing elsewhere, and the reasons are clear why so many come and stay, producing the highest density of poor people in San Francisco, squeezing them into an area less than a third of a square mile, bordered by Market Street, Powell, Post, and Van Ness, the "official" boundaries of the Tenderloin. In reality, the culture spreads onto Market Street, crosses over, and travels a few blocks south into the 6th Street corridor, aka "Winery Row."

Forty percent of San Francisco's parolees live in the Tenderloin. The Tenderloin Police Station, patrolling the smallest area of any precinct in San Francisco, typically makes more arrests than any other station in the city. It is here, more than anywhere else in San Francisco, that the visibly homeless, mentally ill, and drug-ravaged walk the streets. But it may be behind closed doors that the real danger lurks.

The Megan's Law Web site reports 997 registered sex offenders living in San Francisco, with the highest concentration in the Tenderloin.

With its affordable apartments and high concentration of residential hotels, the Tenderloin has become a haven in the last 20 years for sex offenders, as well as immigrant families and those down on their luck.[7]

Recently, a growing number of Latino families have added to the community of poor refugee families from Southeast Asia, Eastern Europe, Africa, and the Middle East (especially poverty-stricken Yemen, even before the Arab Spring uprising[8]). Gentrified out of the historically Mexican Mission District by hipsters and young hi-tech workers, pushed out of large, multi-bedroom flats—especially in the old Victorian buildings that survived, relatively unscathed, by the 1906 earthquake and fire, or equally large living units in post-earthquake Edwardian flats that replaced the buildings that *did* burn or fall down—many displaced Latino families have wound up crammed into tiny units in the Tenderloin. So many poor, dislocated, relocated families from all over the world have taken up residence in the Tenderloin—built to be a workingman's neighborhood (housing the single men who came to rebuild the city after the 1906 earthquake), evolved to be a containment zone, never meant for families—it now has the highest concentration of children of any neighborhood in San Francisco.

That's not all bad.

* * *

I like to take guests on tour of the Tenderloin: fellow professors, jour-
nalists, community activists, students from other schools, members of civic
organizations, and my own family members. One stop I always enjoyed
was the pink IHDC building on Eddy Street. Passersby easily miss the
doorway. It's a basement entryway, covered by a steel gate bolted to the
brick wall. Four cameras monitor what's going on inside and outside the
building. Open the gate. Watch your step! A wooden staircase leads down
to the concrete floor. A heavily used pool table stands off to one side. The
click of wooden balls competes with street noise outside. Tough-looking
young men pause from the game to see who is coming in. They peer at
us with Asian eyes that have seen way too much suffering: parents' lives
wrecked by war, siblings dead from suicide, friends in jail, families destroyed
by everything. My tour guests freeze for a moment on the wooden staircase. Their initial thought, "What have I got myself into?" turns into,
"What has *he* gotten me into?" Their wide eyes shift to me. "Follow me,"
I say cheerfully, as I slap hands, awkwardly (I never seem to get it right),
with the young "toughs," who are taking a break from mentoring little
kids in the back rooms. The basement is full of children happily using
computers in one room, or sitting at a conference table doing art projects
or homework. Further back in the basement, tutors help with reading, or
writing, or spelling, or math. Older girls are teaching younger ones traditional Cambodian dance. The smell of food wafts from the tiny kitchen:
after-school snacks. A neon "Smoothies 'R' Us" sign glows in a window,
part of a healthy food, anti-soft drink program. A wall is covered with this
month's "Cool Words": CLIMATE, SACRIFICE, POWER, COMPOST,
RECYCLE, OXYGEN, PEACE, DEFEND, DESTROY. Out back kids
scale the climbing wall, or play basketball, or sit in the tree house, or
work in the garden. Nothing here is fancy, but it works. This is IHDC's
Tenderloin Achievement Group (TAG), an after-school program.

The Tenderloin is full of pockets of wholesomeness, scattered throughout the neighborhood, drawn to where the children are. Some, like TAG,
are tucked away in basements or storefronts with little or no signage indi-
cating what's inside. Others have prominent signs on or over their doors
or large photographs of children in the windows, announcing what's
going on inside, hoping to move along whatever is—but isn't supposed to
be—going on outside. IHDC's TAG; Tenderloin Children's Playground;

Vietnamese Youth Development Center (VYDC); The Boys and Girls Club—Tenderloin Clubhouse; Tenderloin After-School Program (TASP); Bay Area Women's & Children's Center (BAWCC); Janice Mirikitani/Glide Family, Youth, and Childcare Center; Cecil Williams-Glide Community House; Larkin Street Youth Center (for homeless kids); De Marillac Academy; San Francisco Christian Academy; The Salvation Army's after-school program; and Tenderloin Community School are some of the organizations that we've developed programs or participated in events with. What they all have in common is an absolute commitment to serving disadvantaged children, a dedicated staff, expertise in working with inner-city youth, and being deeply connected with the communities that they serve. Many of their workers grew up in the neighborhood or have long-term ties. Diana Chin was senior playground director at Tenderloin Children's Playground when she "retired" (a controversial departure, in response to the way the City managed budget cuts), after more than 20 years in the neighborhood. Kay Rodrigues, another longtime director, immersed her own children in celebrations and educational programs at the playground. Sammy Soun, a Youth Director with the Boys and Girls Club, was born in a refugee camp in Thailand, but grew up here, as did his older brother, Sam (the name "Sam" is part of many Cambodian names, male and female, even in the same family: "Sambat," "Sambath," "Samnang." It means "good fortune"), my former student, who worked for years at VYDC and IHDC before heading off to college in Oregon. Midge Wilson, Executive Director at BAWCC for more than 30 years, lived here for 20 of those years. Her office manager, Nancy Ong, was 11 years old in 1979, when her parents and their eight children—a "boat people" family—moved in with eight relatives in a two-bedroom apartment in the Tenderloin. Judy Young was a teenage member of VYDC; now in her 30s; she is Executive Director. Tom Heath, a relative newcomer, was Program Director at IHDC from 1999 to 2013, a position he assumed after regularly volunteering at the after-school program when he was a banker, a career that, for him, is now ancient history. He left IHDC to become a supervising social worker for the County of San Francisco. These dedicated youth workers—and others working with the prostituted, homeless, drug addicted, mentally ill, poverty-stricken, and refugees—are all core street teachers for Tenderloin U.

Intensifying the bonds between service providers and children, and the children with each other, is the tension that is always palpable in the neighborhood. While the crime, insanity, and extreme deprivation that walk these streets may be "normalized" by the children who live here, it is normalized as ever-present danger. Bad things happen here, and when people are threatened, they cling together.[9] Combine this with the same village-based heritage of many of the people in the Tenderloin and the actual extended family relationships that exist among so many of them, and the result is a deep, emotional bond between members of the various communities and the people who work with them. So much so that children *want* to be here and take pleasure in being here, as was expressed by Laura Soun, Sam and Sammy's little sister, now a teacher at San Francisco City Academy on Eddy Street, who told me in 1999, at our first College Night event, when she was 13 years old, and many times since, "I love living in the Tenderloin."

Many of my students love the Tenderloin, too, as they bond with the children, service providers, and others, and the community becomes embedded in their souls.

* * *

Hökūao squeezed into the tiny elevator, already packed with five children and Diana Chin, still, then, the senior program director at Tenderloin Children's Playground. Over three years, Hökūao had taken every class I offered in the Tenderloin, and for the past year had tutored these kids as part of an internship with Diana. As our school year was ending, the children took him to meet their father and see their home. The building on Larkin Street looked OK from the outside, but inside, not too good. "Well," Hökūao told me later, "I thought the kids were always clean and well cared for. The apartment was probably neat and tidy, just like they are."

When the sliding door closed, one of the children pushed a button and the elevator lurched down. "Down?" Hökūao wondered, "Why down? The apartments are all upstairs."

The elevator came to an abrupt, bone-jolting halt, and the door creaked open. Five kids bolted out and signaled for Hökūao and Diana to follow. Hökūao looked around. It was a dark and dirty basement that the children led him into. "Man, what's this all about?" he said aloud. The giggling kids ran across the littered floor and pushed open a door. "In here," they shouted. "This way, Hökūao."

Hökūao entered the basement apartment. He was met at the door by the children's father, who bowed his greetings. He was honored by this visitor's presence. Hökūao had become an important person in his children's lives. He was their teacher. Hökūao looked around. The apartment was a disaster. Clutter was everywhere. Black mildew grew on the ceiling and walls. And everywhere, there were shoes. In every nook and cranny, on top of the furniture, stuck on shelves, on countertops, everywhere, shoes. Dozens of pairs of shoes. Why so many shoes for five kids and their dad?

The father waved his hand around the room. "This is my home. This is where we live. Follow me," said the hands of the man who could only speak his native tongue. He walked across the packed living room and opened the doors to the two bedrooms so Höküao and Diana could see where the children, who they tutor every day, sleep every night. Höküao poked his head through the doorways, but couldn't enter the rooms. The floors were covered with mattresses. Lots of mattresses and more shoes. "How many people sleep here?" he asked the children. "Fourteen," he was told. "Fourteen people!" Höküao repeated to Diana, "In two tiny bedrooms."

The kids were so excited to show their home to Diana and Höküao. Höküao and Diana were devastated. When they got back to the playground, Diana, a seasoned veteran of working with inner-city kids, cried for these and all her children. So did Höküao, who would soon be leaving them. He was graduating in a few days and returning to his native Hawaii.

Before he left for home, Diana and the children of the Tenderloin held a goodbye party for Höküao. Latino, white, African-American, but mostly Cambodian and Vietnamese children cut slits in newspapers, wrapped them around their waists as grass skirts, and did a hula for Höküao, his family and me, to Don Ho singing, "I'll Remember You."[10]

It only took the first stanza for the tears to flow, again.

* * *

Höküao's tears tell the story of the Tenderloin. His deep sadness over the living conditions of the children he tutored reflects what most people from outside perceive all the Tenderloin to be and what they see when they drive (few walk) through the neighborhood: poverty, filth, chaos. But his tears of joy were in response to what he experienced here, too: the relationships he established over the three years that he took CBL classes, helped organize service-learning projects, and volunteered at Tenderloin Children's Playground. He found a powerful, loving community that helped him become what he became.

On the afternoon of his graduation from the university, as he was packing to go home to Hawaii, Höküao sent me a card, with a photograph of himself, happily posing with two kids at the Tenderloin Children's Playground on the cover, and this note inside:

Aloha Dr. Don,

Well, I guess this is somewhat it! It's time to go back to Hawaii to my
next aspect on my journey. Thank you so much for inspiring me, immersing
me, and guiding me in the Tenderloin. It truly has had a huge impact on my
life and was a life changing experience. I will never forget all that has happened and I will treasure those memories in my heart forever. I have been
asking the Gods lately what to do, for I am so very passionate about both
worlds. I know the Tenderloin exists everywhere, but each one is unique in
its own way. I have formed a connection here in S.F., especially at the playground that I don't want to lose. This fire burns hotter and hotter within
me and I know that I will come back someday, but the T.L. is a place of
healing and a deep sense of care. Both are beautiful!! Both are spiritual!!
Both are full of love! I can see why you were so drawn to the Tenderloin so
much. I appreciate all that you have done for me Dr. Don and I will never
forget it. Words truly cannot describe how grateful I am for having you and
the Tenderloin in my life. We will be in touch!
    Mahalo. Mālama pono. Na ke akua e ho'opōmaika'i iā 'oe a me a hui
hou!
    (Thank you. Take care. God bless you always until we meet again!)
    Me ke aloha,
    Hōkūao

Hōkūao Pellegrino did go home to Hawaii, where he obtained a second Bachelor of Arts degree in Hawaiian Language from Ka Haka 'Ula
o Ke'elikōlani, Hawaiian Language College at University of Hawai'i at
Hilo, and followed that up with a master's degree. He studied indigenous
cultures on Rapa Nui (Easter Island) and Tahiti; received a Hawai'i State
Foundation Grant on Culture and Arts and apprenticed under master
craftsman Kana'e Keawe to research and craft traditional implements used
in kalo farming and poi making; taught Hawaiian Studies at his alma mater,
St. Anthony's High School, and Kamehameha Schools, Maui Campus;
and was a part-time instructor for the Hawaiian Language College at UH,
Hilo, where he taught Hawaiian Ethnobotany and an interdisciplinary
course on traditional and modern kalo cultivation. Hōkūao also worked as
the Cultural Landscape Curator at 'Imiloa Astronomy Center of Hawai'i,
where he managed and maintained one of Hawaii's largest native plant
landscapes, developed educational curriculum surrounding the many rare
and endangered species still growing there, propagated native plants, and
archived and curated the Center's native Hawaiian artifacts collection.

In 2008, Hōkūao was awarded a fellowship in the First Nations' Future Program, a year-long intensive indigenous leadership training program, where he joined fellow Hawaiians, Native Americans, and Māori at Stanford University and the North and South Islands of New Zealand.

Hōkūao went to work for Kamehameha Schools' Enrichment Department as the Hawaiian Cultural Resource Coordinator—Maui Region, and he's currently its Land Education Specialist. With his new wife, Alana, with whom he has a young daughter, and his parents, he is a wetland-kalo farmer and cultural resource specialist for the family's kuleana land (Noho'ana Farm) in Waikapū, Maui, and is an activist on Native Hawaiian water rights with Hui o Nā Wai 'Ehā, Earth Justice Environmental Law Firm, and The Office of Hawaiian Affairs.

The year after graduating from NDNU, Hōkūao flew back to the Tenderloin to participate in Halloween in the Tenderloin, one of the projects he helped develop. For years, a space on the roof of the playground included "Hōkūao's Garden," filled with exotic plants he sent from Hawaii. And at the playground, children enjoyed pineapples he mailed from home. Diana smiled and shook her head, when the first batch arrived. "I coulda bought 'em at Safeway for less than the postage, but it's the thought that counts."

Hōkūao's life was shaped by his time in The TL, as he helped shape the lives of the children he worked with. For students who study here, it is a remarkable place. What they learn in the Tenderloin are not abstract lessons in sociology. What they learn here are lessons immersed in *their own* reality; they are lessons about life—and death. For good or ill, this is *real*. There is great joy in this neighborhood, and great sadness.

NOTES

1. Mental Illness Policy Org. (http://mentalillnesspolicy.org) reports: "At any given time, there are many more people with untreated severe psychiatric illnesses living on America's streets than are receiving care in hospitals."
2. Davey, Joseph Dillon, *The New Social Contract: America's Journey from Welfare State to Police State*, Westport, CT: Praeger: 1995, p. 47.
3. An aide to the mayor told Anthony Miller, an immersion student staying a week with us in the Seneca Hotel on 6th Street, "It is not the policy of the City to contain crime." But looking out of the Mayor's own City Hall office window, the consequences of just such a policy, the many bodies sleeping in Civic Center Park, are plain to see.

4. Cf., www.virtualtourist.com: *Areas to Avoid in San Francisco and other Warnings* and www.streetadvisor.com: *Tenderloin Guide*.
5. The term "skid road" dates back to the nineteenth century, when it referred to corduroy roads made of logs, used to skid or drag logs through woods. The term came to refer not just to the corduroy roads themselves, but also to the logging camps.
6. Carter, Tom, Marjorie Beggs and Others, ed. Geoff Link, San Francisco: Study Center Press: 2012, p. 3.
7. Martin, Adam, "Police resist sexual predator's S.F. placement," *San Francisco Examiner*, Jan 13, 2007.
8. Yemen is one of the poorest countries in the Middle East, with 40 percent unemployment, dwindling natural resources, rapid population growth, political turmoil, internal warfare, and no functional government.
9. Erickson, Kai, *Wayward Puritan: A Study in the Sociology of Deviance*, Upper Saddle River, New Jersey: Prentice Hall, 2004, presents a sociological explanation on group formation in response to threat, real or perceived.
10. Words and music by Kui Lee.

CHAPTER 4

It Was a Terrible Time

U Sam Oeur

Poet/Survivor

© The Author(s) 2017
D. Stannard-Friel, *Street Teaching in the Tenderloin*,
DOI 10.1057/978-1-137-56437-5_4

More than two decades after they fled the Khmer Rouge reign of terror, most Cambodian refugees who resettled in the United States remain traumatized, a study funded by the National Institutes of Health's (NIH) National Institute of Mental Health (NIMH) and National Institute on Alcohol Abuse and Alcoholism (NIAAA) has found. Sixty-two percent suffered from Post Traumatic Stress Disorder (PTSD) and 51 percent from depression in the past year—six-to-seventeen times the national average for adults. The more trauma they endured, the worse their symptoms.

NIMH press release[1]

* * *

The poster on bulletin boards at Tenderloin Children's Playground, The Boys and Girls Club, TASP, Salvation Army, and VYDC, and in the window of BAWCC read:

**Indochinese Housing and
Notre Dame de Namur Tenderloin University
Present**

**CAMBODIAN POET
U SAM OEUR**

READING FROM HIS NEW BOOK
Crossing Three Wildernesses

MONDAY MARCH 6, 2006
6:00 - 7:30 P.M.
375 EDDY STREET (left door)
for more info call Tom 441-2873

U Sam Oeur was born in the Svey Rieng province of Cambodia. He received his
MFA from the Iowa Writer's Workshop in 1968. He was elected to the Cambodian
National Assembly in 1972 and in 1973 was appointed Secretary of the Khmer
League for Freedom. In 1975, he and his family were imprisoned in the first of six
concentration camps they endured over the next four years. It was a terrible time.

Dinner will be served

Illustration 4.1   IHDC flyer

Not all street teachers in Tenderloin U come from the streets, or even the inner city. On two occasions, the authors of scholarly books we were using in class came to the Tenderloin to talk about their work, because they were intrigued by the concept of CBL in this particular neighborhood, and that some of the classes included Tenderloin youth as students. Some other outsiders, with expertise in various fields related to work in the inner city, met us at Wild Awakenings, or conference rooms in Tenderloin service agencies, or at their own offices scattered throughout the city. And not all Tenderloin U students come from the university. People from the neighborhood can enroll in the 4-unit Inner City Studies classes for $30 instead of the $3896 it would cost them if they were regularly enrolled part-time students. And, in addition to the classes and community events, we put on occasional educational programs for kids in the neighborhood. The poetry reading at IHDC was one such event.

U Sam Oeur's expertise as a street teacher was the knowledge he gained in suffering the horrors of the dictator Pol Pot's Khmer Rouge regime. Emerging from the Cambodian Communist Party, which was formed in the 1940s to fight French colonization, the Khmer Rouge seized power in 1975, in the turmoil at the end of the Vietnam War, and initiated a program designed to eradicate Western influences and impose an "agrarian civilization." More than 1.7 million Cambodian people, out of total population of 7.9 million, were executed or died in concentration camps or on forced community evacuations from disease, starvation, or exhaustion.

I first met Sam at NDNU in 2002, when a colleague, the artist Charles Strong, brought him to speak to my campus-based cultural anthropology class. He told us his story and read from his book, *Sacred Vows*, a collection of poems that describe the beauty of Cambodian culture and the terror that emerged from within after the end of the Vietnam War. This time, four years later, Sam was back in town promoting *Crossing Three Wildernesses*, his memoir of three of those terrors: death by execution, death by disease, and death by starvation. With some trepidation, because of the stressful impact hearing about these horrible experiences might have on a young audience, I invited him to come into the Tenderloin and read to the youth at IHDC, many of them regulars in our service-learning projects and the offspring of Cambodian refugees.

On the day of his reading, I met Sam and Charlie at Wild Awakenings and we walked the three and a half blocks through the Tenderloin to IHDC. It was a sunny day, not unusual here at this time of year. With Twin Peaks, the double-crested hill to the west, blocking much of the fog coming in off of the Pacific Ocean, if it's going to be sunny in San Francisco, it's going to be sunny here. The streets were crowded with street people enjoying the beautiful day, hanging out or doing their thing; lost tourists wondering where they were and why they were here; merchants, residents, government workers, others. The usual inner-city sounds—music, emergency vehicles, people shouting, traffic noise—filled the air. Charlie's been here before (he's lived in San Francisco a long time and in 1997 we team-taught "Language, Culture, and Image," an interdisciplinary art/photography-English-sociology CBL class here, with Ardavan Davaran, a popular professor of English at NDNU, and visiting artist, photographer Douglas Kent Hall), and he seemed comfortable enough. Sam was absolutely serene. The TL is a peaceful garden compared to what he's been through.

Sam is short, stocky, balding—Buddha-like in appearance and attitude. With his glasses on, he looks like the learned scholar that he is. That almost cost him his life in Cambodia. He told us in class on campus, back in 2002, that he threw away his glasses when he was trying to escape persecution in his own country. "Eyeglasses are the sign of an intellectual in a country of illiterate people who have no need or access to them," he said. And intellectuals were deemed to be enemies of the State by the murderous Khmer Rouge.

When we arrived at IHDC, I was worried about whether many or *any* young people from the neighborhood would show up to hear an aging poet read. And I worried, if they did show up, would they be too young to handle what he had to say? I had put the word out beforehand that this could be a difficult subject for younger children, and encouraged program directors to promote the reading to older teens. I knew that this would likely cut down on the number of attendees, so I worried about that, too. When we entered IHDC's basement, I could hear many voices coming from the back room, where the reading would be held. Very good. When we got to the back room, I could see that it was packed, but mostly with younger kids, ten, eleven, twelve years old, a few even younger. Not good, at all. I assumed Sam would tailor his reading to their age, but he was here to talk about what happened in Cambodia, and what happened to him and his family and the families of many of the young children sitting right here, in this basement, waiting to hear what this man from Cambodia had to say.

I introduced Sam to the audience, then moved off to one side. The children sat right in front of us, some within touching distance, in rows of metal folding chairs lined up across the concrete-walled "Program Room." Sam took center stage.

"As Professor Don said, my name is U Sam Oeur, but when I was your age," he motioned to a boy of about ten in the front row, "I didn't have a name. I was just called 'Ok-Ok.' It means 'little boy.'" It was when he went to school that he learned his given name.

He told his young audience that when he was young only boys were allowed to go to school, so they didn't wear any clothes. "We went naked." Little eyes got very big and a few giggles erupted. "It was very hot, not like here in San Francisco," Sam continued. "Clothes just got in the way." Because the school was a five-mile walk away, Sam and his brother had to get up very early to get there on time. There was a river in the way that they had to swim to get across. No clothes, no problem. They made lunch boxes out of woven palm leaves. If lunch got wet, they just hung it up to dry on an angkanh tree.

I looked at the children to see how they were taking in Sam's talk. Clearly, some had not yet recovered from the "naked" news.

"How many of you are Cambodian?" Sam asked. More than half the hands in the room went up. Sam nodded his head at them and said, "The people of the Kingdom of Khmer—Cambodia—are an ancient people. Very old, many wars." Cambodia was colonized by the French in 1863. They stayed until 1953, a long time ago for many in the room, but not for Sam. In spoken words in English and a singsong chant in Cambodian, he told the story of a very personal journey and what happened in Cambodia.

He told the children about growing up on a rice farm, about his schooling in Cambodia, and—through the intervention of spirits, ever-present entities in his life (as they are in the lives of the Cambodian people in the Tenderloin), his admission to and graduation from the industrial arts program at California State University, Los Angeles. Then, in a radical shift in his education, he was accepted into University of Iowa's prestigious MFA Writer's Workshop to study poetry. For seven years, from 1961 to 1968, he lived and studied in the USA. This was the time of the 1960's Cultural Revolution, which he enjoyed very much ("I wasn't ready to be a monk"[2]). It was in the watershed year 1968—when Martin Luther King, Jr. and Bobby Kennedy were assassinated, Richard Nixon was elected President of the USA, Apollo 8 took off for the Moon, and the North Vietnamese and Viet Cong launched the horrific Tet Offensive (although a military failure, it so shocked the American public, it ultimately contributed to US withdrawal from Vietnam)—that he returned home to Cambodia, married his fiancée Dy Yen, who waited at home while he studied abroad, set aside his poetry, became successful in business and politics, and fathered a son. In 1975, seven years after coming home, he was appointed to Cambodia's delegation to the UN, just before the Khmer Rouge entered Phnom Penh, the country's capital, and the horror of the Pol Pot regime began. Sam was among 2.8 *million* citizens driven out of the city by the Khmer Rouge. During the next four years, he and his family survived an unbelievably brutal life in six different forced labor concentration camps. He pretended to be an illiterate farmer to avoid the fate that would befall them all if the truth of Sam's background in America and service in Cambodia were known.

It was at this point in the telling of the story that Sam took out *Sacred Vows*, his book of poems, and read one of the passages that I worried about him reading. It told the terrifying story of the forced evacuation of Phnom Penh, when Sam had to ignore suffering all around him, including that of a dying, disemboweled cousin, and keep moving, trying to get his family to safety. First in chanted Cambodian (sounding, to my American ears, like song), then in spoken English, he told the children of the Tenderloin a horrific story that many of their parents, grandparents, and aunts and uncles endured.

> Once the Blackcrows had usurped the power
> They started to evacuate the people from Phnom Penh;
> They threw patients through hospital windows
> (women in labor and the lame), drove tanks
> over them and bulldozed them under.
>
> The sun shone bright, as if it had come close to the earth.
> The ground was dried and cracked.
> Millions of panicked Phnompenhards jostled each other,
> Desperately overflowing along prescribed routes.
>
> Out! Out! Phankphankphank! My cousin's guts were hanging from his belly.
> Over there! Pap– pap–
> The corpses floated face up, face down in the Bassac River–
> Those who refused to give up their Orient wristwatches.
>
> Twenty meters a day
> For the first three days
> The journey without purpose;
> lost to wife and children,

separated from your loved ones,
repeated night and day,
wandering in circles.

There is crying and wailing
and the elders are groaning–
no one bothers with them;
everyone stampeding
to reach a destination,
any destination
away from Phnom Penh.

I watched the children watch Sam as he recited his poem in Cambodian and English, and continued the story of his life in what was, for many of them, their ancestral home. They were attentive, respectful, but I had no idea if they knew what he was really talking about or how the words were sinking in. Then he got to the part that I dreaded most, even more than the evacuation of Phnom Penh. I looked closely at the children as he began his Cambodian chant, then switched to English, as he read his poem, "The Loss of My Twins."

Deep one night in October, '76
when the moon had fully waxed,
it was cold to the bone;
that's when my wife's labor pains began.

I searched for a bed, but that was wishful thinking;
I felt so hopeless. Two midwives materialized–
one squatted above her abdomen and pushed,
the other reached up into my wife's womb and ripped the babies out.

What a lowing my wife put up
when she gave birth to the first twin.
"Very pretty, just as I'd wished, but those fiends
choked them and wrapped them in black plastic.

Two pretty girls...
Buddho! I couldn't do a thing to save them!"
murmured my mother.
"Here, Ta!" the midwives handed me the bundles.

Cringing as if I'd entered Hell,
I took the babies in my arms
and carried them to the banks of the Mekong River.
Staring at the moon, I howled:

"O, babies, you never had the chance to ripen into life–
only your souls look down at me now.
Dad hasn't seen you alive at all, girls...
forgive me, daughters; I have to leave you here.

Even though I'll bury your bodies here,
may your souls guide me and watch over your mother.
Lead us across this wilderness
and light our way to the Triple Gem."[3]

As I watched the audience, children of the Tenderloin, I wondered and worried, *What is going through their minds?* Most sat up, paying attention. What are they thinking? Was this a big mistake? I shook my head and felt pangs of guilt for bringing this terrible suffering to them, these agonizing words to their young minds. Sam finished his story of his life in the Killing Fields, told of coming to America, getting a job in Minnesota, then settling with his wife and son in Texas, among Cambodians relocated there, as other refugees settled here in The TL. He read one last poem, describing his time at the Douglas Corporation in Minneapolis, where he worked on an assembly line, putting urethane on nameplates. It read it part:

Cambodians, Vietnamese, Thais, and Mexicans
work side by side, like vegetables stirred in a soup
here in this beneficent place, which enchants them all
like rain resurrects parched grasses.

Even during the day shift, when almost
every worker's lips and tongue blab ceaselessly
from dawn to dusk, the harmony of
"I Hear American Singing" is all-pervasive.

After a day of work I feel
like standing on my head,
but genuine bliss sustains my hope
of seeing my boy in the chorus of "I Hear America Singing,"

that he will pursue his true dreams
rather than casting his lot
in the Communist Circle of Indochina,
that he will acquire more wisdom than I.

At lunchtime, while eating Oscar Meyer sandwiches,
I feel pity for the King of Cambodia,
the progenitor of the Khmer Rouge in the '70s–
I wonder what will become of him in his next incarceration.

The children and their program directors, here in the basement of
IHDC, applauded politely. Sam and I stood together at the head of the
"classroom" and I asked this question, "What would you like to know?"
But, before anyone could answer, maybe because I wasn't ready to hear
what they had to say, I asked, "How many of you could understand Sam
reading in Cambodian?" Almost half the children and a few of the program directors raised their hands. Great! I thought to myself. They heard
the horror stories *twice*. "What questions do you have?"

One of the youngest raised his hand and asked, "Where is your son?"

"He is with me in Texas. He is a technical engineer. He has his own
family, my grandchildren, three boys, Edward, John, and Daniel." Sam
smiled broadly. American boys.

"How is your wife?" one of the girls asked, her face scrunched up as if
in pain from asking this very difficult question.

"She is OK. She was blinded in one eye in the camps, but she is OK. She
has her grandsons."

"How many of you knew this story of Cambodia, before today?" I
asked the children, and was surprised to see so many hands go up.

"We wrote a book about it," Tom Heath, IHDC's after-school program director, called out from the back of the room.

"Of course," I said, "*Stories of Survival.*"

NOTES

1. National Institute of Mental Health (NIMH) press release, August 2, 2005.
2. Oeur, U Sam, translated by Ken McCullough, *Sacred Vows*, Minneapolis:
   Coffee House Press.1998, pp. 47, 55, 202.
3. "The Triple Gem" refers to the three objects of Refuge (inspiration and
   devotion) for Buddhists. They are Buddha (Enlightened One), Dharma
   (Eternal Truth), and Sangha (Assembly of monks).

CHAPTER 5

Stories of Survival

IHDC

© The Author(s) 2017
D. Stannard-Friel, *Street Teaching in the Tenderloin*,
DOI 10.1057/978-1-137-56437-5_5

I saw them chop off a person's head, arms, legs, and even cut a person's body in half. They killed them when the people were still alive. Blood was flowing in the road. They used butcher knives that are sharp and a machete. I was scared.

Cambodian IHDC resident
recalling her childhood
in *Stories of Survival*

* * *

Stories of Survival: Three Generations of Southeast Asian Americans Share Their Lives is a book written and published in 2001 by Tom Heath and the community of IHDC. Originally, the plan was for young people, living in the two buildings that IHDC operates, to interview their elders, parents and grandparents, about their lives as Southeast Asian refugees. But many of the older people found that the stories were just too painful to share with their offspring. Also, even though IHDC is a well-managed, well-maintained, and nurturing environment, their homes, for many of the residents, are extremely crowded studio or, for a very few, one-bedroom apartments, and many of the youths were uncomfortable asking intimate questions of close relatives, especially when surrounded by siblings and cousins whom they lived with. So, it was decided that, for many, they would interview elders in other families. As the project unfolded, some of the refugees asked if they could write their stories, rather than tell them. Lisa Margonelli, a professional writer and the book's volunteer editor, conducted writers' workshops for the individual authors, and sons and daughters and IHDC youth program directors translated the stories. As word about the emerging book spread among the tenants of the two IHDC buildings, interest in participation increased, including people from all age groups. In the Introduction, Tom Heath and Sam Soun, who was Oral History Assistant for the project, explain,[1]

> As more people from all age groups expressed a desire to be included, it became apparent we needed to represent all of the experiences across three generations. We added the second generation of U.S. born children and the "one-point-five" generation of young adults born in another country, and brought at an older age to live in America.

Sam, Sammy, Phanna Phay, and many of the young people I know in the Tenderloin are Cambodian "1.5ers."[2] Since they were born in Thai refugee camps and emigrated with their families to the USA as toddlers, they never knew the ancestral home and have no sense of community with Thailand, but often feel—and have been—marginalized here, in America. Still, many of the guys I know, arriving here as little boys, as Sam, Sammy, and Phanna did, had an easier (not easy) time assimilating than their older friends or siblings, especially brothers, who, because they were older, struggled more with the foreign English language and American culture as adolescents in American middle and high schools.

Tom and Sam go on to say,

> We endeavored to tell their stories with dignity while retaining the origi-nal voice of the storyteller. This yearlong journey revealed heartbreak and healing…regret and redemption…loss and appreciation…crime and educa-tion…death and birth.

> You will read stories of surviving against great odds, adjusting to life in a new land, and navigating between two cultures, with the recognition that we all have something to share with each other, no matter our age or background.

> We hope these stories will help you align your life with theirs to realize the importance of friendship, family, community…being alive!

It was in 2003 that Sam brought the book to my attention. For ten years, it was required reading in Streetwise Sociology, until the stock ran out. (Then a new "10th Anniversary Edition," updating most of the sto-ries, came out, and is now back on my required book list.) It gives a lot of background on the people we study in the community, partner with in Halloween in the Tenderloin, College Night, and many other projects, and learn from as street teachers. It's a collection of deeply moving stories of people we *engage* with, come *face-to-face* with, in the pink and the lime-green buildings on Eddy Street, and elsewhere in the Tenderloin. There is incredible depth to the lives of these people, and the others who walk these streets, a depth of experience that is rarely considered by passersby—the rest of us who may dismiss inner-city folks as lazy, good-for-nothing, dope-addicted, ne'er-do-wells. Sometimes—often—it is a horrible depth that has shaped *who* they have become, and the generations that follow. For example, "A Daughter's Story," by a "Cambodian female, age 35"[3] (all of the older storytellers asked for anonymity), begins, "My teenage years in Cambodia were during the war so I don't know much about happiness."

Another woman, a "Cambodian female, age 32," writes in "Lucky Escape,"[4]

When I was small, I got taken away from my mom to be an orphan with the Khmer Rouge. They took me because I was getting older and they wouldn't let you stay with your parents anymore. During the Pol Pot time I would grow crops for the Khmer Rouge and I was living in a Khmer Rouge orphanage. I was about 8 or 9 years old when the Khmer Rouge took me. They made us pull weeds, plant potatoes, rice, wheat and go to the Khmer Rouge meetings. They talked about killing, raping, etc. If you don't go they'll kill you and you can't do anything about it. For two years, I was with the Khmer Rouge. I did not run because they already killed some of my family. Even little kids had been hurt or killed.

I finally ran away to the Crocodile Road, and I stayed there overnight. I had escaped but the Khmer Rouge still came looking for all the other orphans that ran away. I saw them chop off a person's head, arms, legs, and even cut a person's body in half. They killed them when the people were still alive. Blood was flowing in the road. They used butcher knives that are sharp and a machete. I was scared. I was lucky to get away because the Khmer Rouge captured some of the kids back but not me.

A 50-year-old Cambodian male told an interviewer that after the Khmer Rouge took over, "At that time in my life there was never any happiness. One sadness after another and another. I carry it all inside me. It still haunts me now, even as I talk about it."[5]

And a "Cambodian female, age 18," told a story of her mother in "My Struggle, Too,"[6]

My mom has lived through a struggle of pain. She and her family struggled to come to America when the Khmer Rouge were killing their own kind of people. It turned out that all of her family died leaving just my mom and my uncle alive. Some died of starvation and others died of sickness.

My mom and uncle tried to survive with little food. My uncle was begging to spare food for my mom and taking care of her. Soon, my mom was separated from my uncle. My mom followed a family of strangers because she was sick. Luckily, she met a kind-hearted person who was a doctor and he helped cure her. He fed her and let her stay until she found her brother. The day the Khmer Rouge found out that he was a doctor, they killed the whole family including the 8-month-old baby. They hid my mom under the house in the basement. If the baby had hidden with her they would have killed both my mom and the baby. My mom felt pain and wished she could save them somehow, but she was so little and so scared she didn't know what to do. If they were alive today she would pay her respect to them.

These or similar accounts are family stories of children who sat in the audience when U Sam Oeur read his poetry and told his story of survival and death under the Khmer Rouge. This is why they raised their hands when I asked, "How many of you knew this story of Cambodia, before today?" The terrible suffering was their parents' and grandparents' suffering. The "Cambodian female, age 35," the "Cambodian female, age 32," the 50-year-old Cambodian male, and the "Cambodian female, age 18" were not strangers to the children. They lived upstairs in the pink building at 375 Eddy Street and across the street in the lime-green apartment building at 340 Eddy. The blood that ran so easily in Cambodia continues to flow down the stairs and elevator shafts of the two buildings, running down the wooden staircase into the basement after-school program, spreading out on the concrete floor into the Game Room, the Computer Room, the Program Room, the kitchen, and the backyard, pooling in the hearts and minds and souls of the children who play and study here. The Khmer Rouge atrocities crossed the Pacific and entered the Tenderloin as familial PTSD.

* * *

In an article published in the *UC Davis Law Review*,[7] Professor Bill Ong Hing, of the University of San Francisco School of Law, wrote about how the USA drew Cambodia into the Vietnam (American) War through secret bombings in that country in 1969, and support for rightist groups there in 1970. After we lost the war, and pulled out of Southeast Asia, the Khmer Rouge began its genocide of its own people. Thousands of refugees, including the Soun, Phay, and all the Tenderloin 1.5-generation's families, fled to refugee camps. Eventually, 145,000 Cambodian refugees were admitted to the USA. Professor Ong Hing observes,

U.S. resettlement policies provided public assistance and job training for low-income jobs. Refugee families, however, were not provided with the tools necessary to raise their children in inner-city environments, where crime was rampant and culture was radically different from where they came. As a result, many of the refugee children, products of their U.S. environment, have turned to crime.

* * *

Phanna Phay is one of a group of young Cambodian men I have become friends with over the years. The network includes VanSok (Snoop) Chil, David Mack, Sophal (Paul) Meas, Boun (Bee) Nhey, Sophannara (Ra) Sek, Samnang (Sam) Soun, Sambath (Sammy) Soun, Kim Soeun Tek, and Veasna (Vee) Chea. Most of them have hung out on the 200 block of Leavenworth Street, at one time or another, some with Donal, before he left town. Others joined that ever-evolving street scene later on. Many of them enrolled in, or informally audited, one or more of my Inner City courses.

Phanna is taller than most of his friends. Broad shouldered, muscular, and tattooed, he walked the streets of the Tenderloin with confidence, often leading a troupe of kids back and forth from the Tenderloin Boys and Girls Club main clubhouse and its Educational Center on Jones Street, when he was the club's Teen Director, helping out with the younger children. In the evening, after the little kids went home, he'd meet with the teens and work with them on leadership skills, getting into college, and other transition-to-adulthood activities. At the time of U Sam Oeur's talk, Phanna, himself, was taking, what he described as, "the ten-year plan" at City College, finishing up his AA degree in criminal justice. He started community college as he was completing his GED (high school equivalency) around the same time that Sam Soun did. He audited, but never formerly enrolled, in a few of my inner-city classes, worked with me on a number of community activities over the years (College Night, Halloween in the Tenderloin, sports clinics, Youth Philanthropy Workshops), and has been a street teacher, telling my students about The TL, his work, and his personal life. Phanna was raised in the projects in the Western Addition, on the other side of Van Ness Avenue, but spent a lot of his adolescence hanging out in the Tenderloin with other Cambodian youth. In his 20s, he moved, for a while, into an apartment in the pink IHDC building, that members of the Soun family have lived in over the years. He's doing well, but he's had his own struggles.

In 2001, as IHDC was completing the first edition of *Stories of Survival*, Chet Phay, Phanna's older brother, agreed to write a poem for the book, but before it was completed, he committed suicide. Tom and Sam decided, with Phanna, to print a poem that Chet had previously written, have Phanna reflect on his brother's life, and write his own poem in response to his brother's death. The section of the book is called "Two Brothers Search For Freedom." Chet's poem titled "What is Freedom?"[8] revealed his state of mind before he hung himself:

Freedom is like a wild horse running around,
It is like a bird flying in the sky.
It's like a river flow passing by.
To be able to do what I want to do.
To eat what I want to eat.
To play when I want to play.
To sleep when I want to sleep.
To say what I want to say.
To be whoever I want to be.
This is Freedom to me.

But Freedom is hard when you're in a society and have to do what you're
told to do.
I'm not free but I want to be.
I'm still in a ship that's in a sea and about to sink.

To me I will have Freedom, but I'll never be free inside.
Freedom is like a bullet releasing from the shell.
It's like a fish swimming in the sea,
and like the monkey on the tree.
Like a dog off a leash,
A cat on a fence.
Like a waterfall from the mountain,
like an island in the middle of nowhere.
Like a wind passing by.

Freedom..........
To me the world is not free.
It's like a dog chasing a cat.
A cat chasing a rat.

Kingdom is fight Kingdom.
This world will never be free,
till it burns up into flames.
Then the world is free.

Freedom is like a fire burning without rain.
Rain without sun.
That is Freedom.

But this world is a greedy ass world,
there will never be peace.

There will never be Freedom.
Everyone will kill each other till the world ends.
So to me I'm still
Not free.
Like the book said, "Life is like stepping into a ship that's about to sail and sink."
How can I be free if I don't know if I will make it across the sea?
That's how I feel about being free.

Chet Phay
Born Nov. 28, 1976
Died March 9, 2001

In his reflection in *Stories of Survival*, and in addressing my classes as a street teacher, Phanna told Chet's story and aspects of his own.

"My parents fled Cambodia, because they wanted a better life for their kids," he told my Streetwise Sociology students. "One of my brothers died of starvation when he was just a baby and the Communists were killing everybody. We fled to a refugee camp in Thailand. That's where I was born. When I was three, we went to the Philippines, then to America. My parents thought we had finally made it, but what they found here is not what they hoped for. We went from poverty in Cambodia to poverty in America. I wasn't raised here in the Tenderloin. My family didn't want to live here. Too dangerous. We lived in the Western Addition,[9] but there weren't any Cambodian or other Asian kids there, so I hung around the Tenderloin. My father didn't want me to come here, but I did anyway. This is where my friends were."

In his essay, "Freedom," in *Stories*,[10] he said the same about his brother, Chet.

It was hard for my brother, he would get ridiculed at school because he never had any nice clothes. He'd get into a lot of fights. He'd get suspended and miss a lot of school days. When he entered high school, he started hanging out in the Tenderloin. Our family doesn't live in the Tenderloin, and my parents would forbid us to go anywhere near there. My brother started making his own money, selling drugs. By age 16 he'd dropped out of school, and was on the street day and night. He'd come home to sleep, and then be out in the morning. There was nothing my parents could do or say. They beat him, kicked him out of the house, they did everything but it was the life he chose.

He was incarcerated many times. Each time, he'd call the house telling my mom that he'd change. He'd go back to school, find a job. But when he was released, he couldn't go back to school because he was too far behind. He couldn't find a job because he didn't have any experience, he didn't want to work for McDonald's.

The last time he got caught up, they sent him to San Quentin, for 2 years, then the INS held him for another year. He would call the house, and he'd talk about being Free. He'd come out this time and really try to get his life straight. But we heard all this before. My brother and I weren't close, but we talked. And all he ever talked about was Freedom. Freedom from poverty, Freedom from jail, Freedom from his street life. He wanted to change, change for good.

Chet got out of San Quentin in February of 2000. He got a job delivering fish to restaurants, and talked about going back to school, but everyone—including his parents and friends—told him he wouldn't make it. He registered for classes at City College in spring 2001, but never attended. He went back to his old life. In his essay, Phanna continued,

There was so much going through his mind, but he never shared it with anyone. All people ever did was say he was no good, there was no shoulder for him to lean on. I for my part should have been a better brother, should have showed support, but I was too busy with my life, that I couldn't recognize he had problems.

One morning, Chet came home and he had a strange look about him. He disappeared for two days, then came back, still acting weird, talking to himself about wanting to be free from this life. At Phanna's urging ("my parents weren't worried about it, but I was"), he was checked into a psychiatric hospital for evaluation. A 72-hour hold became seven days, but "we never found out what was wrong with him." When his mother and sister visited, all he would talk about was being "tired of it all; he wanted to be Free." Phanna wrote,

On March 2nd, 2001 in the bathroom of the psychiatric ward, my brother attempted to gain his Freedom, with a noose around his neck. But he wouldn't achieve Freedom until March 9, 2001.

I wish this could have been a happy story about how he was able to change, and lead a good life. But in life you don't always get what you want. There is always something that keeps you down. Makes you feel trapped.

In memory of his brother, Phanna wrote this poem, "Life Ain't Free,"[11]

> A life full of pain and sorrow,
> Hopes that faded.
> You lived for today,
> Never cared about tomorrow.
> We never saw those Demons inside,
> You hid them away.
> Didn't let us know,
> Cuz you had too much pride.
> You lived a life of misery,
> No one knew it but you.
> Outside you smiled,
> Inside you wanted to be free.
> No shoulder to lean on,
> Inside you cried for help.
> We couldn't hear you,
> And now you're gone.
> Like a bird you wanted to fly,
> Society kept you grounded.
> They said you were nothing,
> You bought into their lies.
> But you held onto your dream,
> They couldn't take it away.
> You chose your own road,
> And now you are FREE.
> Fly away my brother,
> Fly away from this negativity.
> Never forget I love you.
> Rest in peace.
>
> Phanna Phay
> Cambodian male, age 20

Chet's life was composed of poverty, parental cultural incompetence, familial PTSD, violence at home, violence at school, failure at school/failed schools, street life, prison culture, ex-con status, being unemployed, lack of encouragement from parents and friends, low self-esteem, mental illness, and feelings of being trapped in a world of pain and suffering: "Life is like stepping into a ship that's about to sail and sink." And he killed himself.

* * *

Chet died on March 9, 2001. I never knew him. But I have known Phanna since around the time of his brother's suicide, and I've watched him and a generation of other young Tenderloin people transition from teenagers into adults. Not all are in the survival mode. Phanna is a married man, now, a dad of two, and in his early 30s. At this writing, he is working at San Francisco's Exploratorium, a hands-on learning laboratory for kids, and has contemplated emigrating to Cambodia (not "returning" since, like the Soun brothers, he was born in a refugee camp in Thailand) to farm a plot of land his family owns. After graduating from Oregon, Sam went to work as a counselor for kids involved in, or at risk for, gang membership in Sacramento, 75 miles north and a world away from The TL. Some of the younger kids in the neighborhood were preteens when I first met them. Elizabeth is now a graduate in business administration from UC Santa Cruz. Munie has attended City College, worked as a staff member at IHDC's after-school program, and now is learning the hotel business. David works for Tenderloin Neighborhood Development Corp. And a new generation is just coming up. Munie's little sister, Monica, born after I met the family, has always seemed to be a happy, outgoing child, as are many of her friends who participate with her in neighborhood youth programs, go to school every day, do their homework at IHDC or the Boys and Girls Club's Education Center or the Tenderloin Children's playground or VYDC or TASP, and do community service projects, such as raising money for field trips by selling lemonade on Eddy Street to cops, drug dealers, street people, merchants, and other passersby. The most recent arrivals include babies being born to the 1.5 generation.

U Sam Oeur's hope,

> of seeing my boy in the chorus of "I Hear America Singing,"
> that he will pursue his true dreams
> rather than casting his lot
> in the Communist Circle of Indochina,
> that he will acquire more wisdom than I

is being realized by many of the children of the Tenderloin. Not all.

NOTES

1. Heath, Tom. et al., *Stories of Survival: Three Generations of Southeast Asian Americans Share Their Lives*, San Francisco: Indochinese Housing Development Corporation, 2001, p. 8.

2. The term "1.5 generation" refers to people who immigrate to a new country before or during their early teens. They are the "in-between generation," bringing with them characteristics from the old country as they assimilate into the new. Many in the 1.5 generation retain, to a greater or lesser extent, a bicultural orientation.

3. Cambodian female, age 35, "A Daughter's Story," in Heath, Tom et al., *Stories of Survival: Three Generations of Southeast Asian Americans Share Their Lives*, San Francisco: Indochinese Housing Development Corporation, 2001, p. 31.

4. Cambodian female, age 32, "Lucky Escape," Heath, Tom, et al., *Stories of Survival: Three Generations of Southeast Asian Americans Share Their Lives*, San Francisco: Indochinese Housing Development Corporation, 2001, p. 37.

5. A 50-year-old Cambodian male, "My Country, My Children," *Stories of Survival: Three Generations of Southeast Asian Americans Share Their Lives*, San Francisco, Indochinese Housing Development Corporation, 2001, p. 47.

6. Cambodian female, age 18, "My Struggle, Too," Heath, Tom, et al., *Stories of Survival: Three Generations of Southeast Asian Americans Share Their Lives*, San Francisco: Indochinese Housing Development Corporation, 2001, p. 67.

7. Hing, Bill Ong, "Detention to Deportation – Rethinking the Removal of Cambodian Refugees." *UC Davis Law Review*, Vol. 38, 2005.

8. Phay, Chet, "What is Freedom?" Tom Heath, et al, *Stories of Survival: Three Generations of Southeast Asian Americans Share Their Lives*, San Francisco: Indochinese Housing Development Corporation, 2001, p. 87.

9. The Western Addition, as the name implies, is a neighborhood to the west of the original city boundaries that was added on in 1800s. Neighbor to The TL, it is socioeconomically mixed, with gentrification changing much an area that once included one of San Francisco's largest, predominantly black neighborhoods, including the Fillmore District with its rich jazz history. It still houses pockets of poverty in low-income housing developments, of the kind that Phanna was raised in.

10. Phay, Phanna, "Freedom," *Stories of Survival: Three Generations of Southeast Asian Americans Share Their Lives*, San Francisco: Indochinese Housing Development Corporation, 2001, p. 89.

11. Phay, Phanna, "Life Ain't Free," *Stories of Survival: Three Generations of Southeast Asian Americans Share Their Lives*, San Francisco: Indochinese Housing Development Corporation, 2001, p. 91.

CHAPTER 6

RIP Josh Mann

COLLEGE NIGHT IN THE TENDERLOIN 1999

© The Author(s) 2017
D. Stannard-Friel, *Street Teaching in the Tenderloin*,
DOI 10.1057/978-1-137-56437-5_6

I look at the poster board from … our first College Night. Photographed sitting in the front rows are three bright young Cambodian faces, two six-teen-year-old boys and a thirteen-year-old girl. During the next few years, the youngest will be orphaned, the second will be stabbed in the stomach, the third will be dead.

The Author

* * *

Over the years, in the late 1990s and the first half of the 2000s, Donal came in and out of my life (more precisely, I in his). I interviewed him about his own life and got to see The TL through his eyes. I stopped by the 200 block of Leavenworth with my classes, as we walked or drove through the neighborhood. Often, they were spontaneous meetings, but sometimes previously arranged. He enjoyed telling stories, true or not, that had the potential of shocking my students: "I remember the first time I killed someone," he began to tell a carload of us one evening, as he leaned in the window of the van I was driving. "*Donal*, probably not a good topic," I suggested. He had told me this story, before, and—though I suspected it was more bravado than reality—I thought that it wasn't in his interest to share it with my students, or my students' to know it. He gave me a look, but changed the subject.

My relationship with Donal ended one afternoon when I was walking up Leavenworth Street to BAWCC to talk to Nancy Ong and Midge Wilson, two longtime community activists and Tenderloin U street teachers. That, by now, familiar, deep, soft, menacing voice came out of nowhere, though I didn't recognize it at first, "*Professor.*" I looked around. Nothing. Just a disembodied voice. Calling me? Was it real? "*Professor.*" A movement caught my eye, four stories up, on the other side of the street. The big man was standing on a fire escape, his hands wrapped around the railing. He looked like a sea captain, standing on the prow of a ship, or, more precisely, a Tongan chief in the bow of a war canoe. Or maybe a king on his royal balcony, looking over his domain, Leavenworth Street. "Hey, Donal," I called back. He nodded and gave me that smile. I never saw him again.

In the years leading up to that last encounter, I had learned a lot from Donal and his friends. I came to know young men in the neighborhood that many call "street thugs" or "gutter punks," who I knew to be good people, even if they sometimes got into trouble. I lost track of Kevin, the dread-locked Cambodian kid, shortly after I met him, but in the years since, some of the Fish Stick Gang, or their younger siblings, enrolled in my Inner City

Studies classes, or participated in our service-learning projects, like College Night in the Tenderloin. I've gotten close to some of them, like Phanna and Sam and Sammy Soun. It's been a pleasure to see them grow and develop, and come into their own. It's also been heartbreaking to watch their, sometimes, desperate struggles, and see others lose their lives.

* * *

**Tenderloin Youth College Project:
A workshop on getting into college**

Thursday November 18, 1999
5:00 – 7:00 p.m.

At the Tenderloin Children's Playground

570 Ellis St.
(between Hyde and Leavenworth)

fun!

Meet with Students, Faculty, and Staff from College of Notre Dame

Eat pizza, have fun, and learn important information about going to college!

fun!

APPLYING TO COLLEGE
FINANCIAL AID
CHOOSING A MAJOR
LIFE ON CAMPUS

prizes!

meet new people!

free food!

RSVP by November 11 to Diana Chin at the Tenderloin Children's Playground
(415) 292-2162
or
Dr. Don Stannard-Friel, College of Notre Dame
(650) 508-3770
(Sponsored by the CND Streetwise Sociology class and Tenderloin Children's Playground)

Illustration 6.1 College Night Flyer 1999

* * *

November 19, 2009:
It's College Night in the Tenderloin. Students are setting up in the upstairs Computer Room in Tenderloin Children's Playground. College Night is a Streetwise Sociology production. Students in the class organize, promote, manage, and present information on getting and staying in college. It begins with pizza. NDNU people mingle with Tenderloin youth as they arrive, alone or in groups led by staff members from IHDC, VYDC, Salvation Army, De Marillac Academy, San Francisco Christian Academy, Galileo High School, Boys and Girls Club, and Tenderloin Children's Playground. A mom or dad may come, but usually it's just Tenderloin kids, 25 or 30 of them, with half-dozen grown-up program directors. Most of the attendees have been Southeast Asian, but more Latinos have been coming in recent years, as their families are pushed by gentrification out of the Mission District and into the Tenderloin. I've brought along poster boards, put together by previous Streetwise students, decorated with flyers, handouts, and photographs from past College Nights. Tonight is the ten-year anniversary of the event. I look at the poster board from November 18, 1999, our first College Night (NDNU was still called College of Notre Dame [CND]). Photographed sitting in the front rows are three bright young Cambodian faces, two 16-year-old boys and a 13-year-old girl. During the next few years, the youngest will be orphaned, the second will be stabbed in the stomach, the third will be dead.

* * *

Wednesday May 22, 2002:
I'm sitting in Wild Awakenings, going over my notes from interviews with Donal. I'm scheduled to meet him at 11:00 a.m. to talk some more about his life and the possibility of him speaking to my Criminology class this summer. There is no doorbell for his apartment, so his buddy, Larry, Donal's "Assistant Apartment Manager" ("Assistant Manager in Crime," a cop told me. It doesn't matter which he was, Larry was killed the following year), is supposed to be waiting for me at the gate to the building, just around the corner and two blocks up the hill. I look up at the big clock on the back wall of the coffeehouse. "Uh, Oh." It's 10:55 a.m. Damn, I'm cutting it too close. It's time to go.
I hurry up Leavenworth Street hill. As I get close to Donal's apartment building, the door of a white SUV parked at the curb whips open,

blocking me, stopping me dead in my tracks. Out of the corner of my eye, I see a figure lunge out of the SUV, right at me. Loose-fitting black pants, covered in silver dollar-sized, yellow happy faces distract me from the threat of danger. Then a big, smiling, white happy face on the chest of a bright yellow sweatshirt stares at me, eyeballs-to-eyeballs. The driver of the SUV towers over me. A bright yellow baseball hat sits on top of his head, a head that is six and a half feet above the ground. At 350 pounds (he tells me later), Donal is bigger than ever. The black and yellow colors may have replaced the reds he often wears as a Norteño ally, but even with the happy faces, he's intimidating.

The big man's smile matches the happy faces. "How you doin', Professor?" he says, extending his hand. I laugh as I take it. "You crazy, man," I say. "Crazy!" Shaking my head, relaxing, I look him over. What's *this* all about?

We begin small talk when Donal calls across the street to a small knot of young men hanging out against the wall by the Laundromat. "Hey, Johnny, cum 'ere."

A young white man breaks free from the otherwise Asian group. He's dressed all in black, including a black, knit watchman's cap. A good-looking guy, light-colored hair, hard features, he and Donal call to each other as he crosses the street.

"Hey, you OK, dog?" Donal asks the young man.

"I'm OK," he answers, hurrying through a break in the traffic going up Leavenworth Street hill.

"What happened? You know wha's goin' on?" Donal asks.

"No, I dunno," Johnny replies. "Jason says it's the Samoans."

"Fuck that!" Donal says. "Ain't no Samoans. Jason's full of shit."

Donal turns back to me. "Kid hung himself last night," he says. "Fuckin' brother blames it on the Samoans, but ain't no Samoans did nothing."

The young white man gets to our side of the street. "Hey," Donal says as they clasp their hands in a gladiator greeting. "This here's The Professor. This Johnny, Professor."

Johnny and I exchange a conventional handshake.

Donal and Johnny continue their conversation as we head into the Leavenworth Street apartment building. "What you think happened?" Donal asks Johnny. "Why you think he done it?"

"I dunno. Jason says it was the Samoans. I think Josh just killed hisself. Hanging in the stairwell by a rope. He was dead when they found him."

"It was no fuckin' Samoans," Donal says. "He was a big guy. There'd be some bruises on his hands or face. There was no bruises, was there?"

Donal asks, as he rubs the knuckles on his clenched fist to show where bruises would be.

"I didn't hear about none."

"Fuck, no! It was Jason's fault, if anybody's. Josh was easy goin', but Jason and Ray was always getting into people's faces. They shoulda known better. Fuckin' with the Mexicans, fuckin' with the Samoans. The blacks. Josh wasn't into that shit, but he stood up for his brother. Did *mano-a-mano* with a Samoan. Big motherfucker. Bigger than him. Did his brother's business. Jason cut out, but Josh defended him, one-on-one. Samoan kicked his fuckin' ass, but said he respected that. Standin' up for his brother. Said Jason shouldn't a run. Fuck, Josh was just a good guy. Got too much for him."

"Yeah, he was a good kid," Johnny says. He looks distraught.

We walk up the steps to the third floor of the apartment building and down the blotchy-white corridor to number 32, Donal's apartment. The big man opens the red door and the three of us file in. The place looks about the same as the other times I've been here. Two couches in the small living room, facing each other. Two big, maybe four feet high, speakers on either side of a CD sound system. A computer tucked into a nook on the other side of the room. Doors going off the hall to the bedroom and kitchen. A closet in the foyer that Donal rummaged through the last time I was here, looking to show off his AK-47. When he couldn't find it, he stood up, scratched his head, gave an "Oh yeah!" look when he remembered that he had lent it out, then pulled out a machete. He whipped it over his head, like the giant in the *Raiders of the Lost Ark* movie, just before Indiana Jones shot him dead. But I'm no Indiana Jones, have no gun, wouldn't know how to use it if I did, and this giant with a sword was between me and the door. But Donal was just having fun.

Johnny and Donal talk some more about the dead youth, then Donal wraps it up by giving Johnny some instructions on working out in the gym Donal has set up in the basement for neighborhood youth. "I'm training him," Donal says to me. "He's a natural in the ring." He turns back to Johnny and says, "Go do the treadmill and the rowing machine. Work out on the body bag. We'll talk later. I'll be down later." They exchange a handclasp. Johnny reaches over and shakes my hand.

"See you later, Professor," he says.

"Nice meeting you, John."

Donal and I talk for another hour or so. Willie, Donal's "Mexican big brother," joins us. He's jumpy, but friendly enough. He agrees with Donal that the Samoans didn't kill Josh. "I heard he tied a fuckin' rope around his neck and just jumped over the fuckin' railing," Willie tells us. Joe, an African-American janitor in the building, tool belt wrapped around his waist, comes in. He nods a hello when he is introduced, but doesn't say anything at all. He just listens.

I say goodbye to Donal and his friends and head on over to the Tenderloin Children's Playground, up on Ellis Street. Kay Rodrigues is on duty in the Administration Room. When Boeddeker Park, down on Eddy and Jones, failed as a playground—because its open design resulted in children getting stuck with hypodermic needles tossed in the sand; little kids picking up used condoms, thinking they were balloons; and drug dealers, periodically, taking it over—Children's Playground was built with access control in mind. To get to the play yard, the gym, the activity area, the Latchkey Room, or up the stairs to the Computer Room, Music and Craft Room, kitchen, and outside garden (popular activity areas whose functions were, later, cutback or eliminated in the 2009 budget crunch, and the permanent full-time staff was reduced from seven to one), a visitor has to pass by the Administration Room. With windows on all sides, the staff can see who comes and goes. And at least one of them is usually playing a board game or doing something else with kids in the foyer, anyway. Kay is an energetic, passionate, Chinese-Portuguese, born in Hong Kong, mother of three boys (a fourth would come along, later). She is small, but a force to be reckoned with if someone who doesn't belong tries to enter the playground or tries messing with the kids. She's teary-eyed.

"You OK?" I ask.

"One of our boys died last night. Killed himself," she says. "You know him. Josh. Josh Mann. He was such a sweet kid."

"*Josh?* Josh *Mann?* Damn, I just heard about it, but I didn't know it was Josh *Mann.* Didn't connect it. What happened? Do you know what happened?" I hadn't put it together that one of the street kids that Donal runs with was one of the kids who hangs around Children's Playground and IHDC. Josh Mann *was* a sweet kid. Cambodian, still he was taller than most of his friends. He had a horrendous scar that ran down the side of his head, the result of being smashed with a milk crate by one of his brothers. Right after that incident, Josh came to the playground and asked Kay to look at the bleeding wound. She told me she picked out what she at first thought were white plastic splinters from the milk crate, but discovered that they were actually skull bone fragments. Josh came to Kay for help because he, essentially, grew up in the playground. Kay, Diana Chin, and the other staff members were his nurturing surrogate older siblings or parent figures, like they are to a lot of kids here. Sam Soun told me that Diana was the most consistent adult in his life since he was five years old.

Kay starts to rummage through drawers in the office for photographs of Josh. Lots of photos of the kids from the playground appear: Disneyland trips, river rafting, camping, sporting events, Christmas, Halloween. "I'll find one," she says, determined. She is interrupted by the door buzzer, used during school hours to manage the flow of people coming in and out when fewer staff members are on duty. Kay looks down the hall to the glass front door, "Oh, it's Phanna." Phanna, like Josh, and a lot of the other young adult Southeast Asian men, helped out with the younger children in the playground or just stopped by to visit.

Phanna comes in. "Hey, Dr. Don," he says. "What's happenin', Kay?"

"Hmm, can you tell him, Dr. Don?" Kay asks. "I can't." Her voice breaks as she focuses on rummaging through the drawers.

What can I say? "Josh died."

"What? No way!" says Phanna. "What happened?"

"He took his own life," I say. "No one seems to know why." I look at Phanna to see how he is handling this news. It's only been a little over a year since his own brother committed suicide.

"No way," Phanna says. He is taken aback and we're all quiet for a while.

The conversation returns to Josh. I tell Phanna what little I know and where I heard it. We reminisce a bit, and then go onto other topics, his studies at City College (his final exams are looming) and his interest in journalism. My son, Matt, is a reporter for *The Chronicle*, and we talk about Phanna shadowing him for a day. Then I head over to IHDC. This is where Josh and many of the 18- to 23-year-olds he hung around with hang around, since they are not officially allowed to spend time at the playground or most of the other programs in the Tenderloin, designed to serve 17-year-olds and younger. Like aged-out foster kids, we seem to think that 18 is old enough to be on your own. We leave them to their own devises, *knowing* that that's not a good idea.[1]

I can hear the sounds of lots of kids in the back rooms at IHDC as I open the gate and go down the wooden staircase. No one is at the pool table. The sound of a piano being played is coming from the back of the basement. A bunch of kids are talking in the Computer Room. Sam is there, working on a grant of some kind. Tom is typing on a computer with one hand, holding a small child on his lap with the other. We talk about Josh. There are pictures of him on the computer screens. "There's a service on Friday," Tom says. "I'll call you with the details." Laura Soun comes into the room, hits me on the arm. "Hi, Dr. Don." She is smiling her usual big smile, but her eyes are red. Tek, a tall, lanky friend of Phanna and Josh, comes through the door a minute later. "You heard?" he asks.

"I did."

"Sucks."

"Yes it does."

Friday morning. Tom leaves me a voicemail about the service today, "Open casket showing of the body. Small private service tomorrow, with the Buddhist monks and the cremation."

I go to the showing at Driscoll's Funeral Parlor on 1400 block of Valencia Street, out in the Mission District. I park my VW camper alongside the Salvation Army store at 26th and Valencia, and walk the half-block back to the funeral home. About 25 or 30 kids are hanging out in front. Most are Asian. Most are dressed in black. A lot of the boys have black tee shirts on, with gold necklaces glittering in the Mission District sunshine. A few have big, gold crosses hanging from the chains. Most of the girls have black dresses on. Some, very tight black dresses. A few are wearing black berets, jauntily perched on the sides of their heads. A lot of posturing is going on, the sexual energy of youth revealing itself even under such trying circumstances. Just teenage stuff, set on edge by the horrible death of a friend. David Mack, one of Josh's crew, comes over to say hello. I remember the two of them at the first College Night we did at the playground, sitting in the very front row, in front of Laura Soun. (At the time of the funeral, David had yet to be stabbed in the stomach and Laura had not yet been orphaned, but Josh was now dead.) David, like Phanna and some others in their "Band of Brothers" (many of them actually are brothers, or cousins, or have roots in the same village in Cambodia), enrolled in or informally audited a number of my classes. David even brought his girlfriend along a couple of times. He gives me a handshake and a semi-hug. "You OK?" I ask.

"I'm OK," he says, but he doesn't look OK.

Inside the funeral home, there is a poster with a picture of a smiling Josh, with his name underneath. The small chapel is full. Tom, Diana, and some of the playground and IHDC kids are sitting toward the back. I nod at the group and sit with them. Diana points to the front. "That's his family, there," she whispers. "His mother and brothers." I see a very distraught gathering of people huddled together in the front pew.

People are lining up in the aisle to pay their respects. Tom takes a white rose from a bunch at his feet and gives it to me to bring up to the casket. I get in line. When I get to the front, I put the flower in the casket, adding it to the bouquet that is accumulating. I was apprehensive about approaching the open casket, because of the hanging, but Josh looks pretty good. Pictures of him are mounted on poster boards. One says, in street script, R I P Josh Mann, It reminds me of graffiti at a street memorial in the projects at Hunters Point this week, commemorating the shooting death of a 12-year-old boy. The target was his older brother.

Josh's mom thanks me for coming, shakes my hand as I head back down the aisle. "I'm so sorry for your loss," I say, not able to say what is really on my mind: *I am so sorry for all the suffering that you and your family endured here and in Cambodia, that produced this terrible tragedy, the horrible neck snapping, self-strangulation of your sweet, young son.* "So very sorry." I walk back down the aisle and sit with Diana and Tom. We whisper about Josh and the TL kids. Laura and some of the others come in. They sit in front of us, turn and smile, exchange hugs, take a flower from Tom and go up to pay their respects. Diana points out Jason, Josh's older brother, sitting up front. Jason, who Donal blames for this dreadful mess. Black knit watchman's cap pulled down low over his forehead. Black tee shirt showing off muscles and tattoos. Agony over the loss of his brother apparent on his face.

Six months later, Jason will be dead, found hanging in his jail cell.

How does a mother cope when two of her sons hang themselves six months apart? What was going on inside Josh's mind when he tied the rope around his neck, threw himself over the railing, broke his neck, and choked himself to death? Is this how he reconciled the two lives that he lived: the sweet teenager, who attended our first College Night—participating with enthusiasm when admissions counselors played a form of Jeopardy, howling with joy when he won a CND tee shirt—and the street warrior who defended his brother's honor? What value was the prestige he earned when he fought the Samoan "*mano-a-mano*," and got "his fuckin' ass" kicked? What was he doing, living in the Tenderloin, anyway, put here by our government? Donal said it, "Fuck, Josh was just a good guy. Got too much for him."

Two dead sons. More to come? This is not the life his family sought. They could have stayed in Cambodia.

NOTE

1. Before Josh died, legislation was passed to, at least, begin to address this problem. The Child Welfare League of America (www.cwla.org) reports: "In an effort to assist youth in their transitions to adulthood, the Foster Care Independence Act of 1999 established the John Chafee Foster Care Independence Program (Chafee Program), allowing states more funding and flexibility to help young people transition to adulthood. States received increased funding and were permitted to extend Medicaid eligibility to former foster children up to age 21.

"Additionally, the Chafee program allows states to use up to 30% of their federal funds to provide room and board services to youth 18–21 years of age. This includes young people who move into independent-living programs, age out, or lose touch with the child welfare agency and then return for assistance before reaching 21." But Josh was not a foster child.

CHAPTER 7

One Sadness After Another and Another

CEMETERY REUNION

© The Author(s) 2017
D. Stannard-Friel, *Street Teaching in the Tenderloin*,
DOI 10.1057/978-1-137-56437-5_7

A mom told me about her child's after school playtime in the hallway of their SRO. "I found my son huddled up in the corner." She asked him, "What are you doing?" "Playing shoot up," he said. He had his belt tied around his arm and was sticking a stick in his arm.

Dina Hilliard
Then teacher at City Academy
elementary school

* * *

"I know all about NDNU. I went to Catholic schools, myself." We're standing in the Community Room in the Mission Police Station on Valencia Street. This semester, the Analyzing Social Setting class is studying the historically Latino 24th Street corridor in the Mission District. Our street teacher today is the bicycle beat cop on 24th Street. "The Mission is the opposite of your life in Belmont. Norteños, Sureños, drugs, crazy people. Check out the scene at the 24th Street BART [Bay Area Rapid Transit] station. It's a different world from the life of white college students."

"Wait, wait a minute!" I raise my hand. "How many of you are white?" I ask my students. Of the 22 standing in the room, 2 raise their hands.

NDNU was recently designated as a "Hispanic-serving institution," which means that at least 25 percent of our student body is Latino. Thirty percent actually are. Of the incoming freshman class, 60 percent are non-white. In Analyzing Social Settings today, there are three African-Americans, a Palestinian, a Filipino, a Hawaiian, and the two Euro-Americans, but most of the students have Latin American, mainly Mexican, ancestry. Latino students are attracted to NDNU because of its Catholic roots and its small, nurturing community, and they are particularly drawn to the sociology major, especially Latinas, because of the social justice, community-engagement orientation of the program, often involving children. But the external perception of the student body studying at this small, private, Catholic university, located in the suburbs of San Francisco, is that it is white, privileged, and wealthy. Some are, the vast majority are not. Yet today, and on other occasions, even when standing before them, people "see" my students as white. And "privileged," which, if what they mean is "untouched by real life," I've never met that student.

Earlier, I listed some life experiences of my students: substance abuse, being homeless, family violence, family incompetence, prison time served, sibling in jail, parent in jail, sibling on death row, alcoholic parent, drug addicted parent, parent murdered, sibling murdered, sibling suicide, sexually abused, physically abused, emotionally abused, emancipated teen, aged-out foster child, abandoned as a child, trafficked as a child, mentally ill, victim of a crime of violence, poverty stricken, undocumented immigrant, refugee from an oppressive regime, gross learning disability, crippling disease, life-threatening disease, and disfigurement. Included on the list are the life experiences of students who are "privileged."

Many people, who don't know them, see the young Cambodian men on the streets of the Tenderloin—and friends of other nationalities and ethnic groups, who hang out with them—as "bad." Many of the young Cambodian men I know in the Tenderloin—Phanna Phay, David Mack, Paul Meas, Bee Nhey, Sam and Sammy Soun, Kim Soeun Tek, Veasna "Vee" Chea, others—are well known for their work in the community: tutoring kids, community beautification, safe streets programs, coaching sports, running youth leadership and healthy nutrition programs, helping to organize holiday celebrations (Cambodian New Years, Halloween in the Tenderloin), and helping teens with college applications and elders with citizenship applications. I am so impressed that so many of these street-smart, street-hardened young men are so involved, in meaningful, positive ways, in the lives of young kids in the neighborhood, even the littlest one. But some of them *have* gotten into trouble. And they've all faced really tough times, as have their friends, and many of my students. Where they end up in life—in jail or college, high on drugs or high on life, dead or alive—*always* depends upon the context of their lives, which, for the most part, has been determined by others.

* * *

From: Diana Chin
Sent: Thu 6/17/10 9:37 PM
To: Don Stannard-Friel
Re: Sad News

I don't know if you have heard. Nicky Huertas passed away on Sat. June 12 …. I watched Nicky grow up since he was only 5 years old. He was really engaged with the center esp. w/ Don's [another playground director] board games. It was only in the last few years that he became … more to himself and hanging with the kids on the street. He would only ask to use the phone when he came by…. didn't say too much but I've always made him feel welcome like it was still his second home. I feel so sad for Emelina [his sister] for they were the closest. He always looked out for her. The wake is on Friday and Saturday is the funeral at St. Boniface Church. Kay has more info if you want to attend. I thought my funeral days were over [Diana is retiring in two months]. From Sam's graduation to this …. life can be so unbelievably harsh.

* * *

Summer 2010:
I was a month into summer break from NDNU, reading the morning *Chronicle*, when I first heard about Nicky's death[1]:

Teenager shot and killed in own home
Jill Tucker, Chronicle Staff Writer
Monday, June 14, 2010
(06-13) 20:37 PDT SAN FRANCISCO -- San Francisco
A San Francisco teen was shot dead in his home Saturday evening, apparently while his mother and her boyfriend were in another room, police said.
William Huertas, 17, was shot once in the back of the head at about 8:45 p.m. inside the residence on the 1100 block of Turk Street, said San Francisco police spokesman Samson Chan.
It was not clear Sunday night how the shooter entered the home, what led up to the shooting or how the killer or killers escaped.
No arrests had been made and there was no description of a suspect available, police said. Calls to the victim's home were not answered Sunday.

"Damn, William Huertas? That's Nicky!"
Nicky was one of the kids from Tenderloin Children's Playground. A Halloween in the Tenderloin regular, with some of his sisters, and a College Night in the Tenderloin attendee. Diana made sure of that.
Three days later, I got Diana's "Sad News" email. I replied: "See you at the funeral."

* * *

Saturday, June 19, 2010:
I arrive at St. Boniface Church at 10:55 a.m. for the 11:00 a.m. service. There are no mourners in the church at all. A couple of dozen homeless people are scattered in the pews. A few are sleeping, others are arranging their bundles or watching a priest busy himself around the alter. I am, as always, stuck by the incredible beauty of the church, its openness to the homeless, and the faint smells of incense, burning candles, and the street people. I ask the priest, dressed in a simple, white work garment, if there

is a funeral for William Huertas, today. He answers, "Well, we're waiting for someone. We don't have a name."

"It's Nicky ... William Huertas. He should be here."

"How do you spell his name?"

I'm not sure. "I think it's, H-u-e-r...."

Just then, two tough-looking white women come up to the alter rail and look around the church. "We're here for the funeral. Where is everybody? We're Nicky's mother's best friends." They look very angry.

"Do you know how to spell Nicky's last name?" I ask them. "He's supposed to be here. They don't have his name."

"H-u-e-r-t-a-s," one of the women spells it out. She turns to her friend, saying, "They don't know his *name?*"

I feel a pull on my sleeve. It's Diana. "What's happening? Where is everybody?"

"Hey. I don't know. We're waiting for Nicky and his family, I guess. These two ladies are his mom's best friends." Diana and the women exchange nods and we all go sit down in the front pew. A line of young people files in the door off of Golden Gate Avenue. They are all dressed in black tee shirts and jeans or black slacks. A few of the girls have on black dresses. Most of them come over to greet Diana, who cries. I know some of them, and we exchange handshakes or hugs. A family comes in. More young people, dressed as the others: a black Oakland Raiders' jacket, more than a few black Giants baseball caps. More adults appear. Finally, at 11:20 a.m., the funeral procession appears at the door: the coffin, Nicky's mom, her boyfriend, Nicky's sisters, Emelina, Andrianna, Scarlet, and Gina, one of them very pregnant (new life entering the Tenderloin as another young one leaves). Like Nicky, I know most of the sisters, especially Gina, from College Night or Halloween or just hanging around the playground. Some of the mourners, walking behind the coffin, look worn-out, beat up by life: missing teeth, sunken cheeks, skinny bodies, hollow eyes. Bewildered little children cling onto grown-ups' hands. Nicky's coffin leads the way up the center aisle. The pallbearers are all dressed in white dress shirts. Muscular men, for the most part, tattooed, long-haired, or buzz cut, or pig-tailed hairstyles with the sides of their heads shaved. One has a flat-brimmed white baseball cap on; another wears his Giants cap on backwards. This is Nicky's crew, his homeboys from The TL and Western Addition, where he and his family lived in what we no longer call "the projects." How many of these young men will be carried in here by the others?

A priest in mass garments emerges from the back of the altar. It's a Vietnamese priest who I interviewed years ago. I didn't think he was a good fit for St. Boniface, then, when he told me that the Cambodian people were "not like Vietnamese. Cambodians uneducated. Don't want to work." I wondered at the time, What's he doing *here* at this (along with Glide Memorial up the block), the most diverse, most liberal, most social justice-oriented church in liberal San Francisco? Maybe time, the Tenderloin community, and the good work of the friars have opened him up to a new perspective.

The priest begins the funeral mass. Everyone stands up, including a few of the homeless men. Following the opening ritual, the priest begins, what I assumed was going to be, a reflection on Nicky's life and death: "I didn't know William, but I spoke to him last night." He talks about the difference between "knowing" and "understanding." "I didn't know him," he says again, "but I understand him. I spoke to him last night."

I turn to Diana and whisper, "He didn't even know his name last night."

The priest goes on. He makes no personal references to Nicky, on his life, or how he died. No comments on social justice or the injustices that produced such a horrible end to a vibrant young life, which would have been how Fr. Louie Vitale, the Franciscan priest who just retired as pastor of St. Boniface, would have reflected on the murder of a kid from the neighborhood. This priest's focus is on redemption (saving one's self, and soul, from personal wrongdoing) and asking for forgiveness. He gives an illustration of a conversation between the wife of a man who committed suicide and her priest.

"The wife say to priest that she is suffering because she know he is burning in hell," he tells the mourners. "You know, Catholic doctrine: 'commit suicide, go to hell.' The priest say to the wife, 'No, he in Heaven. On way down, you know, from the bridge, he say to God, "I make mistake," and asks forgiveness. So he is in Heaven!'" He looks at Nicky's family, and nods at them.

"What has this got to do with Nicky?" I ask Diana. Nicky was shot in the back of the head. He wasn't thinking of asking for forgiveness. He was murdered!

The priest continues, "Every week, I was beaten by my father. I wouldn't do what he wanted. My mother say to me, 'Do you love me?' 'Yes.' 'Will you do me *one* favor?' 'Yes. *Many* favors.' 'Just one,' she say. 'Obey your father, so he won't beat you.'"

"You know, I didn't want to obey him. Wanted to have excitement, fun. But we *must* obey. Rules! Like," he stares at Nicky's mother, "*You were 20 minutes late!*"

I think, thankfully, the mom looks too distraught to catch what was going on.

"I understand William," the priest concludes, without ever revealing what that means.

At communion, he says, "If you are Catholic, please come up for communion. If you are not Catholic, do not come up!" He repeats it for good measure, "If you are Catholic, please come up for communion. If you are not Catholic, do *not* come up!" Most Catholic services I attend, especially with Fr. Louie at St. Boniface and the chapel at NDNU, the priests invite non-Catholics to come up to be blessed during the communion rite.

As the mass ends, the priest spreads incense over the casket. Then he stands at the head of the coffin and flips his hand, back side up, the sign of *dismissal*. Take it away! The service is over.

The funeral directors, a man and a woman, tough, squat-looking people in ill-fitting long, black jackets, organize the pallbearers, who line up and take the coffin out. The mourners follow, with the family in the lead. Diana and I are just joining the line when shouting erupts in the vestibule. A woman's voice, "Get the fuck outta here! Get your hands offa him!" I pull Diana back. A mass of people is swaying back and forth around the coffin. A shoving match is going on.

We wait until the commotion dies down, then leave by the front door. We see Nicky's little sister, Gina, standing outside, holding someone else's baby. Gina is a very sweet kid of 13 or so, a regular attendee at playground events. "Thank you for coming to Nicky's funeral," she says. She hugs us. Another sister walks by, livid, says, "Bitch spit on me." Diana calls me later, "Scarlett [Nicky's oldest sister] got in fight with Nicky's dad—not hers. She didn't want him there. Says he was never around when Nicky was alive. He has no right being there, now."

* * *

July 1, 2010:
"Ring, ring, ring...." I'm calling Diana.
"Hi, Dr. Don"
"Hi, Diana. How's it going?"
"Not too good. Another death. I really think it's time for me to leave. One of our girls drove her car into a truck on the Bay Bridge. I think it was suicide. It sounds like suicide. She was having a really hard time."

I go online, at SFGate.com, to check out what happened:

Motorist dies in fiery Bay Bridge crash
July 01, 2010|By Henry K. Lee, Chronicle Staff Writer
(06-30) 12:19 PDT SAN FRANCISCO — A woman died on the Bay Bridge early today in a fiery crash with a recycling truck, briefly shutting down eastbound traffic on the lower deck, authorities said.
  The crash happened when the woman, driving a Volvo at high speed, ran into the back of a recycling truck in the eastbound direction in the Yerba Buena Island tunnel shortly before 3:50 a.m.
  The car became pinned underneath the tractor-trailer truck, and both vehicles caught on fire, according to the California Highway Patrol.

The next day, I check the paper's website again:

Woman killed in fiery Bay Bridge wreck is IDd
July 02, 2010|By Will Kane, Chronicle Staff Writer
(07-01) 11:24 PDT SAN FRANCISCO — The woman killed in a fiery wreck on the Bay Bridge early Wednesday was identified today as 28-year-old Clara Cisneroz of San Francisco.
  Cisneroz was pronounced dead at the scene after her eastbound Volvo rammed the back of a recycling truck and burst into flames in the Yerba Buena Island tunnel shortly before 3:50 a.m., said Officer Herman Quon of the California Highway Patrol.
  Witnesses told the CHP that the Volvo had been going about 100 mph when it hit the truck.

Clara Cisneroz, another playground kid. 100 mph. 3:50 a.m. Pinned under a garbage truck. Burst into flames. DOA. 28 years old. She left behind two little girls and a life she no longer deemed worth living.

* * *

July 20, more news of Nicky's murder[2]:

S.F. man, 18, charged in teen's slaying
Jaxon Van Derbeken, Chronicle Staff Writer
Tuesday, July 20, 2010
A San Francisco transient was charged Monday in the shooting death of a 17-year-old boy who police believe had invited the suspect home possibly to sell a rifle, authorities said.

William Huertas was fatally shot with that rifle on the evening of June 12 while his mother and his stepfather were upstairs in their Turk Street residence, authorities said. On Friday, police arrested Robert Griffin, 18, on suspicion of robbery, burglary and homicide.

Police said surveillance video from the development where the boy lived shows him bringing Griffin to his residence.

Huertas' family said the teenager had a sport rifle and police theorized that he was trying to sell it or show it off when he was killed.

Griffin is shown on another video tossing the rifle over a nearby fence three days after the killing, authorities said. On June 18, police arrested Griffin on suspicion of an attempted burglary of a cell phone in a Fifth Street shopping center. He was not charged.

"It's very tragic," said Lt. Mike Stasko of the San Francisco police homicide detail. "The victim had this rifle, he apparently tried to show it to him. (Griffin) ended up using it on him."

* * *

From: Kay Rodrigues
Sent: 8/31/2010
To: Recipients
Re: Tenderloin Families Need Help

Tenderloin families need help to pay for headstones for very needy families. We've got 2 young men who've recently passed away by lethal gun shot wounds. William Nicholas Huertas and now, Logan Kaufman. Funds to help pay for their tombstones can be made to Woodlawn Cemetery in Colma. If you know of any agencies that provide special prices or services to aid low-income families with this need please contact me asap. Kay

*"Logan Kaufman...*dead?" I said aloud to myself, as I read the email. Another one?

* * *

From: Don Stannard-Friel
Sent: 8/31/2010
To: Kay Rodrigues
Re: Tenderloin Families Need Help,
What is the story behind Logan's shooting?
Don

* * *

From: Kay Rodrigues
Sent: Tue 9/1/2010 11:13 AM
To: Don Stannard-Friel
Subject: Tenderloin Families Need Help

Logan shot himself in the head, but lived on life support for at least 3 weeks, but passed away just days ago according to Scarlett (Nicky's sister) and Sammy Soun. He shot himself in his apartment after having an argument with his girlfriend, they just had a baby together...apparently baby was in the house so CPS has custody. It's not pretty to say the least. Kay

* * *

Summer "vacation" is over. Fall semester begins. I'm sitting in my office in Ralston Hall. NDNU is located on the old estate of nineteenth-century banker, builder, and Comstock silver mine magnate William Ralston. Ralston Hall was his summer mansion. Surrounded by beautiful lawns that are populated by graceful trees, small herds of deer, and quick, black squirrels that fascinate the Tenderloin kids when they tour the campus as part of the College Night program. The contrast with The TL couldn't be more striking. I'm at my desk, looking at a poster board put together last semester by students in the Promise of the Inner City class. Pictures of Tenderloin scenes are taped to the board. So are brochures from service agencies, a photo of the students sitting in Celtic Coffee Company (the new name for Wild Awakenings), neighborhood demographic statistics, crime rates, and Phanna's poem from *Stories of Survival*, reflecting on the life and death of his brother. A former student appears at my open door. "Hi, Dr. Don. How was your summer?"

It's Jamie Moraga,[3] a May graduate, now a new graduate student at the university.

"It was, well, OK. It was... mixed. Come, take a look at this."

I show Jamie the poster board, and point out Phanna's poem. I tell her about the summer deaths of the three young people. I shake my head. "Tragic."

Jamie's eyes glisten. "Do you remember my brother?"

Jesus Christ! I say to myself. "Yes, of course. I am so sorry." Her brother committed suicide. She told me the family story when she was a freshman. I think his death is one underlying cause of Jamie's passionate drive to be an activist in service of humankind. She has an impressive list of social justice accomplishments since arriving at NDNU, four years ago.

We sit together in silence, looking at Phanna's poem and pictures of children playing in the playground. There's a photo of Diana Chin, surrounded by little kids. Which of them will die too soon?

I say goodbye to Jamie, and walk down the hall to class, past a row of administrative and faculty offices. I see a friend, a staff member, sitting at her desk, and stop to tell her the story of the summer deaths, and that a former student just reminded me of her brother's suicide. A shadow passes across her face. "My sister committed suicide six months ago," she tells me. "But I didn't even find out until three months later. She was caught up on drugs."

I go to teach "Deviant Behavior," a popular on-campus class for, if nothing else, its title. I tell the story of my summer break, that a former student reminded me of her brother's suicide, and that a school employee just told me about her sister's overdose death. A young woman in the class bends over, sobbing, jumps up, and runs out of the room. In a little while, she comes back, gives me a little thumbs-up sign, and returns to her seat. After class, she comes up to the podium and tells me that a friend in the Army just committed suicide. "He put a gun in his mouth," she sticks her index finger into her own mouth, "and pulled the trigger." Her eyes fill up, but she doesn't cry.

I take the Exploring the Inner World of the Inner City class to San Francisco County Jail. We sit with 50 inmates in a pod[4] and share stories. Mario, a clean-cut, hardworking sophomore sociology student in two of my inner-city classes, raises his hand. "My brother was a Sureño," he says, his voice shaking. "He was killed a few years ago." A student who was supposed to attend this jail gathering was denied access because his name showed up on a background check as "Actively on probation or parole." That was wrong. A computer error. He finished parole a year before, after completing a three-year prison sentence for the manufacture of drugs. One of the best students I have ever had, he went on to law school.

My Sports, Service and Society class is planning a sport clinic in The TL. El, a basketball player in the class, comes into my office to get a signature. I'm just getting to know El this semester, and I ask where he is from. "Sacramento," he replies. "Well, Baltimore, until I was two, then my mother gave me away to my aunt to raise. I never saw her again. My father was in prison. I didn't meet him until I was ten, then he went back to prison. It's OK. My aunt is my mom. She's taken good care of me."

Ashley tells her classmates and inmates at another jail gathering that she just reunited with her dad at Thanksgiving, after he was released from a long prison sentence. He's back in prison, now. Maria, a new student in sociology, has visited relatives and friends in prison her whole life. Rebecca, on a tour of San Quentin with the Deviant Behavior class, points to the second tier in the Reception Center. "That's my brother's cell."

* * *

Gretchen Wehrle is another longtime CBL professor at NDNU. She offers "Building Community Through Diversity" and "Community Psychology," and runs the Sr. Dorothy Stang Faculty Scholars Program,[5] teaching other NDNU professors community-engagement practices. For two years, we were California Campus Compact-Carnegie Foundation Fellows for Political Engagement together, developing community-engagement curricula with 21 other professors from throughout the state, and we often co-present at conferences, sometimes with students who have taken our classes. In many conversations about our teaching lives, we have asked each other, "Has it always been like this?" Has so much suffering always been sitting right before us in our classrooms, as we taught Deviant Behavior, Social Problems, Criminology, Social Psychology, Soc of the Family, and other, *campus-based* courses that deal with life's struggles? Or is there a new cohort of college students coming to college, one that has experienced more pain and suffering than earlier generations? I think it is both. Students have always confided with their professors about personal issues, and those issues have often been profound. But today, students, in general—in this Age of Communication, of Facebook, of increasing transparency, and a societal-wide interest in making public what was once private (e.g., blogs, tweeting, YouTube, cell phone videos/photography, reality shows, the personal lives of politicians, Edward Snowden) —seem more willing to share their stories, especially in CBL classes, where levels of intimacy are enhanced by the nature of the classes (meeting in off-campus sites, hanging out in coffeehouses, walking the streets together, engaging in conversations with street teachers, doing community service, traveling in carpools to, and, especially, from inner-city engagements, par-ticipating in organized reflection) and the topics we encounter often hit home, stimulating personal reflection. And, perhaps of more significance, students from more varied backgrounds, including those with physical, emotional, or learning differences—who were previously *denied access* by a society that discriminated against them (labeling youth with learning or emotional disabilities as "stupid" or "troublemakers," and institutionaliz-ing or at least not mainstreaming those with significant physical disabilities, before ADA legislation) —are coming to college in far greater numbers than ever before. As a college education became a more expected and necessary goal in society at large, we, as a society, began redefining who should (and *could*) go to college, beginning with the GI Bill after World War II. Since then, the number and variety of attendees have soared. The percentage of people enrolling in college immediately after high school increased from 20 percent in 1950, to 40 percent in the 1960s, to 50 percent in the early 1970s, to 70 percent today, and as the cohort expanded, so did a rich mixture of life experiences within it. Non-traditional age students returned to school in ever-increasing numbers, more women than men are now enrolled, and there is far more racial and economic diversity than ever before. And more challenges.

Recognition that many new students often had to overcome, or are still struggling with, previously unseen or unrecognized significant obstacles to achieving educational goals caused the federal government to add these inquiries to its Free Application for Federal Student Aid (FAFSA) checklist:

- Both your parents are deceased, or you were (until age 18) a ward or dependent of the court
- You were a foster child after the age of 13
- You are an emancipated child as determined by a court judge
- You are homeless or at risk of homelessness as determined by the director of a Department of Housing and Urban Development (HUD)-approved homeless shelter, transitional program, or high school liaison

And according to a report in the Archives of General Psychiatry, discussed by Lindsey Tanner, Associated Press (AP) (December 2, 2008),[6]

Counting substance abuse, the study found that nearly half of [5000] young people surveyed [age 19 – 25 years old] have some sort of psychiatric condition, including students and nonstudents.

Personality disorders were the second-most-common problem behind drug or alcohol abuse as a single category. The disorders include obsessive, anti-social and paranoid behaviors that are not mere quirks but actually interfere with ordinary functioning.

Add to the list all the learning disabilities spread throughout the population, and the turmoil, illnesses, and stresses that take their toll on family and individual life everywhere, and the opportunity to connect students' experiences, or the experiences of someone they love, with the lives of the people of the streets, becomes apparent. That the new FAFSA inquiries, the common application for financial aid for students going to college, were added to the form, acknowledges that qualities that we associate with "troubled" lives in the inner city are *not* contained there.

When we recognize that aspects of the suffering that we see on "skid row" are, in fact, all around us—in the dorms and communities we live in, and the families we come from—we can appreciate that the root of the problem is not *individual* in nature, but *social*, demanding a social response, and insight into the actual foundations of the struggles people face can be achieved. When we connect our own lives to lives in our tenderloins, we walk in their shoes.

* * *

"Dr. Don, my sister is a prostitute. A streetwalker in the Tenderloin," a well-dressed business major tells me after class one day.

"I can't go on to San Quentin with you, Dr. Don," a reentry student says. "My daughter's rapist is there."

A student tells me that her father, an ex-con, is now running a well-known rehab program. "You must be very proud of him," I said. "He put me through hell," she replies. "I remember when I was 11, cops breaking down the door, making me and my little sister lie on the floor with our arms stretched out, while they searched for drugs."

Melissa, a young mom, meets with me to talk about her term paper. "What's your topic?" I ask. "Homelessness," she replies. "I was homeless last semester. I lived in a tent with my two boys."

Wendy, another reentry student and mother, is also a very accomplished artist. She gave me one of her photographs. "You'll understand," she said. On the bottom it read, "A View from my Bedroom Window." It was a silk screen of buildings. "Do you recognize it?" she asked. It looked familiar, but I couldn't put my finger on it. The colors were altered and washed across the page in artistic distortion. "It's the courthouse in the Tenderloin. Civic Center Park was my bedroom when I was strung out. I lived there with my kids."

Dre's brother is on death row in Guam. Samantha's mom is mentally ill. Christian was shot in the back, three times.

* * *

November 15, 2005:

It's College Night in the Tenderloin. The agenda for the evening has stayed about the same throughout the years: after the pizza and intro-ductions, Admissions and Financial Aid counselors offer guidance to Tenderloin teenagers, play a game of College Facts Jeopardy with the youth, and NDNU student speakers tell personal stories and explain how they got in college and what's it like being there. Recently, Tenderloin youth who have gone on to college come back to tell their stories to the next generation of college-bound hopefuls. The event reflects the "real-life learning" philosophy of community-based education. In fall semester 2005, the real-life learning got way too real.

Vamsey, whose family emigrated from India, emceed the College Night gathering in the multipurpose room at Tenderloin Children's Playground. Very intelligent, with a great sense of humor, he has a thin skin when it comes to the kinds of confrontations that young men sometimes find themselves in, and that's gotten him into trouble. He's working on chang-ing that. Katie, born in Ukraine, came to the USA with her family after the fall of the Soviet Union. Raised right across the street from Children's Playground in Reverend Glenda Hope's San Francisco Network Ministries apartments, she enrolled at NDNU after attending several College Nights as a Tenderloin kid and taking two of my inner-city classes, while still a senior in high school. Her topic this night was "From The Tenderloin to NDNU." Theresa, an effervescent Filipino-American, talked about clubs and campus life. Eno, whose family is from Nigeria—very tall, very ele-gant, very nervous—invited the attendees to a campus visit trip. Christian, a basketball player, introduced the sports program and told his story of growing up in Bayview-Hunters Point, a San Francisco neighborhood notorious for drug wars and drive-by shootings. Raised in the poor, iso-lated community—cut off from the rest of the city (including hospitals and supermarkets) by freeways, industry, abandoned warehouses, and a municipal transportation system that, at the time, took forever to get any-where—he explained that he understood how difficult it is *not* to enter street life, but that going to college changed everything for him. He had no doubt that doors were going to open, that would otherwise be closed. In a Streetwise class meeting before College Night, he told his story to the rest of us, and we related it to Robert Merton's theory, "Social Structure and Anomie."[7]

Decades before the 1960s Cultural Revolution, Merton focused on social injustices and oppression of many kinds, although he didn't use that vocabulary. For Merton, "structural inequality" in America was apparent in the systematic denial of access to "institutional means" (jobs, education), which are the legitimate pathways to achieving "cultural goals" (meaning, in America, material success). This means–goals disjuncture produces "anomie" or "normlessness," a state of anxiety and confusion resulting from the individual's desire to achieve the American Dream, but being systematically denied access to socially acceptable ways of doing so. This state of tension, Merton said, can be mitigated through "innovation," the production of illegitimate means ("lower-class crime") to attain the culturally expected economic success. In other words, in attempting to achieve society's most cherished objectives, those denied access to the legitimate means to the goals may *deviate to conform* to cultural expectations. An obvious alternative, of course, is for society to open up institutionalized means to success to those who have been previously redirected: education, jobs, and access to people and places that make a difference in the world of material success. Later, this became popularly known as "civil rights," "desegregation," and "affirmative action."

Christian's upcoming graduation in May—and that nearly 60 percent of his fellow traditional-age undergraduates enrolled at NDNU were drawn from non-white communities—we said, demonstrates social progress in American society, the broadening of access to means to success (in this case, higher education and the higher-paid jobs that follow), although roadblocks and discrimination of many kinds remain. Then, just a few weeks after College Night, as Christmas vacation was about to begin, one semester before he was going to graduate from college, Christian was dead, shot in the back three times.

* * *

Two Bay Area Men Killed, Third Arrested in Clearlake Home Invasion
(CA) December 8, 2005 | AP
By GLENDA ANDERSON
THE PRESS DEMOCRAT[8]
CLEARLAKE, Calif.--Two Bay Area men are dead and a third in custody in what police say was a botched home invasion robbery in Clearlake. Authorities say 21-year-old Rashad Williams of Pittsburg and 22-year-old Christian Foster of San Francisco died of gunshot wounds after authorities say residents of the home mounted a counterattack.

A third man who also allegedly participated in yesterday's early morning invasion, 21-year-old Renato Hughes Junior, was hospitalized with head injuries in the attack.

Because two people died in the incident, Hughes has been arrested and booked for two counts of murder and other charges.

At least one of three Bay Area men involved in an alleged home invasion that left two of them dead in Clearlake on Wednesday was armed with a shotgun, according to charges filed against the surviving suspect Friday.

Two of the men were shot and killed by the homeowner, Shannon Edmonds, during what police described as a thwarted home invasion robbery. Authorities said the incident was drug-related.

An undisclosed amount of marijuana and a medical marijuana card were located at the residence, police said.

The third robbery suspect was arraigned Friday in Lake County Superior Court on murder, attempted murder and burglary charges.

The three men allegedly broke into the 11th Street home Edmonds shares with his daughter, his girlfriend and her two sons at 4:25 a.m. Wednesday.

It appears they attacked Edmonds and the woman in their bedroom, then beat the woman's 17-year-old son, Dale, with a metal baseball bat when he came to their rescue, said Lake County Chief Deputy District Attorney Jon Hopkins.

"I think he was trying to help his mother and Shannon. Someone hit him in the head with a baseball bat," he said.

Hopkins said he does not know which of the men dealt the blow, which seriously injured the boy.

The condition of the teen, who remains at Santa Rosa Memorial Hospital, was not available.

Police believe the suspects obtained the bat from the residence, Hopkins said.

During the assault, Edmonds grabbed the 9 mm handgun believed to have been used to kill two of the intruders, Hopkins said.

It has not yet been determined whether Edmonds shot the men while they were inside the house, outside the house or both, a factor that will help determine whether Edmonds will be prosecuted, he said.

The gunshot victims fell about 30 feet from the house.

Edmonds dropped the gun in the street near one of the bodies when police arrived, Hopkins said.

* * *

A few days after Christian's death, we sat in a circle in the university's Cunningham Chapel—people from NDNU and some of his friends from Bayview-Hunters Point—to remember him: funny, smart, handsome, athletic, focused, a good person, a great smile. No one—except the people who were there, and two of them are dead —really knows what happened in the middle of that night, at the home of a drug dealer in Clearlake, a rural town 132 miles north of NDNU. Whatever happened, Christian was definitely in the wrong place at the wrong time.

"He was a victim of racism," a voice from the circle in Cunningham Chapel said. No matter what actually went down in Clearlake that night, there is no doubt that Christian was a victim of racism. That black men make up 6 percent of the country's population, but 40 percent of its murder victims[9] speaks volumes to blocked opportunity, anomie, and the social consequences of raising children in a society that produces and maintains communities steeped in violence, drugs, and poverty, neighborhoods like Hunters Point and the Tenderloin. And rural Clearlake, aka "The Meth Capital of California."

But the two young men who were killed that night, and their friend who was sent to prison, were not "gangbangers" or "thugs" as some have claimed. Christian Foster, Rashad Williams, and Renato Hughes grew up together and were elementary school friends. All came from stable, supportive families. They enjoyed success in Tae Kwon Do martial arts, track, and basketball, and were active in church and community service activities.

Christian aspired to become a guidance counselor for underprivileged and underrepresented kids. He had participated in feeding the homeless programs through his church and tutored and mentored junior high school students. He was about to become engaged to his longtime girlfriend. A communications major at NDNU, he was a popular, outgoing student. He had won awards in Tae Kwon Do and played high school basketball so well that he earned a basketball scholarship to NDNU, but was no longer on the team when he took Streetwise Sociology. He told me he had some kind of falling out with the coach, and was bitter about the situation. I was worried that this might taint his presentation to the Tenderloin youth on College Night, but he gave a stellar performance, promoting NDNU, its sports program, including the basketball team, and college athletics in general.

When Rashad, the other boy killed, was a 15-year-old high school freshman, he became a national hero. He read about 16-year-old Lance Kirklin, a Columbine massacre victim who was shot in the chest, face, and legs. Lance would need multiple surgeries, but he didn't have the insurance to pay for it. Rashad, a track star, figured, since he was already running in San Francisco's Bay to Breakers race, maybe he could turn his involvement into a fund-raiser. The result: he raised $40,000 for Lance's medical bills. Six days before the race, *San Francisco Examiner* columnist

Rob Morse wrote about the story and it went national. Rashad appeared on *The Oprah Winfrey Show*, CNN, *Good Morning America*, MSNBC, and was a contestant on *To Tell the Truth*. He was honored with an award from the National Alliance of Black Schools and received a US Senate Certificate of Commendation. San Francisco Mayor Willie Brown declared May 24, 1999, Rashad Williams Day, and a year later, Williams was grand marshal of the Bay to Breakers.

Then, something happened. His mother said his celebrity status interfered with his everyday life. His grades dropped and he started falling behind in his college preparatory work. He was traveling the country, being interviewed and honored for his good work, but his life was falling apart at home. It seemed Rashad had hit rock bottom when he was convicted of two unarmed bank robberies in nearby Contra Costa County, but the bottom was yet to come. He was staying at his grandparents' home in Clearlake, waiting for the start of his three-year prison term, when he was killed.

Renato, the sole survivor of the three friends, graduated from Mission High School in San Francisco. An all-around athlete, as a youth he was involved in football, basketball, baseball, and track and field. He had stopped out as a business major at San Jose State University, but was planning on returning, soon. He was working as a cashier at Trader Joe's supermarket, played cello with the Golden Gate Philharmonic Orchestra, and taught at San Francisco Christian Center. He had a daughter who was two years old at the time of the shooting.

The Lake County District Attorney (DA) charged Reynato with murder, responsible for the deaths of his two friends, because, he said, they were killed in commission of an "armed home invasion" attempt to steal marijuana. The charge was based on a controversial application of California's Provocative Act doctrine, which says that someone who provokes another to kill can be charged with murder. Shannon Edmonds, the shooter, was cleared as acting in self-defense. Christian's friends and Renato's defense lawyer, Stephen Carter, claim it was a late-night marijuana purchase from a dealer with a history of violence and racial confrontations that turned into a terrible altercation. Carter insisted that Edmonds was not an innocent victim. "When you shoot someone who is fleeing, it's not self-defense," he said at Renato's trial. "It's an execution."

As news of the killings and the charges against Renato circulated in the Bay Area, a community of support emerged for what became known as the "Clearlake 3." The National Association for the Advancement of Colored People (NAACP), in a November 14, 2007, press release, said:

According to Alice Huffman the President of the California NAACP, "The NAACP strongly feels that this is a current civil rights injustice case that should not be occurring in this day and time. There are elements of the case that make no sense and it is clear that justice for the murdered victims will not be vindicated until the true culprit is punished, and it is equally evident that the rights of the young man [Renato] accused in this case have been compromised. We feel it is urgent to bring this civil rights case before the public."

The California State Conference of the NAACP has enlisted the services of attorney, Stratton Barbee to file an amicus brief in support of Renato Hughes receiving a change of venue in this case. It is believed that this young man cannot receive a fair trial by a jury of his peers.

On Thursday, November 15, 2007, a judge granted the defense's motion for a change of venue. Renato's lawyers successfully argued that he would not be able to get a fair trial, because of extensive local media coverage and the likelihood that he could not get a jury of his peers in a county of 3000 inhabitants, 91 percent of whom are white, and 2 percent black.

* * *

What did happen that night in Clearlake? According to the prosecution in Renato's murder trial, it was a home invasion robbery. According to the defense, it was a drug deal gone bad. What is known is that a 17-year-old boy was beaten with his own baseball bat in the home that night, that he suffered serious brain damage, and that two of the alleged robbers were killed by Shannon Edmonds. Edmonds was a certified user of marijuana for his own medical purposes. Police found five gallon-sized bags of processed marijuana in Edmonds' house, along with a half-bucket of freshly picked pot, an awful lot of weed for "personal medical use." A few nights before the killings, there was an altercation of some kind between the Edmonds' household and two black teenage neighbors, specifically involving Dale Lafferty, the 17-year-old who was beaten with a baseball bat. On the night of the shooting, Edmonds had smoked marijuana (as had every other person in the house that night) and had taken Lexapro, an antidepressant, and Neurontin, a drug used to control seizures. After Edmonds shot Christian and Rashad in their backs as they were running away from his home, he told police officers that seeing Christian run out of the house with his sagging pants falling down "was funnier than shit to see him fall with his ass hanging out." Two signs posted on Edmonds' property warned, "Private Property Keep Out" and "This house guarded by a shotgun three nights per week. You guess which three." The shotgun that was purportedly used in the alleged home invasion was never found by police, but several weeks later Edmonds turned one in that he said he found in some bushes. It was never connected to the events of that evening.

In the months following the killings, news stories and web postings demonstrated widely divergent views of the case held by people directly involved in the tragedy and other observers.

Renato's mother, Judy Hughes, a San Francisco schoolteacher, called the trial against her son "a legal lynching.... This is a mother's worst nightmare. This community here has a good old boys regime." She acknowledged that her son and his friends may have been out "partying" and looking for marijuana, but that's very different from being involved in murder. "Only God knows what happened in that house," she said. "But this I know: My son did not murder his childhood friends."[10]

Sheila Burton, Rashad's mother, said of Edmonds, "This man shot my son in cold blood."[11] She protested the way Renato was being treated, "There are questions I need to have answered. I can't bring closure to my son's death when they have incarcerated my son's best friend."[12] She was furious when she proclaimed, "I can't believe that the judicial system is treating [Rashad's death] this way.... Instead of my heart mending, it's being torn apart."[13]

From the other side of the story, Deborah Besley, grandmother of the badly beaten Dale Lafferty, said,[14]

"If there's a living nightmare, this is it."

On Dec. 27, I kept saying I was waiting for my hug from Dale for my birthday, Besley recalled. "The therapist picked up his arm and put it around my neck. ... It's heartbreaking. You live through the sadness, the numbness, the grieving. You live through the not knowing and constantly wondering. We want Dale back the way Dale was."

Lori Tyler, Dale's mother, had this to say,[15]

"Dale was a wonderful young man with a great future and everything going for him," she said.

Today, he has to have 24-hour daycare after suffering eight skull fractures during the incident. Tyler said he had to have surgery to remove part of his brain in order to survive.

"The counselor told me that I have lost my son," she said, adding when she took him home after his hospitalization, it was like bringing home a 170-pound infant.

Edmonds's defense of his own actions was reported in the press[16]:

> the unemployed car mechanic said since the shootings, he's been ostracized in the small town, abandoned by his fiancee and is about to lose his home, which he can't afford on his own.

> "I didn't do anything wrong. All I did was defend my family and my children's lives," said Edmonds, 33. "I'm sad the kids are dead, I didn't mean to kill them. But this has destroyed my life."

Edmonds was not completely ostracized, however. In response to the shootings and the news stories that followed, Ironmagazine.com (March 16, 2007) posted comments from his supporters:

> Posted by KelJu:

> Civil rights groups are claiming racism, but seem to ignore the fact that the gang of nigger thugs broke into Shannon Edmond's house and beat his son to the point of brain damage.

> Posted by DOMS:

> If a black man isn't handed everything on a silver platter, it's racism. I'm trying very hard not be racist towards blacks, but shit like this makes it hard.

> Posted by Little Wing:

> People in the U.S. are so used to hearing "shooting" it doesn't have much effect. Maybe if pieces of shit like this started getting hacked to death by machete people would stop and think twice before they commit home invasions.

On the Free Republic blog, responding to a comment by Renato's sister, quoted in a newspaper article,[17] that her brother "was active in several youth and community groups in San Francisco," HEY4QDEMS posted: "Let me guess, Crips or Bloods?" Another Free Republic posting, commenting on Christian and Rashad's deaths, "Two out of three ain't bad!"

* * *

On August 8, 2008, Renato was found not guilty for the murder of his two friends and the attempted murder of Dale Lafferty, the boy who was beaten. The jury also found him not guilty of attempted voluntary manslaughter, and not guilty of robbery of an inhabited dwelling, but they did find him guilty of assault with a firearm on Edmonds, and guilty of burglary with a weapons enhancement.

During the trial, Renato's defense attorney called witnesses to testify about Edmonds' credibility as a key witness in the trial, and his own propensity toward violence. Paul Edmonds, Shannon's brother, testified about a fight the two had in November 2006—almost a year after Christian and Rashad's deaths—at Paul's mobile home in Mendocino County. *The Press Democrat*[18] reported on the brother's testimony,

> Paul Edmonds, a small-engine mechanic in Ukiah, said his brother threw him on a hot stove, fired as many as 10 rounds from a shotgun and struck him on the head with the butt of the gun.
>
> Shannon Edmonds was knocked unconscious during the fight, which resulted in Paul Edmonds being charged with assault and other crimes.
>
> Paul Edmonds said he was convicted of cultivating marijuana after authorities discovered 75 pounds of pot at his home, along with digital scales and receipts for money paid and owed. He said the marijuana was to be used by him, his brother, [Lori] Tyler and a fourth person for medical reasons.

A total of *75 pounds of pot*, to be used by Paul, Shannon, Lori, and a fourth person. That's about 19 pounds apiece. That should take care of any medical condition.

Dale Lafferty's (the beaten boy) mother, Lori Tyler, who was in the house on the night of Christian and Rashad's killing, was another witness testifying to Edmonds' violent history. She sobbed on the stand when she told the court that Edmonds tried to kill her in August 2007, by forcing her to ingest about 150 pills.[19]

> She said he forced her to write suicide notes and that if she didn't go along with the plan, that he would find another way to kill her.
>
> "Why did you think he'd find another way to kill you?" Hanlon [Renato's defense attorney] asked.
>
> "Because he was, how do you describe it, it was like he'd lost his mind and I believed him," Tyler replied. "He was scary."

Tyler obtained a restraining order against Edmonds. She said she tried to have him arrested for attempted murder, but the police and DA refused to do so.

Edmonds admitted during cross-examination that he had given marijuana to at least three juveniles to smoke and gave the drug to at least one
juvenile to sell. Teenagers at the trial testified that Edmonds hired them
to trim marijuana buds, smoked weed with him on numerous occasions,
sold marijuana for him, and even, on one occasion before the night of the
shooting, *drove with Rashad Williams to Edmonds' home to make a marijuana purchase.*

According to Ken Nelson, chair of the California chapter of the NAACP,
the NAACP tried to get prosecutors to charge Edmonds for these crimes,
but they refused.[20]

Was the DA trying to protect Shannon Edmonds' reputation and
keep him out of jail during the time that Renato was on trial? DA Stuart
Hanlon suggested that Edmonds was receiving favorable treatment from
Clearlake police and the prosecution because of his importance in testifying against Renato.[21]

Then, on Thursday, March 11, 2010, the following was reported[22]:

Clearlake man, cleared in one slaying, convicted of murder in another
Lake County Sheriff's Office
**Shannon Edmonds, 35, of Clearlake was convicted Thursday of
using a knife to kill Shelby Uehling, 25.**
By GLENDA ANDERSON
THE PRESS DEMOCRAT
March 11, 2010
A Clearlake man who gained national attention in 2005 for killing two
men as they fled a break-in at his home was found guilty Thursday of second-
degree murder for another killing.

Shannon Edmonds, 35, was convicted on Thursday of using a knife to kill
Shelby Uehling, 25. He also was found guilty of charges that he assaulted
the victim with a police baton and inflicted great bodily injury.

Edmonds faces 15 years to life in prison, said Lake County Deputy
District Attorney Art Grothe, who prosecuted the case.

Edmond's co-defendant, Melvin Dale Norton, 38, was convicted of
being an accessory to murder and assault with a golf club. Because he has
two prior "strike" convictions, Norton likely is facing 25 years to life in
prison, Grothe said.

Uehling was stabbed and beaten to death Sept. 22 along Old Highway
53 in Clearlake.

Prosecutors said that Edmonds killed Uehling because he had been
phoning and texting his girlfriend. Uehling had had a week-long, drug-
fueled relationship when Edmonds and the woman were separated.

* * *

In Streetwise Sociology classes since the Clearlake incident, we have talked about the tragedy of Christian's death and the confusion surrounding it, and that even some of the people living in Hunters Point, who were in Christian's circle of acquaintances, said that they heard it *was* a home invasion robbery. But when Edmonds was convicted of the brutal murder of Shelby Uehling—clubbing and stabbing him to death because Uehling had been seeing a woman who Edmonds had dated—the accumulated injustices in the case seemed, to us, to be overwhelmingly outrageous. It seemed obvious that a miscarriage of justice had occurred, racism still has a powerful place in American society, our management of illicit drug use is a terrible failure that increases the likelihood of violence, and, after 250 years of responding to crime the way we do (punishing the individual with incarceration), it's time for significant change.

Still, in spite of what we learned, Renato was still imprisoned, and Christian and Rashad were still dead.

What were the forces that shaped Christian's life and death? What really happened in Clearlake that night? Who is Shannon Edmonds and what life experiences made *him* the man he is today? What forces shape the lives of inner-city kids or any of us who walked the streets of the Tenderloin with Christian Foster, before Shannon Edmonds shot him dead? This was no abstract lesson in sociology. This was real!

* * *

Sunday, May 15, 2011:

I'm sitting in Farley's Coffeehouse, celebrating the end of another semester with a double cappuccino. I turned in my grades on Friday and summer break began. I check the news on SFGate.com,[23] to see what's going on:

SAN FRANCISCO: Triple Shooting Rattles Quiet SF Neighborhood
    Posted: 8:18 pm PDT May 14, 2011 -- Two victims died in a shooting Saturday evening in San Francisco's Bernal Heights neighborhood, a police spokesman said. San Francisco medical examiner's office Monday identified the two men as Pacific Som, 21, and Rathanak Chea, 26. Officers responded to reports of a shooting at about 7:20 p.m.... Arriving crews found Som and Chea suffering from life-threatening gunshot wounds and a third male victim whose gunshot wounds were not believed to be life threatening.

Uh, oh! I know a Chea family in the Tenderloin, but this took place in Bernal Heights, on the other side of town, and Rathanak Chea is not a familiar name. The next day, I check the news again. The story's been updated,[24]

> **SF Bernal Heights Birthday Party Brawl Leaves 2 Dead**
> **SAN FRANCISCO: Triple Shooting Rattles Quiet SF Neighborhood**
> **Posted: 8:18 pm PDT May 14, 2011**
> **Updated: 2:32 pm PDT May 16, 2011**
> SAN FRANCISCO – ..."The victims were found in the street and in a nearby courtyard," he said. Som and Chea were taken to a local hospital. They later died of their wounds. Multiple suspects have been arrested in connection to the shooting. Witnesses said two warring groups clashed Saturday around sunset. The fight began with fist then quickly escalated to gunfire resulting in the death of two men, one 21 and the other 26. "The man who was killed he grew up in the projects," said Bernal Dwellings resident Alan Best. "He was a good young man and now his life is over. His parents are devastated, and for what? The bravado of gangs."
>
> Police said shootings aren't the norm in Bernal Heights. Some neighbors have speculated about what incited the shooting. "There's a Cambodian family that lives on the block, and they were getting harassed," said neighbor Dena Grim. "Their son was getting harassed and he called his friends from the Tenderloin to come over and help fix the problem."

I read the last line a second time, "Their son was getting harassed and he called his friends from the Tenderloin to come over and help fix the problem." "*he called his friends from the Tenderloin.*" Damn! I check out the victims' names again, "San Francisco medical examiner's office Monday identified the two men as Pacific Som, 21, and Rathanak Chea, 26." "Rathanak." I didn't catch it the first time around. I knew him just as "Anak."

* * *

From Tom Heath
To: Don Stannard-Friel
Date: 5/16/2011

Anak was Sam's cousin and his daughter came to our program often. His brother, Palou survived [he was the third victim, who was wounded] but was also the one with Tee [Soun – Sam, Sammy, and Laura's brother, convicted of manslaughter] when the other death happened four years ago. Talk to you soon and I'll let you know if I hear funeral plans. Tom

From: D Chin
To: Don Stannard-Friel
Sent 5/17/2011 8:58 PM

Hello Dr. Don ....I just received the bad news today....Yen (Anak's wife) called me this morning. She told me it happen last Sat. during a party in Bernal Heights. She was beside herself. I watched Anak grow up at the center...the last couple of times when I visited the TL [Diana retired from the playground], I would always somehow bump into him. He would give the biggest warmest smile with a huge hug...saying how much I meant to him and his family. And I felt he was like family. Yen tells me the viewing will be this Thurs. from 3-8pm at Duggans (in Daly City, close to the Theatre) and the funeral service will be Fri. from 9 am to 1:00 pm.

And so summer "vacation" begins with Anak's funeral.

★ ★ ★

How fine is the line that divides the tragedies of the streets and tragedies *not* on the streets? Even here, as I sit in my office in the beautiful Ralston Hall mansion, I am reminded of the commonality of the human experience when I recall the death of William Ralston, the man who built this majestic building as his weekend and summer home. He named his estate "Belmont," now the name of the town it is in. The busy road that runs by the university is Ralston Avenue. In 1875, his Bank of California stock crashed and Ralston lost his fortune. The next day, he was found dead, floating in the Bay, a possible suicide.

What was Ralston's "privileged" life like that it could lead to such a tragic end—the decision that living like the rest of us would be a life not worth living? He normalized an amount of consumption that few of us achieve. What will become of the underprivileged Tenderloin children, who normalize the horrors of the streets by standing "in somebody else's shoes and see[ing] through their eyes," as President Obama encouraged in *The Audacity of Hope*, when those shoes and eyes lead them astray?

Dina Hilliard, a street teacher for the Promise class, told us, "When I was a teacher at City Academy, I asked my children, 'What frightens you when you walk around the neighborhood?' One child said, 'When someone is shouting.' Another said, 'When someone touches me.' One little boy said, 'When someone gets shot in the head,' an attack he actually witnessed. A mom told me about her child's after school playtime in the hallway of their SRO. 'I found my son huddled up in the corner.' She asked him, 'What are you doing?' 'Playing 'shoot up,'' he said. He had his belt tied around his arm and was sticking a stick in his arm."

NOTES

1. Tucker, Jill, "Teenager shot and killed in own home," SF Chronicle Staff Writer, June 14, 2010.
2. Van Derbeken, Jaxon, "S.F. man, 18, charged in teen's slaying," *SF Chronicle*, July 20, 2010.
3. Not her real name.
4. A pod is a housing unit in jail. One configuration is a circular room with locked bedrooms (not barred cells) on the perimeter, and a command desk in the center, with computer screens monitoring all activities on the unit, and sheriff's deputies watching and managing the goings-on.
5. Dorothy Stang, a Sister of Notre Dame, the founding order of NDNU, and a 1964 graduate of the then CND, was murdered in 2005 in Anapu, in the state of Pará, in Brazil, for her work protecting the Amazon forest and poor farmers who live there.
6. Tanner, Lindsay, Associated Press, "Personality disorders affecting young adults," *U-T San Diego*, December 2, 2005.
7. See, for example, "Anomie Theory, Merton's Theory of Social Structure and Anomie," http://main.socprobs.net/Theory/Anomie.htm
8. Anderson, Glenda, "Two Bay Area Men Killed, Third Arrested in Clearlake Home Invasion," *The Press Democrat*, December 8, 2005.
9. According to the *St. Petersburg Times* (see Politifact.com, August 12, 2009), a 2009 Pulitzer Prize recipient, using the Census Bureau's population estimate of 304,059,724 for the entire country in 2008, "We determined the number of black men in America by taking the 2008 population estimate for African-Americans as a whole and multiplying that number by .477. (For various actuarial reasons, the Census Bureau found that 47.7 percent of African-Americans were male and 52.3 percent were female in 2007.) This left us with 18,631,063, or 6.1 percent of the U.S. population.... The percentages for the two prior years were 42 percent in 2006 and 41 percent in 2005."
10. CBS 5 CrimeWatch, "Change Of Venue Approved In Lake Co. Murder Trial," November 16, 2007, http://cbs5.com/local.
11. Anderson, Glenda "Clearlake robbers shot from behind," *The Press Democrat*, January 12, 2006.

12. Yollin, Patricia, "Families agonize over bizarre murder case / Hearing on killings of troubled ex-hero, friend wrapping up," SFGate.com, February 07, 2006.

13. Yollin, Patricia, "Bayview success story's tragic end / Heroic track star shot dead after failing school, turning to crime," SFGate.com, January 18, 2006.

14. Yollin, Patricia, "Families agonize over bizarre murder case, Hearing on killings of troubled ex-hero, friend wrapping up," *SF Chronicle*, Tuesday, February 7, 2008.

15. Larson, Elizabeth, "Hughes sentenced to state prison; appeal expected," *Lake County News*, September 8, 2008.

16. CBS 5 CrimeWatch, "Change Of Venue Approved In Lake Co. Murder Trial," http://sanfrancisco.cbslocal.com, November 18, 2007.

17. Anderson, Glenda, "Clearlake robbers shot from behind," *The Press Democrat*, January 12, 2006.

18. Yollin, Patricia, "Families agonize over bizarre murder case, Hearing on killings of troubled ex-hero, friend wrapping up," *SF Chronicle*, Tuesday, February 7, 2008.

19. Moore, Derek J., "Hughes' attorney turns tables on Edmonds, Defense calls witnesses who say alleged victim is really violent drug dealer," *The Press Democrat*, Wednesday, June 25, 2008.

20. Williams, Rita, "A CASE OF MURDER?" KTVU.com Special Report On Clearlake Murder Case, July 8, 2008.

21. Moore, Derek J., "Hughes' attorney turns tables on Edmonds, Defense calls witnesses who say alleged victim is really violent drug dealer," *The Press Democrat*, Wednesday, June 25, 2008.

22. Anderson, Glenda, "Clearlake man, cleared in one slaying, convicted of murder in another," *The Press Democrat*, March 11, 2010.

23. KTVU.com. "Triple Shooting Rattles Quiet SF Neighborhood," Posted: 8:18 p.m. PDT May 14, 2011.

24. KTVU.com, "SF Bernal Heights Birthday Party Brawl Leaves 2 Dead: Triple Shooting Rattles Quiet SF Neighborhood," Posted: 8:18 p.m. PDT May 14, 2011, Updated: 2:32 p.m. PDT May 16, 2011.

CHAPTER 8

The Drug Store

SAN QUENTIN STATE PRISON

© The Author(s) 2017
D. Stannard-Friel, *Street Teaching in the Tenderloin*,
DOI 10.1057/978-1-137-56437-5_8

Walking up Leavenworth Street hill, the Streetwise Sociology class gets a heavy dose of weed on the wind. At first, we can't tell where it's coming from. Then we come across a little cluster of two women and three children – two chubby babies sitting in strollers, and a 10-year-old boy perched on a box, sucking hard on a great big doobie. The moms pass a joint between the two of them, as they bustle around the babies, who silently sit there, side-by-side, Tweedledee and Tweedledum, in a cloud of marijuana smoke, wide-eyed and open-mouthed, gulping in the intoxicating air.

In the Tenderloin

* * *

The telephone rang, startling the assembled, as if someone had slammed a door. A button was pushed on the phone and a voice came out of a speaker, "This is a collect call from Mr. Stanley Williams, an inmate at San Quentin State Prison. Your phone call is being recorded and monitored. Will you accept the charge?"
"Yes, yes, we will. Hello?"
"Hello?" A man's voice on the other end of the line.
"Hello? Hello, Stan?"
"Yes, this is Stanley Williams."
"Hello, Stan, this is Phil Gasper."
"Oh, hi, Phil. How are you doing?"
"I'm fine, thank you."
Thus began a teleconference call between Stanley Tookie Williams and a group of NDNU students, faculty, and staff. We were in the old Belmont community Catholic Church, now the renovated Taube Center on campus. Tookie was in his Death Row cell at San Quentin State Prison. Phil Gasper, chair of the Philosophy and Religious Studies Department, had arranged the call.
Phil had a previous relationship with Tookie and Barbara Becnel, coauthor, with Tookie, of nine award-winning antigang, antiviolence books, most for young people. Barbara was with us in Taube and, before the phone call, talked to us about Tookie's life and the efforts to save him from death inside San Quentin's execution chamber.
Stanley Williams, a five-time nominee for the Nobel Prize[1] (2001–2005), was cofounder of the notorious, violent Crips street gang that emerged out of South Central Los Angles. In 1979, Tookie was convicted of four brutal murders, of a 7-Eleven store clerk and three members of a Taiwanese family that owned a motel in South Central LA. A jury found him guilty of all four murders with special circumstances (murder during the commission of a robbery and multiple murders in the case of the Taiwanese family) and

found that he, personally, fired the shotgun used in the crimes. The jury recommended the death penalty and the judge ordered his execution. Tookie
denied involvement and Barbara was working hard to prove his innocence.

"What would you like to know?" The voice on the other end of the
telephone line—coming out of the mouth of a man found guilty of exe-
cuting four innocent, hardworking people, a man who was, by his own
admission, a "predator," an incredibly vicious street fighter, a violent drug
dealer, a gang leader involved in numerous shoot-outs with the police
and other gangs, and who, witnesses claimed, was guilty of many more
murders and laughingly referred to the dead family he was found guilty of
slaughtering as "Buddha-heads"—sounded nice.

"Tell us about yourself," Phil said.

And Tookie Williams did.[2] In a calm, pleasant, strong voice, with a
prison-enhanced vocabulary, learned from studying the dictionary (as
Malcolm X had done while he was in prison), he told his story of a troubled childhood; his incarceration for more than half of his life; the likelihood that he would die behind the walls of San Quentin State Prison and,
if events continue the way they have been going, probably inside the death
chamber, although Tookie still hoped for exoneration.

"I was convicted because of prosecutorial misconduct, exclusion of
exculpatory evidence, and things of that nature. Here I was, from the streets
of South Central, founder of the Crips, extremely muscular, a black man,
being judged by an all-white jury, and prosecuted by a corrupt DA. What do
you think would happen? My conviction was a paradigm of racial injustice."

The audience, I think, was taken off guard. They expected to hear the
voice of a gangster, a street thug, a scary monster of some kind. Instead,
the voice coming out of the speaker sounded like that of an articulate,
wise, courteous *grandfather*.

"I was wrongfully convicted. I am innocent. There was not a shred of
tangible evidence connecting me to the crimes. Everything presented was
predicated on hearsay evidence from individuals facing execution for murders that *they* committed. I've done many bad things in my life, I admit, I
have been a pathetic person, but nothing of this magnitude."

"Stan?" It was Phil talking into the telephone.

"Yes, Phil?"

"A student has a question."

"Go ahead."

"What will you do if you do win a stay of execution?"

"If I am allowed to live, if I receive clemency or an indefinite stay, I
will continue proliferating my message to young adults and other indi-

viduals, keeping them out of gang life, getting them out of that life. And eventually, I believe that if I'm allowed to live, with the help of Barbara Becnel, who is there with you tonight, and so many others on the outside, I'll prove my innocence. I *am* innocent. Yes, I have been a wretched person, but I have redeemed myself. I will continue to write my children's books with Barbara. I will continue to write and speak out for *redemption*, something I deeply believe in. Whether others believe me or not, I have redeemed myself. I am at peace with myself."

The conversation with Stanley Tookie Williams was supposed to end in 15 minutes. It lasted more than an hour. "I guess they forgot about me," Tookie said. "Any more questions?"

NDNU students, faculty, and staff lined up to speak into the telephone. Tookie was gracious, respectful, and patient. His story sounded reasonable and truthful, although there remained doubters in Taube Center when the conversation was done. Few spoke of it that night, right after the conference call, but, later, some of my students wondered, "What really happened?" Some asked how such a miscarriage of justice could have occurred. One asked me, "Do you think he really did it?" Another said, "What's he supposed to say, 'I'm guilty. Kill me!'?" Others told me, "I think he killed them!" For Phil Gasper, our chair of Philosophy and Religious Studies, the important point was that "Stan turned his life around. He's risen above his situation. Even from his isolated, Death Row cell, he's made a difference. He's making a contribution."[3]

* * *

On November 15, 2005, a semester after the teleconference call, I took my Deviant Behavior class on our annual tour of San Quentin. We were met at the gate by Lt. Vernell Crittendon, Public Information Officer and, for a longtime, my contact at the prison. I've been taking students on these tours most years since the 1980s, and, no matter how many times I go, it's always been a sobering and fascinating experience. But Vernell, personally, added a lot to the tour: he enjoyed storytelling, was good at it, and was deeply interested and informed about San Quentin and its history.

San Quentin is California's oldest prison, and it looks it. On the surface, there is nothing modern about it. But, behind some of its most ancient walls is a new medical center, and tucked away in another old building is the new, and as of this writing, unused, death chamber. The old one was decommissioned in 2006, when a moratorium on executions was ordered by the courts, because of poor record keeping; concern that the chemical cocktail used to kill the contemned was not rendering them unconscious before the actual lethal drug was administered, possibly causing excruciating pain; and that prison personnel were not properly trained. The new death chamber was completed, using inmate labor, at a cost of $853,000, in 2010.[4] But, when we went on tour in November of 2005, the old chamber was still in use. And Tookie was scheduled to die in it, in exactly four weeks, under the old procedures, which soon after would be deemed "cruel and unusual."

The tour with Vernell took us through two checkpoints, to make sure that we are who we say we are, and that we understood prison policies. Photo identification was examined (background checks were run weeks before), and the inside of our wrists were stamped with a mark, visible under ultraviolet light, to make sure that the person coming out was the same person who went in. We were checked to see that we were appropriately attired (not too much skin showing; no blue clothing, the standard color of inmate garb; no other clothing inappropriate to the situation). And we were informed of the prison's "No hostage policy" (all efforts would be made to secure our release, should we be taken captive by prisoners, but there would be no trading inmates' freedom for hostages). We walked by the Adjustment Center, where the "worst-of-the-worst" are held in solitary confinement, and were told the controversial story of the George Jackson shoot-out that occurred right here, on this spot, where a memorial to correctional officers (COs), slain over the years, is now laid out. We were met in the chapel area (Catholic, Protestant, and, remarkably, a combined Jewish-Muslim temple. "Works just fine," Vernell told us) by three lifers, who told us their stories of before and after incarceration and why they were here (two were murderers, the other a strong-armed robber/kidnapper, with a prior conviction for murder). We went to the Dining Hall, with its beautiful and remarkable prisoner painted murals; chatted with another kidnapper, about to be released after 20 years of being incarcerated, entered the neat, tiny, 6' × 7' cell where he shared every intimate detail of his everyday life with another inmate (open toilet, a sink, bunk beds, and shelves on a wall full of books and personal items),[5] and walked past the other cell blocks to see the death chamber.

"Move over to the wall, please," Vernell told us, as three COs, escorting a large, black man in prison blue, passed by. The inmate's legs were shackled, his arms were chained to his waist, and COs, on each side, held his arms. The arms were huge. The man, gray-haired, bespectacled, and distinguished-looking in spite of the prison garb and chains, looked at us and turned to his guards. "You *have* to parade me past these kids?" he asked. It was Tookie Williams.

"He's a Condemned Row inmate, going to see his lawyers," Vernell said, without mentioning Tookie's name. He waved us on. "Let's go see the execution chamber."

We went back through the second checkpoint that we had passed through on the way into the prison yard, the backs of our hands were looked at under the ultraviolet light, and we walked along the long, castle-like, exterior wall, past a guard tower with views of the prison on one side and the beautiful San Francisco Bay on the other, to a little alleyway. Vernell opened a gate, led us down the walkway, unlocked a steel door, and waved us into the death chamber room.

The chamber looked like the diving bell it once was, made of riveted lime-green steel plates, with thick glass windows. The students and I formed a semicircle around the death chamber, as witnesses do during an execution, and imagined what it must have been like for the 207 who have died inside, 196 by gas, 11 by injection. Tookie Williams would be number 208. Vernell helped us visualize what went on inside by pointing to a sturdy, blocklike chair, set off to the side, outside of the chamber. "That's the chair—actually, one of two that were originally inside the chamber—that inmates were strapped into when we used gas. The chair you see inside, now, is a modified dentist chair, with wings added to strap the condemned arms to, to facilitate the lethal injection." We all looked wide-eyed at the chairs that so many people died in for killing so many others.

"This was constructed as a gas chamber by convicts in 1937," Vernell told us. "The master welder on the project was released after his term was up, but he committed a murder on the outside and was returned to San Quentin. He was executed inside his own creation, looking at the airtight walls that he had so expertly welded."

"Do they fight back?" a student asked. "Do they resist at the end?"

"Usually not," Vernell said. "In the early days, a double-jointed inmate wriggled free of the restraints and ran around inside the chamber. The gas had already been released, so the warden let the execution continue. As horrified witnesses watched, the condemned man frantically tried to escape the lethal fog before he finally collapsed and died." We all stared into the chamber, horrified ourselves at what happened, so many years before.

In 1937, gas was deemed to be more humane than the previous method of execution by hanging, but the chamber was converted for lethal injection executions in 1996, after death by gas was then considered, by many, including Supreme Court Justice John Paul Stevens, to be, "in essence asphyxiation by suffocation or strangulation."[6] Justice Stevens' opinion, however, was in the minority when the court decided such executions were *not* "cruel and unusual," but, still, most states, including California, converted to lethal injection. In California, the decision was left to the condemned to decide on his or her (of 733 inmates on California's Death Row, at this writing, 19 are women) own method of execution: gas or lethal injection. If they won't or can't make the decision, the State directs execution by injection. Since 1996, only one chose his own way of death: by injection. The State directive was carried out for all others. Then, in 2006, Judge Jeremy D. Fogel, of the US District Court, blocked the execution by lethal injection of convicted murderer Michael Morales, while *its* infliction of pain and suffering was evaluated, and, in December, he declared that California's death stature violates the Eighth Amendment of the US Constitution (forbidding cruel and unusual punishment). Governor Arnold Schwarzenegger ordered a moratorium on executions, but that was more than a year after our tour in 2005, which was four weeks before Tookie was scheduled to die.

On December 1, 2005, I sent out the following notice to the NDNU community

WITNESS

to the

SAN QUENTIN DEATH RITUAL

At 12:01 a.m. (one minute past midnight) on the morning of Tuesday, December 13, 2005, **Stanley Tookie Williams** is scheduled to be executed at San Quentin prison. As we did with the executions of Thomas Thompson, Jay Siripongs, Manny Babbitt, Darrell Rich, Robert Lee Massie, Stephen Wayne Anderson, and Donald Beardslee, Notre Dame de Namur University students, staff, and faculty will stand together to witness the death ritual outside the prison gates. **Witnesses will meet at the prison gate beginning at 10: 00 p.m. on Monday December 12.** (A protest/vigil by various other organizations will begin outside the prison gates at 8:00 p.m.).

The goal of the Witness Program, as with our community-based learning program, is to become deeply involved in important social events that are part of our culture, and to motivate ourselves to act in the service of humankind. One need not be for, or against, or have a clearly formed opinion about the death penalty to attend the Witness event. We do this to become informed and to be more directly involved in one of the most important debates in our society, concerning the decision to take the life of another human being.

Be sure to check the evening news to determine if a stay of execution has been granted before going to San Quentin.

Dress warmly. Bringing an umbrella and flashlight is recommended.

For more information about the Witness Program, contact Dr. Don Stannard-Friel, X3770.

Illustration 8.1 Witness flyer

On December 13, 2005, Stanley Tookie Williams did die, and we stood outside the prison gates during his execution.

Since 1998, we have conducted the "Witness to the San Quentin Death Ritual" gathering. "You don't have to be for or against or even have a position on the death penalty," I tell my students. "The point is to be as close as we can to the most serious action our society takes against an individual: taking their life. Killing them. If you have been with me on tour of the prison, you have been in the death chamber, and can visualize what's going on. If you were with us last month, you saw the man who is going to be executed, Tookie Williams. If you attended the conference call last semester in Taube Hall, you heard him speak. Maybe you talked to him yourself. Now, we'll stand outside the gates, while he is executed inside, witnessing the ritual that takes place every time an execution takes place. But this time, there will be a lot more people and a lot more media attention than usual."

It was a cold, damp night—not unusual on Point San Quentin, the little peninsula, on the Marin County side of the Golden Gate Bridge, that sticks out into San Francisco Bay—when some of us arrived early to catch the beginnings of the vigil. As usual, when our carpools pulled up, Highway Patrol officers directed us away from the prison, down a long road to curb-side parking and corporate parking lots closed for the night. It's a mile or so walk along the roadside, back to the gates. As we passed through San Quentin Village, the little cluster of homes occupied by prison employees and regular citizens ("The safest place on earth," one of the guards once told us), we could hear Joan Baez singing "Swing Low, Sweet Chariot." It was not a recording. She stood on a makeshift stage near the prison gates and spoke to the growing crowd, "Tonight is planned, efficient, calcu-lated, antiseptic, cold-blooded murder and I think everyone who is here is here to try to enlist the morality and soul of this country."

Already, a thousand or more demonstrators of one ilk or another clus-tered around the gates, in an area boarded by the Visitor Center—a low, single-story building with a gift shop, offering prisoners' art and craft proj-ects for sale, and two tiny, beat-up bathrooms—and a post office with a sign on the wall, "San Quentin California 94964." More than a thousand more protesters would arrive before the evening was over, spreading out from the gate, down the road, into the Village. A row of porta-potties was set up for a crowd much, much smaller than was forming. Television cam-eras—more than we have ever seen at any of the seven other executions we have attended—were on the roof of the Visitor Center and scattered alongside the roadway full of protestors. TV newscasters, from local and national stations, were already speaking into cameras plugged into trucks with satellite dishes on their roofs. Small planes circled overhead, more news crews. Guards, in riot gear, stood in formation behind the gates. Speakers took turns protesting the execution of a man many declared was a "victim of a racist society."

Mike Farrell, the actor, spoke out against capital punishment in general, and the execution of Tookie Williams, in particular: "A wise man once said the death penalty is about three things: politics, politics, and politics and what we have seen today is that Governor Schwarzenegger is another cowardly politician." So did Jesse Jackson, and Barbara Becnel, Tookie's coauthor, who attended our teleconference call. Snoop Dog (a former Crip) wore a white tee shirt saying "Save Tookie Williams."

Signs in the crowd read "End the Racist Death Penalty," "Queers Against Execution," "Save Tookie: International Socialist Organization," and "Thou Shalt Not Kill – Ever!" Priests and nuns, Buddhist monks and Rabbis mingled with giant puppets, young people, and old-timers, protesting the execution.

But not everyone in the crowd was against capital punishment and the execution of Tookie Williams.

"Hang the Bastard," read one sign. "An Eye for an Eye," said another. A man near that sign held up a forensic photograph of Yu-Chin Yang Lin, one of the victims that Tookie had been found guilty of killing. The photograph showed the dead man with a bloody hole in his face, where one eye used to be.

As the evening wore on, a few confrontations between supporters of Tookie and those supporting his execution broke out. Speakers called for calm. I found two of my students standing in a line, arms locked with others, separating the two sides. "You OK?" I asked them. "We're good, Dr. Don. Just trying to help keep the peace," said one, a lacrosse player.

Finally, the time came. Word from inside. I knew it would come from Vernell, standing inside the death chamber room, but it was later than I expected it to be. What took so long? The news was passed on by a friend of Tookie's, Fred Jackson, who told the crowd, "It's all over."

"Now what?" one of my students asked.

"It's OK. It should be OK," I said, only a little worried about what might follow.

A woman's sob, angry shouts, curses, but Fred Jackson urged calm. The crowd sang, "We Shall Overcome," and, slowly, it dispersed, taking the long, cold walk back through San Quentin Village, out to the roadway and line of parked cars.

Stanley Tookie Williams was the 13th person executed in California since the death penalty was reinstated in 1978. A month after Tookie's execution, on January 17, 2006, we stood outside the gates as Clarence Ray Allen, 76-years old and confined to a wheelchair, would become the last to die before the moratorium was put into effect. At the time of Tookie's execution, 651 inmates were on Death Row. Now there are 751, with an expected net increase of 13 a year ("based on a six-year annual average of 20 new arrivals partially offset by condemned prisoners who either die while incarcerated or have their sentences overturned"[7]).

Tookie Williams is dead. Who was Tookie Williams, alive?

Stanley Tookie Williams III was born to a 17-year-old girl in New Orleans Charity Hospital on December 28, 1953. He was named after his father, who abandoned the family when Tookie was a year old. When he was six, Tookie's mom, in search of a better life, moved the two of them to South Central Los Angeles. Growing up, while his mom worked two jobs, Tookie played in the streets of the poverty-stricken, crime-infested neighborhood.

Organized dogfights were commonplace entertainment in South Central LA. After the dogs were done killing each other, the men would often turn to organized kid fighting as sport, betting on children as they did on the dogs. A good bet, it turned out, was Tookie Williams. As his reputation grew, he was bullied by older boys. So he fought them, too. This only strengthened his prowess and reputation for violence. Fighting, vicious street fighting, became his *raison d'être*. Before long, he was expelled from high school, sent to juvenile detention, and became a leader among his peers.

When he was 16, Tookie was arrested for auto theft and sent to Los Padrinos Juvenile Hall, in Downey, California, where he was introduced to weightlifting. When he was paroled a year later, he was bigger, stronger, and angrier than ever. Upon his release, when asked about his future, he told the review board that he planned to become "the leader of the biggest gang in the world." And he did. He cofounded the Crips, which, eventually, spread throughout the country and grew to more than 30,000 members. Tookie grew, too. While still in his teens, he weighed in at 300 pounds of muscle, with 22″ biceps.

The sheer size of the man contributed to his larger-than-life reputation, but made his exit from life more difficult than it might have been. Kevin Fagan, our frequent street teacher from *The Chronicle*, a regular media representative at San Quentin executions, was in attendance at Tookie's. Looking through the death chamber window, he wrote about what happened,[8]

With a chest like a barrel and bulging arms the size of toned thighs, Williams had to squeeze with his guards along the 7 1/2-foot-wide chamber's glass window just to get to the side of the gurney. There, he lay down slowly, and after the guards unlocked his wrists, he helpfully spread his arms along the gurney and became still. In two minutes, the team had him lashed down tight: black straps with buckles at his shoulders, chest, waist, knees and feet, and brown-leather Velcro straps at his wrists.

The first catheter slid in messily at the crook of Williams' right elbow, taking just two minutes to seat but spurting so much blood at the needle point that a cotton swab was soaked, shining deep red before it was taped off.

Then came the real trouble. A medical technician, a woman with short black hair, had to poke for 11 minutes before her needle hit home.

At the first stick, at 12:04, Williams clenched his toes. At 12:05, he struggled mightily against the straps holding him down to look up at the press gallery behind him, dishing out a hard stare for six long seconds. By 12:10 a.m., the medical tech's lips were tight and white and sweat was pooling on her forehead as she probed Williams' arm.

"You guys doing that right?" Williams asked angrily, frustration clear on his face. The female guard whispered something back; it was hard to hear anything through the thick glass walls of the death chamber. One guard, jaw clenched tightly, patted Williams' shoulder as if to comfort him.

The main complication in the death chamber this time was the excruciatingly long wait for the poisons to work.

It made sense. Williams was the most muscular man put to death in the modern era of executions in California, and it appeared as if his bulky body was fighting off the inevitable, even after consciousness and the ability to move had fled.

This was not a man who went meekly.

Thus, the explanation of why we had to wait so long before Vernell sent out the word and Fred Jackson announced to the assembled outside the prison gates, "It's all over." Tookie was a hard man to kill.

The troubled life that began 52 years before in New Orleans Charity Hospital was over. A life full of potential—an intelligent, articulate, charismatic man with natural leadership abilities—was over, for a crime spree that, court records say, began with four men smoking cigarettes laced with PCP and ended with the cold-blooded murder of four innocent, hardworking people.

* * *

"Who was Tookie Williams?" I ask students in Deviant Behavior classes, in the semesters following his execution. I show his picture to the class, the one with Tookie's hair teased into a big "natural," and showing off his huge, muscular body and massive arms, and hand out a personal history of the life and death of Tookie Williams. "How does resilience theory relate to his life? How did he become the man that he became?"

(Resilience theory is discussed in several of my classes. It seeks to answer why people raised in very difficult situations often overcome their pasts. The essential elements of the theory include: involvement by a *caring adult*, who has *high expectations* for the behavior and ability of the child, and helps provide *opportunities* for success. This is discussed in detail in Chap. 16.)

"His mom was a 'caring adult,'" Tyree answers, "but she was at work most of the time, so the street people in South Central became his mentors. They had 'high expectations' for his ability to fight, deal drugs and conform to the rules of the street, which he did do. He succeeded in the 'opportunities' that were given him."

"Yes, great, Tyree. His is a case study of resilience theory, headed in the wrong direction. He *was* highly regarded in his community for his violence, intelligence, and charisma. He was a disciplined person, as evidenced by his remarkable bodybuilding regimen, and he had a natural talent for leadership, as evidenced by his cofounding of the Crips. But he didn't transcend his early life; he was a product of it. His caring adults were criminals, who had high expectations for his ability as a gangster and 'appropriate' behavior as a street soldier, and they offered him opportunities in drug sales, street warfare, and crime. Tookie was a 'success,' in the context of his life, until it was taken from him."

Tookie Williams is dead, but the legend and the gang he founded live on.

"The 30,000-membership Crips gang is actually a loose network of factions or 'sets,' spread throughout the country," I tell my students, as we prepare for another tour of San Quentin. "Crip on Crip rivalries" are common, often producing violence. Tookie, himself, was stabbed in the neck, inside San Quentin, by a young member of a rival set. But they still share a bond produced by lives immersed in impoverished, violent, drug-filled neighborhoods, hatred for rival gangs, especially the 'Bloods,' and involvement in criminal activity, including homicide, drive-by shootings, assault, robbery, auto theft, burglary, and extortion.

"But they have, what shall I say—'matured' may not be the right word—*evolved?* Over the years the Crip's have diversified. They launder money through real estate investments and cash-based businesses: bars and barbershops, concert promotion companies, recording companies, and music groups. And they are very involved in identification fraud. But their most lucrative business continues to be distribution of drugs. So successful have they been, they've been a major reason for the nation's continuing 'War on Drugs.' "And how's *that* going?" I ask. "When 'The War' was started by President Richard Nixon in 1971, about 200,000 Americans were in prison, compared with about 1.7 million today. Including county jails, the number of incarcerated is 2.2 million. This is called 'mass incarceration.' "Now look at this," I pass out a list of "Drug War Facts".

Sociology 2317   Don Stannard-Friel
Deviant Behavior   don@ndnu.edu
                                                                   X3770

Drug War Facts

Amount spent annually in the U.S. on the war on drugs: **More than $51,000,000,000**

Number of people arrested in 2011 in the U.S. on nonviolent drug charges: **1.53 million**

Number of people arrested for a marijuana law violation in 2011: **757,969**

Number of those charged with marijuana law violations who were arrested for possession only: **663,032 (87 percent)**

Number of Americans incarcerated in 2011 in federal, state and local prisons and jails: **2,266,800** or 1 in every 99.1 adults, the highest incarceration rate in the world

Fraction of people incarcerated for a drug offense in state prison that are black or Hispanic, although these groups use and sell drugs at similar rates as whites: **2/3**

Number of states that allow the medical use of marijuana: **18 + District of Columbia**

Number of people killed in Mexico's drug war since 2006: **70,000+**

Number of students who have lost federal financial aid eligibilitybecause of a drug conviction: **200,000+**

Number of people in the U.S. that died from an accidental drug overdose in 2009:**31,758**

The Centers for Disease Control and Prevention found that syringe access programs lower HIV incidence among people who inject drugs by: **80 percent**

One-third of all AIDS cases in the U.S. have been caused by syringe sharing: **354,000 people**

U.S. federal government support for syringe access programs: **$0.00**, thanks to a federal ban reinstated by Congress in 2011 that prohibits any federal assistance for them

(Source:http://www.drugpolicy.org/drug-war-statistics)

Illustration 8.2   Hand Out Drug War Facts

"*You* know," I say to my students, "many of you, firsthand, how available drugs continue to be, and how prevalent their use is in American society. And our response, obviously, has been to lock people up, punishing them for breaking a law. It's a system that, just as obviously, doesn't work. A way of looking as this, I learned from *my* old Deviant Behavior professor, Pete Garabedian at San Francisco State, is that crime statistics can be interpreted as '*indicators of needed social change.*' What's that mean when, as the hand-out shows, two-thirds of the people locked up for drug offenses are black or Hispanic, while, combined, they only make up 25 percent of the population? What's that say about our society and its criminal justice system, especially when you see that blacks and Hispanics sell drugs at similar rates as whites? What does it say that our solution to a major social problem produces the highest incarceration rate *in the world*, with one out of every hundred adults behind bars? And a few more facts, not on the chart: the USA houses nearly 25 percent of the *world's* prisoners, despite having less than 5 percent of the world's total population. By the end of 2010, the USA had 1,267,000 people in state prisons, 744,500 in county jails, and 216,900 in federal penitentiaries. More than 2.2 million people were locked away.[9] More African-American men are in prison or on parole today than were enslaved in 1850, before Emancipation. And a black child has less of a chance of being raised by his parents than he or she did during slavery.[10] What does all that say about American society? What does all that *indicate* about needed social change?"

* * *

Deviant Behavior isn't my only class studying the causes and consequences of drug sales and abuse. Although it does do the San Quentin tour and participates in the Witness Program (as do many other students), it is more likely to study the problem from a macro-level perspective, looking at national and international statistics and trends, while the Inner City Studies classes look at it on the micro-level. Literally, *look* at it:

Walking up Leavenworth Street hill, the Streetwise Sociology class gets a heavy dose of weed on the wind. At first, we can't tell where it's coming from. Then we come across a little cluster of two women and three children—two chubby babies sitting in strollers, and a ten-year-old boy perched on a box, sucking hard on a great big doobie. The moms pass a joint between the two of them, as they bustle around the babies, who silently sit there, side by side, Tweedledee and Tweedledum, in a cloud of marijuana smoke, wide-eyed and open-mouthed, gulping in the intoxicating air.

* * *

Promise of the Inner City is rounding the corner of McAllister and Leavenworth, heading up the hill to VYDC. Standing in the middle of the sidewalk, blocking our way, is a big, muscular, white guy in a tee shirt. At first, he looks like he's playing an invisible violin, but as we get closer, we can see that he's actually sticking a needle in his arm. The class parts into two lines, walking around him on either side, as if he's an immovable boulder in a rushing stream. He is. Most of us take a look back, to see what we can see. The big man is too preoccupied with the task of emptying the syringe into his vein to notice us, or even care that we are there, but his buddy, a skinny, white, long-haired young man, leaning against the brick wall of the Hasting College of Law dormitory, once the old Empire Hotel, says, "Move on, move on, nothing here to see. Mind your own business. Mind your own business. Keep moving." He waves us on, annoyed with our interest. "Mind *our* own business?" a student whispers to me. "He should take *his* business somewhere else." But this is the Tenderloin, The Drug Store, a containment zone. It *is* the place where junkies go to do their business, and everyone knows it and, for the most part, tolerates it. And that's why *we* are here, walking *these* streets, instead of in the more affluent neighborhoods where this kind of behavior isn't allowed, at least on the streets. This is where the rubber hits the road, ground zero for open-air drug sales and use. It is ironic, though, that the Promise class is here to study *positive* aspects of the neighborhood, the programs and people who offer hope and inspiration to the downtrodden and those growing up in the neighborhood. We are here, today, to learn from street teachers at VYDC who are the "caring adults" who have "high expectations" for, and offer meaningful, legitimate "opportunities" to, at-risk youth. But first we have to get to the program, and this means walking the streets and passing by the action, the magnets that suck and hold people into lives of desperation. The guy with the needle in his arm is on one side of the Tenderloin "coin." VYDC is on the other. The Promise class continues its walk up the hill to the Promised Land, past indicato rs of needed social change.

* * *

Analyzing Social Settings is walking along Turk Street, near Taylor. The sidewalk is packed with people dealing and doing dope or just socializing. Every one of them is black, although African-Americans make up only 12 percent of the neighborhood. Marijuana smoke is thick in the still air, and people are exchanging money for pills, packets of drugs, and rocks of crack cocaine. Loud voices and laughter drown out the noise of trucks and cars passing by and the sounds of buses and streetcars on Market Street. Many of the street people are very animated, *too* animated; others are zombies, pressed up against the wall or plopped down on the sidewalk. Some are just regular folk. We weave in and out of the pockets of people and scattered bodies. There are 16 of us, but it's as if we don't exist. Other than an occasional glance our way, or a smile, or a step aside to let us by, we are totally ignored. For most of the street people, we just don't matter. One jolly, young, hip passerby does laugh when he sees us and asks if we are on "a ghetto tour," but to the dealers and the users, near Turk and Taylor, we don't exist. No money? No drugs? No badge? No matter!

* * *

Exploring the Inner World of the Inner City is sitting in the Community Room at the SFPD-Tenderloin Station. Captain Joe "Big Red" Garrity is talking to us, along with Officer Irene Huey Machaud, a patrol cop. I met (actually re-met) Irene a dozen years or so ago, when I had a "Tenderloin U" display set up at an educational street fair in Boeddeker Park. My table had stacks of course descriptions, a list of NDNU activities in The TL, and a poster board of photographs of students, community partners (including Captain Joe, who was then Sergeant Joe, who would later become Commander Joe), and Tenderloin kids engaged in service-learning activities: Halloween in the Tenderloin, College Night, the "A Christmas Carol" play performed, then, at the Seneca Hotel, and sports clinics at the playground. A small, Asian woman, in a blue cop uniform, came up to my table, her torso thickened by body armor underneath her shirt, an eight-pointed star, nametag, and a microphone all attached to the front of it. From her belt hung a baton, handcuffs, gun, walkie-talkie, pepper spray, and whatever else cops carry with them. It seemed like an awful lot of gear to be piled on such a small person, but she handled it with ease. As she looked at the pictures, I asked, "Have you ever heard of College of Notre Dame?" the name of NDNU then.

"Yes, I have," she answered. "I was in your Cultural Anthropology class, Dr. Don."

I looked at the nametag. It said, "Irene Machaud."

"I was Irene Huey, then."

I looked at her again. "Irene? Irene Huey!" I remembered that face on a small, quiet Chinese-American girl, sitting near the front of class in the little theater in Wiegand Art Gallery on campus, a room that I like to teach Cultural Anthropology and Deviant Behavior in, because its walls of stone blocks, quarried right here on the old Ralston estate, and the natural wood ceiling, give it an almost cave-like feeling, appropriate, in my mind, to the subject matter I teach there: who we are, where we come from, why we are the way we are? I never would have predicted that Irene Huey would become a cop. But she did. In the Tenderloin! And, I was to find out in the years that followed, a highly admired cop in the Tenderloin. As we chatted, another police officer, a man, strolled up to join in. But before he could, a commotion broke out on the walkway through the park, a path the locals called "The Gauntlet." A tall, disheveled man began to shout and wave his hands, "Fuck you! Fuck you! Gedda way from me, fuckin' asshole!" He was screaming at a menace only he could see.

"Excuse me, Dr. Don," Irene said, and she walked over to the big man, who towered nearly a foot over her. He didn't even notice her as he went on shouting obscenities and waving his long arms in the air, fending off the invisible threat.

I turned to the other cop. "Um, you think you should, you know, *go over there?!*"

"Nah," he said. "She's fine."

Fine? I asked myself. *Fine?* I don't think so! It seemed to me she could use some backup. But within a very few minutes, the big man was sitting on a bench, and Irene was patting him on the shoulder, chatting with at him.

"You're her partner?" I asked the other cop.

"Yeah, that and her husband," he laughed.

Irene and Brian Machaud are the only husband–wife street cop team on the SFPD force. A few years after my reintroduction to my "quiet, little Chinese-American student," I opened *The Chronicle* and read,[11]

Two police officers are walking down Leavenworth Street in San Francisco's Tenderloin district when they spot a tall young man popping something in his mouth.

They're only a few feet from him. One officer takes two steps and clamps his hand around the man's throat, pushing his thumb into the tiny muscle behind the man's jawline. His partner grabs the man's arm in one hand and holds on to his jaw with the other.

"Spit it out!" she barks at the man. "Spit it out now!"

The man shakes his head, and the three engage in a violent little dance on the corner of Leavenworth and Turk for a few moments. The officer releases his grip on the man's throat, and the man spits a small white pill onto the sidewalk.

The pill turns out to be a prescription medication that the man, a heroin user, had bought to get a small high. He's wanted in connection with a domestic violence dispute from the day before, and a police van arrives a few minutes later to take him in for booking.

The officers walk back to the Tenderloin Station to complete the paperwork on the bust. Later, they'll drive home together, make dinner and put
their kids to bed.

Brian and Irene Michaud are San Francisco cops – and married to each
other. This does not make them rare in the department. But they are also
partners on the street, and no one knows of another such team in the city.

Irene Michaud is 33 and a San Francisco native. She grew up in the
Sunset, went to Mercy High School and ... Notre Dame de Namur
University in Belmont.[12]

I've run into Irene and her husband, Brian, on a few occasions on the
streets of the Tenderloin. Brian even escorted us for a while, when we
walked the streets doing the 2011 Point-in-Time Homeless Count. And
Irene has talked to my Exploring the Inner World of the Inner City class,
as she is today. Exploring studies social problems in the streets, including
the rampant use of drugs in The TL.

Captain Joe just finished telling us about his nearly 20 years in the
Tenderloin, as a street cop, Sergeant, and coming back as Captain, after a
few years as a lieutenant on the Tactical Squad. Soon after this talk, he was
promoted to Commander, bringing on a slew of "Big Red" recollections
and human-interest stories about him online and in the media. Two of my
favorites revealed his personality:

"Some time in the 1980s Garrity and I were in a foot pursuit in the
Tenderloin," [his old partner, Roger] Battaglia said. "Suddenly the suspect
bolts into St. Boniface Church with Garrity and I right behind him. John
Joseph, the good Catholic boy he is, abruptly stops at the holy water basin,
blesses himself, and then recommits to the pursuit. We got the guy."[13]

And another story,

Two years ago Garrity came upon a street brawl on Turk Street. When he
intervened, one of the participants sucker-punched him. But rather than
going down, the 53-year-old Garrity locked the punk in an arm bar and
pinned him to the sidewalk until help arrived.[14]

"My question," Joe asked at the time, "is can we book him for elder
abuse?"

That's Joe. Today he is our street teacher.

"The Tenderloin station makes more arrests than any other station in
the city," Joe tells the class. "It has more people on probation, sex offend-

ers, homeless, and addicts living here, and mentally ill people wandering the streets, than anywhere else in San Francisco. There's also more than 3000 kids living here, too, with hardworking, mostly immigrant parents, too poor to live anywhere else in the City. Good people. Really good people. The Tenderloin is home to both saints and sinners. There's a lotta good here, I love it, but a lotta suffering too, and some *very bad guys*."

Irene picks up where Joe leaves off. "People come from all over to sell and buy drugs here. Look at the cars that pull up on the corners at night: BMWs, Lexus."

"Marin housewives," Captain Joe chimes in.

"And people from down the peninsula, where you come from," Irene continues. NDNU is in Belmont, a half-hour south of the city, down the San Francisco peninsula. "And the East Bay," she says. "Probably 90 percent of the dealers come from Oakland, Richmond, the other side of the Bay Bridge."

Whenever I hear Irene or anyone else talk about dealers coming from the East Bay, I am reminded of Sergeant Kenny Sugrue, a popular bicycle patrol cop in The TL, who participated in Halloween in the Tenderloin, sports clinics (he was an athlete, himself), and other neighborhood events (before he died suddenly at 39 of a heart attack), who told me, "I take BART from Concord. I remember seeing this guy coming in with me, every day. I figured he was a commuter, like me, sitting there reading his paper, coming and going to his job in San Francisco. Then I saw him at work one day, selling drugs at Turk and Taylor. He was a commuting dope dealer. Busted him. 'I know you,' I told him. 'We commute together.'" Kenny laughed, "Haven't seen him since."

Captain Joe asks the class if there are any questions.

"What are some of the drugs sold here?" a student asks.

"Why *you* wanna know?" Captain Joe teases him. The class laughs. Joe responds to the question: "Heroin, black-tar heroin, methamphetamine, marijuana of course. Cocaine, powdered cocaine and crack. MDMA, Ecstasy. We're seeing a lot more prescription pills: OxyContin, hydrocodone, codeine. Pharmaceuticals like Adderall, Vicodin. Street sales of pharmaceuticals are becoming more prevalent than heroin and crack cocaine, especially on lower Leavenworth Street, the Tenderloin's 'Hall of Shame.'"

"The 200 block of Leavenworth?" I ask.

"Yeah, *you* know! Old farts," he tells the students, "like Dr. Don and me, have seen a lot of change." He turns to me, saying, "How long we known each other? Twenty years?"

I have to think for a minute before I answer, "Since '98." I met Captain Joe at the first Halloween in the Tenderloin planning meeting that I attended. In that meeting, Joe agreed to ask the Hilton Hotel to donate 200 hotdogs, chips, and boxes of juice, which they did do, and continued to do for years. When the Hilton eventually declined to continue the donation, Joe arranged for the Police Officers Association (POA) to pick up the tab.

"Yeah. Lot's changed. Lot's the same," the Captain continues. "Lower Leavenworth's been a problem for a long time. And of course, with drugs comes violence. Not just gang violence, that's not so bad here, now. Other neighborhoods, but not so much the Tenderloin. But you've got drug-related violence, robberies and assault, especially when young people are mixing drugs or don't even know what their taking. They can get crazy, lose it. And there still are turf issues and rip-offs, sometimes spilling over here from other neighborhoods, Bayview-Hunters Point, Western Addition. We're still losing kids in the Tenderloin."

* * *

It was few months after our meeting with Joe and Irene that I got this email from Tom Heath, the after-school program director at IHDC:

From: Tom Heath [theath@ihdcsf.org]   Sent: Sat 9/8/2012 10:38 AM
To: Don Stannard-Friel
Subject: Another tragedy in the TL

Sorry to report another loss. Jimmy Sokheang was shot on Leavenworth on Sept 6. His family removed him from life support on Sept 7. Jimmy lived with his family in our green building until his Mother passed and then moved with his brother Vessna to Bayview where his life took a wrong turn. He was 21 and had a good spirit. In fact he was the only one of the "street crowd" that we allowed to come into the program. He was not a bad person; just never had good opportunities come his way. I will let you know when I have details on the service.

Tom
Tom Heath, MSW
Program Director
Tenderloin Achievement Group
Indochinese Housing
theath@IHDCSF.org

I knew Jimmy. He was a real nice guy. Around me, he was quiet, but friendly and respectful. Always offered to shake my hand when we ran into each other in the basement of IHDC. I knew he moved out of the neighborhood years ago, but he was often around, a part of the IHDC community. It was after his murder,[15] on the 200 block of Leavenworth—Captain Joe's "Hall of Shame," where Donal, "Big D," and the Fish Stick Gang hung out years ago, some of them and their younger counterparts still do—that I learned about why Jimmy moved. I was checking for funeral arrangements online when this notice came up[16]:

Jimmy's light was prematurely dimmed at the hands of a violent crime & his family is calling out to you to help put his soul to rest.

A fifth grader's biggest worry is when recess will commence, at this age, Jim Sokheang, had witnessed his mother lose a 2 year battle to cancer. Never knowing his biological father, he became a ward of the state at the age of 10. Jim bounced around homes of different family members for years, until he was finally taken in by his barely legal older brother, Vess and his brother's girlfriend, Tee, at the age of 12. By no means did they live in the lap of luxury as Vess and Tee had struggles of their own to face with raising a new born and trying make ends meet as ripe young adults. None the less, Jim's care givers, and family members provided him with love and comfort the best they could, while instilling hardwork and stern family values in him. Jim matured into a sincere, warm, and respectful young man over those years into adulthood.

One fateful night, after visiting family members in the Tenderloin District of San Francisco, Ca, Jim- alone and on his way home- was heartlessly gunned down and robbed. He suffered a bullet wound to his head that would penetrate his frontal lobe, find it's way through both hemispheres-snapping the brain stem, and come to a stop cracking the back of his skull. He was rushed to S.F. General Hospital where doctors ran several tests determining that Jim was brain dead. Doctors seeing no other feasible alternatives, made their own decision to pull the plug on little Jim at midnight on September 7 of 2012. Little 12 year old Jim had barely begun his life at the age of 21.

Despite the harsh realities and sometimes bitter coldness that life threw Jim's way, he grew into and remained a respectful younger brother, a dependable uncle, loving cousin, faithful boyfriend, and genuinely warm and kind hearted young man to everyone around him until he was violently ripped from this world. The only thing we, his family and friends wish for him now, is to be able put him to rest and pray that he finds peace in a new home. In order to be able to provide Jim this last gesture, we call upon your generous and open hearts- to give and to share Jim's story. Jim grew up with many struggles and few things handed to him, now that he has departed this life, our only hope now is to send him on his way properly.

Any amount will help. Credit card donations can be made through this website. All friends and family members are encouraged to make monetary donations toward this cause in place of flowers or material gifts.

If you have any information on this shooting please contact SF police.

Illustration 8.3 Jimmy funeral notice

But I still didn't know what happened. He was shot in the head, but no one I asked seemed to know why, or, at least, was willing to say.

On Saturday, September 15, 2012, I went to the funeral of Jimmy Sokheang, 21 years old, murdered on the 200 block of Leavenworth, the very place where I used to hang out waiting for Big D, 16 years before. The service was at Duggan's Sierra Mortuary in Daly City, down the peninsula, up on a hill, just over the San Francisco border. As I got there, I could see lots of young people in black outfits of one kind or another. In vivid contrast was Norman, an 18-year-old, recent high school graduate and longtime member of the IHDC community. Norman climbed out of the car next to mine in the parking lot, wearing a perfectly pressed and tailored US Marines uniform. As he stood by the car, his buddy went over his jacket with a lint remover.

"Hi, Dr. Don," the Marine said to me.

"Norman? Norman, is that you? When did you join the Marines?"

"Right after high school. I just got out of boot camp," he said.

"You look great!" He did. "Thank you for your service, Norman," I said, meaning it, though, with the expert rifleman's badge pinned to his shirt, I worried if he had just jumped out of the frying pan, into the fire.

"Thank you, Dr. Don." And Norman, his buddies, all of whom I knew from the Tenderloin, and I walked over to the funeral of 21-year-old Jimmy Sokheang, who I would never have to worry about being killed in Afghanistan.

A lot of young people were hanging around outside the funeral parlor, waiting for the service to begin. I said hello to those I knew. Some, not so young anymore, were at the service for Josh Mann in 2002. Ten years later, here we were again. How many funerals have they been to in between? How many more to come? Who here today will be in the coffin tomorrow?

A group of guys were passing around a bottle of hard liquor. It's 11:00 a.m. They made no effort to hide it, but didn't offer me any, either. I wasn't offended. I knew it wasn't a sign of rejection, but respect for an elder, a teacher, at 11 o'clock in the morning. They're good guys performing a macho death ritual. They gave me a friendly welcome. I've been on the edge of their lives for a long time. Elizabeth came up to say hello. A tall, strikingly beautiful Cambodian, she was just a little girl when I met her. "How's it going, Elizabeth?" I asked. "Good, Dr. Don. I'm working at a bank. Maybe I'll go back to school to get my MBA." She's a recent graduate of UC Santa Cruz. There's a lot of movement at the door of the chapel. It was time to go inside.

I signed the guestbook and found a spot midway down the aisle. Thai, the father of Munie, Meng, and Monica, IHDC kids, came over and sat with me. The family lives in the lime building, where Jimmy and his mom lived before she died. They spend a lot of time at the after-school program. Monica is still a participant in after-school activities. Meng is a Youth Worker there. And Munee, the oldest at 22, with a long history of doing everything we do in The TL—Halloween, College Night, Campus Visit, the Christmas celebration, philanthropy projects—is Program Assistant. She is also one of our street teachers now.

Young men wearing oversized white tee shirts walked by. The words "Rest in Paradise Jimmy" were emblazoned, graffiti-style, on their backs under a photo of a tougher-looking Jimmy than I remember, wearing a blue shirt, black SF Giants hat, and flashing a peace sign at the camera. The same picture, enlarged and framed, was on an easel next to the coffin.

It was time to go up to pay respects. I joined the long line of mourners. An ancient Asian lady was handing out incense sticks at the end of the aisle, just before the coffin. I looked at the others to see what to do: light it off a candle there and stick it in a bowl of sand. A bouquet of smoldering sticks spread the smell of incense around the coffin. I imagined the ancient roots of this tradition, back in hot, tropical Cambodia, when preparing the dead for viewing wasn't what it is today. I waited for my turn to view Jimmy, wondering what he'll look like after having a bullet pass through his head. When my turn came up, I was happy that he looked so good, handsome, with his thick, black hair combed straight back, a young man's mustache on his upper lip, wisp of a goatee on his chin, and no mark at all where the bullet penetrated "his frontal lobe, find its way through both hemispheres—snapping the brain stem, and come to a stop cracking the back of his skull." Two packs of Newport cigarettes lay on his chest in the coffin. No worry about lung cancer in the afterlife, Jimmy. The viewing went on for some time; Jimmy had lots of friends and a large extended family. Many of these connections weave back to the village in Cambodia where his parents came from. I waited for a formal service of some kind to begin, but it never did. "What's happening?" I asked Vee, whose own murdered brother, Anak, was buried just a few months before. "His brother was too upset to do it," Vee answered. "No one else came forward. I offered to do it. I know what to do. I just did it, but he said no. Thought it was his job, but he couldn't do it."

At the time of the funeral, I still didn't know what had happened, what the circumstances were in Jimmy's killing. Then I ran into a cop that I know keeps tabs on the streets. "It was about 1:00 a.m.," he told me.

"Jim was walking on Leavenworth Street, to catch a bus home to Hunters Point, when a car stopped, guy got out, put a gun to his head, and shot him. Blew his brains out. It was an assassination. He was the *intended* victim."

"Do you know why?"

"Why you think?"

* * *

Dr. Nadine Burke Harris runs the Center for Youth Wellness, a pediatric clinic in San Francisco's Bayview-Hunters Point, the district Jimmy moved to after his mother died, a neighborhood known for drugs, drive-by shootings, and poverty, though it has been slowly gentrifying over the years and recently took a giant leap in that direction with the construction of the 3rd Street MUNI light rail line that connects the area with downtown. A strip of condominium buildings is rushing its way up the 3rd Street corridor, like a line of domino tiles righting itself, bringing in new restaurants, shops, coffeehouses, and other services for the new residents, changing the character of the community and, apparently, raising the consciousness of city leaders about this chronically neglected neighborhood. A farmers' market, new playgrounds, expansion of the local YMCA, a privately funded entrepreneurship training program for neighborhood youth, and a new Boys and Girls Club chapter have been added, and the school district transformed some low-performing schools into "Dream Schools," with more resources, counselors, and after-school programs. All good things.

Still, it remains a high-crime area, noted for gang violence, including street shootings and drug trafficking.

Jimmy survived the streets of Bayview-Hunters Point, though it may have been his involvement there that got him killed on the streets of the Tenderloin.

An article in *The Chronicle*[17] about Bayview-Hunters Point, written in 2006, a few years after Jimmy moved there, reported,

"A lot of these kids don't get to go out of their houses at all when they get home after school because of the danger," said Tareyton Russ, principal of Willie Brown Academy elementary school.

"I've been to at least 20 funerals in the [nine] years I've been in this district," Russ said. "I could have been to many more, but it just got to the point where it was making me sick. Going and seeing 14- and 15-year-olds in boxes is a very hard thing to do. And I've had to apologize to many parents because students I knew had gotten killed, and I didn't go to their funerals because I just couldn't do it anymore. I don't do it anymore."

– [The neighborhood] has higher rates of asthma than any other ZIP code in the city. One-sixth of Bayview-Hunters Point children have asthma, according to a 1999 and 2000 community health survey.

– The neighborhood's leading cause of premature death is homicide, according to a 2004 city survey. Indeed, half of the city's 31 homicides this year took place in Bayview-Hunters Point.

– Infant mortality was 2.5 times higher than in the rest of the city and the highest of any ZIP code in California, according to a previous Chronicle analysis of state births and deaths between 1992 and 2001.

– The hilly, mostly treeless, landscape has more liquor stores than grocery stores.

– Public-school enrollment has been dropping, and low-performing schools have been recommended for closure.

When *The Chronicle* reporter who wrote this article told one neighborhood boy that she didn't know anyone who had been killed by gunfire, his mouth dropped open. "You mean they all died because they were sick or old?" the astonished boy asked.

It was in 2006, the year that that article was written, that Dr. Nadine Burke Harris opened her pediatrics clinic. In 2013, another *Chronicle* reporter, Jill Tucker (who has been one of our street teachers), wrote about Dr. Burke Harris becoming a key figure in Hillary Rodham Clinton's first philanthropic effort after stepping down as Secretary of State. Clinton's "Two Small to Fail" campaign is designed to promote research into child development, including brain development and early nutrition, publicize the results, and make recommendations to politicians, parents, and caregivers. Dr. Burke Harris was featured with Clinton in a video launching of the effort. In *The Chronicle* article,[18] Jill wrote:

Each day, children file through pediatrician Nadine Burke Harris' clinic in San Francisco's Bayview neighborhood, 1,000 patients a year with the typical childhood complaints: an earache, a fever or maybe headaches, a recurring cold or tummy troubles.

But Harris doesn't just peer in ears and dole out the occasional antibiotic.

With years of experience in urban pediatric medicine, she knows she has to look at her patients closer and ask questions, a lot of questions, about their lives, their homes and what they've seen or heard.

That's because 2 of every 3 children who come to see Harris have witnessed what she calls adverse childhood experiences.

In plain language that includes physical or emotional abuse. Domestic violence. Depression or mental illness. Sexual assault. Substance abuse. Neglect. The absence of one or both parents. Incarceration. Death.

And more than 1 in 10 of the children she sees have experienced not just one of those traumas, but four or more.

The trauma can travel through their brains and into their bodies, where it can cause physical harm.

Some initial research out of a suburban San Diego community has already offered insight into the long-term health effects of trauma and adversity.

The study found that children who had four or more adverse childhood experiences were more likely to suffer from a range of chronic diseases as adults, including heart and lung disease, as well as increased risk for depression, alcoholism, suicide attempts and drug use.

Harris noted that the study didn't even include community violence on the list of possible adverse experiences.

She recalled one patient who was diagnosed elsewhere as having attention deficit hyperactivity disorder and other health problems.

No one had evaluated her for exposure to trauma and adversity. But Harris identified seven areas of trauma, including violence in the home, a mother with depression and an absent father, as well as sexual abuse.

"Then she's struggling in school, and they say it's ADHD," said Harris, her anger visible.

Screening for trauma or adverse childhood experiences can help identify the root causes of many physical and behavioral issues that can be both expensive to treat and life threatening, Harris said.

Childhood trauma: violence in the home, violence in the streets, violence in school, physical and emotional abuse, sexual assault, substance abuse, neglect, the absence of one or both parents, parental incarceration, parental depression or mental illness, alcoholism, suicide attempts, the prevalence of death in one's life. These are the adverse childhood experiences suffered by many of the children of Bayview-Hunters Point, the Tenderloin, and other communities historically neglected by the greater society. For many of the families involved, these same adverse childhood experiences or comparable debilitating experiences (e.g., long-term serial colonial oppression or the physical and emotional consequences of being intentionally exposed to nuclear fallout in the Marshall Islands, or the inhumane, barbaric, murderous conditions in Khmer Rouge concentration camps in Cambodia) were previously suffered by these young people's parents and grandparents, aunts and uncles and cousins, passing on the consequences of their PTSD to the next generation, which is developing its own, personal relationship with the condition. And then we contain them in ghettos, and blame them for their "misbehavior," and put them in "guidance" centers, rehab programs, jails, prisons, mental hospitals, or we just kill them, seemingly not able to give sincere and effective due consideration to what one inmate on a panel of five lifers in San Quentin told us on a tour. "What we all have in common," he said, gesturing to his fellow panelists, "is that we come from poverty, foster homes, and violent communities." (His crime? He killed a man in a bar who refused to pay for a round of drinks when it was his turn.)

* * *

"Hey, Dr. Don."

"Rob!"

I'm sitting in Farley's coffeehouse. I just finished writing this chapter, or so I thought, when in walks "Big Rob" Harrison, a recent graduate of NDNU. We've met here before, my "office" on Potrero Hill. NDNU students, faculty, and staff, and Tenderloin colleagues have met with me here to talk about whatever it is we want to talk about. Today, Rob is just stopping by to say, "Hi."

Rob is half Samoan, half African-American, and big. He used to be bigger, but he went on a health-kick and lost 100 pounds. Now, he's down to 200, and, on his 6'3" frame, he looks good, strong, and healthy. He's still "Big Rob." We talk about what he's been up to since graduating ("working with little kids, learning to be a physical trainer") and what his longer-term plans are ("Not sure, maybe the Peace Corps"). We chat about his mom (she is the new director at Tenderloin Children's Playground), and talk about how ironic it is that she is now involved in Tenderloin U as a street teacher, after her son's participation as a student.

Rob and I talk about the book I am writing (the one you hold in your hand), and I tell him about this chapter. I summarize Jill Tucker's article on Dr. Nadine Burke Harris and her clinic in Bayview-Hunters Point, the neighborhood where he was brought up and still lives. Rob has strong families ties and a supportive community there. But he has also had his share of adverse childhood experiences, just by growing up where he did.

"I remember getting on a bus and looking at some guy's jacket in front of me, because it was a cool jacket. 'Wha'chu lookin' at?' he said to me, pissed off. Next day, he gets on the bus with ten other guys, ready to beat the crap outta me. This was just normal stuff. You look someone in the eye, and they're ready to shoot you. I got into that, too. Look me in the eye, '*Wha' chu lookin' at?*!' It's normal. But it's *not* normal! It wasn't until I got to NDNU that I really realized how normal it *isn't*! There's other ways of dealin' with people."

I remember that it took Rob a while to learn to deal with other people in other ways. I first met him in class, where he was a charming participant in classroom discussion, but not living up to his academic potential. Then I got a call from the Dean of Students to see if I would mentor Rob (or monitor him, I'm not sure which she said), who was about to get kicked out of school for fighting. He would get into altercations, especially at school dances and parties, where drinking and young men's egos can mix like gasoline and fire.

Big Rob was a big problem.

"This is his last chance," the dean said.

Fortunately, Rob was ready to do what he had to do to stay in college and make some changes in his life. He began to take on his studies seriously, and curtailed his partying. He participated in Halloween in the Tenderloin and sports clinics in The TL, and was scheduled to attend a "Meeting of the Minds" discussion between students in the Exploring the Inner World of the Inner City class and inmates at SF County Jail that my former student, Phelicia Jones, and I were facilitating. But he called at the last minute. "I can't go," Rob told me. "I gotta study for finals."

"Good!" I said, hoping that's actually what he was going to do. I learned later that he did, and did well.

Phelicia was disappointed that Rob wasn't coming to the jail. She had met him on campus, when she talked to my Deviant Behavior class about her life and work in the community. She had lived in Hunters Point, until her family moved to San Mateo to escape increasing violence in the projects. (Still, after their move, her two sisters were murdered.) When Rob told her that he, too, lived in Hunters Point, she took a special interest in his life. So, when he didn't come to Meeting of the Minds, she was disappointed. "I'll come back with him after finals," I told Phelicia, "if that's OK with you and he wants to come." It was, and he did.

A few weeks later, Rob and I went to the jail to have our own conversation with the inmates. On the way, Rob told me that he had been to the jail many times, visiting friends. "My father's been here, too. He used to tell me that he was going to Mexico. He went there often. Then, one time he was in Mexico, I went to jail to visit my friend and there was my dad. I found out that when he 'went to Mexico,' he was actually going to jail."

When Rob and I got to the jail, it was kind of a homecoming for him, although he was never incarcerated, himself. But he knew, or had a connection with, about a third of the 50 inmates who sat in a circle to tell their stories and hear from Rob and me: they lived in Hunters Point, went to the same schools as he did (until they didn't), played basketball at the same gyms, hung around the same spots.

"You know, this was all just normal to me, growing up," he told me, as we sat having coffee at Farley's. The violence, the looking or not looking in people's eyes, learning which streets to walk on and on which ones you could get shot. This was all "normal."

"I remember washing the car. Two other people were washing their cars on the same block. Someone starts shooting a gun. In any other neighborhood, people would dive for the ground or run away. Wha'd *we* do? *We washed our cars.* We looked up to see what was going on, but we went on *washing our cars!* That's crazy! That's *not* normal! I started to get real anxious. Anxious all the time. Nervous and paranoid."

"Paranoid?" I said. "Rob, when people are shooting guns and threatening to kill you for *looking* at them, that's not being paranoid. That's being *aware!*"

Dr. Nadine Burke Harris told Jill Tucker that screening for trauma or adverse childhood experiences can help identify root causes of many life-threatening physical and behavioral issues, and that treatment can mitigate a lifetime of health problems. "We are at a tipping point when it comes to this issue," she said in the interview. "This is a massive, massive public health issue." It is. And underlying that is a massive *social* issue.

* * *

In Deviant Behavior, I pass out Jill Tucker's interview with Dr. Burke Harris and review it and the War on Drugs incarceration chart and fact sheet with my students. "The USA spends more than $51,000,000,000 a year on the War on Drugs," I say, referring to the hand out. "In 2011, 1.53 million people were arrested in the USA for nonviolent drug charges. And we house nearly 25 percent of the *world's* prisoners, in spite of having less than five percent of its population. How's all that all working?" I ask my students.

"Not very good," Eddie answers.

"What makes you say that?" I ask.

"Oakland."

"Oakland! Tragic, but good answer," I say.

Oakland is just across the San Mateo Bridge from NDNU, on the other side of the Bay. It's been in the news, a lot, for drive-by shootings and related drug violence.

"Oakland is a good example of the War on Drugs *not* going well," I say. "So is Hunters Point. So is the Tenderloin."

"In 2012," I continue, "64 percent of inmates released from California's state prisons were returned within three years, which is an *improvement* over previous years. A two-thirds failure rate. How would NDNU be judged if we only had a one-third graduation rate? And what about drug rehab? How successful is that? The relapse rate for people completing substance abuse and addiction programs in the USA is anywhere between 50 percent and 90 percent.[19]

"The Department of Justice says that the illicit drug market in the USA is dominated by 900,000 criminal gang members affiliated with 20,000 street gangs in more than 2500 cities,[20] and Mexican drug cartels directly control drug markets in at least 230 American cities.[21] On top of all that, Al-Qaeda and nearly half of the organizations on the State Department's list of Foreign Terrorist Organizations have ties to the illegal drug trade.[22] For example, the Taliban and Afghan warlords collect nearly half a billion dollars a year from illicit drug farming, production and trafficking,[23] while the FARC in Colombia finances its activities with $300 million a year in illegal drug sales.[24]

"Why is there so much demand for drugs in the USA?" I ask my students. "Why do people use in the first place? Why do people *you* know use drugs?"

"Boredom," one answers. "Depression," says another. "Peer pressure." "Family problems." "Genetic." "Stress." "To get high."

"All of the above," I say. "You're all right. And there's more. While the National Institute on Drug Abuse[25] and others say that home, family, peers, and schools are *the* 'environmental factors' increasing the risk of drug addiction, they don't explain *why* home, family, peers, and schools pose such negative influences. In what context do *they* exist? What gives shape to the networks of relationships that are most intimate to us, the social institutions we all belong to: family, economy, education, religion, and politics? The institutions that shape *us*?"

Until we accept that the *root cause* of the "life-threatening physical and behavioral issues" that Dr. Burke Harris so nobly struggles with is actually in *our culture*, in the way our society is organized and the way we treat and relate to each other, there will always be Tookie Williamses. Until we *believe* that crime rates and other forms of "deviance" are indicators of needed social change, not much will change, at all.

* * *

November 7, 2013, San Quentin State Prison:
Deviant Behavior is touring San Quentin. Lt. Sam Robinson, the new Public Information Officer, is our tour guide. Sam took over the office when Vernell retired. Sam is, as Vernell was, an articulate, interesting, and charismatic storyteller of San Quentin's history and culture, drawing on a wealth of experiences from his 17 years at the prison. He meets us at the gate and tells us of the prison's no-hostage policy. He takes us through the gates and the two security checkpoints and our wrists are stamped with the ultraviolet ink. We enter the interior of the prison, the area between "Heaven and Hell," and hear Sam tell the story of George Jackson and of other notorious inmates who have tried, often succeeding, in creating havoc inside, and in the case of Jackson, just outside the most secure lock-down in the prison, the Adjustment Center. I can see a group of inmates forming over by the chapels. "Good," I say to myself, knowing they are there to talk to us. Most years the tour guides have arranged such a meeting, but last year, Sam was called away at the last minute, and his substitute, a retired CO, had not known to arrange such a meeting. After the Adjustment Center talk, Sam said, "This is your chance to hear from the other side." He walked us over to the chapel area. "I'll step aside and you can ask these men whatever you like. They will tell you their point of view on San Quentin. Feel free to ask them anything you want." I could see apprehension and excitement on the faces of my students. This time, six men in blue denim waited for us.

One was white, one was Asian, two were African-American, one Hispanic, and one looked mixed race, white and black. I recognized two of them from pervious tours: Troy, a big black man, and Curtis, a small white man, smaller than I remember. He'd lost a lot of weight since the last time I saw him. Troy greeted us. "Welcome to San Quentin," he said. "You'll have a chance to ask us anything you want, but before you do, let us tell you about San Quentin, from our point of view." The big man smiled at us. Troy seemed a lot more mellow than the last time I saw him. He told us about life inside San Quentin. It was pretty positive report. "Compared to other prisons we've been in, Folsom, Soledad, or Pelican

Bay, San Quentin is OK. When I first got here, I was ready for the worst. I heard about 'Blood Alley,'" he gestured over his shoulder, "where a lot of people died. You'll walk through it today." I could see a few students grimace. Troy noticed that too. "It's not like that now. Stuff happens, but not like the old days. In other prisons, maybe. You wouldn't have guys like us standing together. Blacks, whites, Hispanics and … what *are* you?" He pointed at one of his comrades, "Asian? Samoan? You an island boy?" They all laughed. "It's not that we don't have trouble between the races, but not like other prisons. Questions?"

Eddie, a tall Mexican-American, a future cop, dressed in a sport jacket and tie, raised his hand.

I had spent a lot of time discussing "appropriate attire" in the weeks leading up to the tour. Still, two female students were deemed "inappropriately attired" for the tights one had on and the short skirt worn by the other one. Fortunately, we were able to dig some oversized men's pants out of the trunk of one student's car for both of them. (I was inspired, the following year, to begin bringing extra "appropriate" clothing.) They looked a little ridiculous, but it worked. Eddie, however, was the only one in the class, including me, with a tie.

"You the teacher?" Troy asked. It was the tie. "What's your question?"

"Does the 'R' in CDCR mean anything?"

Troy laughed, "Rehabilitation? (The acronym stands for "California Department of Corrections and *Rehabilitation*.") Actually, here at San Quentin, it does. We have job training programs, anger management, GED, drug treatment. Patton University offers college courses. We have our own newspaper."

Larissa raised her hand.

"Yes?" Troy smiled at her.

"How long are each of you here for? When will you get out?"

I butt in, "And what was your crime?" A student may eventually ask that, but it seems like the right time for them to talk about it, as they tell us about their sentences.

"Ah, *the* question! We've been waiting for that one. Let's go down the line."

Each inmate gave us the date of his crime, the name of his victim(s), and his sentence. Three were murder one, one was second-degree murder, one was aggravated kidnapping, and one was a third-striker ("But I was innocent of the first crime"). The stories included drive-by shootings, carjackings, gang warfare, and strong-armed robbery.

A seventh inmate joined the line, an older, black man, with gray hair and a cane. Troy explained what we were doing. "I'm in for murder one," he said. "Been in for 36 years." "I know you," I said. "I know you, too," he said. "I talked to your class a long time ago. Late 80s, early 90s." We checked each other out. Both had grayed since then, and, now, he had the cane. Decades had passed and he was still here. And I was at Notre Dame all that time. "My name is Lonnie," he said. "I grew up in Oakland. I got into this life when I was 12 years old, when my mother died. I wound up on the streets. I was surrounded by grown men into criminal activity. It was the way it was. They taught me how to survive. It made sense. It's all I knew. Eventually, I killed two people in a jewelry store. I've been here ever since." Lonnie nodded at me and I nodded back.

Troy turned to the class and said, "I don't want to dismiss what we've done. We done the crime and we doin' the time. But *this*," he waved his hands through the air, taking in the prison, "is no solution! We gotta do something for that 12-year-old boy *before* he gets into trouble. We gotta change the world around him *before* he kills someone."

NOTES

1. Tookie Williams was nominated four times for the Noble Peace Prize, once for the Literature Prize.
2. There was no recording of Stanley Tookie Williams' teleconference call conversation with us. Because the man's vocabulary and intelligence were so apparent in his spoken words, rather than paraphrase, I matched my notes and memory with the vocabulary he used and explanations he gave in online interviews to reconstruct what he said in his own words as accurately as possible.
3. See Williams, Stanley Tookie, *Blue Rage, Black Redemption, A Memoir*, Pleasant Hill, CA, Damamli Publishing, 2004.
4. See http://blogs.kqed.org/newsfix/2011/02/08/judge-fogel-tours-san-quentin/ for a discussion of the controversy and video tour of the new death chamber.
5. See San Quentin Cell Tour—YouTube video for an illustration.
6. Stevens, JD, John Paul, US Supreme Court Justice, dissenting opinion in *Gomez v. United States*, April 21, 1992. "Execution by cyanide gas is 'in essence asphyxiation by suffocation or strangulation.' As dozens of uncontroverted expert statements filed in this case illustrate, execution by cyanide

gas is extremely and unnecessarily painful. 'Following inhalation of cyanide gas, a person will first experience hypoxia, a condition defined as a lack of oxygen in the body. The hypoxic state can continue for several minutes after the cyanide gas is released in the execution chamber. During this time, a person will remain conscious and immediately may suffer extreme pain throughout his arms, shoulders, back, and chest. The sensation may be similar to pain felt by a person during a massive heart attack.' 'Execution by gas … produces prolonged seizures, incontinence of stool and urine, salivation, vomiting, retching, ballistic writhing, flailing, twitching of extremities, [and] grimacing.' This suffering lasts for 8 to 10 minutes, or longer."

7. Gorman, Steve, "California's death row faces no-vacancy situation," *Reuters*, March 30, 2015.
8. Fagan, Kevin, "Eyewitness: Prisoner did not die meekly, quietly," *SF Chronicle*, Wednesday, December 14, 2005.
9. https://www.aclu.org/issues/mass-incarceration
10. Padgett, Juliaglenn, "Author: Politics Responsible for Mass Incarceration," *San Quentin News*, December 2011, about the work of Michelle Alexander, author of *The New Jim Crow: Mass Incarceration in the Age of Color Blindness*.
11. Koopman, John, "Husband and wife—partners both on the beat and at home," *SF Chronicle*, October 14, 2007.
12. See a series of photos of Irene and her husband making the arrest at http://www.sfgate.com/bayarea/article/Husband-and-wife-partners-both-on-the-beat-and-at-home
13. Nevius, C.W., "Tenderloin police captain will be missed," *SF Chronicle*, May 11, 2013.
14. Nevius, C.W., "Tenderloin top cop reluctantly accepts promotion," C.W. Nevius, *SF Chronicle*, May 7, 2013.
15. Fugitive Watch, "21-Year Old Man Suffers Life-Threatening Injuries In Tenderloin Shooting," http://www.fugitive.com/2012/09/06/21-year-old-man-suffers-life-threatening-injuries-in-tenderloin-shooting/
16. Duggan's Sierra Mortuary, http://www.duggans-serra.com/obituary/Jimmy-Sokheang/San-Francisco-CA/1109354
17. Lelchuk, Ilene "BAYVIEW-HUNTERS POINT / S.F.'s invisible majority / Area with highest density of children is most underserved," *SF Chronicle*, May 31, 2006.
18. Tucker, Jill, "Hillary Clinton turns to S.F. doctor to help kids," *SF Chronicle*, June 23, 2013.
19. http://www.caron.org/current-statistics.html
20. U.S. Department of Justice. National Drug Intelligence Center. February 2010. *National Drug Threat Assessment 2010*. http://www.justice.gov/ndic/pubs38/38661/38661p.pdf

21. U.S. Department of Justice. National Drug Intelligence Center. December 2008. *National Drug Threat Assessment 2009*, http://www.usdoj.gov/ndic/pubs31/31379/dtos.htm#Top

22. U.S. Department of Justice. Drug Enforcement Administration. *Dateline DEA: DEA's Biweekly E-mail Informant*, December 2009.

23. United Nations Office on Drugs and Crime. *Afghanistan Opium Survey 2008* http://www.unodc.org/documents/crop-monitoring/Afghanistan_Opium_Survey_2008.pdf

24. US Department of State. Bureau for International Narcotics and Law Enforcement Affairs. *International Narcotics Control Strategy Report*, March 2002. http://www.state.gov/p/inl/rls/nrcrpt/2001/rpt/8475.htm

25. http://www.drugabuse.gov/publications/science-addiction/drug-abuse-addiction

CHAPTER 9

Tender Loin

SEX IN THE CITY

© The Author(s) 2017
D. Stannard-Friel, *Street Teaching in the Tenderloin*,
DOI 10.1057/978-1-137-56437-5_9

"Dr. Don, my sister is a prostitute," she paused, "a streetwalker in the Tenderloin."

Student in Deviant Behavior class

* * *

It was early in my return to the Tenderloin. I was talking to my Deviant Behavior class on campus about life in the inner city, specifically, on this day, prostitution. The Tenderloin streets were still loaded, then, with streetwalkers. Desperate, strung out, beaten-up and beaten-down loners sold sex on the lower blocks of the hill (they still do). Further up, clusters of women, especially in Tendernob, where Tenderloin meets Nob Hill, the well-to-do neighborhood to the north, crowned by the majestic Grace Cathedral, the stately Flood Mansion, home to the über-exclusive[1] Pacific Union Club, and the three "landmark luxury" hotels: The Fairmont, Mark Hopkins, and The Huntington. A hilltop of affluence overlooking the downtrodden, below. A medieval arrangement. The schizophrenic merging of two unlike communities produced a border strip of dope dealers and art dealers, upscale apartment houses and niches for the homeless, and "Ho Ro" (Whore Row): Tendernob.

I remember riding with the police late at night and seeing women prance around the bus stop near Leavenworth and O'Farrell, or driving by myself to see what was going on at commute time (morning and evening), along the busy street corridors that move workers in their cars to and from homes in the outlying neighborhoods and their work in the financial or tourist or retail sales districts downtown. Groups of, mostly, young black women—wearing short dresses or tight leather miniskirts with tailored holes cut into the garments at strategic places to show off shiny, oiled skin—gathered where they would most likely be seen by the commuters. The grinning women would bend over and push out their rear ends, covered in the leather, stretched to its limits, at oncoming cars. These were the upper-echelon streetwalkers of Tenderloin society.

Lower down wound "Ho Stroll," the well-worn route where more worn-down women and male-to-female (MTF) transgenders strutted their stuff, as did the "boy toys" in Polk Gulch, the old gay district that lost its prominence when Eureka Valley, at the foot of Twin Peaks to the west, became "The Castro." Still, the old reputation lingered. Upscale cars cruised by, looking for young male prostitutes.

I concluded my lecture-discussion and students came up to the front of the classroom to ask about term projects, upcoming midterms, or to ask a question about The TL. One, a well-dressed young woman (in casual business attire favored, at the time, by many students in the business major), waited patiently for her turn. When all the others were done, she stepped forward. "Dr. Don, my sister is a prostitute," she paused, "a streetwalker in the Tenderloin."

Looking back, I am not sure how I reacted to the news. I'm used to the unexpected, and long ago learned that many of my "privileged college students" had their own stories of personal or family suffering and pain, struggle, and tragedy. They had their own trauma. Still, those words coming from this particular student took me off guard.

"Would you like to find time to talk?" I asked.

"Yes, I would," Connie[2] said.

And we did. On a later occasion, her mother would join us, but that was after the sister and her pimp came to class to share their experiences and tell us their story of selling sex on the streets of the Tenderloin.

* * *

Deviant Behavior settled down in Cuvilly 1, the ground-floor classroom with big windows on two sides, overlooking the main campus walkway. Students passing by easily see the goings-on inside. I had made no announcement to the students in the class, or anyone else, that our guest speakers today would be a prostitute and her pimp. I didn't want to attract any attention to this particular class meeting, didn't want anyone there but my students, but wasn't sure what the sister or pimp would look like, how they would be dressed, how they presented themselves, and wondered if their appearance would draw the attention of passersby. I met briefly with them before the class, and figured everything would be OK. Connie had asked to introduce them.

I began, "We have guest speakers today. Connie will introduce them. Connie?"

Connie began. "This is my sister, Marty, and her pimp, Joseph." She got right to the point. "Marty is a prostitute in the Tenderloin." Connie had a troubled look on her face, but gave a sweet, little smile to her sister and sat down. Enough said.

Everyone in the class sat upright, paying attention, not always the case, I am sorry to say, when I am talking. Marty smiled back at her sister and began.

"Hi everyone!" Marty waved at the students and grinned. A white woman in her mid-20s, maybe. Maybe a little younger. Or older. Good-looking, but with a slightly weathered look to her face. Hard, but not too hard. Short-cropped, light brown or dark blonde hair. Tight jeans, but no different than many of the female students sitting in front of her. A snug, short-sleeved blouse with a floral print. Tennis shoes. She could walk across campus, as she just did, without drawing any more attention than any attractive student would. The man standing next to her was young, too. Maybe late 20s or early 30s. Slender, average height. Jeans, a brown fatigue jacket, black tee shirt, and a brown crocheted Rastafarian hat on his head. Light brown skin. He wasn't smiling, but seemed comfortable being there, moderately interested in what was going on. He, noncha-lantly, looked around the room. Just another day: pimp in a classroom.

"Thanks, Connie. I just love my sister," Marty said. "Gonna graduate from *college*! So proud. Well, what should I say? I like my work. Been in it for a while. Mostly in the Tenderloin, Mission. Tried LA, not my thing, came back home." She smiled at Joseph, saying, "He's my man!" She pat-ted him on the back, then gazed toward the ceiling. "Let's see." Marty looked at the students, all of whom were staring at her. She laughed. "You're funny," she said to the class. "What would you like to know?"

"Uh, what's it like?" one said. "Being a ..." he hesitated.

"Prostitute? Streetwalker? Hooker?" Marty finished the sentence for him. She laughed. "Hah, you're cute." His eyebrows popped up. She was high energy, almost bubbly, charismatic, friendly. "I like it. It's interesting. Has its ups and downs." She laughed at what appeared to be an unin-tended joke, but was probably told many times before. Some of the stu-dents laughed. Others didn't get it. "It's a job. It's a lifestyle. It's my life." And for 75 minutes, Marty taught us what it was like to be in "The Life," at least from her perspective.

She saw herself as providing a service, not just sex. Men sometimes just want to talk, share their hopes and dreams, or their problems, "but mostly, it's the sex. Almost always." She seemed to be happy being able to be of service. The men she had sex with were "johns" or "tricks," sometimes sad, lonely people, "or just someone who wants to get a laid." She smiled at the students and turned to Joseph. "He's my Daddy."

"Daddy?" one of the students repeated.

"Yes, my Daddy. Joseph is in charge." Another smile. "He makes things happen. Protects us, his family. Me and the other girls, when there are other girls. We're family, me and the other girls and Joseph. Just me and Joseph, right now, but not always. I like it when there's another girl or two. Someone to talk girl talk to. Another 'wife-in-law,' that's what we call each other. We're in 'The Life' together. Same family. We understand each other. But not always. Some of the girls are crazy, too strung out. Not a good 'in-law.'"

"What do *you* do, Joseph?" one of the female students asked. More of a confrontation than a question.

"I take care of her and the money," he replied.

"*Her* money!" the student said.

Joseph ignored her. "I protect them. Make sure they're safe on the track."

Marty jumped in, "The 'track,' or the 'stroll,' is the place on the streets where we hook up. Hyde Street in the Tenderloin. Or Leavenworth. Turk. Pretty much anywhere in the Tenderloin." She laughed again. "Not just The TL. Capp Street in the Mission. But everybody knows what's happenin' in The TL and where to go if you want to get some." Marty was enjoying herself. "Joseph makes sure other pimps don't beat on us. Or 'Renegades'—that's women without pimps—work our stroll. She's 'outta-pocket,' on her own. That's some dangerous shit, excuse my French. A 'Renegade.' Workin' without a pimp is just asking for trouble. Even with a pimp, you gotta be careful. Be careful who the tick is. Be careful with other pimps. Makin' eye contact with another pimp is dangerous, 'reckless,' we say. Could mean you wanna change pimps, 'choose' a new one." Marty made quote signs with her fingers around the spoken word "choose."

"Makin' eye contact may make your pimp *think* you want to change. Not, usually, a happy ending, there, if you know what I mean. You hang out on the corner with other girls and their pimps, you *do not make eye contact* with the other pimps. 'Reckless eyeballing' we call it." Marty looked down and shaded her eyes with her hand.

"Did you ever change pimps?" A question from the back of the classroom.

"Not me. I love Joseph. He's my man." She gave him a little hug. He looked at her, noncommittal. "A girl can," Marty continued. "But you gotta pay an 'exit fee.' A lot. $10,000?" She turned to Joseph, her "banker," for confirmation. He nodded. "It's best to keep your eyes down," Marty said.

Another question, "How much do *you* get paid?"

"On the streets? Me? $50, $100. Maybe more. Maybe less. Depending on what I do. Depending on the day, who's in town. Doctors' convention? Lawyers? Nobody? Time of day. How close I am to quota."

"Quota?"

"How much I have to make that day. $300. $500. A thousand. It depends."

I looked at the big clock in the front of the room. It was almost noon. Class ends at 12:05 p.m. "I'm afraid we have to wrap up. One last question."

A young woman in the front raised her hand. "Marty, what are your plans? What's your future?"

Marty nodded at the student. "Good question." She looked at Joseph. He turned toward her and she put her hand on his arm. "We're both getting tired of the streets. It's gettin' old. We do have plans. We're thinking of massage parlors. Workin' in massage parlors. Much safer."

"More money, too," Daddy says.

* * *

The TL is still ground zero in San Francisco for sex sales on the streets, but cells phones and the Internet have replaced much of Ho Ro and Ho Stroll. Some women, MTF transgenders, teenage boys, and young men still walk these streets, but many now advertise online, moved their work into massage parlors, as Marty did, or promote their work on the back pages of alternative newspapers such as *The Bay Guardian*.

"**Nasty Girls! Hardcore, Live 1-ON-1**," reads one advertisement; "**Yarna, 100% Sexy Functional Transsexual, Beginners Are Welcome**," another; "**Interracial Kink, A Swinger Party, Gangbang w/Latina Luna**"; and "**Mature Dominatrix with Pretty Feet, All Fantasies Welcome**" are accompanied by suggestive photos showing bare bottoms and lots of skin.

Still, there are enough prostituted walking these streets to catch our attention as *we* walk these streets, providing plenty of evidence that our society still hasn't figured out what to do about sexual exploitation.

* * *

High school English teacher: "Well, class, today we finalize decisions on our American Experience field study projects. What social issue do you plan on studying?"

Sarah: "I'm going to study prostitution."

Teacher: "Well, uh, what a good topic, Sarah. But, this is a field research project. Interviews. Stuff like that. How will you study, uh, prostitutes?" Sarah: "No problem. My grandfather knows lots of prostitutes."

I am Sarah's grandfather, and I do know lots of prostitutes or—as Reverend Glenda Hope, a neighborhood activist, street minister, founder of Safe House for women leaving prostitution, and street teacher, has taught us—"prostituted." And I did help her study the subject, firsthand, when I brought her into San Francisco's South of Market and Tenderloin Districts and introduced her to people who could explain street life in a way that I never could.

I took my granddaughter to The Standing Against Global Exploitation (SAGE) Project, a "survivor-centric" organization, founded and run by "CSE" (commercial sexual exploitation) survivors, "with one primary aim: bringing an end to the commercial sexual exploitation of children and adults." She was introduced to program directors, toured their site on Mission Street, and interviewed Rose Arnold,[3] a former prostituted and current street teacher for Tenderloin U, who told her, "It was always a disgusting thing to do, but it became sort of an addiction."[4] After saying our goodbyes, we walked the streets of the 6th Street corridor, past street-walkers (including one standing right outside the SAGE front door), porno stores, hockshops, and the Henry Hotel, looking about the same as we did when Sarah's grandfather and great-uncle stayed there our first night in San Francisco. We crossed over Market Street, and entered the Tenderloin.

In the Tenderloin, Sarah met service providers and young people in some of the programs scattered throughout the neighborhood, many tucked away in storefronts or basements, operating to prevent entry into the kinds of lives that SAGE is trying to get people out of. We went to St. Boniface Church to see the "Sacred Sleep" program. But the doors were closed early, the outer gate chained, an outcome of Fr. Louie's recent departure and the impact of new, competing priorities and limited funds at the church. We walked by the long line of hungry people outside St. Anthony's Dining Room, "The Miracle on Jones Street," founded in 1950 by Fr. Alfred Boeddeker, who was challenged by those who wondered if this soup kitchen was really needed. After 36,000,000 meals later, his dark vision has proven prophetic, many times over. We wound our way up the aptly named Jones (aka "Jonesin'") Street hill. Clusters of jumpy addicts crowded around dealers, blocking the sidewalk in front of the big windows of The Boys and Girls Club and Up and Away Café. I pointed out the old Lyric Hotel—right across the street, now a residential treatment facility for the formerly homeless and mentally ill—where Sarah's grandfather lived, when I was just a few years older than she is now.

We crossed the street and entered Boeddeker Park, on the corner of Eddy and Jones. The Franciscan friar hoped that his namesake park would be a sanctuary for the old and young, a place where the tired and poor could spend time in safe and secure surroundings. "May it be peaceful," the old man said at its opening on May 1, 1985. But the kid-friendly mission was thwarted by the hypodermic needles and used condoms tossed in the sand. The pathway through the park, lined with benches meant for the old and tired, taken over by dealers, became "The Gauntlet"; the freestanding, self-contained, self-cleaning, public toilet at the park's entrance, used as a mini-shooting gallery by street addicts, "The Vertical Coffin." Sometimes, when there is nowhere else to go, streetwalkers use it to hook up with johns.

Sarah and I continued our tour of the Tenderloin, passing by smoke shops, massage parlors, strip joints, X-rated movie houses, porno stores, liquor stores, drug treatment programs, soup kitchens, health clinics, AIDS clinics, check cashing stores, and SRO hotels. Streetwalkers were starting to come out in number. Drug dealers, homeless people, the mentally ill, the aged, and physically disabled were everywhere. And in the midafternoon, the children who live here—white, black, Latino, Native American, Samoan, Tongan, Russian, Asian Indian, Middle Eastern, Filipino, Chinese, but especially Southeast Asian: Vietnamese, Lao, Cambodian, Thai—flooded the neighborhood, as they went from school to home, or playground, or after-school program, or to hang out on the streets with friends already there, school dropouts, as many who join them soon will be. Sirens wailed, people shouted, horns honked, engines roared, and music blared.

Sarah got an "A" on her paper, "Prostitution." In the opening paragraph,[5] she asked,

Here's a question for you. Have you ever been walking through the San Francisco streets and happened to pass a massage parlor where you see a scantily dressed, tired-looking woman standing there, possibly smoking, and acting as if she is looking or waiting for someone, and you think, "Oh, jeez, there's a prostitute," so you walk a little faster? Now, have you ever thought about how and why she got there, or what was so wrong in her life that she would sink this low?

Sarah's researched answer? Poverty, rejection, neglect, physical abuse, emotional abuse, sexual abuse (especially in childhood), isolation, humiliation, degradation, depression, substance abuse, and rejection by a society that doesn't seem to care about causation ("what was so wrong in her life…") once a woman turns a trick ("…that she would sink this low?"). Sarah cited one study that reported, " police in a southern California community closed all rape reports made by prostitutes and addicts, placing them in a file stamped 'NHI'…No Human Involved."[6]

* * *

My introduction to the world of the San Francisco sex worker began in 1968 when I was, by day, an undergraduate in sociology at San Francisco State, and, by night, a cabbie for Yellow and DeSoto Cab Companies. The sexual revolution was in full swing. Topless (later, for a while, bottomless) joints lined Broadway in North Beach. Carol Doda, with her silicon-enhanced breasts (34″ became 44″), writhed on top of a white piano as it was lowered from the ceiling at the Condor Club (the same piano top a club bouncer and a dancer made love on, until the lift was accidently activated, asphyxiating him and pinning her under his dead body for three hours). Polk Gulch was still the gay mecca. "Boy Toys" were everywhere. In New York, the Stonewall riots erupted in Greenwich Village, protesting a police raid on the gay bar, launching, many say, the gay liberation movement. But two years earlier, "drag queens" (ostracized by society for who they are, therefore, with few work options, many prostituted) rioted at Compton Cafeteria in the Tenderloin, angered by the treatment they suffered at the hands of the owners and police. This, many who were there say, was the spark that ignited the raging fire that became Stonewall.[7]

In addition to "regular" fares, I was picking up drug dealers, making deliveries; pimps and the prostituted, heading to wherever they wanted to go; sometimes the prostituted and their johns, often too eager to get started before the ride was over; tired strippers, heading home after the clubs closed; and tourists, looking for action on the streets or in the bars.

When I came back to the Tenderloin in 1995 to write a book, advertising on the Internet was just beginning. Online solicitation for sex did not yet exist. The Mitchell Brothers' O'Farrell Theater was the most famous strip club in the country, even though Jim Mitchell was convicted of killing his brother, Artie, four years before. Massage parlors were everywhere, so were strung out streetwalkers, many lingering victims of the crack epidemic that hit the Tenderloin hard in the 1980s. Both City Baby and

Star (the principals of my earlier book on the Tenderloin) sold sex on occasion to support their habits (City Baby's crack addiction, and Star's drug of choice was heroin). I wasn't sure what I would write about in the Tenderloin, but knew something about its culture from my cab driving days and, years before, my on-and-off living in the neighborhood. I was riding with the cops, talking to service providers, hanging out on the streets, and attending community meetings, but I was too inhibited to engage directly with the sex culture. I didn't want to be seen, especially by the young Tenderloin residents I was just getting to know, chatting with a streetwalker or entering a strip joint or massage parlor or porno store, even if it was (really) to do research. So I called up Call Off Your Old Tired Ethics (COYOTE), and asked for Margo St. James.

Margo is well known in San Francisco, and beyond, for her activism as a "sex-positive feminist." A former prostitute (she would not apply the term "prostituted" to herself), she has a long history of promoting sex work as legitimate work, and has agitated to change cultural attitudes toward sexuality, in general. She filed a lawsuit against the State of Rhode Island for selective prosecution of its antiprostitution laws: far more prostitutes were being arrested than johns. She sought the Republican Party's nomination for President in 1980, with the legalization of sex work in her platform. And in 1996, she finished seventh for a position on the San Francisco Board of Supervisors in an election that seated the top six vote getters (she received 78,669 votes). It was her nearly successful run for office that caught my eye, reminding me of her long, colorful, and passionate work for sex workers, and I made the call to COYOTE.

COYOTE was one of Margo's most enduring accomplishments. The goal of the organization that she founded in 1973 was "the repeal of the prostitution laws and an end to the stigma associated with sexual work."[8] Its work included public education, crisis counseling, support groups, referrals to legal and other services, testifying at government hearings, serving as expert witnesses in trials, helping police with investigations of crimes against prostitutes, and providing sensitivity training to government and private nonprofit agencies that provide services to prostitutes. It worked to ensure the rights of all sex workers including strippers, phone sex operators, prostitutes, porn actresses, and others. Furthermore, "the laws against pimping (living off the earnings of a prostitute) and pandering (encouraging someone to work as a prostitute) should also be repealed, to be replaced with labor laws dealing with working conditions in third-party owned and managed prostitution businesses," such as massage parlors, brothels, escorts services, and on the streets.

"Hello, Ms. St. James. My name is Don Stannard-Friel. I'm a professor at College of Notre Dame. I'm working on a book about the Tenderloin, and wonder if I could meet with you to talk about some ideas."

"I'm pretty busy right now. Maybe you could come to one of our meetings?"

"That would be great."

She told me when and where COYOTE meets, and I was at their next gathering.

* * *

The COYOTE meeting was held at the Institute for Advanced Study of Human Sexuality, then, as I remember, on Van Ness Avenue, the busy north-to-south boulevard that runs by City Hall. The sidewalk outside the front door was covered by a long awning, giving the entrance the appearance of a nightclub. The building, itself, was a distinguished one, probably built a couple of decades after the earthquake and fire that destroyed virtually everything across the street and east of here. Inside I was greeted by a pleasant-looking middle-aged woman, "How can I help you?"

"Uh, I'm going to the COYOTE meeting," I said, not without some discomfort, wondering what she was thinking about who I am and what I was doing going to a COYOTE meeting. I was more comfortable hanging out with drug dealers on Leavenworth Street than meeting with a bunch of sex workers.

"Sure, right that way." She pointed to a set of large doors down the hall.

I entered a lecture hall. A desk and lectern were on the floor. Chairs were set on rises, half-circling the room. Margo St. James (I recognized her from the many news stories about her), seated at the desk, was smiling broadly (she usually is) at several women clustered around her. Other women, a few MTF trans, and a couple of men were seated in the chairs above them. Everyone was engaged in a lively conversation about "best condoms."

"Sheik rubbers got my vote," said one young white woman, sitting in the second tier. She looked like a secretary from the financial district, with her sleeveless gray dress, dark green shawl, and modest silver jewelry. "Did you see the 'Angry guy' commercial?"[9] The television ad showed a furious young man screaming that he wasn't going to use a condom. "They're a tool of the establishment, just to bring us down," he shouts, "they want to control us, with their condoms," until a pretty young woman comes up behind him, hands him a condom, and says, "Sheik, use one or get none!"

producing an instant conversion to safe sex. "They're cool, I mean, I'd use one.... Thank you, thank you, Mr. Sheik!"

The women in the room looked like everyday people. Most in jeans and casual attire, except for the "financial district secretary." It turned out she was a call girl, working out of her apartment in the Avenues. I recognized one of the men, an older white guy, with long gray hair tied back in a ponytail. He wore a colorful kaftan. I had seen him before, off and on over many years, leading a group of young commune members through the Haight-Ashbury and Golden Gate Park.

Most of the conversation involved developing plans to encourage the city to adopt a Board of Supervisors' task force report that had recommended decriminalizing prostitution. COYOTE had been a big part of the process and had the backing of DA Terrence Hallinan, who had proposed the Task Force in 1994, when he was a member of the Board of Supervisors. The final report came out in 1996, and it was being examined and debated throughout the halls of city government. I was impressed by the knowledge the women had of the issues and their thought-through arguments for decriminalizing sex work.

Toward the end of the meeting, a frazzled, somewhat disheveled, transgender woman stood up to complain about police brutality and how she was abused in a recent arrest for solicitation. "They strip-searched me, humiliated me, hit me, hurt me, and threw me in with the men. I am suing them!" she said—hands on her hips, chin jutted out showing a "six-o'clock shadow" of whiskers—"for half a million dollars. Maybe more."

Good luck with that, I said, sarcastically, to myself. Some months later, I saw on the front page of a local gay newspaper that she had won her case and was awarded $500,000.

I went to several COYOTE meetings, and even volunteered to be part of the phone tree, reminding people about upcoming meetings, but didn't think I was really accepted by the group. I didn't fit in. I was something of an intrusion, an observer, not there for the same reasons as everyone else. People were polite, but didn't connect with me beyond basic courtesies. Except for Margo. She welcomed me, remembered my phone call to her, and that she had invited me to the meetings. It turns out she was housesitting on Potrero Hill, a few blocks from where I live. I invited her out to lunch at Aurora's, a new neighborhood "comfort food" spot, and met her there one afternoon.

Margo was, as she always seems to be, upbeat. We talked about our lives, the uniqueness of San Francisco, and the changing neighborhood that we both lived in (I still do). Then we talked about COYOTE, and her passion for recognizing sex workers as valuable contributors to society, needing legal protections.

She told me that her work for sex workers' rights began on Mother's Day in 1973 with "WHO," Whores, Housewives, and Others. The first meeting of WHO was held on Alan Watt's, the famous philosopher and 1960s icon, houseboat in Sausalito. The name COYOTE came from Tom Robbins, the novelist, who called her a "Coyote Trickster." At one of her parties, she asked Sheriff Richard Hongisto, a politically connected, liberal, former Haight-Ashbury community liaison street cop, advice on spreading the word about sex workers rights. He said she needed a victim to speak out. "So, that was me." And COYOTE was born.

Margo's work, and that of COYOTE, focused on legitimizing sex work. The group's website argued,[10]

> The laws prohibiting the soliciting or engaging in an act of prostitution, or patronizing a prostitute, should be repealed. The laws against pimping (living off the earnings of a prostitute) and pandering (encouraging someone to work as a prostitute) should also be repealed, to be replaced with labor laws dealing with working conditions in third-party owned and managed prostitution businesses.
>
> Commissions, a majority of whose members should be prostitutes or ex-prostitutes, including individuals who have worked on the street, in massage parlors and brothels, and for escort services, should develop guidelines for the operation of third-party owned and managed businesses, including but not limited to health and safety issues, commissions, and employer/employee relationships.

Margo was very serious about her commitment to sex work as a regulated and protected *profession*.

The SAGE Project, where I took my granddaughter, Sarah, to begin her high school field study project, had a different take on the industry.

* * *

Rose Arnold meets us at the door of The SAGE Project. She smiles and hugs me and says hello to each student coming in off of busy Mission Street, as if she's a friend's mom welcoming them into her home, instead of a former Sacramento–Las Vegas–San Francisco "pipeline" prostitute.[11] There are 23 students, a large enrollment for an inner-city class. I try and keep it at around 15. Walking the streets in too large a group attracts too much attention, and can be a problem when we try to squeeze into some of our street teachers' places of operation.

To the disappointment of some in the class, the walk from the coffee-house was low-key compared to most of our travels through The TL. The SAGE Project is actually not in the Tenderloin, but just outside of it, on the other side of Market Street in the SoMa District, on Mission Street, between 8th and 9th.

We did pass homeless hangouts on the side of the Main Library. The library offers one of the few "full service" bathrooms available to the homeless in The TL (separate men's and women's rooms, sinks and toilets, soap and paper towels), so homeless gatherings happen here every day. And a trio of animated transgender women walked by. One said to us, "What's with the parade?" But most of the folks that we pass near the library, at this time of day, are tourists or working stiffs, going about their business.

It's April. We've been walking these streets as a class for three months now. Eight of the students have been in inner-city classes before, another works here, and another one lives here. So, it's a pretty seasoned class. But, still, going to The SAGE Project excites the group.

This is a modified Promise of the Inner City class. The general educational goal of Promise is for students to learn about *positive* qualities of the Tenderloin, and, sometimes, other inner-city neighborhoods (Chinatown, the Haight, the Mission). But this time, added to the regular "learning outcomes," it's a focus on "political engagement."

With my NDNU colleague, Gretchen Wehrle, I was a Campus Compact-Carnegie Foundation Fellow for Political Engagement. With 21 other California Fellows, from many disciplines, we met periodically with Campus Compact and Carnegie leaders and facilitators to collaborate and explore community engagement pedagogies that encourage students to become politically involved members of society. It didn't take much tweaking of the Promise class to meet the program's criteria.

In addition to introductory, reflection, student presentation, and wrap-up meetings on campus, we attended a talk by civil rights leader Angela Davis on "Building Communities of Activism" in the NDNU Theater, and met at City Hall with County Supervisor Chris Daly, who talked about "Inner City Politics." Chris was a Mission District housing activist before his election to the Board. His confrontational style produced a lot of turbulence during his ten-year tenure. One of his first acts was to get into a near fistfight with Mayor Willie Brown, 38 years his senior, but no pushover. In his closing months in office, Chris promised to say "Fuck" at every meeting of the Board, which he did. But he was effective in increasing housing for the homeless and very poor. Carol Chetkovich, author of one of our textbooks, *From the Ground Up: Grassroots Organizations Making Social Change*, joined us in The TL to talk about "Grassroots and Deliberative Democracy."

Columnist C.W. Nevius and reporter Jill Tucker met us in the *San Francisco Chronicle* newsroom and spoke about "The Politics of Homelessness"; Angela Alioto, former President of the Board of Supervisors and Chair of the Mayor's Task Force on Homeless, met us in an SRO hotel and explained "San Francisco's Response to Homelessness"; and Jennifer Friedenbach, Executive Director of the San Francisco Coalition on Homelessness, discussed "The Grassroots Response to SF's Response to Homelessness" at the Coalition's offices on Turk Street.

Sgt. Guytano Caltagirone, Community Liaison Officer for SFPD, Tenderloin Station, explained "Community Policing"; and Penny Schoener, of California Prison Focus, discussed "The Policed Community."

We also toured The TL, visited a permanent supportive housing site at the Cecil Williams/Glide Community House; volunteered at PHC; produced three Youth Philanthropy Workshops with DonorsChoose/YouthChoose; organized the panel discussion on "The Hidden Face of Homelessness"; studied Proposition, a measure on the upcoming November ballot in San Francisco to decriminalize prostitution in San Francisco; and met with Rose Arnold and her colleagues at The SAGE Project to learn about "The Politics of Prostitution."[12]

Rose, my first contact at SAGE, is a highly regarded program director here, but today she is not going to be our street teacher. She introduces us to Norma Hotaling, the founder and executive director of SAGE, who greets us, expresses her appreciation for our interest, and passes us on to three other women, Maggie, Joan, and Susan.[13] I don't know if they are former sex workers. Not everyone here is. And these three don't look like they have ever been in The Life, but then, few who work here do. They're well dressed, well groomed, articulate, informed, and friendly. (After class, the students say Maggie looks like a social worker, Joan a lawyer, and Susan an NDNU student.) The three women tell us about the origins and mission of SAGE, some of its accomplishments, and show us a film about their street outreach program.

Maggie (the "social worker") begins, "SAGE was founded by Norma Hotaling, who you just met, a survivor of commercial sexual exploitation and substance abuse. Norma was sexually abused as a child, beginning when she was three years old, a child prostitute beginning at five.

Beginning when she was twelve, she was put in juvenile halls, jails, psychiatric hospitals, and drug treatment programs. By the time she was eighteen, she was a homeless streetwalker, addicted to heroin. For twenty-one years, no one ever asked her about her personal life, about being raped, about being kidnapped, about the metal plate in her head from being beaten, about her suicide attempts. Norma says, no one ever treated her like a person. She was just a whore, a drug addict, and a criminal. Then in 1989, she changed her life. She kicked heroin and devoted her life to helping others. Joan will tell you about that."

Joan (the "lawyer") takes over. "In 1993, Norma started The SAGE Project, Standing Against Global Exploitation, to help women, and men, too, leave prostitution. She began meeting community leaders, arguing that the women were not on the streets out of choice, but exploited by others. She used her life to teach others about prostitution, telling them it was *not* a choice, but violence against women. Women become prostitutes because they are exploited by others, to perform sex for money. Or they are overcome by drug addiction or poverty and see no way out. SAGE shows the way.

"The staff of SAGE is made up of women who are survivors of commercial sexual exploitation. Most of the staff members are survivors, including the three of us."

There's my answer to "I don't know if they are former sex workers." I look at the students to see their reaction. A few glance at each other, but most are just taking it all in.

Joan continues, "The exploited are trafficked by pimps and others who turn out little girls and vulnerable young women. Our experience allows us to provide support and gain trust without re-traumatizing them. We give them role models of who they can be. Role models who truly care about them. Believe in them. *Were* them! More than 350 women and girls receive our direct services each week.

"This is what we learned from the women we meet at SAGE: The average age of entry into prostitution is thirteen to fourteen. Sixty to seventy-five percent have experienced domestic violence in their personal relationships. Seventy-five percent have experienced violence in their community, including gun violence, gang violence, physical assaults getting to school, while in school, and in their neighborhood. Between forty and sixty percent have experienced sexual assault. Ninety-five percent have used drugs. PTSD, post-traumatic stress disorder, is the norm. Violence and sexual abuse are the norm.

"At SAGE, women and girls receive assistance in exiting the criminal justice system, escaping prostitution and pornography, and recovering from abuse. They also receive medical and mental health care, peer counseling, substance abuse treatment, housing, intensive case management, education, and vocational training."

Joan continues, "In addition to providing direct services, SAGE engages in advocacy, educational programs, and outreach activities. Staff reach out to prostituted women living on the streets of San Francisco, inviting them to enter programs and receive services. Susan will talk about our street outreach program."

Susan (the "NDNU student") begins, "Hi, everyone. Actually, I am going to show you a movie about our street outreach program and more." She turns on a DVD player, and the video begins.

"Endangered Species: The Women of SAGE" is a remarkable film.[14] It begins with Norma and one of the SAGE graduates doing street outreach in the Tenderloin, talking to Theresa on what I think is Taylor Street, who is known to them from her previous involvement with SAGE. They are encouraging Theresa to come back to the program. To get the life that they tell her she deserves. Theresa says she can't believe that she is back on the streets and promises to come to the SAGE offices "tomorrow."

The video goes on to Norma and several SAGE graduates telling their stories. Most striking to me, and to many of the students, is the appearance of some of these women as they are now—attractive, professional, well dressed, happy, clean, and sober—compared to their mug shots, shown on the screen: skinny, toothless, unkempt, stung out, spaced out women being processed into jail. It's hard to believe that they are the same people. They tell their stories of being prostituted, being addicted to drugs, going to jail, living on the streets, being used and abused.

One story is that of Tracey. The video includes a portion of an earlier documentary, "Black Tar Heroin: The Dark side of the Street,"[15] shot five years before, showing a strung out, streetwalking Tracey, sitting in a storefront doorway, pulling her pants down around her ankles, searching for a usable vein in her legs to shoot heroin into. She then wanders off as the drug takes hold, looking for another trick. In the new video, a sober Tracey says, "I used to think I was prostituting to buy the drugs. Then I realized, I had to be on drugs to prostitute."

Tracey says, "Let me take you on a walk into my past." The camera follows her back to "her" corner and she recalls, "This is my spot. Sometimes, you know, if it was nice, because in the afternoon the sun would be shining down so I would be all nodded off on heroin and I would sit right here," she says, pointing to a spot in an alley. "And sometimes the date would come and shake me and wake me up, because, you know, I was so sexually enticing, passed out on the sidewalk, they just *absolutely* had to have me."

Tracey got off the drugs and off the streets and is now a counselor at The SAGE Project.

Early in the film, Norma cries as she tells her story, but later, she shows anger as she shares it with men at the "john school."

In 1996, Norma cofounded the First Offender Prostitution Program (FOPP), also known as the "john school," with the DA's office and police Lt. Joe Dutto, known as a no-nonsense cop, "who would arrest his own mother."[16] Lt. Dutto, who had repeatedly arrested Norma for prostitution and drugs, suggested to her, after she became the Executive Director of SAGE, that johns needed to be educated about the consequences of their crime. So, began the john school.

The john school is a court diversion program designed to curb the demand for CSE by reducing recidivism among those who solicit prostitution. It allows first offenders to have their charges dropped if they pay a $1000 fine and participate in a first-of-its kind, six-hour course, featuring speakers, mostly CSE survivors, who explain the negative impact prostitution has on women, the johns, and the community. "The men who seek out prostitutes don't like to think they're part of exploiting someone," Norma says. "They like to believe it's a victimless crime."

In the video, Norma speaks to a roomful of men, sitting in chairs with their backs to the camera. She is at a podium, looking out at the audience, with a look on her face that shows disgust and outrage. "I was waiting for one of you to take me out somewhere and get a little crazy or make me do something I didn't want to do or push my head down a little hard on your dick and I was gonna kill your ass.... I was so full of rage."

One by one, former prostituted women tell the men what their lives were like before getting into sex work, of the horror of their lives, of being victims of all kinds of abuse, of getting addicted to drugs and what that does to you, and of the role that johns play in perpetuating a system that wrecks people's lives.

The FOPP and SAGE have been recognized many times over the years. By the time of our visit, they had received the Innovations in American Government Award from the JFK School of Government at Harvard and the Ford Foundation, the Peter F. Drucker Award for Innovation in Non-Profit Management, and Oprah's Angel Network Use Your Life

Award. Norma accepted the Angel award, which included $100,000 for the SAGE Foundation, on Oprah's show. Shortly after she spoke to our class, she received the Cheyenne Bell Award from the Center for Young Women's Development, honoring her work helping young women escape street prostitution.

But the work of SAGE was not without its critics. Most prominent of those opposed to the work of Norma and her colleagues was Margo St. James.

The john's school "is taking a very negative tack by trying to shame men," Margo told a reporter for AP.[17] "It's a waste of time and money." Margo's approach, of course, was to legalize and regulate the sex industry, which was the point of Proposition, a measure on the San Francisco election day ballot, seven months after our, then, most recent visit to SAGE. A year earlier, leading up to her run for county supervisor, Margo launched a poster campaign promoting the issues that she cared about, including one of a naked woman photographed from behind that read: "If Prohibition couldn't stop alcohol, how could it stop something like this?" She may have narrowly lost her bid for office, but she was still fighting for what she believed in.

Proposition K was San Francisco's latest attempt to legislate prostitution, an effort going back to the city's earliest days. In 1848, gold was discovered in Sutter Creek, resulting in the Gold Rush that increased the population of what was then known as Yerba Buena from 850 to 36,000 in four years. Among the earliest settlers were 200 "pioneer prostitutes."[18] In 1850, another 2000 women arrived, many of them prostitutes, who were generally welcomed by the male population that exceeded the number of females by a ratio of fifty to one.[19] But by 1854, legislation was already being written to purge the city of its prostitutes, especially Chinese prostitutes (and Chinese people in general). Ever since, San Francisco, as Yerba Buena came to be known, has had a love–hate relationship with the prostituted. "Red light" districts have come and gone. "Women of the night" have been celebrated and demonized. In the days leading up to the Proposition K vote, Margo reminded San Franciscans that well-known prostitute Tessie Wall accompanied Mayor James "Sunny Jim" Rolf to the Policeman's Ball every year from 1911 to 1930; Madam Sally Stanford's bordello was credited by San Francisco's beloved columnist Herb Caen as being the founding place for the United Nations, because so many delegates to the 1945 conference frequented her business (in 1976, Sally became Mayor of Sausalito, San Francisco's neighbor to the north); and Margo's own Hooker's Ball was celebrated on Halloween in the city from 1974 to 1979, then replaced by the Exotic Erotic Ball[20] until 2010, reported to be the "Wildest Party on Earth,"[21] with 15,000 partygoers. The vast majority who went to the balls were not prostitutes, just San Franciscans looking for fun, many dressing up as what they imagined streetwalkers or pimps looked like. Others wore little or nothing at all. Two mayors (Brown and Newsom) issued proclamations recognizing "Exotic Erotic Ball Day" in San Francisco.

But others pointed out that women actually working the streets were not having fun.

Elizabeth Fernandez, of *The San Francisco Examiner*, reported[22] on the murders of two young women working the streets during Thanksgiving week, a third was in her seventh week in a coma after a vicious beating that broke her skull, shattered her teeth, and fractured her eye sockets, and a "fourth young prostitute," Fernandez wrote, "a 15-year-old from the East Bay who reportedly worked the Tenderloin, was raped Oct. 28 and repeatedly jabbed in the eyes to prevent identification of her assailants. The attackers then shot her in the back of the head; the bullet exited through her right ear."

In 2007, AP reporter Kim Curits wrote,[23] "Two women were accused of soaking a homeless, drug-addicted prostitute with gasoline and burning her to death after she reported that one of them had robbed her."

And on April 27, 2010, AP reporter Lisa Leff, in an article headlined, "Man charged in transgender prostitute murder,"[24] wrote,

> Prosecutors said Donzell Francis, 41, of San Francisco, has pleaded not guilty to charges of murder, forcible oral copulation, sodomy by use of force and other charges in the death of 27-year-old Ruby Ordenana. She was raped, strangled and left naked near a freeway.
> The charges in the slaying carry allegations that would make Francis eligible for the death penalty or life without the possibility of parole if he was convicted. He already is serving a 17-year sentence for sexually assaulting and beating another transgender woman six months after Ordenana's death.
> The victim in that case, like Ordenana, was a prostitute who worked in the city's Tenderloin district.

Proposition K actually grew out of earlier efforts to legalize or decriminalize prostitution.[25] In 1993, *The New York Times* reported,[26] "Responding to complaints from merchants and residents, city officials are considering whether to establish city-run brothels that would rent rooms to prostitutes, check their health and collect taxes on their earnings." Then supervisor, soon-to-be DA, Terence Hallinan, proposed a task force to study this and other issues related to the city's response to prostitution. The following year, the Board of Supervisors established a Task Force on Prostitution, made up of people from many perspectives, including three prostitutes. One was Margo St. James. In its 1996 Final Report, the task force did not recommend a city-run brothel (that was too much even for liberal San Franciscans. Mayor Willie Brown said at the time, "San Francisco's first black mayor is not going to be San Francisco's first legal pimp"), but did recommended decriminalizing prostitution, removing it from criminal justice oversight. It was this report that was the topic of discussion when I attended COYOTE meetings in 1997. They knew then that the report was controversial. Some of the Task Force members had resigned rather than support the final outcome. Eventually, it was not embraced or implemented by city leaders. But the movement did not die. One recommendation, in an effort led by Supervisor Chris Daly in 2003, did eventually become policy: the city transferred the regulation of massage parlors from the police department to the Department of Public Health. This, many say, resulted in de facto decriminalizing prostitution in the massage parlors, since oversight shifted to focus on matters relating to cleanliness and health, not crime. Police raids on parlors did continue to uncover and prosecute trafficking, but the goal was not to ferret out sex workers. The unofficial–official position was expressed when one police lieutenant told me about the cops aggressively enforcing prostitution laws on the streets, especially against pimps and johns, to push it indoors, "If it's outta sight, it's outta mind." Marty, my student's sister, made her move off the streets and into the massage parlors at just the right time.

The 1996 Task Force report also recommended creating an anonymous hotline for sex workers. It took a decade, but this was implemented in 2006 by the Department of Public Health. Not much else changed. Margo and her allies did continue the fight for decriminalization of prostitution. And that effort led to Proposition K on the November 2008 ballot. It generated a lot of discussion and passion on both side of the issue.

Those in favor of decriminalizing prostitution argued that prostitutes would no longer have to worry about criminal charges being lodged against them for reporting being assaulted or raped during their work activities. It would free the police and the DA's office to spend more time and effort investigating and prosecuting crimes committed *against* sex workers and others. Prostitutes who operate out of their homes would no longer be subject to eviction for their work (unless other laws, not specific to outlawing prostitution, were enacted allowing landlords to do so); this would reduce the need for these sex workers to operate on the streets. Decriminalization would save on the costs of investigating and prosecuting illegal sex work. In the year preceding the vote on Proposition K, that came to nearly $11.5 million. Proposition K would enable the City to spend those funds prosecuting other crimes or providing services for prostitutes.

Those against Proposition K claimed that by decriminalizing prostitution, including pimps and clients, and eliminating funding for related investigation and prosecution, Proposition K would make it more difficult to prosecute coercive pimps and to pursue charges against human traffickers, including those who coerce minors and children. The Early Intervention Prostitution Program, which offered support and treatment for prostitutes, and services for prostitutes resulting from SAGE's FOPP, both funded by fines levied on johns, would be eliminated because the fines would be eliminated, making it more difficult for prostitutes to exit the sex industry or deal with traumatic experiences and such issues as substance abuse. Prop. K would also result in San Francisco becoming a destination for prostitutes, pimps, and johns.

On November 4, 2004, the following was on the ballot. It read:

Proposition K: "Shall the City stop enforcing laws against prostitution, stop funding or supporting the First Offender Prostitution Program or any similar anti-prostitution program, enforce existing criminal laws that prohibit crimes such as battery, extortion and rape, regardless of the victims status as a sex worker, and fully disclose the investigation and prosecution of violent crime against sex workers?"

Illustration 9.1   Proposition K

It was a passionate and hard-fought battle between two perspectives, each fighting for what they believed to be the pathway to honor the dignity and wellbeing of women and men engaged in prostitution.

The final vote: No: 202,235 (59.06%)
                       Yes: 140,185 (40.94%)

Margo and Norma were central figures in the fight, charismatic leaders of opposing sides. Norma's effort won, but a month later, she lost another battle. On December 16, 2008, she died of pancreatic cancer. In an article published in the *San Francisco Chronicle* (December 20, 2008), reporter Meredith May wrote,[27]

> Although she was struggling with her illness, she led a successful opposition to Proposition K on the November ballot, which would have decriminalized prostitution in San Francisco.
>
> "She used her own experiences to educate advocates, policymakers, government officials and other survivors by calling prostitution a form of violence against women instead of a job," said Melissa Farley, director of San Francisco's nonprofit Prostitution Research and Education.

A posting on the Women's Building Home Page read[28]: "When asked how she managed to work with women with complex problems, Norma said: 'It's like caring for orchids. They die so easily. But you take the dead-looking stem to someone who knows orchids and that person can look at the root and say, 'Look! There's still a little bit of life here.'"

Even before the Proposition K election, sex worker rights activists from Margo's COYOTE organization and the Erotic Dancer's Alliance formed the St. James Infirmary, providing "free, compassionate, and nonjudgmental healthcare and social services for sex workers [current or former] of all genders and sexual orientations while preventing occupational illnesses and injuries through a comprehensive continuum of services,"[29] and COYOTE, as an independent operation, suspended business.

Margo retired to a cabin on Orcas Island, off the coast of Washington state. But she is still the feisty advocate for sex worker rights. *Bitchmedia* interviewed her in 2013, and reported the following[30]: "with chickens clucking and a rooster crowing in the background, St. James, 75, still hosts regular visitors ('My neighbors probably think I'm turning tricks!') to talk about the ongoing 'War on Whores'.

"Bottom line [Margo said] we need to engineer a repeal of the war on whores and the war on drugs. These prohibitions are the mechanisms by which sexism and racism are maintained. Examining these bad laws will show clearly how stigma is used to disenfranchise minority women and men, especially."

* * *

Courtesan, harlot, escort, whore, hooker, sex worker, streetwalker, call girl, women of pleasure, scarlet woman, tart, shank: these are some of the names we have used to describe prostitutes. Rudyard Kipling was the first to declare them representative of the "the most ancient profession in the world" in his 1888 essay, "On the City Wall."[31] I tell my Deviant Behavior students. "Actually, it wasn't until Kipling's times, the Victorian era in England, that the now common view of streetwalkers emerged, when health officials grew increasing worried about the spread of venereal disease in the massively urbanizing societies, with its widespread poverty."
Who were the Victorian prostitutes? Author Magara Bell writes,[32]

They were primarily young, single women, between the ages of 18 and 22. Their first sexual experiences were not extraordinary, usually serial monog-amy within their own social class. Most had previously held low wage jobs, primarily as domestics (maids). Few supported illegitimate children. Their health was generally superior to other working women, who suffered under 14 hour workdays. They had a higher standard of living than others of a similar class background; they had money, clothing and could afford their own rooms.... Prostitution offered the young woman more independence, economically and socially, than could otherwise be available to her.

In Victorian London, which was the better "choice," to work 14 hours a day in a factory or as a domestic, under oppressive and unhealthy condi-tions, or to work the streets? And how much of a "choice" did a young, poor woman actually have? The opposing perspectives, "choice" versus "coerced," put forward by Margo and Norma, were not unfamiliar to the Victorians. In *Prostitution and the Victorians*, Trevor Fisher says,[33]

For most of the nineteenth century, the prevailing establishment view was of prostitution as a necessary evil; many argued that no government restric-tions should be placed on the way in which a person wished to sell their labour.... A vociferous puritan minority led an ultimately victorious assault on these *laissez faire* attitudes, basing a large part of their campaign on the claim that prostitutes were not willingly selling their services, but were enslaved.

In today's lingo, that would be "trafficked."
In my own meetings with prostitutes/the prostituted, some have con-vincingly argued that their career choices were, in fact, choices. Others made it clear that they are victims of their pasts. If choice, what brings a woman to that decision in a society that has only scorn for the profession,

even as it romanticizes it in such movies as *Pretty Woman*? If coerced, why have we criminalized them? What are the risks the women of the streets take, and why would they take such chances? Leslie Bennetts, in an article for *Newsweek* magazine, answered both questions[34]:

> Prostitution has always been risky for women; the average age of death is 34, and the American Journal of Epidemiology reported that prostitutes suffer a "workplace homicide rate" 51 times higher than that of the next most dangerous occupation, working in a liquor store.

Bennetts reports, as Norma and the women of SAGE have told us, that most prostitutes were sexually abused as girls, typically enter prostitution between the ages of 12 and 14, have drug or mental illness problems, and "one-third have been threatened with death by pimps, who often use violence to keep them in line."

This coerced perspective is the "abolitionist" viewpoint, Norma's point of view.

But Bennetts also presents the other side, the one that Margo has long argued:

> But other feminists defend pornography on First Amendment or "sex-positive" grounds, and support women's freedom to "choose" prostitution. Tracy Quan, who became a prostitute as a 14-year-old runaway, says that many women do it for lack of better economic opportunities. "When I was 16, it's not like there were great high-paying jobs out there for me," says Quan, the author of *Diary of a Manhattan Call Girl* and a spokeswoman for a sex workers' advocacy group.
>
> "My view of the sex industry is that if we treat it as work and address some of its dangers, it would be less dangerous," says Melissa Ditmore, an author and research consultant to the Sex Workers Project of the Urban Justice Center in New York.

It's been more than a century since the debate about "choice" versus "coerced" emerged. Not much has changed.

NOTES

1. "The Flood Mansion was the only great Nob Hill house to survive the 1906 Fire, saved just barely by its Connecticut brownstone walls. The Pacific Union Club purchased the shell, and William Bourn, who was on the building committee, secured the reconstruction commission for Willis

Polk…. The Flood Mansion remains the home of the Pacific Union Club and is decidedly not open to the public. Not ever. Not under any circumstances. It is barely open to the wives of the members" (www.noehill.com/sf/landmarks/sf064.asp).
2. Not the student's real name, or that of her sister or her sister's pimp.
3. Not her real name.
4. Walton, Sarah *Prostitution*, Hillsdale High School, San Mateo, CA, 2007.
5. Walton, Sarah, *Prostitution*, Hillsdale High School, San Mateo, CA, 2007.
6. Farley, Melissa. *Prostitution: Factsheet on Human Rights Violations.* Prostitution Research and Education. November 2, 2006. <http://www.prostitutionresearch.com>.
7. See "Screaming Queens: The Riot at Compton's Cafeteria" (Frameline) DVD.
8. http://www.walnet.org/csis/groups/coyote.html
9. See https://www.youtube.com/Sheik Condom Commercial
10. http://www.walnet.org/csis/groups/coyote.html
11. "Pipelines" keep women moving from city to city to keep them from supportive networks and to bring "fresh meat" to customers.
12. See also Lloyd, Rachel, *Girls Like Us*, New York: HarperCollins Publishers, 2011, and the video, "Very Young Girls," produced by Nina Alvarez, 2007, for a program similar to SAGE and a story similar to Norma Hotaling.
13. Not their real names.
14. See it on YouTube as "The SAGE Project: Part One."
15. See "Black Tar Heroin: The Dark side of the Street," an HBO production (Steven Okasaki/Farallone Films).
16. Sward, Susan, and Jaxon Van Derbeken, "Internal investigator who ruffled the SFPD/Cop transferred off probe of fracas is known as straight-talking, duty-bound workaholic," *SF Chronicle*, January 19, 2003.
17. Clifford, James O., "School for 'John's' a Reality Check on Prostitution," *Los Angeles Times*, March 2, 1997.
18. "The San Francisco Task Force on Prostitution Final Report," http://www.bayswan.org/1TF.html March 1996
19. "The San Francisco Task Force on Prostitution Final Report," http://www.bayswan.org/1TF.html March 1996
20. See YouTube "Exotic Erotic Ball."
21. See http://www.sfweekly.com/sanfrancisco/exotic-erotic-ball-wildest-party-on-earth-very-nsfw/Slideshow?oid=2688881
22. Elizabeth Fernandez, "Murder stalks S.F. prostitutes," *San Francisco Examiner*, December 10, 1995.
23. Curtis, Kim, "San Francisco prostitute kidnapped, burned to death," *Press Democrat*, February 16, 2007.
24. Leff, Lisa, "Man charged in transgender prostitute murder," *Ventura County Star*, April 27, 2010.

25. Legalization regulates prostitution by law. Decriminalization simply eliminates laws regulating prostitution. See, for example, Donna M. Hughes, PhD, in "Women's Wrongs," *National Review*, October 20, 2004.
26. "San Francisco Considers a City-Run Brothel," *New York Times*, November 28, 1993.
27. May, Meredith, "Norma Hotaling dies – fought prostitution," *SF Chronicle*, December 20, 2008.
28. http://www.womensbuilding.org/twb/
29. http://stjamesinfirmary.org homepage
30. Fischer, Anne Gray, "Forty Years in the Hustle: A Q & A With Margo St. James," *Bitch Media*, February 11, 2013.
31. Cf., Kipling, Rudyard, "On the Wall," *Soldiers Three*, Gloucester, UK: Dodo Press, 2005.
32. Bell, Megara, *The Fallen Woman in Fiction and Legislation*, Boston: University of Massachusetts at Boston.
33. Fisher, Trevor, *Prostitution and the Victorians*, London: Palgrave Macmillan, 1997, p.164.
34. Bennetts, Leslie, "The Growing Demand for Prostitution," *Newsweek*, July 18, 2011.

CHAPTER 10

The Mental Hospital Without Walls

LAURA WILCOX. MARCH 5, 1981–JANUARY 10, 2001

© The Author(s) 2017
D. Stannard-Friel, *Street Teaching in the Tenderloin*,
DOI 10.1057/978-1-137-56437-5_10

Alice...tried another question. "What sort of people live about here?"
"In THAT direction," the Cat said, waving its right paw round, "lives a
Hatter: and in THAT direction," waving the other paw, "lives a March
Hare. Visit either you like: they're both mad."
"But I don't want to go among mad people," Alice remarked.
"Oh, you can't help that," said the Cat: "we're all mad here. I'm mad.
You're mad."
"How do you know I'm mad?" said Alice.
"You must be," said the Cat, "or you wouldn't have come here."

Lewis Carroll,
Alice's Adventures in Wonderland

* * *

It's 12:30 p.m. I'm walking down Jones Street hill:
"Diamond eagle, diamond go, American eagle, American Express,
you're my financial, you're my legal attorney of rights, information data
sheet, legal board of information, go to my driver's license."
The man sits on the sidewalk. His face is turned away from the sun that
lights up his crinkly silver and black hair, which sticks out every which way
as if a bolt of lightning is coursing through his head. His beard is white
and wild, but his face is smooth and serene. His eyes are distant and he
doesn't pay me any attention at all as I walk by.
"California DMV, you legally serve me now, bring my identification, information, DMV, 1,4,1,1,8,3,2. Diamond eagle, legal rights,
1,4,1,1,8,3,2."
His voice is not that loud, but it projects up and down the block, a corridor of stone buildings, reaching the long lunch line shuffling into Glide's
soup kitchen; traveling across the street to the clusters of men, and a few
women, dealing and doing dope in front of the gate at the back end of the
walkway through Boeddeker Park. The gate itself is chained closed on this
side, to cut off the easy escape route taken by dealers who enter from the
"Vertical Coffin" side, and use the interior of the park as a retail outlet for
crack, pills, weed, heroin, and methamphetamine. The man's chant finds
its way into the open doorways of Jonell's and Cinnabar, the two busy
neighborhood bars on the far corners of Ellis and Jones.
"Diamond eagle, diamond go, 1,4,1,1,8,3,2."
I write down his words, and continue my walk down Jones Street hill.
Suddenly, street noise ratchets way up as a fire engine shrieks down
the hill. A second one, its horn blaring, turns the corner a block away,

and brakes to a stop at Eddy and Jones. A third comes wailing up Eddy, going against the flow of traffic, and a City ambulance joins the noisy congregation. The four emergency vehicles converge on two cops frisking a bloodied old man, cane in hand, propped up against a wall, calmly whispering to himself or to an unseen acquaintance. Blood is streaming down his face from, what another bystander tells me is, a self-inflicted head wound. The cops switch from frisking the man to sitting him down on the sidewalk as EMTs take over. The three fire engines take off in a roar.

Half a block further down the hill, a skinny, toothless white woman runs into the traffic in front of Hung Phat Bakery and Pink Diamond Gentlemen's Club. Her long, jet-black hair is streaked with red. She has on a denim jacket over a long, purple-and-red, floral-print dress; a maroon scarf is wrapped around her neck several times, its ends whipping about as she dances in circles. She waves to the cars coming right at her and holds up her hands. "Stop! Stop!" she yells, laughs as they do, and skips in circles, flapping her arms like a bird. She runs up onto the sidewalk, flapping away. "Fuck it, fuck it!" she shouts, as she spins, out of sight, around the Turk Street corner, only to reemerge seconds later, leaping, gazelle-like, into the traffic, laughing, shouting, stopping to talk into an imaginary cell phone. Screams "Fuck you!" into her hand. Snaps it closed. Laughs and dances some more.

It's 12:55 p.m.

* * *

Valentine's Day 2013. Analyzing Social Settings is headed over to the Seneca Hotel on 6th Street. Of all the gentrifying blocks that shoot out along the south side of Market Street, like ribs from a spine, 6th Street is the lone holdout. Late nineteenth-century maps describe this part of San Francisco as "Skid Road," and, in spite of all the urban renewal/ slum removal efforts over the years, 6th Street still is. A radical transformation has squeezed street people out of much of what is now known as SoMa, but 6th Street is part of the Tenderloin containment zone, even if it isn't officially included in the neighborhood boundaries. Hockshops, SROs, porno shops, drug dealers, homeless people, mentally ill, and the lowest-echelon prostitutes are still well represented here. The Seneca is a 204-room SRO, harm reduction hotel run by Tenderloin Housing Clinic (THC).

As we cross Market Street and round the 6th Street corner, we encounter a group of about a dozen young men passing around joints and a couple of bottles in brown paper bags. We have to squeeze between some of them and through the cloud of marijuana smoke to make our way to the Seneca. The students' easy chatter that has accompanied our walk since we left the coffeehouse stops. My classes have walked through groups like this for nearly two decades, and nothing bad has ever happened. But few of these students, here with me today, have yet to spend any appreciable time in the neighborhood. This is our fourth week off campus, but our first on 6th Street. And this is a particularly scary-looking group of street guys. As usual, of the 15 students in the class, most of them are women.

"Hey, happy Valentine's Day, Ladies," one of the men shouts. A gold front tooth glitters in the sun.

"Be mine, Valentine," says a big man with a knit watchman's cap pulled down around his head to eyebrow level, a tight black tee shirt showing off bulging biceps and black slash tattoos on his muscular forearms, a big gold ring in each ear, and a thick gold chain around his thick neck, a neck that is heavily tattooed. He feigns a swoon and laughs.

"Hey, cutie," says another one, patting his chest. "You make my heart sing!" All the guys crack up over that one. Even some of the students smile.

"He talkin' to you, Dr. Don?" one of my students asks. A few other students laugh. They know the story.

"Yeah, *right!*" I told a story in Deviant Behavior last semester, as we were prepping for our tour of San Quentin, about an earlier visit to the prison. Fifty or so inmates had rushed over to see us, spreading out along a long, white line that, if crossed, could get them shot. Twenty-six of us passed them by: 18 college-age women and eight men, including me. The inmates were as close to us as prison rules and that white line would allow. Still, they were a good 25′ away. They couldn't make physical contact, but they could tease. "Thanks for making my day, pretty ladies!" or "New COs? I sure hope so!" There were a lot of whispers and giggles and occasional outbursts of laughter, but no one was rude or crude, as far we could hear. The shouted comments were flirtatious, but not inappropriate, and not directed at anyone in particular until one inmate called out, "Hey, cutie! Cutie! *You!* You with the beard!" That would be me. Everyone—inmates, COs, and students—thought that was a good one.

The 6th Street guys are just teasing, too, and they part to let us pass. A few make swooping hand gestures, waving us by, as if to say, "Right this way." And they all chuckle at the game.

A little further down the block, I point out a spot in the middle of the street, near the Seneca, where, a few semesters back, a young woman advertised her availability (and state of mind) to passing pedestrians and motorists by waving money and cavorting back and forth across the street with no pants on. I nod down Stevenson Alley, where the dancing lady had disappeared, and say, "It's a place to take johns, shoot up, and go to the bathroom. Maybe all at the same time. Happy Valentine's Day."

We walk by the popular Tu Lan Vietnamese Restaurant, a hole in the wall so highly regarded that Julia Child is said to have recommended it, now temporarily closed because of "live mice and cockroaches in the cooking areas, standing water in the kitchen, improper refrigeration and unsanitary food handling."[1] Next door is Dottie's True Blue Café, a dining spot that Studs Terkel frequented when he was in town. He loved to greet and entertain the other patrons with his comments about the world, often quoting himself and his books. Of the American breakfast that the restaurant specializes in, he told a reporter in 2003 that his cardiologist told him, "At your age, cholesterol is as relevant as the truth is to George Bush."[2] Everyone in the joint liked that one. Dottie's took over the recently renovated Passion Café, a French restaurant that tried to make a go of it here, until, among other happenings, someone came into the restaurant, ripped the television off the wall, and walked away with it. For 20 years, Dottie's was very successfully located on Jones Street in The TL. A crowd of mostly young people would patiently wait an hour for good American food in a friendly, efficient environment. But the owner wanted to expand and the 6th Street location looked good. It was, after all, "Tenderloin South." Part of the charm of Dottie's was that it was good eats in an edgy neighborhood. 6th Street would maintain that tradition. Shortly after they reopened, I asked a waitress if the 6th Street location was different than Jones. "It's the same, and it's different," she said. "On Jones Street, panhandlers would ask the customers in line for change. Here, they demand it." She laughed. "It's cool. Customers don't seem to mind."

We crossed Stevenson, and entered the Seneca.

The Seneca Hotel, and other programs that contract with the city to deliver various social services, is required to operate under harm reduction guidelines.[3] The City of San Francisco was a pioneer in requiring harm reduction for contracted social services. When it was first launched, Ulysses Torassa, medical writer for *The San Francisco Chronicle* (January 15, 2001), wrote,[4]

Quietly last September, San Francisco became the first city in the nation to adopt harm reduction as its official policy. That means the dozens of agencies the city hires to provide drug and alcohol treatment must have harm-reduction programs and policies in place.

Among the signs of the new philosophy:

– The Department of Public Health last year began offering care at the city's needle exchange sites and at a special clinic, treating injection-related skin infections before they grow into raging, life-threatening wounds.

– The city is teaching jail inmates how to perform CPR on their friends who may be overdosing on drugs. A media campaign aimed at teaching addicts how to reduce deaths from heroin overdose is in the works.

– And a pilot project is expected to start in a few months that will put the prescription drug naloxone – a heroin antidote – in the hands of addicted couples, so they can administer it to their partners in case of an overdose.

"The war on drugs has encouraged users to lie to their providers (drug counselors) and not seek out help when they are struggling with addiction," said Dr. Joshua Bamberger, medical director for housing and urban health at the San Francisco Department of Public Health. "Harm reduction opens the doors to honesty and allows providers to move addicts one positive step at a time toward better health."

Proponents of harm reduction focus on the ill effects of addiction, from homelessness to the spread of AIDS and hepatitis and overdose deaths. They seek to treat clients "where they are," instead of insisting that they be clean and sober before getting services.

Thirteen years before our Valentine Day visit in 2013, four months before San Francisco adopted its harm reduction policy, a group of us from the then CND—five students, three faculty members, the Director of Health Services, and the Director of Campus Ministry—stayed for a week at the Seneca. THC had just begun master-leasing[5] the hotel a year before and was already operating in a harm reduction mode, although, we would find out in many visits over the years since that, there was a lot more to harm reduction than what was available in May of 2000, but it was a start.

The group of us met at Wild Awakenings. I had been hanging out there for five years then, and meeting students there for three, but this is the first time we showed up with luggage and a weeks' worth of clothing and necessities. "Necessities," as always, depended on perspective. The one male student, Anthony, had a backpack; female students had wheeled luggage. But everyone had packed conservatively. No need for much more than jeans, a few layers of upperwear to deal with the ever-changing San Francisco weather, and the basics. Our plan was to "experience the experience" of living in an SRO, walk the streets of the Tenderloin, day and (early) night, eat at a different ethnic food restaurant for each meal (Thai, Chinese, Mexican, Japanese, Indian, American, etc.),[6] except for breakfast, which would be bagels and cream cheese in our rooms, since no one wanted to get up early (this was a wise decision, since early bedtimes were not an option). We would also do service of some kind every day.

We all had some anxiety anticipating the week ahead. Most of the students, but none of the faculty or the Director of Health Services, had participated in our Tenderloin events or classes. The Director of Campus Ministry had partnered with me in various events, and even came in drag— he was about 6′3″ with very thick, black eyebrows and broad shoulders— to our Halloween festival. The hour-long ride on the train and bus from our campus in Belmont to The TL resulted in no noticeable reaction from fellow travelers, he said, but on his walk through the Tenderloin to the playground, he was a big hit, "Hey, big mama, got some for me?"

Even with all my time in the neighborhood, I was anxious, not only for my students' and colleagues safety, but for my own. Sleeping at the Seneca was a new experience for me, and I had spent very little time there before our stay. What I had seen before were swarms of drug dealers and users outside the front door, and strung out people inside. But I had worked with THC before, and knew them to be competent. If we were going to have a meaningful immersion experience, this would be as good as it gets. And it was.

Checking in was like crossing the border into a new country. The "native" population was as fascinated by the new arrivals as we were of them. One, a tiny, skinny lady came up and said, with a big gap-toothed smile, "Welcome to the Seneca. What the hell are you doing *here?*"

"We're students and faculty from College of Notre Dame," I said. "We're here for a week."

"Well good for you! I'm Irma." She nodded down the line of arriving guests. "I'll be right here if you need me. Good people here…mostly."

So far, so good, I think, I said to myself.

We checked into our rooms. The men, Bob, Anthony, and I, took single rooms, but all the women teamed up with one or two roommates. Some of the students rearranged their mattress, because of the stains they found on some. And we all settled in for come-what-may.

Come-what-may was inspiring, but not without its moments of us experiencing inner-city life at its near depths. The actual depths could be seen from Anthony's window overlooking the corner of Stevenson Alley and 6th Street. We would gather there most nights to talk about the day, and look out the windows at the goings-on. Streetwalkers hung around on the corner, so did drug dealers. Homeless people slept in the alley. People shot up. Others shouted at their demons. A fight broke out one night. Cops made arrests. Street people congregated on the corner, socializing and shooting the breeze.

We were told that 180 people occupied the 203 rooms available during our stay (one was closed for renovation), and most of the residents had lived on the streets before moving in here. The rooms were about 10' × 12', with a sink, a chest of drawers, and a bed. A few were slightly larger, with two beds. There was a total of six men's bathrooms, six women's bathrooms, and six showers, one of each on each floor. No cooking facilities were available in the hotel.

I had a room overlooking 6th Street. Across the hall was a little lady who kept to herself. She was short and round, I think Asian, with jet-black hair, cut in a bowl-style. She always seemed to be smiling, but distracted, never acknowledging my presence, even when I was standing right in front of her, saying hello. She talked in what I think was gibberish. In any case, I couldn't understand what she was saying, even though she was always talking. She rarely came out of her room. I worried about her when I heard a garbage truck come down Stevenson Alley, early one morning. The grinding and screeching noises sounded horrible. They made me think of the Chief in *One Flew Over the Cuckoo's Nest*,[7] who heard a humming, menacing Combine in the walls of the mental ward, threatening to make machines out of everything and everyone. I could hear my neighbor through the door, the sound of her gibberish rising to compete with the sounds of the garbage truck. As it got louder, she got louder. What was my little neighbor thinking when that bone-crunching sound bounced off the walls of the Seneca Hotel? What horrible menace lurked in the hall? Or was she just having a conversation with the machine?

The manager took me to a room where an old man recently died. He had lived in the Seneca a long time, well before THC took over the hotel. The window was covered with tinfoil, and the walls and ceiling were plastered with pornography. The rug smelled of urine.

A ride on the creaky elevator down to the lobby to see what my students were up to was a ride on a Ship of Fools. One man was talking to someone not on the elevator; another was just staring at him. A third was tweaking out. A fourth grinned at me, rolled his eyes, and tilted his head at the other three. When the elevator stopped, I stepped out into a room full of normal-looking people going about their business. More were missing more teeth than is typically seen in most places. Some of the conversations seemed a little too animated. But it was a pleasant scene. People were chatting, lots of laughter, some were reading, others headed out the door or up the stairs or were talking to the desk clerk. The TV was on and a dozen or so residents were excitedly watching a show.

A group of my students, the four women, were sitting with a nice-looking man, probably in his late 30s. "Hey, Dr. Don, Dr. Don, come over here," Stephanie called. Stephanie is an enthusiastic, upbeat, Latina, passionate about doing service-learning activities.

"Hi, guys," I said to the group.

Stephanie introduced me to the man. "This is Raymond.[8] Raymond, this is Dr. Don. Dr. Don is our teacher. Raymond graduated from UC Berkeley, Dr. Don."

I smiled, Raymond stood up and we shook hands. He was nicely dressed in a sport jacket and open-collar dress shirt.

"Call me Don," I said.

"How do you do, Dr. Don," he said. "You'll have to excuse me for a minute. I'll be right back." Raymond left the group and headed up the stairs off the lobby.

"He keeps doing that," Monica, one of the other students, said. "He's an alcoholic and has a bottle in his room."

Two of the main principles of harm reduction are to minimize the harmful effects of drug use and "meet the drug user where they are at."[9]

Before harm reduction was introduced as a concept, housing for the very poor and homeless depended on the addicted giving up drugs or alcohol. With harm reduction, use is allowed, as long as it is taken in private places and the user exhibits no violent or aggressive behavior. The goals are to minimize the harmful effects of drug use in a nonjudgmental and noncoercive environment, stabilize the individual's life, and encourage positive social relationships.

Monica continued, "He's a genius, Dr. Don. He can answer all the questions on *Who Wants to Be a Millionaire?*." The then new television show, hosted by Regis Philbin, was extremely popular at the time, emerging as one of the highest-rated game shows in television history. A crowd of Seneca residents sat around the television, rooting on the contestants, and calling out their answers to the multiple-choice questions. Raymond and the students sat off to the side, but within easy viewing and listening distance to the TV.

Raymond came back from his room and rejoined us. I was skeptical of his UC Berkeley credentials, and even more so of Monica's claim. "The students have been telling me about your ability to answer the 'Who Wants to Be a Millionaire?' questions," I said.

Raymond shook his head. "Yeah, well, I just have a good memory."

"Go ahead, Raymond, show him," Rebecca, another student, said.

Raymond looked reluctant to do so. I didn't say anything to encourage or discourage him, but I didn't expect much to happen.

The residents watching the show groaned over a missed answer. "Shit, *I* knew *that*," one of them claimed. Regis went on to the next contestant, explained the game, and asked the first question. All the students, with grins on their faces, looked back and forth from Raymond to me. And Raymond began. He answered every question asked correctly, until it was time for another trip to his room. I was totally blown away. He could have made thousands! He could have been a millionaire! And here he sat in the lobby of the Seneca Hotel, an SRO on "Winery Row."

Over the years, we made many connections with the Seneca, but didn't do another immersion there. The following year, we stayed at a decommissioned homeless shelter in the basement of the Salvation Army Hotel on Turk Street. We did begin doing a Christmas celebration at the Seneca that year, called "A Miracle on 6th Street," and have continued the event in the neighborhood ever since.

CND/NDNU has performed an extremely well-reviewed musical version of Charles Dickens' *A Christmas Carol* on campus since 1985, and Mike Elkins, the head of our Theater and Dance Department (who also plays Scrooge), volunteered to bring scenes from the play—and presents for residents and neighborhood kids—to the Tenderloin. The story is one of redemption. A rich, old miser finds the Spirit of Christmas and is awakened to do good deeds and provide hope and charity to the downtrodden. Streetwise has coordinated the celebration, beginning in 2001 at the Seneca, when Ana "Star" Bolton took over as manager. Then, after several years, when the hotel was being remodeled, we relocated it to Boeddeker Park ("A Miracle on Eddy Street"); then to the Tenderloin Playground ("A Miracle on Ellis Street"), before returning to the Seneca a few years ago. The hotel is a perfect venue for *A Christmas Carol*. Physically, as an Edwardian structure, it inherits some of its architecture from Dickens'

Victorian England. Poor people are everywhere, in a city of abundance. Struggle among plenty.

* * *

Thirteen years after our immersion experience, on Valentine's Day, 2013, the Analyzing class walked into the lobby of the Seneca to meet with Sam Meki, the hotel manager and our street teacher for the day. Our encounter with the "Valentine's Day Gang," though uneventful, rattled some of the students, and a group hanging out in front of the hotel, though older and quieter than the guys down the block, had obviously been through some hard times. Passing through them added to the unsettling of community engagement rookies in the class. It's a rite of passage in this kind of CBL. Most of the tough-looking people moved aside to let us by and nodded their hellos. The potential to understand is enhanced by intimacy.

I pushed the buzzer next to the door and looked at the video camera mounted on the wall so the desk clerk could see who was there. The lock clicked and we filed into the Seneca.

Sam met us in front of the desk clerk's window, a large plate of glass with a teller's slot in the bottom to pass mail and paperwork through, and, higher up, a round slotted opening to speak into. The lobby was, as usual, a social scene. It had been spruced up over the years. There was a new wall on the south side of the lobby, opening into a community kitchen. A caseworker's office door was where an entrance to a manager's apartment once was. Sam explained that the Seneca now included support services. I had already passed out handouts from the THC's website.[10]

THC Supportive Service Goals

- Help residents maintain enough stability to retain their housing.
- Augment tenants' ability to enrich their self-respect, confidence and awareness as well as improving their quality of life.
- Ensure that all tenants are aware of and have access to the full range of support services available to them.
- Provide thorough, effective and dependable case management on a voluntary basis to every tenant who requests it.
- Work collaboratively with tenants to minimize, modify or resolve is sues that may jeopardize their housing.
- Infuse each hotel with a strong sense of community through conflict resolution, social events and workshops that foster a culture of health.
- Support tenants and provide access to information about their rights.

Illustration 10.1   THC Supportive Goals

Sam said that the caseworkers were there to assist, not to intrude into people's lives, and the way that worked was to develop relationships with hotel residents.

He took us upstairs to check out a couple of rooms. We climbed the staircase, but I could see that there was a new elevator. People in the hallways were friendly and several invited us into their rooms. The rooms had been painted and cleaned up since our immersion stay, and attached to walls in the halls on each floor were needle disposal boxes, part of the harm reduction philosophy, to protect users from unclean needles. Most of the people we talked to reported being happy at the Seneca, "Got me off the streets, my home for *years!*" one resident told us. "Saved my life." (A few months later, a small group, on the street outside of the hotel, did complain about the conditions and management and posted their video-taped protest on YouTube.[11])

We entered one room that was being renovated and treated for bedbug infestation, an epidemic problem in San Francisco's SROs at the time. "The wiring is old and we have blackouts when tenants plug in too many appliances into a socket, but it's clean and safe." We could see from the wood molding and refinished hardwood floors that the Seneca was once a very nice hotel.

"How long can people live here?" one student asked.

"This is permanent housing," said Sam. "As long as they do their part, it's home."

"How much does it cost?" asked another.

"One-third of their welfare checks. It's deducted from the check before they get it."

"Is there any violence?"

"None that we can't handle," said a voice coming from behind us. A large, smiling man walked into the room.

"This is my assistant manager," Sam said. "We don't have many problems, but we are trained to deal with whatever comes up." Looking at the size of the two men, I had no doubt that they can, indeed, "handle" whatever comes up.

The Seneca was THC's first master-leased hotel. Today, they operate "the City's largest permanent housing program for single homeless adults and is a leading provider of legal services to low-income tenants,"[12] and manage 1600 permanent, supportive housing units in 16 hotels. THC is not without its critics, and the debate over housing, treatment, and other services for the very poor, the addicted, and the mentally ill, particularly the severely mentally ill, in San Francisco continues.[13] The play *A Christmas Carol* was inspired by Charles Dickens' own life in Victorian England; his father was locked away in debtors' prison. What would the son write about life on 6th Street and in the Tenderloin? Why, in spite of the work of THC and other service providers, are there still so many mentally ill people wandering the streets of San Francisco?

* * *

I'm walking up Hyde Street to check out the playground before going over to Celtic Coffee to meet the Sports, Service, and Society class. Today is our annual Tenderloin Sport Clinic. If recent years' clinics are any indication of what will happen this afternoon, a hundred neighborhood kids will show up to play dodgeball. When students originally proposed dodgeball as a "sport" for the clinic, I objected, "Dodgeball is *not* a sport. Tenderloin kids have it hard enough, without us promoting throwing balls at their heads."

"But kids love it," I was told by my students.

"Let me check with the playground directors," I said, sure that they would support my insistence that dodgeball was *not* an appropriate sport for the Tenderloin, and that it was not even a sport.

"Great idea," said Tom Heath, director of IHDC's TAG, an afterschool program.

"Kids love it," said Kay Rodrigues, Tenderloin Playground director.

"OK," I told my students. "But this is a clinic. You have to *teach* it. Rules and all. *Are* there rules in dodgeball?" I asked.

"Sure. Great. Let's do it!"

Since 2002, Sports, Service, and Society has held clinics in the Tenderloin. The program was suggested by Midge Wilson, Executive Director of BAWCC. Working with the legendary UCLA basketball coach, John Wooden, she started the program as part of a larger sports initiative, and even brought some of The TL kids to meet "the Wizard of Westwood" in LA.[14] We partnered with her, and, for the first six years, lacrosse was our sport. NDNU's lacrosse coach, Tony Romano, and his teams would come to the Tenderloin, demonstrate the game, talk about its Native American roots, put headgear on little Cambodian-American (and Vietnamese-American, and African-American, and Euro-American, and Mexican-American) heads, put a long-handled lacrosse stick in their hands, and play the game with them. In year three, after being hit on my Birkenstock-ed foot by a rock-hard lacrosse ball, I asked the team to switch to a tennis ball, after their orientation. In the years following lacrosse, we held clinics in basketball, volleyball, soccer, and kickball. But by far, the most popular sport has been dodgeball.

The purpose of the Sports class is not, really, to teach a sport, but to *engage* the community, in particular, the youth and their program directors. For the NDNU student, this is an eye-opening experience, meeting and learning about the well-behaved, enthusiastic, bright, fun-loving children of the Tenderloin and their passionate, hardworking, talented service providers. For the Tenderloin kids, this is an opportunity to meet and engage a group of college student role models that is as ethnically diverse as they are (although NDNU students are drawn more heavily from Latin American ancestry and Tenderloin kids are more likely Southeast Asian, but as the Mission District gentrifies, The TL's Latino population is rapidly growing).

Walking up Hyde Street to the playground, I pass by the usual mix of Tenderloin pedestrians: government workers heading to City Hall or the courts or the library in Civic Center and students and faculty going to and from Hastings Law School. Sidewalk vendors, displaying goods for sale on sheets of cardboard or blankets or tablecloths or just on the sidewalk, gather along the fence that lines the parking lot where The Blackhawk jazz club used to be. A drug sale takes place right in front of Faithful Fools Street Ministry. A young woman, probably in her mid-20s, dressed in wrinkled, brown military fatigues and a dirty white tee shirt, is propped up against the wall. Her hair is stringy. Her face is blank. Her eyes stare up as she slides down the wall, pulls her pants down to her ankles, goes into a squat, and pees. The liquid runs between her legs and spreads out across the sidewalk, the same sidewalk that children coming from Tenderloin Community School will soon walk on, going to our dodgeball clinic. Most passersby don't pay any attention to her, except to step over or around the stream. A few look at the young woman with disgust. An old woman tilts her head and grimaces in apparent sympathy for the young woman, who stands up, pulls her pants on, leans back against the wall, and stares at nothing at all. Like everyone else, the old lady walks on by. So do I. What happened to our caring society, our Good Samaritans? How can this *abandonment* of the mentally ill be so accepted in this, the USA?

* * *

I'm finishing up the semester in Deviant Behavior. I set up a table on the low stage at the front of the small auditorium in Wiegand Art Gallery Projection Room. Five sheets are carefully folded on top of it. Three are draped lengthwise over the table, spread open, with each end folded over about 6″. On top of them, two more sheets, folded several times lengthwise, are also draped over the sides of the table. Two more, folded the same way, hang over the back of a chair nearby. An eighth sheet, a set of leather ankle restraints, a set of cotton and nylon restraints, and a roll of white hospital tape sit on a small table, next to the lectern. Students in the red velveteen theater seats in front of me look at the set up with expressions of interest and confusion on their faces. "OK, Andrew," I say, waving to a student in the back of the room. "You ready?"

"Sure," says a voice from the back of the room, as Andrew walks down the aisle. A tall, thin young man, I know Andrew well, and asked if he would participate in this demonstration.

I pat the sheets on top of the table and say, "Lie down right here."

Andrew complies. Another student comes up to give me a hand.

"This is called 'sheet restraints.'" I tell the class. "In the years I worked in psychiatry, this was the main way, besides medication, that we used to control patients, whether they were out of control or not. Normally, this would be a hospital bed, not a table, but you get the idea. OK, let's begin."

With the help of my student assistant, I wrap Andrew up, one sheet at a time. The first loops around his arms from behind, securing them to his body. The second is wrapped around his legs.

The three bottom sheets go over his shoulders and are wrapped completely around his body, one at a time. Andrew looks like a mummy. Then one of the long sheets, from the back of the chair, is draped over his chest, the other one over his knees. "These would be looped under the bedframe," I say. "We'd step into the loop and push down with a foot to tighten the wrap, and then fold the sheets into the frame. They'd be held tightly in place by the tension of the bedsprings pushing up, pressing the patient to the bed." I pick up the white tape. "This would be taped over the patient's shoulders to keep them from wiggling out. The leather restraints...." I hold them up. "These are old school. I never used leather restraints, but with these," I hold up the nylon and cotton restraints, "we'd tie the patient's ankles to the foot of the bed if they were particularly resistive. Then, we'd put a sheet on top, just like we all do when we go to bed. But underneath, the patient is totally restrained, except when they're not."

"Except when they're not?" Andrew asks, looking up at me from his seemingly helpless position.

"Sometimes patients, especially teenagers, chewed their way out, tore the tape and wiggled free, if their feet weren't tied. Once I saw a man, a very big man, rip right through the sheets. They must have been old and worn, but it was freaky. Tore them apart. We just stuck him with a needle, right through the sheets, knocked him out. Usually patients didn't fight back. Which said to me, they didn't need to go into sheets in the first place."

I look at Andrew. "You OK?"

"I'm good, Dr. Don." He looks fine, but this isn't't real.

* * *

"For five years, from 1969 to 1974," I tell my students, "I worked on the psychiatric wards of a hospital whose 'catchment area'[15] included the Haight-Ashbury, undergoing its radical experiment with altered states of consciousness; the historically African-American Fillmore District, experiencing street riots as the struggle for civil rights continued; and other neighborhoods near Golden Gate Park, home to many homeless people and hippies tripping in the bushes and overdosing at concerts at Frisbee Field and Hippie Hill."

I was studying at San Francisco State (and participated in the student-led strike of 1968–1969 that helped change higher education in America), and then at UC Davis, while I worked to support my growing family. Working on the mental ward was one of the most enriching and exciting experiences of my life, even though I disagreed with some of its "therapeutic" methodology. At the time, the paradigm was changing in our culture, redefining some *centuries*-old ways of thinking (e.g., women and minorities as second-class citizens; sex as something only to performed in the sanctity of marriage, unless you were male), when a generation was challenging the status quo, and cultural gurus were promoting altered states of consciousness (Timothy Leary, "Turn on, tune in, drop out"[16]; Carlos Castaneda, "To seek freedom is the only driving force I know. Freedom to fly off into that infinity out there"[17]; R.D. Laing, "Insanity – a perfectly rational adjustment to an insane world"[18]). Here I was, living and working in the Haight-Ashbury, which was at the center of a transformative way of thinking; working in the mental hospital that served the Haight, as some of it citizens entered altered states of consciousness and couldn't find their way back; and studying sociology as the world was undergoing fundamental social change. Working on the ward was an amazing and intimate experience. Many on the staff, and even some of the patients, became my family of friends. (I met my wife, a nurse working on the children's unit, there.)

Still, the new paradigm emerging never did completely take hold (think of race relations and related socioeconomic conditions in twenty-first-century America), and understanding society's contribution to such "individual" states as "mental illness" was not making much of an impact in mainstream psychiatry at the time, though this is better understood today.

I wrote about working on the wards in *Harassment Therapy: A Case Study of Psychiatric Violence*.[19] In the book, I explored the emergence of a particularly aggressive form of "assertive therapy," which was made popular at the time by Synanon, the hip, drug treatment program that attracted celebrities as well as regular folks, well known for its confrontational "games," until it all unraveled as the founder and his cadre went well beyond the boundaries of acceptability, as did some of my colleagues, I argued, with their "harassment therapy."

One question, I asked in the book, was, how could such a "therapy" happen—making patients scrub the floor with a toothbrush; throwing garbage on them while they did so; spilling the wash pail over, blaming the patient for the mess, and making them clean it up; forcing them to make and remake beds, until the sheets were "perfect," which they never were; sometimes double-teaming the patient: one staff member making one demand, while another made a contradictory one, and on, and on, and on, all the while, verbally demeaning the patient. Then putting her or him in street restraints for "not following through" with impossible tasks. How could this be allowed in an era of emerging civil rights, which increasingly included the rights of the "mentally ill."

Madness Network News, a newspaper-type publication, modified *The New York Times*' motto, "All the news that fit to print," to reflect their own concerns, "All the fits that news to print." They wrote extensively about the rights of the mentally ill and stories of patients suffering at the hands of the psychiatric establishment and an uncaring, oppressive society. The paper demanded that the civil rights movement of the era include the mentally ill. Thomas Szasz, MD, in *The Myth of Mental Illness*,[20]challenged fellow psychiatrists to rethink their practice of labeling people "disabled by living" as "mentally ill." In his *Psychiatric Justice*[21] and in *Law Liberty and Psychiatry*,[22] he called for recognition of mental patients' rights as constitutionally guaranteed civil rights. The American Civil Liberties Union (ACLU) published *The Rights of Mental Patients*,[23] and sociologist Thomas Scheff wrote that "societal reaction" is a significant part of channeling people into "careers" of mental illness.[24] Societal reaction, such as harassment therapy.

In *Harassment Therapy*, I examined how such "treatments" as harass-ment therapy could be imposed on mental patients, typically *voluntary* patients who objected to the treatment, in an era so concerned with civil liberties. On July 1, 1969, a month before my arrival on the unit (called "Ward 3A" in the book), a law redefining the rights and treatment of the mentally ill, originally passed by the California legislature in 1967, was implemented. The Lanterman–Petris–Short (LPS) Act defined the rights of individuals involuntarily and voluntarily housed on psychiatric wards, and was to develop a system of community-based mental health centers that would provide psychiatric care near the clients' home, thus increas-ing their quality of life, while reducing the costs by closing or reducing the patient population in California State (psychiatric) Hospitals. A main reason inspiring the community mental health movement—which actually began with the Eisenhower administration's Joint Commission on Mental Illness and Health that published a report in 1961 called *Action for Mental Health: Final Report of the Joint Commission on Mental Illness and Health* that was advanced by John F. Kennedy's Community Mental Health Act of 1963–was the development of psychotropic drugs that were believed to allow patients to live more independent and productive lives.

How'd this all work out?

The National Alliance on Medical Illness (NAMI) analyzed the early impact of LPS and community mental health in California,[25]

The release of thousands of individuals into the community from the State's asylums and institutions began in 1970 and continued throughout the decade. One example vividly illustrates what it was like and what would hap-pen in communities, large and small, across the State. Over 3800 mentally ill people were released from Agnews State Hospital on June 30, 1972 into the San Jose area. This resulted in the creation of a "mental health ghetto" overnight as various service providers converted vacant buildings and aban-doned fraternity houses into board and care homes. Between 1969 and 1970, California counties would be required to provide mental health ser-vices to over 45,000 inpatients and 120,000 outpatients. While the authors of the legislation thought they were improving lives, what they actually did was release thousands of ill, confused and vulnerable individuals into com-munities that were simply unprepared to provide the services and support envisioned.

E. Fuller Torrey, MD, founder of the Treatment Advocacy Center and executive director of the Stanley Medical Research Institute, writes,[26]

[D]einstitutionalization has helped create the mental illness crisis by discharging people from public psychiatric hospitals without ensuring that they received the medication and rehabilitation services necessary for them to live successfully in the community. Deinstitutionalization further exacerbated the situation because, once the public psychiatric beds had been closed, they were not available for people who later became mentally ill.

Deinstitutionalization was based on the principle that severe mental illness should be treated in the least restrictive setting.... [T]his ideology rested on "the objective of maintaining the greatest degree of freedom, self-determination, autonomy, dignity, and integrity of body, mind, and spirit for the individual while he or she participates in treatment or receives services." This is a laudable goal and for many, perhaps for the majority of those who are deinstitutionalized, it has been at least partially realized.

For a substantial minority, however, deinstitutionalization has been a psychiatric Titanic. Their lives are virtually devoid of "dignity" or "integrity of body, mind, and spirit." "Self-determination" often means merely that the person has a choice of soup kitchens. The "least restrictive setting" frequently turns out to be a cardboard box, a jail cell, or a terror-filled existence plagued by both real and imaginary enemies.

And what about the impact of LPS on the wards? When I left "3A" in 1974, it was, to a significant degree, being ignored, in part, because of the stipulation that these rights may be denied for good cause "only by the professional person in charge of the facility or his designee." Neither, "good cause" nor "designee" was defined, resulting in a situation where any employee on the unit could and did ignore the "rights" of the patient. Besides, except for me, who was studying the law and its impact on the ward, none of the nursing personnel (psychiatric technicians and nurses), actually coming into daily contact with the patients, really knew much about what it said. And those who did know (e.g., the nursing supervisor) said that they discouraged disseminating patients' rights, "for the patient's own good." One discovery I made about implementing the law was how the hospital followed through on the requirement that patients' rights be "prominently posted." The nursing supervisor did "prominently" post them on 3A, on the bulletin board in the room where patients were wheeled into on gurneys, when they received shock treatments.

Since then, mental patient advocates have worked hard to successfully implement the spirit and the letter of the law by ensuring the expansion of rights, the requirement that patients be regularly informed of them, and that they have access to a patients' rights advocate.[27] SRO hotels, like the Seneca, have been converted into supportive permanent housing for homeless people, most struggling with substance abuse or mental illness. NPOs have opened inner-city clinics, and organizations have rallied for increasing funding and support for those who suffer on the streets.[28]

How has all this affected the situation on the streets?

It's worse than ever.

The Mental Illness Policy Org., whose mission is to report "unbiased information for policymakers + media," says,[29]

> People with untreated psychiatric illnesses comprise one-third, or 250,000, of the estimated 744,000 homeless population. The quality of life for these individuals is abysmal. Many are victimized regularly. One study found that 28 percent of homeless people with previous psychiatric hospitalizations obtained some food from garbage cans and 8 percent used garbage cans as a primary food source.
>
> At any given time, there are many more people with untreated severe psychiatric illnesses living on America's streets than are receiving care in hospitals.

Robert Tilford, in GroundReport, wrote,[30]

> At any given time in America, approximately 50% of all "seriously men-tally ill" (SMI) individuals are not receiving any mental health treatment whatsoever.
>
> These people often end up living on the street or worse put into pris-ons and jails (which have become de facto mental health treatment centers) where they are often victimized or mistreated not only by the system (jails) but by other inmates as well.

And Matt Ford, in *The Atlantic* magazine (June 8, 2015), wrote,[31]

> At least 400,000 inmates currently behind bars in the United States suffer from some type of mental illness – a population larger than the cities of Cleveland, New Orleans, or St. Louis – according to the National Alliance on Mental Illness. NAMI estimates that between 25 and 40 percent of all mentally ill Americans will be jailed or incarcerated at some point in their lives.
>
> What sort of crimes had these people been arrested for? One kid on the list had a tendency toward aggression, but officials emphasized that the over-whelming majority were "crimes of survival" such as retail theft (to find food or supplies) or breaking and entering (to find a place to sleep). For those

with mental illness, charges of drug possession can often indicate attempts at self-medication. "Even the drugs of choice will connect to what the mental illness is," Petacque-Montgomery told me. People with severe depression might use cocaine "to lift their mood." Those who hear voices and have schizophrenia or bipolar disorder often turn to heroin to regulate their sleep. Marijuana use "is just constant for kids with ADD and depression," she notes. "I'll ask, 'Can you eat or sleep without this?' and they'll say no."

What happened?

* * *

"There was a collision of two ends of the political continuum," I tell my students. "The Right wanted to cut back on spending, the Left wanted to increase civil rights. The result was a disaster."

The community mental health system did save the State money, since it never was adequately funded, producing the "Mental Hospital Without Walls," that became one of several Tenderloin monikers, as mental patients were discharged from State hospitals and new patients were never even considered for admission in the scaled back institutions. A high concentration of inner-city clinics, soup kitchens, shelters, and SROs drew those needing their services to the Tenderloin and 6th Street corridor, creating San Francisco's containment zone, a mental health ghetto, as other neighborhoods rejected the programs and their clients' presence in their own "backyards."

Civil rights legislation did increase the rights of the mentally ill, enabling them to be more in charge of their own lives, and eliminated the easy involuntary hospitalization practices I encountered on "3A." A noble effort, as was the articulated reasons for creating a community mental health system in the first place. It just didn't work out very well.

The combined efforts of the two political opponents resulted in the young woman in beat-up military fatigues taking a leak on Hyde Street, oblivious to the world passing by, one among many disastrous outcomes, many far, far worse, of a society that just can't seem to get it right, or refuses to do so.

* * *

"On Jan. 10, 2001, our daughter, Laura, was at work at California's Nevada County Behavioral Health Clinic. A client appeared for a scheduled appointment. Without warning or provocation, he drew a handgun and shot Laura four times. When the rampage at the clinic and at a nearby restaurant ended, Laura and two others lay dead and two were injured."

Thus wrote Amanda and Nick Wilcox, Laura's parents.[32]

"The Nevada County Board of Supervisors expresses its deep regret about the tragic circumstances that unfolded January 10, 2001, causing grievous injury to many, and the death of three cherished individuals—Laura Wilcox, Pearlie Mae Feldman, and Michael Markle.

"The County acknowledges that it failed to predict and therefore prevent the violence perpetrated by a mentally ill patient."

Thus wrote Nevada County Executive Officer Rick Haffey.[33]

At this writing, it's been 15 years since Laura's death. Her killing provoked intense discussion and debate in the mental health community among State legislators, families, and friends of the mentally ill, people who have been victimized by mentally ill individuals, and people with mental illness, themselves. One outcome was "Laura's Law," passed in 2002, designed to prevent the kind of situation that led to Laura's death. But, for nearly a decade and a half, it had little impact on the lives of violent, severely mentally ill people or those who suffered at their hands.

Who was Laura Wilcox, what happened, and what is Laura's Law?

This is what her father told the Nevada County Board of Supervisors on September 28, 2004[34]:

> For the record, my name is Nick Wilcox. I wish to speak to Item 44 on your agenda. I ask your indulgence to hear me out.
>
> I will begin by recalling my last conversation on January 8, 2001, with my daughter, Laura Wilcox. The image of Laura curled in the blue wing chair by the wood stove while she quietly spoke of her day at the Nevada County Behavioral Health clinic is burned into my consciousness as if by a hot iron. She had worked at the clinic the previous summer and was helping out for a few days during her college winter break.
>
> After one day on the job, she observed deterioration in staff moral since the previous summer. She noted that department had no director, there were vacancies on the psychiatric staff and the prospects of filling these positions were dismal due to lack of funds. She had felt during her summer employment that patients were not always treated with respect and that this attitude was even more pronounced in January. Treating people with respect was an issue of great importance to Laura. She conveyed a sense that the department had become dysfunctional and was on the verge of collapse. Less than two days later, Laura was lying dead on the clinic floor, shot four times at close range by a patient, Scott Thorpe, who was being ignored by a department that had indeed collapsed.
>
> We have said on many occasions in the past that what happened on January 10, 2001, was both predictable and preventable. Due to pending

litigation we have never publicly elaborated our reasons for saying this. As of this moment in time, however, the gag order that you and your attorneys have imposed on us is lifted and we are free to speak, and you in turn are required to listen.

We recognize that there was a random element in Laura's death. Scott Thorpe did not enter the clinic that day in January of 2001 with the specific intent to kill Laura. We have come to believe, however, that what happened that day was indeed predictable and therefore entirely preventable.

As you may know, Scott Thorpe had been a client at Behavioral Health since 1996. His first psychotic episode occurred in October 1999. By April 2000, his paranoid delusions were readily apparent to all who had contact with him including his family, his girlfriend, Pam Chase, the crisis worker with whom he became obsessed, and to the treating psychiatrist, George Heitzman. The evidentiary record establishes that Heitzman and others at Behavioral Health and Thorpe's family had in their possession the following information prior to January 10, 2001.

1. Heitzman knew that Thorpe would likely benefit from anti-psychotic medication and that he was refusing to take this medication.
2. Heitzman knew that Thorpe possessed an arsenal of firearms and that he would use them if provoked.
3. Heitzman knew that Thorpe was a heavy user of marijuana.
4. Heitzman knew that Thorpe had developed a sexual fixation on crisis worker Pamela Chase. Heitzman and others, including Laura, knew that Pam was frightened of Thorpe and that she was asking for protective measures.
5. Heitzman knew that Thorpe had developed an elaborate delusion about an FBI plot to cause him harm. Heitzman knew that he himself was the focal point of Thorpe's anger.
6. In the months and days prior to January 10, Heitzman knew that Thorpe's family was calling franticly seeking intervention. Heitzman refused to acknowledge all but one of these calls, even with passive listening. Had he listened, he might have learned that Thorpe had a record of criminal assault. Heitzman might also have learned that Thorpe had converted his home into a military style bunker in preparation for the FBI attack he believed was coming.
7. Furthermore, Heitzman knew that both Thorpe's father and grandfather and committed suicide by firearm, thus establishing a history of violent behavior in the family across generations.

Scott Thorpe came to the clinic in July of 2000 for an evaluation to determine whether he should be involuntarily committed to an institution for treatment. Had he been committed, he would have been required to take appropriate medication and he would have been prohibited from purchasing and possessing firearms for a period of five years. Scott Thorpe taped this interview. He did not specifically say that he was going to kill an identifiable person or himself. He therefore, in the opinion of the interviewers, did not meet the threshold for involuntary commitment. The criteria in California for involuntary treatment are that a person must be, in the opinion of a psychotherapist, a danger to self or others or otherwise gravely disabled. In Nevada County this apparently was interpreted to mean that unless you actually provide specific details of a plan to kill yourself, or another, you did not meet the threshold for treatment.

Two questions must be asked. First, did Heitzman have in his possession sufficient information to make a commitment decision, and second if he did, why was the decision not made? The simple answer to the first question is yes. Refusal to take medication and stalking behavior are known to increase the likelihood of violence. Marijuana is known to amplify the paranoia of those who are psychotic, which in turn can lead to violence. Firearms, though not themselves a cause of violence, greatly increase the chance that potential violence will be fatal. Finally, Heitzman wrote in his medical notes twice in the month prior to the interview that Thorpe was "potentially dangerous and on the verge of needing hospitalization". We can only conclude that Heitzman had sufficient information and that he ignored the accepted standards of his profession.

This raises the second question. Why was Thorpe not committed? The simple answer is that Behavioral Health was unwilling to spend the money on needed treatment. Involuntary services are not available locally. Involuntary services are expensive and not reimbursable under state and federal health programs. Financial resources from the State for mental health services are inadequate. Therefore, there is a strong financial incentive to cut corners. Simply put, the Behavioral Health Department was gambling that nothing bad would happen as a result of withholding needed treatment. Furthermore, those who made these decisions could afford the risk. After all, why spend money on treatment and workplace safety when you have clerical staff to take the bullets for you.

Prior to the shootings, Heitzman, Diane Chenoweth, and Judith Edzards, among others, had raised the issue of workplace safety and the need for a bullet resistant partition. Such materials are costly. Accordingly, no action was taken. Former CEO Ted Gaebler commented to The Union that, "Employees have asked for zillions of things such as cleaner bathrooms and better food in the Rood Center cafeteria. There is an endless list of things people ask for." Put another way, why should money be spent on workplace safety measures when you have a nineteen-year-old clerical worker to act as a human shield? After all, killing a young employee is far more cost effective than injuring her. You do not have the nasty problem of ongoing medical expenses to deal with. Nor did Laura's life have value in economic terms because she did not have dependents.

By now you are probably thinking that you are being confronted with the ranting of an angry and grieving father. I admit that I am angry, and yes, I am still grieving, but what I am saying is not ranting. Heitzman knew in advance of the shootings that the department was on a collision course with disaster.

Heitzman shared his feelings about the deteriorating conditions at Behavioral Health with colleague David Moyer less than three weeks before the shootings. Heitzman told Moyer the department was, " just waiting for a lawsuit. There will be some bad outcome," Heitzman said, "and the cards are going to fall." He went on to say, "We're not providing the support we should to our clients. They're not being managed properly. We need to be spending more resources to track our high-risk adults."

Shortly after the shootings, court appointed psychologist Alfredo Amezaga wrote in his notes, "Unfortunately for a host of innocent victims, Scott Thorpe's mental illness had been poorly managed over an extended period of time, which resulted in his paranoia and delusions escalating to the point of extreme irrational thought and behavior. It is both a professional and personal tragedy that the quality of psychiatric care that Mr. Thorpe now receives (in prison) could not have been provided in the weeks and months prior to his explosive and deadly psychotic rage."

We learned during the criminal trial that Thorpe was among the most mentally ill patients that Doctor Charles Scott had ever examined. So I ask the question, what does it take in Nevada County to receive treatment? It takes a commitment from those in a position of power, such as you, to help those in great need, rather than sweeping them under the rug, as was Scott Thorpe. Recently, former supervisor René Antonson confided to me that in retrospect, he now understands that there was far more that his Board could have done but that it was simply not a priority. You must make this a priority.

As an epilogue, you should know that we learned recently in a conversation with Scott Thorpe's sister-in-law that now that Thorpe is under proper supervision and taking his meds, his behavior is normal. He wakes up every day fully understanding the horrific act that he committed, as do we.

Thank you for your patience.

Two years before Nick Wilcox delivered his message to the Nevada County Board of Supervisors, California passed "Laura's Law," designed to prevent a repeat of what happened to his daughter in 2001. The legislation allowed judges to order involuntary outpatient treatment for people with severe mental illnesses if they have a history of being hospitalized or jailed or show violent behavior toward themselves or others. Short-term involuntary hospitalization was already legal in California, under section

5150 of the LPS Act, if an individual had shown that they were a danger to themselves, to others, or gravely disabled. But unlike the situation I reported on in *Harassment Therapy* in the early days of LPS, as time, the movement toward transparency in all areas of life, and the civil rights movement unfolded, definitions of being "a danger to self or others" or "gravely disabled" were much more stringently applied. The abuses of earlier eras, when a women depressed by her marriage could be involuntarily hospitalized on her husband's recommendation, or an 18-year-old young adult, brought to the psych ward by his well-to-do parent, was "5150'd" for smoking pot—events I actually observed—were over. The civil libertarians of the mental health community were, largely, successful. And because community mental health programs were to be located in neighborhoods where individuals needing their services lived, and that they, therefore, could easily access treatment early in the cycle of mental decomposition, the possibility of *preventing* the need for large-scale involuntarily hospitalization seemed to be at hand. Had we had entered a new level of dealing with the mentally ill? We had. We hit rock bottom by abandoning them. The State hospitals were shut down or scaled back, but the promised levels of funding for community mental health centers didn't materialize. The outcome? The Mental Hospital Without Walls.

Enacted *33 years* after LPS was implemented, Laura's Law was to correct all this by allowing carefully administered involuntary treatment in home communities. This is what *Time* magazine reported[35] actually happened.

[Laura's Law] was touted as a preventative measure allowing family members, mental health workers or parole officers to request treatment for the ill before they do anything harmful, especially in cases where a patient's condition inhibits them from making rational decisions about treatment. The law, however, left it up to counties to decide if they want to implement it, and they've been reluctant to do so not only because it's controversial in terms of civil rights but because of funding problems. Almost a decade later, only one of California's 58 counties has adopted it, Wilcox's Nevada County. A second is running a pilot program.

In 2011, when the *Time* magazine article appeared, Los Angeles was the county running the pilot program. San Francisco was one of the other 56 counties that had not adopted the law. The city's progressives, in this most liberal of cities, railed against the abuses of the past. The idea of involuntary hospitalization was seen as particularly abhorrent, and other approaches were seen as more viable and humane. Jennifer Friedenbach, one of our frequent street teachers over many years, Executive Director of San Francisco Coalition on Homelessness, told the Exploring class that the problem was not with the mentally ill *individual*, but with the availability of mental health *services*. Later, in an article titled "'Laura's Law' a looming disaster for mentally ill," she put her concerns down on paper[36]:

In the past couple of years, long-term San Franciscans have often asked me why folks on the streets are in such mental distress. The answer is quite simple. Mental health and substance abuse services have been decimated in San Francisco.

According to San Francisco's Health Commission, between 2007 and 2012 alone, the health department reduced behavioral health by $40 million in direct services, mostly coming out of civil service. Almost every level of services was impacted – many programs closed their doors.

A frightening reality is that the system was already stretched far beyond capacity, and services had been steadily shrinking since the late 1970s as realignment at the state level and the changing real estate market resulted in the loss of about half our board and care facilities as well as deconstruction of our then-flourishing community mental health system.

The cumulative result has been staggering. The system is increasingly reliant on expensive and traumatizing stays at the locked psychiatric facility at San Francisco General Hospital and emergency room visits.

The increased acuity of people suffering from mental illnesses and addictive disorders has had a dramatic impact across The City, on emergency homeless services and neighbors alike. For the individual in crisis, however, the horror is compounded.

The debate around the mental health system has centered around a long string of tragedies, falsely linking mental illness to violence, and focusing on forced treatment as the silver bullet that will solve the crisis. Most recently, legislation was introduced at the Board of Supervisors to enact Assembly Bill 1421, known as Laura's Law. While this law has been in effect for more than 10 years, until recently, only one small county, where Laura Wilcox lost her life, Nevada County, has implemented it. The majority of mental health providers and advocates oppose the law.

Like most Californians, advocates and mental health professionals do not believe a new bureaucratic process is the same as a new solution. AB 1421 does not address the lack of mental health treatment. It does not add funding. What it does is allow a family member, a roommate, or a police officer to petition the court, and through court order, drag someone before a judge where he or she is mandated into treatment under threat being held in a

locked facility for 72 hours. Concerns around perpetrators of domestic violence being able to use this to control their victims aside, this adds considerable costs – police, transportation, court costs and more. Resources that
could go twice as far by simply expanding our treatment system.

However, this law goes far beyond wasting scarce resources; it trauma-
tizes someone suffering from a health condition by putting him or her into
the hands of our criminal justice system and removes fundamental rights to
voice in health care decisions.

If individuals do not comply with the treatment plan, it will be up to the
police to remove them from their homes. If this individual is a member of
a community with a history of racial profiling and violence at the hands of
the police, it can go beyond being a traumatizing experience to a potentially dangerous one. This law was implemented in New York, and studies
found disturbing disparities among people of color – African-Americans and
Latinos were forcibly treated at much higher rates.

Year ago I authored a study on homeless people experiencing mental illness. We surveyed hundreds of homeless people who self-identified as mentally ill, and we found that they were desperate to get help. They wanted
their situations to change, and they had tried repeatedly to get treatment, to
no avail. We ended up calling the report "Locked Out."

Addressing mental health issues is difficult, but not impossible. A true
solution would be to build up our residential dual-diagnosis programs, and
radically invest in a full array of community based mental health treatment.
Programs must be nimble, as what works for some does not work for others.

A poor therapeutic relationship means little chance for success, whereas
a solid relationship is grounded in trust. Homeless people with mental illnesses want treatment – forcing them instead into involuntary outpatient
programs works against the very dignity and empowerment critical to recovery. AB 1421 would be disastrous for San Francisco.

San Francisco's political leaders had long held the same view as Jennifer,
but on July 9, 2014, the following article appeared in *The Chronicle*[37]:

Laura's Law passes easily in S.F. supervisors' vote
Easy passage belies the years of debate on implementation of state
measure
By Marisa Lagos Wednesday, July 9, 2014
After years of debate, the San Francisco Board of Supervisors overwhelmingly voted in favor Tuesday of implementing Laura's Law, the state
measure that allows mentally ill people to be compelled into treatment by
a court.

The 9-2 vote wasn't a surprise, however: In May, Supervisor Mark Farrell announced he would move forward with implementing the law here, either by taking it to the ballot or, if he could get the votes, at the Board of Supervisors.

Last month, Farrell all but guaranteed a legislative win when he secured the support of progressive Supervisor David Campos by agreeing to amend the law to include creation of an oversight team that will try to get mentally ill people to accept voluntary treatment first.

"Recent studies and reports show that over 40 million American adults have mental illnesses," Farrell said. "People are falling through the cracks ... right here in San Francisco. We see it on the streets, in the community and in families every single day."

Under Laura's Law, courts could only order treatment for those who have been hospitalized or jailed for mental illness twice in the prior three years or those who have been violent to themselves or others or have threatened such violence during the past four years. Though outpatient hospitalization can be court-ordered, medication cannot. Involuntary hospitalization can only be obtained for those who refuse voluntary treatment and have a "substantially deteriorating" condition. Furthermore, the San Francisco Board required that the county mental health director establish a "care team" made up of another person with mental illness, a forensic psychiatrist, and a person who has a family member suffering from mental illness.

San Francisco was not the only county to adopt Laura's Law more than a decade after it was passed by the California legislature. As of May 2015, Los Angeles, San Diego, Yolo, Placer, Orange, Mendocino, and Contra Costa had signed on, while several others were in the process of doing so.

What was so convincing?

First of all, there are so many people suffering in the communities: those who have mental illness, those who love them, and those who fall victim to seriously disturbed individuals.

Second, money. In 2004, California voters passed Proposition 63, a 1 percent tax on incomes above $1 million to fund mental health treatment. In 2008, state officials ruled that counties could use Proposition 63 funds to implement Laura's Law.

Third, Nevada County officials showed that, for them, Laura's Law is cost-effective, reduces violent crime, and helps keep the mentally ill out of jails and prisons. Specifically, they reported these outcomes[38]:

- Hospitalization was reduced (46 percent);
- Incarceration reduced (65 percent);
- Homelessness reduced (61 percent);
- Emergency contacts reduced (44 percent);
- Savings of $1.81 to $2.52 for every dollar spent as a result of reducing incarceration, arrests, and hospitalization.

* * *

San Francisco's experience with Laura's Law is too new to measure, but Barbara A. Garcia, San Francisco's Director of Health, greeted the new law within a statement to families of the mentally ill[39]:

> SAN FRANCISCO (July 8, 2014) – With today's progress toward passage of Laura's Law, or Assisted Outpatient Treatment, San Francisco is closer to providing another intervention for family members who are concerned for the welfare of their loved ones who struggle with severe mental illness. The goal is to help prevent adults with mental illness from cycling through the emergency and acute hospitalizations that could have been avoided with successful engagement in outpatient treatment in the community. This provides the opportunity to improve their quality of life and bring peace of mind to their families.

Still, acutely aware of the multifaceted issues surrounding mentally illness, Ms. Garcia went on to warn the law is limited in its outreach and potential to reach large numbers of individuals.

> While it will be helpful to some patients, Assisted Outpatient Treatment is not a panacea for the problem of mental illness in our society. It is a very specific tool, focused on a narrow population – those with documented severe mental illnesses, whose conditions are deteriorating, and who are not engaged in treatment.
> We expect Laura's Law/Assisted Outpatient Treatment to apply to fewer than 100 people in San Francisco. It will not solve the problem of chronically homeless, mentally ill people.

Chronically homeless, mentally ill people—like, I assume, the tragically spaced out young woman in dirty fatigues, peeing on the Hyde Street sidewalk—make up approximately 2200 of San Francisco's homeless population, people that students in Inner City Studies have "real-life" experiences with, every time they walk the streets of the Tenderloin.

NOTES

1. Lucchesi, Paolo, "Tu Lan shut down by health department," *San Francisco Chronicle*, July 31, 2012. After a one-year shutdown to clean itself up, Tu Lan opened in late 2013 to rave reviews, for example, see Duggan, Tara, "Tu Lan: Cleaned up but still as good as ever," *SF Chronicle*, December 24, 2013.
2. Garchik, Leah, "Breakfast with Studs," *SF Chronicle*, Friday, October 31, 2003.
3. See https://www.sfdph.org/dph/comupg/oservices/mentalHlth/SubstanceAbuse/HarmReduction for San Francisco's harm reduction policy.
4. Torassa, Ulysses, "Method of Treatment for Drug Addiction / S.F. models 'harm reduction' theory," *SF Chronicle*, January 15, 2001.
5. Long-term master leasing from owners is a part of the Direct Access to Housing Program (DAH). "Established by the San Francisco Department of Public Health – Housing and Urban Health Section in 1998, DAH is a permanent supportive housing program targeting low-income San Francisco residents who are homeless and have special needs. A 'low threshold' program that accepts adults into permanent housing directly from the streets, shelters, hospitals and long-term care facilities, DAH strives to help tenants stabilize and improve their health outcomes despite co-occurring mental health issues, alcohol and substance abuse problems, and/or complex medical conditions. In addition to being an effective way to end homelessness, this supportive housing model is also fiscally prudent as it leads to cost savings by reducing overutilization of emergency services." See www.sfdph.org
6. I had a small grant from the college to cover costs, which were minimal.
7. Kesey, Ken, *One Flew Over the Cuckoo's Nest*, New York: Penguin, 2003.
8. Not his real name.
9. http://harmreduction.org
10. http://www.thclinic.org/support_services.php
11. See https://www.youtube.com/watch?v=czg-0umHLtg to see the protest and the Sixth Street scene in front of the Seneca.
12. http://www.thclinic.org/about.php
13. See, for example, http://www.bluoz.com/blog/categories/6-Tenderloin-Housing-Clinic
14. See Salter, Stephanie, "New Team Spirit in the Tenderloin," *SF Chronicle*, June 29, 2003, for Midge's experience starting the Sports Initiative.
15. An area that an institution, in this case, a mental hospital, provides services to.

16. Timothy Leary advised a group of 30,000 hippies at a "Human Be-In" in Golden Gate Park in 1967 to "Turn on, tune in, drop out."

17. Castenada, Carlos, *The Teachings of Don Juan: A Yaqui way of knowledge*, New York: Ballantine Books, 1968.

18. Laing, R.D., *The Politics of Experience and The Bird of Paradise*, New York: Penguin, 1970.

19. Stannard-Friel, Don, *Harassment Therapy: A Case Study of Psychiatric Violence*, Boston: GK Hall/Schenkman Publishers, 1981.

20. Szasz, MD, Thomas S., *The Myth of Mental Illness: Foundations of a Theory of Personal Conduct*, 1961.

21. Szasz, M.D., Thomas S., *Psychiatric Justice: How the psychiatric profession and the legal establishment unwittingly conspire to deny citizens their constitutional right to trial*, New York: The Macmillan Company, 1965.

22. Szasz, MD, Thomas S., *Law Liberty and Psychiatry*, New York: The Macmillan Company, 1963.

23. Ennis, Bruce, and Loren Siegel, *The Rights of Mental Patients*, Avon Books, 1973.

24. Scheff, Thomas, *The Myth of Mental Illness: Foundations for a Theory of Personal Conduct*, New York: Harper Perennial, 2010.

25. http://www.namica.org/about-nami.php?page=history&lang=eng

26. Torrey, MD, E. Fuller, in *Out of the Shadows: Confronting America's Mental Illness Crisis*, New York: John Wiley & Sons, 1997.

27. See "Handbook: Rights for Individuals in Mental Health Facilities" http://www.sccgov.org/sites/mhd/Resources/OFA/Documents/Patient's-Rights-Handbook

28. Cf., Friedenbach, Jennifer, "'Laura's Law a Looming Disaster for Mentally Ill," *SF Examiner*, June 6, 2014.

29. Mental Illness Policy Org. (http://mentalillnesspolicy.org)

30. "No one has any real idea how many seriously mentally ill individuals are homeless in Phoenix, Arizona." Robert Tilford, http://groundreport.com

31. Ford, Matt, "America's Largest Mental Hospital is a Jail," *The Atlantic*, June 8, 2015.

32. Rifkin, Rich "At long last, Laura's Law is being implemented," *The Davis Enterprise*, May 13, 2015.

33. "Laura Wilcox Memorial Dedication," YubaNet.com, September 29, 2004.

34. Public Record.

35. Gould, Jens Erik/Fullerton, "Should Involuntary Treatment for the Mentally Ill Be the Law?" *Time* magazine, October 27, 2011, http://content.time.com/time/nation/article/0,8599,2098044,00.html

36. Friedenbach, Jennifer, "Laura's Law' a looming disaster for mentally ill," *San Francisco Examiner*, June 8, 2014.

37. Lagos, Marisa, "Laura's Law passes easily in S.F. supervisors' vote
38. Easy passage belies the years of debate on implementation of state measure," *SF Chronicle*, July 9, 2014.
39. http://mentalillnesspolicy.org/states/lauraslawindex.html
40. http://www.sfhealthnetwork.org/lauras-law-offers-option-to-family-members/

CHAPTER 11

I've a Feeling We're Not in Kansas (City) Anymore

YELLOW BRICK ROAD

The cyclone had set the house down very gently – for a cyclone – in the midst of a country of marvelous beauty. There were lovely patches of greensward all about, with stately trees bearing rich and luscious fruits. Banks of gorgeous flowers were on every hand, and birds with rare and brilliant plumage sang and fluttered in the trees and bushes. A little way off was a small brook, rushing and sparkling along between green banks, and murmuring in a voice very grateful to a little girl who had lived so long on the dry, gray prairies. While she stood looking eagerly at the strange and beautiful sights, she noticed coming toward her a group of the queerest people she had ever seen.

L. Frank Baum
The Wonderful Wizard of Oz

* * *

It wasn't a cyclone, snaking its way through cornfields, sucking up houses with little girls and dogs inside, delivering them to a very beautiful, strange, and mysterious place called Oz. But it was just as frightening. It was The Muni, The Municipal Railway System, San Francisco's human zoo on wheels. Colorful, exciting, scary: it runs up and down Market Street, and snakes its way all over town.

They came in considerable number, disgorged from trolley cars, members of The Greater Kansas City Chamber of Commerce: well dressed, well groomed, well mannered, eager to learn about the inner workings of the City and County of San Francisco. Of the 65 visitors, 59 appeared to be white. So many, so white, so neat, so concentrated in a single group, they contrasted with the surrounding racial and cultural mix in this city of diversity, where everyone is a minority.[1] We met them at the bus stop, men and women in casual business attire: dress shirts, open at the collar, slacks, some with sports coats or sweaters, a woman or two wearing a dress or skirt. The men had short, neat hair; some had crew cuts. Together, they looked just like what they were, businesspeople, visiting from the Midwest.

A handful of Promise of the Inner City students lined up as escorts: Samantha, always dressed in black. Hair dyed jet-black, contrasting with her pale white skin, nose ring, scar on her chin, tattoos everywhere. Kesha, single mom, sweet, loud, and do not mess with her. Libah lives in the neighborhood at Cecil Williams Community House, Glide's housing for low-income families. Talo, a great big gregarious guy from Hawaii, mixed race: Japanese-European-other; and Adrian, not a student, but one of the guest lecturers from my Deviant Behavior class and a street teacher, here to help out. Adrian is Mexican-American, brilliant, extremely well read, a former dope fiend, and graduate—after a five-and-a-half-year stay—of Delancey Street Foundation's "each one teach one," "mutual restitution" drug rehab program.[2]

We walked as a group into the neighborhood, from the Civic Center side, the backdoor to the Tenderloin. At first, we passed just a few street people and a lot of tourists, but mostly City Hall-types and people going to and from the courthouse, Main Library, Asian Art Museum, Orpheum Theater, Bill Graham Auditorium, Hastings Law School, and Civic Center Parking Garage. Then we hit McAllister Street, walked past Wild Awakenings Coffeehouse, crossed over Leavenworth, and everything changed. Seventy-one of us—students, teacher, visitors, and Adrian— entered the big lobby of Civic Center Residence, an SRO hotel, part of the city's "Care Not Cash" program for the formerly homeless. People in the lobby turned and stared. It was as if the people from Kansas City had been dropped from the sky.

It wasn't a munchkin who met us at the doorway, although he looked like one. It was Charles—small, wiry, sweet, friendly, polite, sincere— who used to live in a cardboard refrigerator box under the freeway on Potrero Hill and hung out in front of Farley's Coffeehouse, where I spend a lot of my time. He was, what *San Francisco Chronicle* reporter Kevin Fagan called, a neighborhood "mascot"[3] (a term that the activist group San Francisco Coalition on Homelessness despises), a homeless person "adopted" by the locals. After four years shining shoes and doing odd jobs on The Hill—where he grew up, attended and dropped out of grammar school, missed learning how to read or write, got inducted into the Army, anyway, with the "help" of a recruiter, did a tour in Vietnam, held a few jobs on his return, but wound up living under the freeway a few blocks from where he was born—Charles had a stroke. Fiercely independent, he was back in front of Farley's within weeks, with his left side severely weakened, his mouth drooping, his foot dragging, and his left arm dangling. The neighborhood gathered around him, providing food, temporary shelter, and encouragement to seek help from San Francisco's welfare system, but he refused, until he wound up back in the hospital, when an infected wound on his arm festered. A social worker talked him into trying out the city's "Housing First" program,[4] and he moved into Civic Center Residence.

"Charles, how are you?" I asked. "You look great!" He did. His body seemed to be working pretty well. Only a hint of the left-side weakness remained.

"Good. It's good here. Nice people," he said softly, not because of the stroke, but because that's his nature. He seemed unperturbed by the large group surrounding him.

"We're here to learn about the program," I said, waving my hands through the air, taking in the hotel lobby.

He looked around the lobby, as if looking for the program. "It's nice here." He still seemed a little spaced out, but much better than the last time I saw him.

"We have a meeting in the library. People are waiting for us. We have to go. See you later, Charles."

"OK."

The 71 filed into the library, just off lobby. It was a big room, Edwardian-style, reflecting the age of the building. The metal folding chairs, stretched in rows across the floor, were quickly filled by the visitors. Behind two long tables, arranged end to end, sat three panelists—there were supposed to be four—which the class had recruited to talk to the people from Kansas City. A student from Promise of the Inner City assumed the moderator's role.

"Hello, my name is Libah, I'm a student in Dr. Don's Promise of the Inner City class. I live here in the Tenderloin, at Cecil Williams-Glide Community House. I am a former drug addict, been in jail, and was homeless for years. I was as low as you could go, but I turned my life around. My passion now is to help others turn their lives around. I am a facilitator of recovery, harm reduction, parenting, and life coaching groups. I was a candidate for the San Francisco Board of Supervisors. I have three wonderful daughters, am working on completing my college degree, and I am very happy to welcome our guests from Kansas City."

The audience applauded.

Libah went on, "I am also happy to welcome you to our talk today, 'Putting a Human Face on Homelessness.' Our panelists are Don Falk, Executive Director of Tenderloin Neighborhood Development Corporation; Kevin Fagan, *San Francisco Chronicle* reporter; Jennifer Friedenbach, Executive Director of San Francisco Coalition on Homeless; and Angela Alioto, Chair of the Mayor's Task Force on Homelessness, but she isn't here."

I called out from the back of the room, "Angela's office says she should be here soon." I called them as soon as I saw the empty chair. Her office didn't know where she was. "She's supposed to be there," I was told. I know that! I said to myself. That's why I'm calling you! Where is she? "I'm sure she'll be there soon," her office person reassured me.

Angela is a longtime activist in the city, a member of an old and prominent San Francisco political family. Her dad was mayor. She was President of the Board of Supervisors, and is an extremely successful antidiscrimination lawyer. She is known for passion, dedication, and eccentricity. Where is she? "Go ahead and start, Libah."

"OK, thanks. We will. Let's begin."

* * *

The panelists represented a cross section of neighborhood homeless-housing politics, but this is San Francisco, so that cross section generally occupies a narrow band on the left end of the political continuum. In a city that rarely votes for a Republican candidate (13 percent voted for the McCain–Palin ticket, a few months after the KC tour), and all elected city and county office holders are Democrats (or an occasional Green), discussions about social issues often become debates between the left and the far left (or "liberals," aka "moderates" in San Francisco, and "progressives," the more extreme[5]). This is a city that, at the time of the Kansas City visit, the police chief, fire chief, and DA were all women; the head of the Police Commission was an MTF transgender; the sheriff's department had the only condom dispensing machine inside a jail or prison in California (the condoms were free); and two of the eleven Board of Supervisor members were openly gay (only four of the eleven were, presumably, straight white males). One of the two State Assembly members and one of the two State Senators were also homosexual, in a city with a gay, lesbian, bisexual population that made up only 16 percent of the total. A few years before the Greater Kansas City Chamber of Commerce came to town, the mayor famously allowed 4000 same-sex couples to marry, although the State Supreme Court overruled his actions. The City has been a sanctuary city for undocumented immigrants since 1984, when the wars in Central America were raging. In my neighborhood, Potrero Hill, St. Teresa's Church recruited "safe houses" for people fleeing the Death Squads. Nervous, but committed, white-haired parishioners—most of the congregation, at the time, consisted of senior citizens—slipped in and out of Good Life Grocery Store, carrying more bags than usual, cautiously looking over their shoulders as they entered their homes. And at the time of our panel discussion, city officials were launching an advertising campaign on television, radio, billboards, and bus shelters, in English, Spanish, Chinese, Vietnamese, and Russian, promising illegal immigrants safe access to city services and a don't-ask-don't-tell policy concerning residency status. It was in this context, from this perspective, that the panel discussed and debated what the visitors from the Midwest came to the Tenderloin to hear: How is San Francisco dealing with the problem of homelessness? As the panel was wrapping up, the introduction of another—very different—perspective, coming from a Kansas City gentleman, stirred up and enriched the conversation.

This is what happened:

The people sitting behind the end-to-end tables, set up in the library at Civic Center Residence in the heart of the Tenderloin, could have been San Francisco State University professors about to present scholarly papers to colleagues. But they weren't university professors; they were Tenderloin street teachers.

Don Falk, with graying hair and a scholar's high forehead, wearing a tweed sport jacket, open-collar dress shirt, and jeans, was the new Executive Director of Tenderloin Neighborhood Development Corporation (TNDC). Soft spoken, but projecting confidence (something like Donal, the King of Leavenworth Street, but, literally, half his size and not menacing), he has a long and admirable history of work in nonprofit housing, a BA with honors in Economics and Urban Studies from Oberlin College, and a master's degree in Public Policy from the University of California, Berkeley. At the time of his talk, with more on the horizon, TNDC had built or rehabilitated—and provided management, on-site caseworkers, an after-school program, and other support services for—28 residential buildings, many with award-winning designs, consisting of 2500 individual housing units for low-income residents, including formerly homeless. One of those buildings was the one that we were sitting in, the rehabilitated Civic Center Residence, a "Care Not Cash" SRO.

Kevin Fagan, *SF Chronicle* staff reporter (once a laid-back street musician in Europe, still looks like one, still performs, but in clubs, now), recently returned from a year-long sabbatical at Stanford University as an honoree of the prestigious John S. Knight Fellowship in Journalism. Kevin writes human-interest stories, including the highly acclaimed "Shame of the City" continuing series that began in 2003 with an exposé of the depth of the San Francisco's hard-core homeless problem as "the worst in the nation." He went on, over the years, to chronicle Mayor Gavin

Newsom's "Care Not Cash" response to the problem, including coverage that it is now considered to be one of the best in the nation, much to the chagrin of the San Francisco Coalition on Homelessness.

Jennifer Friedenbach is Executive Director of the San Francisco Coalition on Homelessness. With long brown hair, jeans, and shirt-jacket over a sweatshirt, she looks like the street activist that she is, or somebody's harried mom, which she also is. Her bearing can shift from composed to combat-ready to fully engaged in a heartbeat in response to a comment or a claim by someone taking a position that affronts her sensibilities about the plight of the homeless, someone like the mayor or the chief of police. I think she and Kevin like each other, but she has told me that she feels that he has overly emphasized or reported on exaggerated successes of the mayor's programs, without giving adequate attention to its limitations. (Kevin has said he wonders, on occasion, if Jennifer is being "practical" in some of her pronouncements.) Just a couple of months before the Kansas City visit, Jennifer received a "Women Making History Award," jointly given by the San Francisco Commission on the Status of Women and the County Board of Supervisors.

Angela Alioto was still AWOL. Her chair sat empty.

* * *

Even before the Greater Kansas City Chamber of Commerce came to town, Tenderloin U classes had met with each of the panelists several times as street teachers, except for Don Falk who, at the time of this meeting, had just recently taken over the helm of TNDC. We did meet on a number of occasions with Don's predecessor, Franciscan Brother Kelly Cullen, and various program directors from TNDC who shared the organizations history and accomplishments with us. Each of the panelists represented different experiences with the controversial issue of homelessness, and, although they all shared the traditional San Francisco leftist approach, they came from different perspectives.

In 2003, Kevin and photographer Brant Ward went out into the streets of San Francisco to explore how the City was—or was not—handling its homeless problem. At the time, San Francisco was spending *$200 million* a year dealing with, what was estimated to be, 8600–15,000 homeless people, of which 3000–5000 were considered "hard core" or chronic. The rest were "couch surfers"—staying a few nights, here and there, with relatives or friends—or other situational homeless taking up temporary residence in shelters, or jail, or vehicles, or hospitals, or on the streets, or in city parks, or under the freeways. All of the homeless census numbers were rough estimates, because nothing approaching an accurate count had ever been done. After the radical upsurge of homelessness throughout the nation in the early 1980s, following President Ronald Reagan's cutback of federal support for low-income housing (this continued throughout the decade as new budget authority for low-income housing dropped by 75 percent,[6] and homelessness grew), and his earlier closure and scaling back of California's state hospitals for the mentally ill when he was governor, San Francisco's dealings with the homeless became known as "the worst in the nation." Reagan's policy decisions were exacerbated by the city's well-known reputation for tolerance, its relatively (compared to other communities) generous welfare system, the temperate climate, and its inability to come up with a workable plan to deal with the problem. Like so many others, for their own reasons (gold prospectors in the mid-1800s, maritime workers in the 1940s, beatniks in the 1950s, hippies and my brother, David, and me in the 1960s), the homeless were drawn to The City by the Bay, beginning, especially, in the 1980s, when, as a nation, we pulled back the safety nets for the very poor and mentally disabled and unleashed a rampant social problem. Willie Brown, wrapping up two terms as San Francisco mayor when Kevin and Brant began their "Shame of the City" series (which continues today), was quoted in *The Chronicle*[7] as saying, "San Francisco cannot solve the state's mental health crisis, or the nation's poverty crisis, alone. As long as we remain the only city in Northern California truly committed to addressing homelessness, we will continue to be the beacon in the fog, and we will continue to see homeless people on our streets. No one mayor, no one city, can change that alone." Kevin's articles attempted to answer a question many visitors and residents began (and continue) to ask: "How did San Francisco, one of the most sophisticated and cultured cities in the world come to have so many people living so blatantly, so visibly, in misery?"[8]

The 1980s saw the rise of a "homeless" problem throughout the country. Before the 1980s, the term "homeless" was rarely used. "Tramp," "hobo," "bum," "vagrant," and, with the increase in the number of homeless women, "bag ladies" (later, "shopping cart ladies") were the more common references. With the explosion in the number of people begging and living on the streets, the more descriptive, neutral, and universal term became the accepted way of describing the problem, but society's reaction to "the homeless" stayed about the same. We criminalized them. In San Francisco, even with its liberal, tolerant attitudes, the homeless were harassed, arrested, and forced to move on.

In the late 1980s, Mayor Art Agnos, a former social worker and a solid San Francisco liberal, initially ordered sweeps of Golden Gate Park, evicting the homeless who had taken up residence there. But he also pledged to end the city's homeless problem within a year, and organized a task force that came up with a "Beyond Shelter" plan that won national recognition. As multiservice centers, envisioned in the plan, were being developed, he allowed the homeless to stay in Civic Center Park. As their numbers grew, so did protests against them being there. Agnos argued that kicking them out would just push the homeless into the neighborhoods and that, as long as they were so visible, right across the street from City Hall, city leaders would be confronted with the urgency of the situation. And they were. But not in the way he hoped. Civic Center Park became known at "Camp Agnos," and his many critics demanded that he use force to close the camp, which he initially refused to do. Eventually the outcry forced his hand, and he began the evictions, but by then he had lost political support, even in this most liberal of American cities. He also lost his bid for reelection. Frank Jordan, his former police chief, who had been in charge of the Camp Agnos dispersal, replaced him.

Mayor Jordan's "solution" was to crack down on the homelessness. In the first few months of his program, he issued more "quality of life" citations than had been issued in the previous five years. He closed the doors of the Transbay Bus Terminal to the more than 100 homeless people who regularly slept there, and locked the gates to parks throughout the city when the sun went down. He put a successful measure on the ballot requiring that single adult welfare recipients be fingerprinted, and he ordered police to arrest homeless people in possession of shopping carts. But an overwhelming number of city residents protested this order, and it was rescinded.

Mayor Jordan called his program "Matrix," which usually means "an enclosure that encourages the origin or development of something," from the Latin word for womb. But Jordan's strategy was not womb-like. Instead, his goal was to disperse, to keep the homeless moving. And move they did. For the first time, San Francisco's middle-class neighborhoods started to see significant numbers of homeless people sleeping and begging on *their* streets (as Art Agnos had predicted). And from across the Bay and down the Peninsula, suburban communities complained about the noticeable increase in *their* homeless populations. Eventually, in San Francisco, the liberal sentiments kicked in and people began to question the harsh treatment that they saw on the streets and on their television screens. Generally considered to be a "nice, regular guy" before Matrix, Mayor Jordan was disparaged in the press and in complaints to City Hall. Defending himself, he argued, "Matrix isn't just a police program. We have social workers getting people into treatment and housing." He insisted that it was a "compassionate welfare response." But statistics released by the city painted a different picture.[9]

> After more than 9,500 contacts with homeless people, Matrix's seven (count 'em, seven) outreach workers have steered a mere 211 people into permanent housing. Only 55 found their way into outpatient mental-health and substance-abuse clinics. Meanwhile, police have arrested or cited more than 22,000 people for so-called quality-of-life crimes such as urinating in public or sleeping in parks. Most of the citations have been ignored by those charged, transforming them into arrest warrants.

In the next election, Mayor Jordan lost his job. (It didn't help that, at his hip, younger wife's urging, trying to loosen up his uptight image, he posed in the buff in the shower with two popular male talk show hosts). The homeless problem intensified under Jordan's successor, Willie Brown, as it did across the nation, as housing costs went through the roof; urban renewal/slum removal eliminated huge numbers of affordable units; the downsizing of the state mental hospitals meant not only that many of the former patients were pushed out the door, but that those doors were now closed to many *new* admissions, forcing helpless, disoriented people to fend for themselves on the streets; and the War on Drugs proved to be a failure in curbing debilitating substance abuse and drug addiction. The 6th Street corridor, the Tenderloin, Golden Gate Park, the cable car turnaround at Market and Powell, the Mid-Market area, and many tourist spots became hangouts, bedrooms, and bathrooms for the homeless. Visitors to the city, the Chamber of Commerce, the Convention and Visitors Bureau, shoppers, and locals complained. Mayor Brown's response: the homeless problem "may not be solvable."

But he tried.

Mayor Brown declared an end to Matrix and spent more money on homelessness and created more supportive housing during his administration than all the mayors before, but he also continued to roust the homeless from the parks, issued tens of thousands of citations, and conducted sweeps of homeless encampments. UN Plaza, a popular hangout near City Hall, was remodeled and all the benches were removed. But he, or any of his predecessors, never developed a comprehensive plan, even though other cities, like New York and Philadelphia, were receiving large federal grants and accolades for doing so.

One significant proposal developed (but not implemented) during the Brown administration was a "Care Not Cash" program, introduced by a young county supervisor. Appointed to the Board by Brown, Gavin Newsom made solving the homeless problem his signature issue when he ran his successful campaign to succeed Mayor Brown, becoming, at 36, the youngest San Francisco mayor in a hundred years. (Later, he would take on the gay marriage cause and receive national attention for issuing more than 4000 marriage licenses to gay and lesbian couples, a move later voided by the California Supreme Court.) Care Not Cash was built on the premise that simply giving the homeless money is no solution to their problem. Giving housing is.

After Newsom assumed office, Kevin (February 1, 2004) wrote the following[10]:

> During his eight-year term, former Mayor Willie Brown essentially threw up his hands amid political squabbling, even as the hard-core homeless people filled the city's sidewalks and alleys with in-your-face human tragedy every day.
>
> But now, as freshly minted Mayor Gavin Newsom takes over, tradition-ally hostile factions seem ready to listen to each other – from City Hall to businesspeople to social workers to homeless people themselves.
>
> All sides agree that the best way to treat the most-troubled homeless people is to route them into "supportive housing" with counseling services for substance abuse and mental problems. And this week, at the urging of federal officials, Newsom is expected to announce the formation of a group to draft a 10-year plan to end chronic homelessness.
>
> Turning this long-awaited opportunity into actuality is the tricky part.
>
> The same business, poverty-aid and government interests that couldn't agree through those eight years are still crucial to resolving the issue. Newsom must rope them together and make them march in the same direc-tion. But their anxieties are surfacing.
>
> Soup kitchens, independent shelters and other emergency programs fear they will shrink if homeless people begin to leave the streets. The Coalition on Homelessness is afraid too much attention will be turned toward the hard core, who make up about 40 percent of the overall population of homeless people, to the detriment of affordable housing for the poor.

At the core of the plan that actually did emerge was the Care Not Cash program.

Care Not Cash, approved by San Francisco voters in 2002, was implemented in May 2004, under the City's Housing First Program. At the time, 2497 homeless people were receiving monthly welfare checks for as much as $410. Under the Care Not Cash program, those payments were reduced to $59 and the homeless were offered permanent housing or shelter instead. Using money saved from welfare, grants, and city coffers, 1531 supportive housing units were created between 2003 and 2007, the time of the Greater Kansas City Chamber of Commerce discussion, most from existing housing stock: SROs and other low-income units in the Tenderloin and other inner-city neighborhoods. The City contended that more than 95 percent of all individuals placed in this program remained housed.[11]

In another program, called Homeward Bound, between 2005 and 2007, 2519 homeless people were given bus tickets to other communities, if someone on the other end agreed to receive them.

Philip Mangano, President George W. Bush's director of the US Interagency Council on Homelessness, said,[12] "We have gathered together over the past several years an unprecedented number of innovative ideas, public will and resources so that now, for the first time, we can actually see the numbers drop. And San Francisco has a lot to do with that. It has served as a real model of some of the best practices in our nation, showing that you must not simply continue to manage homelessness, but you must abolish it."

From the worst to one of the best? How could that be? Mangano cited San Francisco's supportive housing (with on-site counselors), PHC (San Francisco's bimonthly gathering of hundreds of volunteers in an auditorium, to provide vital services to thousands of homeless, replicated in 135 cities throughout the country), and expansion of on-street outreach counselors.[13]

According to an HUD report,[14] the population of chronically homeless people in the USA declined by 11.5 percent, between 2005 and 2006. The actual number, it says, dropped from 175,900 to 155,600. Bucking the trend, in San Francisco, the chronic homeless count *increased* 4 percent between 2005 and 2007, but federal and city officials attributed that to a more thorough count in 2007 when twice as many people were used to conduct the census. But between 2002, when Mayor Brown was still in office, and 2007, the City claimed that San Francisco's homeless population dropped 38 percent, from 4535 to 2771. (These figures have been challenged by the Coalition on Homelessness as significant undercounts. Our Tenderloin U experience participating in the biannual homeless count, described in the next chapter, seemed to support the Coalition's contention.)

HUD reported that the decreases throughout the country were the result of the shift in emphasis to supportive housing and counseling—in what has been called "Housing First," a concept that assumes substance abuse and other problems are better dealt with when people are in structured, caring, permanent living environments—and away from police crackdowns, emergency shelter beds, and the debilitating conditions of life on the streets.

Jennifer (Jenny) Friedenbach, our panelist from San Francisco Coalition on Homelessness, sparred with Kevin during the discussion, challenging some of the conclusions he reported on in his talk and in his *Chronicle* series on homelessness. She had a different take on San Francisco's efforts.

Jennifer, her organization, and their allies have long battled the establishment over its approach to housing and homelessness. In response to Kevin's comments about the HUD accolades for San Francisco's accomplishments, she said, "'One of the best in the nation' is a sad commentary. Between 6[000] and 10,000 are still homeless. And HUD's report is a complete hoax, when what they've done for years is to gut the funding for affordable housing. They *created* the problem!" Media stories, she said, that report HUD's and Mayor Newsom's claims that the homeless problem had decreased substantially don't explain or even give due recognition to the reality that the number of homeless people seeking services continued to rise.

In a report called "The Forgotten: A Critical Analysis of Homeless Policy in San Francisco,"[15] the Coalition maintained:

Across the nation, there has been growing momentum for a "Housing First" model and yet another new buzzword – "chronic homelessness." Housing First is a policy the Coalition on Homelessness has called for consistently during the past 10 years. What it means is that homeless people can be placed in housing directly off the streets, without first going through a "readiness process," shelter, or transitional housing program. This idea challenges popular beliefs in the social work field that you must have a "continuum" whereby homeless people must be "housing ready" before placement in housing. Of course, at the Coalition on Homelessness, we have always believed that all homeless people are housing ready!

However, as good ideas mixed with politics often go awry, so does Housing First in San Francisco. There are two problems with the way Housing First is being implemented in San Francisco. First, the City decides without input or choice from homeless persons that housing is paid for by cutting poor people's programs and benefits. It has been used as a way to garner political points, justify budget cuts and implement paternalistic welfare reform policies. Secondly, this "Housing First" policy has, for the most part, focused on a very narrow portion of the population – those dubbed "chronically homeless." This is defined as an unaccompanied disabled individual who has been sleeping in one or more places not meant for human habitation or in one or more emergency homeless shelters for over one year or who has had one or more periods of homelessness over three years. It typically refers to single adults, and chronic homeless initiatives funded from the federal government are not meant for homeless families. In San Francisco, we were able to get families included in the definition of chronic homelessness, so at least on paper, this is our policy. This has yet to be reflected in most homeless housing developments.

We all agree that housing is a fundamental solution to homelessness, and we welcome the recognition of this fact by the City of San Francisco. But critical questions remain as to how this housing is paid for and who has access to this critical resource. This second question of who gets the housing becomes even more important as we look deeper into how homeless policies are being implemented. The people who are not being housed are paying for the housing of others more fortunate than themselves. As we will demonstrate in this document, poor and homeless people are paying for the housing – not for themselves – but for other, luckier, poor people. They are paying with their [lost] public benefits.

In the panel discussion, Jennifer argued that the focus of San Francisco's homeless programs has been on the most visible, the "chronic homeless," the ones whose *lifestyle* is begging on the streets or on traffic islands as cars stop at red lights, lying or gathering in doorways or storefronts or on the sidewalks, pushing their shopping carts past the rest of us or blocking our way with them, "hiding" (often in plain view) under the freeways or in city parks, or sleeping in the pews of St. Boniface Church. The City's primary attention has been on people who are "obviously" homeless (a not-always-correct assumption, as the newly housed, under Care Not Cash, with their monthly welfare checks cut to $59 a month, continue to beg on the streets, look "disheveled," and often continue to push their shopping carts around the Tenderloin, collecting whatever), who offend the sensibilities of others: tourists, city officials, workers, employers, merchants, and residents. Why focus just on this goal to the exclusion of other homeless populations, who are, in fact, the majority? Jennifer asked. Her answer: to get them out of sight, protect the tourist industry, and meet the demands of a public that is out of touch with the actual causes of homelessness and the depth of suffering in the homeless community. The problem with this policy: while serving the few, it shortchanges the others. The City, they say, is "robbing Peter to pay Paul."[16]

Jennifer argued that the homeless *community* is funding Care Not Cash with lost employment programs and legal services, and cuts in treatment programs and childcare. The misery of homeless children, youth, families, immigrants, the disabled, seniors, veterans, and working homeless people grows as their safety nets are yanked to get the chronic homeless off the streets. "The dirty secret behind San Francisco's new homeless policy is that the City is housing a few hundred homeless individuals literally at the expense of thousands more who are being forgotten."[17]

"And who do you think was living in the SROs before they were converted to Care Not Cash rooms?" Jennifer asked the people of the Greater Kansas City Chamber of Commerce. "Other poor people, that's who! We have empty housing in this city. Use it! And shelter beds are not housing! We have to create decent living situations for families. We have to stop cutting funding for some to pay for others. And we have to stop *harassing* poor, homeless people."

Jennifer put both hands on the table in front of her and leaned forward to emphasize her concluding comment. "We haven't begun to do what we need to do for the homeless. We have to change our way of *thinking*. Government policy decisions *produced* the problem. We have to stop blaming victims, the very poor, the mentally ill *for what politicians did!*" She sat back and nodded at the polite applause.

At that point in the panel discussion, a woman from Kansas City raised her hand.

Libah, our panel moderator from the Promise of the Inner City class, smiled at the woman, African-American like herself, one of only a handful of minority visitors from the Midwest, "Yes, ma'am! You have a question?"

"Not a question," the woman replied. "I have a personal story I want to tell." She looked troubled, nervous. "My name is Edith."[18] She paused and looked down at the floor in front of her. Then, after glancing around at her Chamber of Commerce colleagues, she said, "I know what it is like to live on the edge. I wasn't homeless, but I have been poor. I was on food stamps. People assumed that I was just lazy, or didn't want to get ahead. It was humiliating, being poor and on food stamps." At this point, she was talking directly to Libah. It was, obviously, a very uncomfortable moment for her. She talked about what it was like for her and her family to turn to welfare to survive, but she was not apologetic. "I appreciated the help. It made a difference. I went to school, took college courses, started a business, and here I am. But it was hard. Very hard. Not everyone starts off in the same place, but here I am."

The audience applauded. Libah said, "Thank you, sister. I know what it's like feeling like you don't deserve anything, college, a good living situation. But, yes, here we are. We've come a long way!" She gave Edith a big Libah-smile, and turned back to the panelist. "Our last speaker, I guess, is Don Falk from TNDC." She looked at me, standing in the back of the room.

"Angela's still not here," I said, cell phone in hand. Nearly an hour had passed since Libah welcomed the guests from Kansas City. I was still checking in with Angela's law office and they were still telling me, "She supposed to be there. We're trying to find her. I'm sure she will be there soon." I knew it was not like her. Angela had been a little late on the two previous occasions she had been a street teacher for my classes, but not *an hour* late. I could hear concern in her office manager's voice, and I assumed something very serious had come up or there was some kind of mix-up. It was OK, as far as the panel was concerned. I hoped she was OK. Angela would be missed, but the discussion was going well.

"OK," Libah said. "Mr. Don Falk, as you know, is the head of TNDC. He'll explain what that means." The audience applauded.

Don began, "Hello everyone. Let me join Dr. Stannard-Friel and his students in welcoming you to San Francisco and the Tenderloin. As I am sure you know, the Tenderloin is San Francisco's poorest, most crime-ridden neighborhood, but what you may not know is that it is also a wonderful, diverse, close-knit community of hardworking people, families, disabled, good people from all over the world. Some of them are homeless or formerly homeless. TNDC, Tenderloin Neighborhood Development Corporation, is here to serve them all. We've been around a long time."

TNDC was founded in 1981 by a group of Volunteers In Service To America (VISTA) volunteers, community activists, and people of faith as a pioneering organization in supportive housing. At the time, gentrification was threatening to change the Tenderloin from a place where low-income people were able to live. In TNDC's first decade, they saw immense growth in their organization with the acquisition and rehabilitation of eight buildings, including 400 apartment and residential hotel units, and annual expenses of $1 million.

"Today," Don reported, "TNDC has twenty-eight residential buildings, over two hundred staff members, and $20 million in annual operating costs, yet our mission remains the same: to work with Tenderloin residents in preserving the neighborhood and serving people for whom homelessness is a real possibility." TNDC provides after-school and youth programs, including annual college visits—the year of the panel discussion, to the Chicago area. The previous year to Philadelphia—social work services, community organizing to involve residents in positive social change and decisions that affect their own lives, and tenant activities, such as produce drops and holiday and cultural celebrations. And of course, housing. One of their buildings was the one we were in. Civic Center Residence, an SRO, provides supportive housing for over a hundred formerly homeless individuals. Another was the new Curran House, opened in March of the previous year. Curran is a mixed-income family residence. Forty percent of the residents are at "average affordability"[19] for San Francisco, and 60 percent are Section 8 low- and extremely low-income residents, and formerly homeless.

Curran House is a remarkable place. Consisting of 60 units, including a studio, one- (and particularly notable and unusual for the Tenderloin), two-, and three-bedroom apartments, it features a glass wall in the back of the lobby, showing off a "decompression" garden that greets residents and visitors as they enter the building, a beautifully landscaped and accessible courtyard seen through large windows at the rear of the lobby. On the roof of the building, a vegetable garden offers hands-on access to nature to recently homeless and other residents, including children whose lives are often almost completely contained in environments made up of concrete and asphalt. And, as with TNDC's other buildings, it is staffed with a nurturing, supportive group of employees.[20] The "mixed income" approach is intended to avoid the "residential segregation" by socioeconomic status—meaning, often, racial segregation, too—of the older, familiar "housing projects" concept that places poor people in isolated institutional-appearing settings (large, concrete, or barrack-like buildings, marked with informational signs—building numbers, penal code warnings, designed by government workers—housing and signage more suitable for a factory or a prison or the military than a residential community). While the mixed-income concept has been embraced by many housing activists as possessing the many demystifying and humanizing benefits of social integration (learning through relationships who people from other socioeconomic groups really are, the richness of various other cultures, and what it is like to have friends and neighbors from different racial, ethnic, and social backgrounds by sharing a living environment), it is not without its critics, especially in the Tenderloin, who see it as a form of gentrification, with all its accompanying ills. But no one on the panel that day in the Civic Center Residence challenged TNDC as doing anything other than serving the poor with its award-winning 990 Polk Street Senior Apartments; its Aarti Hotel, housing formerly homeless, at-risk Transitional Aged Youth (TAY), ages 18–24, with serious mental health needs; Antonia Manor, with 100 percent of its residents Section 8 beneficiaries, seniors, and others with disabilities; The Dalt Hotel, offering 179 permanent, affordable housing, SRO units for extremely low-income working adults, seniors, and disabled persons; and 23 other properties (and more on the horizon), meeting housing, counseling, after-school care, community, and other needs of homeless youth, the very poor, low-income families, recent immigrants, seniors, the mentally and physically disabled, formerly homeless, and people with HIV/AIDS.

As Don was talking, I heard a commotion out in the lobby. "I'm here! I'm supposed to be here." A woman's voice was coming through the library door. I peeked out to see what was going on. The woman's long black hair stood out from her head as if she had just come in from a cyclone. Sunglasses, perched on top of her head, were failing miserably to contain the windblown mane. Her coat was draped over her shoulders like a cape. She wore a black dress and knee-high leather boots. And she made her point by pointing her briefcase-sized purse at the stunned people watching her. "The panel! I'm on the panel! Where's the panel?" Everyone in the lobby acknowledged the woman's powerful presence by turning to see what new force had entered their realm. Among the residents stood Charles, astonished, as the munchkins must have been when Dorothy landed in Oz. Or when the Wicked Witch of the West appeared with her army of winged monkeys.

But it wasn't the Wicked Witch of the West. And it certainly wasn't Dorothy. It was Angela Alioto, our missing panelist. She saw me by the library door and said, "Sorry … late. Dog died. Grandkids cryin'. Tears all over. Where do I go?"

I ushered her into the library and sat her down in a chair in the back of the room. "Catch your breath," I said. But this was Angela Alioto, the Energizer Bunny in human form. "No thanks," she said, as she bounced off the chair and dashed across the crowded room to the last empty chair, alongside the other panelists. Don was in the middle of his concluding comments, but he paused to greet her. "Hello, Angela."

She nodded. "Dog died. Never mind. Hi." And she sat down at the long table.

Don went on to talk about the evolution of the neighborhood, and that, despite all the progress that TNDC and others had made, the Tenderloin still suffered from widespread poverty, decrepit housing, street crime, drugs, prostitution, and homelessness. Still, he pointed out, that over 4000 households are now in affordable housing, owned or leased by more than a dozen nonprofit housing developers like TNDC. Vacant store-fronts are nearly nonexistent, and—as a result of community activism—a grade school, playground, and police station now serve the Tenderloin's residents. The Tenderloin is home to 30,000 people, he said, from all walks of life, varying races and ethnicities, trying to improve their lives in a very difficult environment. "What would the people of this neighborhood face today if not for these community efforts?"

Don thanked the visitors for their interest in the neighborhood, and the audience applauded.

And Angela began.

"Hi. Sorry I'm late, long story. I'll just take a few minutes. We've come a long way in San Francisco, dealing with the homeless problem. It hasn't been easy." In the next ten minutes, she summarized Mayor Gavin Newsom's administration's work on the homeless problem, and took on a controversial question by one of the Kansas City visitors.

"I'm Angela Alioto. I've been involved in San Francisco politics a long time. In 2004, the mayor appointed me Chair of the Ten Year Plan to End Homelessness."

Actually, what happened was that Angela was running against Gavin Newsom in his first candidacy for mayor. Matt Gonzalez, the popular President of the Board of Supervisors and one of the first members of the Green Party elected to political office in the Bay Area, was proving to be an unexpected challenger to, what was thought was going to be, an easy win for Gavin. With Angela in the race, the moderate vote was split, and many believed that the progressive Gonzalez might actually win. So, Gavin did what politicians do. He went behind closed doors and negotiated with

Angela. When it was all over, Angela dropped out of the race and endorsed Gavin. He won and one of his first acts was to appoint Angela Chair of the Ten Year Plan to Abolish Chronic Homelessness Council. He also appointed her niece, Michela Alioto-Pier, to his old District 2 Supervisor seat. And Angela went to work on the Plan.

In the three months, between March 19, 2004, and June 30, 2004, when the Plan was presented to the mayor, the Council and its commit- tees, representing a cross section of San Francisco's homeless interest groups, met 85 times. Public hearings were held at City Hall on May 26 and 27. More than 785 individuals and 400 organizations participated in the discussions. In the final report, Angela wrote[21]:

> For the first time in the twenty years that I have been in public life, I feel the united excitement, the electric energy, the profound intelligence, and the strong will to end chronic homelessness in our great City. I credit a lot of that to you, Mr. Mayor, for having the courage to make homelessness a priority in your administration. On behalf of the Council and me, we thank you!
>
> It's time to roll our sleeves up, and get to work on what will be one of the most rewarding accomplishments of anyone's life. I certainly look forward to this particular "victory party!"

On May 2, 2008, in the closing few minutes of our panel discussion, "Putting a Human Face on Homelessness," Angela ran through San Francisco's recent accomplishments:

She told the group that late in the 1980s, San Francisco, and every place else in the country, saw an overwhelming increase in homelessness, brought on by changes in government policies at the federal level. Faith- based organizations were the first to step in, offering sleeping mats and cots in temporary housing, shelters in church basements, and other places. Angela, working with members of the Ten Year Plan task force, met with anyone who was interested, across all political lines. They completed the report in June of 2004. The main recommendation was to reduce home- lessness by shifting from temporary to permanent supportive housing. This, she said, is what happened since then:

There was a 26 percent decrease in overall homelessness and a 40 percent decrease in street homelessness. (Later studies would challenge that.) Within 12 months of people moving into supportive housing, the task force found their use of emergency rooms fell by 58 percent and use of inpatient beds by 57 percent saving huge sums of money. Use of residential mental health programs went from an average of more than two and a half days per person per year to zero. Angela held up her hand, and curled her thumb and index finger into an "O." "Zero!" People placed in supportive housing had a five times higher rate of maintaining employment and twice as many enrolled in employment programs compared to those continuing to be homeless. She said the city in the year of the panel discussion had 1500 year-round shelter beds, homeless prevention programs, a medical respite center, detox centers, and an effective behavioral health treatment system. San Francisco launched the nation's first PHC Program, a one-stop service center for chronically homeless people that engaged over 15,000 volunteers, helping 22,000 homeless, that had been copied by more than 160 cities throughout the world. Since 2004, almost 5000 permanent supportive housing units had been developed, half for chronically homeless, the other half for families and single adults in a welfare to work program. The Housing First program houses 3000 formerly homeless people and a majority of them are employed or in job training programs. A Direct Access to Housing program is a national best practice program, providing permanent housing with on-site supportive services and medical care for approximately 1000 formerly homeless adults, most of whom are struggling with mental health issues, substance abuse, and chronic medical conditions. The supportive housing program has a 90 percent average stability rate, while reducing costs to the system. Finishing her summary of the Ten Year Report, Angela gave a quick nod of her head to the visitors from Kansas City, saying, "I think we've done a great job, but there's lots more to do. But we have a plan and so far, so good." With that, she sat back, having compressed four years of work into a ten-minute presentation.

The audience applauded, obviously impressed by the whirlwind of information given by the late-arriving Chair of the Ten Year Plan. Libah took over, "Thank you, Ms. Alioto." She turned to the audience, asking, "Do you have any questions, to any of our panelists?"

A man in the back raised his hand. He stood up when Libah called on him, and said, "You know, it's great that Edith and Libah pulled themselves up by their own bootstraps, but what about those that won't? What about the guy who has a full-time job, and just decides, 'The hell with this!' Quits his job so he can live off the rest of us. Doesn't want to get up and go to work anymore. It's great that Libah and Edith pulled them-selves up by their own bootstraps, but some people just don't wanna to work. They give it up, go live on the streets, and live off the rest of us. What are we supposed to do with them?"

Angela was first to respond. "Let me answer that!" Halfway out of her seat, arms outstretched with her hands turned backward, as if she was holding back the other panelists, she almost shouted, "Let me answer that!" She turned to the man and said in firm, measured speech, "That...person...does...not...exist! Who would do that? Who in their *right mind* would go live on the streets, risk their life every night, sleep in filth, hun-ger, disease? The cold? Who in their right mind? And even if they were, which they're not, they'd *be* crazy in no time. Living on the streets actually reduces the gray matter in the brain!" She tapped her head with a finger. "It deteriorates! So even if you're not crazy when you 'choose' to become homeless—which nobody in their right mind does, it's *not* a choice—you're crazy soon after. Who would *choose* to live like that? No one that I've ever met, and I've met *plenty*!"

The man, obviously not impressed, sat back down.

"Well," I said, after the Q & A wrapped up, "let's take a walk."

We formed six groups, with the students, Samantha, Kesha, Libah, and Talo, and Adrian and me each taking a group of ten or eleven Kansas City visitors out into the streets of the Tenderloin. We paused between each group's departure to avoid attracting too much attention. Seventy-one of us walking the streets, all together, would be just too bizarre. As it turned out, it was bizarre enough. My group took up the rear.

We walked up Jones Street past St. Anthony's Dining Hall, which was by now closed for the day. Small groups of worn-out men and women gathered on the steps of the vacant, old Hibernia Bank, astonished to see wave after wave of white people in casual business attire. Others, camp-ing out along the fence across the street from St. Anthony's, stared as we walked by. The resident of two shopping carts, with a tarp thrown across them to form a hut, crawled out to see what was going on.

A big man in a business suit, entering the Pink Diamonds Gentlemen's Club on Jones, shook his head at us as we passed by, and three little girls, dressed in white blouses, burgundy-colored sweaters, and navy blue skirts, leaving City Academy, right next door, waved merrily to us. "They coexist," I said of the side-by-side strip joint and Christian school, "*reluctantly*!" We turned at Golden Gate, and walked by the entrance to

Boeddeker Park, its gates chained closed. I paused at the porta-potty on the corner. Noises inside. "Listen," I whispered.

"Mudderfukker ain' no shit!"

"Wassa fuck?"

"Gimme dat!"

Three muffled voices, two male and one female, followed by banging on the porta-potty's inner wall.

"It's a shooting gallery," I whispered. "People shoot up inside. They call it 'The Vertical Coffin.' Door opens and someone's sitting on the john, passed out, nodding out, or worse."

"Hey! Wassa fuck?" A voice from inside.

"I think they mean us," I said, beckoning my group to move on down Eddy Street, past pockets of people hanging out by the Windsor Hotel and Alexander Residence, by now utterly bewildered to see another wave pass them by.

"What the freak is going on?" laughed a youngish, but toothless, white guy with a green-and-yellowish-gold-colored Mohawk, standing in front of Daldas Market. "A white person's parade?"

"That's Oakland A's colors," I tell my group, gesturing to the guy's Mohawk. "Cops'll tell you that most of the drug dealers come from the East Bay. Oakland, Richmond."

We turned the corner and went up the hill, crossed over Ellis Street, and walked alongside the long food line at Glide Memorial Church. Hundreds of hungry people waited patiently as the line, stretching all the way down the block, around the corner, and up the hill, moved slowly into the dining hall. More than 2200 meals—breakfast, lunch, and dinner—would be served that day, and every day. Some of the visitors from Kansas City made eye contact with or nodded to people on the line, but most just looked ahead, or off to the side, as did most of the people in the line.

"There's still an awful lot of homeless here," a woman from Kansas City said to me.

"Yes," I said. "Yes, there is."

NOTES

1. Whites constitute 43.63 percent of the population; Asians, 30.72 percent; Hispanics, 14.11 percent; African-Americans make up 7.44 percent, Native Americans account for 0.26 percent, and other, 3.84 percent.
2. See http://www.delanceystreetfoundation.org

3. Fagan, Kevin, "SHAME OF THE CITY, Homeless 'mascots' find niche in tony neighborhoods," Wednesday, December 3, 2003. Kevin wrote about Charles as being a neighborhood mascot.

4. Housing First: Facts from San Francisco Government webpage http://sfgov.org describing the City's Housing First Program: In 1999, San Francisco began a supportive housing program using SRO hotels that have been renovated by the owners and leased to nonprofit housing agencies under contract with HSA. The housing agencies provide property management, support services, and money management with the main outcome focused on housing retention. This program was established to provide housing options to very low-income homeless individuals. In May 2004, San Francisco implemented the voter-approved Care Not Cash initiative reforming the City's cash assistance program. Homeless CAAP clients receive a reduced cash grant in exchange for permanent supportive housing in the Housing First Program. More than 95 percent of all individuals placed in this program remain housed. The Care Not Cash portion of this program is made available through the clients' CAAP eligibility workers at 1235 Mission Street. Other low-income clients are referred via city shelters and programs serving homeless adults.

5. See Vikingkingq, "Progressives vs. Liberals: What's in a Name?" Daily Kos, February 23, 2008.

6. Davey, Joseph Dillon, The New Social Contract: America's Journey from Welfare State to Police State, Westport, CT: Praeger, 1995, p. 47.

7. Fagan, Kevin, "SHAME OF THE CITY / THE BEST INTENTIONS / The kindness San Francisco extends to the homeless - welfare checks and daily handouts - has combined with political gridlock to allow the problem to persist," SF Chronicle, December 3, 2003.

8. See http://www.sfgate.com/gate/special/pages/2003/homeless/

9. Cothran, George, "Matrix's Happy Face New statistics contradict Jordan's spin on homeless crackdown," SF Weekly News, March 22 1995.

10. Fagan, Kevin, "Chance to solve homeless crisis/New mayor arrives as warring factions agree on solution," SF Chronicle, February 1, 2004.

11. Housing First: Facts from San Francisco Government webpage http://sfgov.org

12. Fagan, Kevin, "Homeless numbers down in U.S.; S.F. called 'model' for outreach," SF Chronicle, November 8, 2007.

13. Fagan, Kevin, "Homelessness czar Mangano now with nonprofit," SF Chronicle, December 1, 2009.

14. The Second Annual Homeless Assessment Report to Congress, March 2008, US Department of Housing and Urban Development Office of Community Planning and Development, https://www.hudexchange.info/resources/documents/2ndHomelessAssessmentReport.pd

15. *The Forgotten: A Critical Analysis of Homeless Policy in San Francisco*, San Francisco Coalition on Homelessness, May 2005, p. 3.
16. *The Forgotten: A Critical Analysis of Homeless Policy in San Francisco*, San Francisco Coalition on Homelessness, May 2005, p. 5.
17. *The Forgotten: A Critical Analysis of Homeless Policy in San Francisco*, San Francisco Coalition on Homelessness, May 2005, p. 5.
18. Not her real name.
19. Also called "AMI," Area Median Income, meaning in this case, 60 percent of the units are formerly homeless or Section 8 families, the remaining 40 percent are what's called "Average Affordability," people in the median-income range of the community, which in San Francisco is around $80,000 a year. See www.dbarchitect.com/projects/slideshow/9.html for a slide show of Curran House.
20. See www.dbarchitect.com/projects/slideshow/9.html for a slide show of Curran House.
21. http://www.sfgov.org/site/planningcouncil_index.asp

CHAPTER 12

Don't Count Me!

Rev. Glenda Hope: Street Minister

© The Author(s) 2017
D. Stannard-Friel, *Street Teaching in the Tenderloin*,
DOI 10.1057/978-1-137-56437-5_12

It was a miserable evening, very dark, muddy, and raining hard. We had forgotten the mud and rain in slowly walking and looking about us, when we found ourselves before the workhouse. Crouched against the wall of the workhouse, in the dark street, on the muddy pavement stones, with the rain raining upon them, were five bundles of rags. They were motionless, they had no resemblance to the human form.

"What is this?" said my companion.

"Some miserable people shout out of the casual ward, I think," said I. We went to the ragged bundle nearest the workhouse door, and I touched it. No movement replying, I gently shook it. The rags began to be slowly stirred within, and by little and little a head was unshrouded – the head of a young woman of three and twenty, as I should judge, gaunt with want and foul with dirt, but not naturally ugly.

"Tell us," said I, stooping down, "why you are lying here?"

"Because I can't get into the workhouse." She spoke in a faint, dull way, and had no curiosity left. She looked dreamily at the black sky and the falling rain, but never looked at me or my companion.

"Were you here last night?"

"Yes; all last night and the night afore."

Charles Dickens
"A Night Scene in London"
The Quincy Daily Whig, February 27, 1856

* * *

Who are the street people? Where do they come from? Why are they here? What are their lives like? Are they lazy? Are they dangerous? Are they drug addicts? Are they all homeless? Are they crazy? Are they no-good people who "choose" to "live off the rest of us"?

* * *

Tuesday July 6, 1999:

The Tenderloin is busy today. There doesn't seem to be any order to the flow of sidewalk traffic at the intersection of Ellis and Jones. I have to zigzag to narrowly avoid bumping into passersby. Am I the only one zigzagging today? Pedestrians are walking every which way, looping around the dealers and beggars who mumble, "Wha' sup, man?" or "Spa' change?" Business-types, street-folk, social service providers and consumers, cops and criminals, residents and tourists walk the intersection of Ellis and Jones, momentarily sharing space in each other's lives, as people have done here ever since the sand dunes, swamps, and marshes were filled in, and rock and then cobblestone and then concrete and asphalt replaced wood planks to form the streets of San Francisco and breathe life into St. Anne Valley as it became Uptown Tenderloin, a "higher class" den of vice and corruption, when the Barbary Coast was still the bottom of the pit in the early days, as Yerba Buena became San Francisco and, in time, "Uptown" was dropped from the neighborhood name.

Crossing Jones, I zig when I should have zagged and nearly collide with a tiny person walking the other way. Light blond hair, touch of gray, clear, intelligent blue eyes, black jacket, slacks and shirt, and white clergy collar: I recognize her not because of the attire, but in spite of it. "Hey," I say. "Reverend Hope. You're in uniform today." Glenda Hope is a well-known presence in The TL, but she rarely wears her minister's garb on the streets.

"A friend died last night," she says. "I'm going to preside at the memorial. Would you like to come?"

"Yes. Yes, I would. Thank you." I reverse directions and tagalong. "I don't see you in the collar often."

"It attracts too much of the wrong kind of attention," she responds. "I just got stopped by a guy asking for money. I didn't give him any, so he accused me of 'not being a very good Christian.'" She tucks her chin in, raises her eyebrows, and peeks at me over the top of her glasses. Glenda has managed to give away a fortune in goods, subsidies, and services in the more than 25 years she's ministered in the Tenderloin. "It's better when I walk the streets without the collar. But," she sighs, "not today."

"Who died?" I ask.

"He was a street musician down in the Powell Street BART station."

"Oh yeah. I read about him in this morning's *Chronicle*." He was very popular with the commuters. Kevin wrote the obituary.[1]

"Well, his friends are saying goodbye today."

As we walk down Jones and turn on Eddy Street, I comment on how noisy the neighborhood is today.

"It's a sunny day. Everybody's outside," she says, "and it's only the Sixth. People still have some money to spend." Government assistance checks are distributed on the 1st and 15th. Glenda draws a lot of attention on the streets. Most of it is friendly, but the collar does attract some nasty reactions. A shout from across the street, "God sucks!"

We enter the Ritz Hotel on Eddy Street, near Taylor. A beaux-arts-era SRO, built in the aftermath of the 1906 earthquake and fire that leveled the Tenderloin, the Ritz was rehabilitated and taken over by TNDC and some of its community partners in 1991, to provide housing for 90 adults with mental and physical disabilities. We're met in the lobby by a small cluster of people, friends of the deceased. Eight of us squeeze into the rickety old elevator. Posted on its wall is a notice, "Maximum Occupancy: 4." On the second floor, we climb out and enter a small community room with a tidy kitchen area and a table off to one side, set up with a fruit punch bowl, paper cups, a vase full of purple lilies, a few sympathy cards, and a sign reading:

In Loving Memory

Paul Decuir

1957 -1999

`"Lift Every Voice and`

`Sing "`

Illustration 12.1   In Loving Memory sign

Kevin's obituary about Paul's life and death is taped to the table.

Chairs are lined up in neat rows in the middle of the room. I sit off to the side and watch the mourners arrive. They're about two dozen of them, mostly black and Hispanic, a few whites. Most look to be in their 40s or 50s, but age is hard to tell when life's been so hard.

Two women sit down. I know them. It's Anne and Tala, a lesbian couple. (Well, lesbian now. Tala used to be a man. In a few years, after this gathering, Anne and Tala would come to my Cultural Anthropology to talk about Tattoos. Anne, who was transcribing audiotapes for *City Baby and Star*, is a well-known tattoo artist in San Francisco, with a master's degree in cross-cultural studies, and both women have numerous, well-done tattoos, all over their bodies.) In the Antho class, they would come to talk about the history and evolution of tattoos: Anne the cultural-historian-practitioner, Tala the "visual aide." After Anne's talk of body adornment/modification (tattoos, piercing, branding, scaring), since ancient times and throughout the world, Tala stood before the class to show off her tattoos. As she started to remove her shirt, so the students could see the artwork on her torso, she remembered, "Oh, shit. I meant to wear an undershirt. What the hell, you've all seen tits before."

After class, a young man came up to me to say, "Before she took off her shirt, I thought she was a man."

"She used to be," I said.

"But she likes *woman*!" he said. "Why would *he* change?"

"Because he realized he was a lesbian," I said.

My student left the lecture, pondering a new idea. Real-life lessons can happen anywhere, even in the classroom.

In the community room of the Ritz Hotel, at the memorial for Paul Decuir, I exchange hugs with Anne and Tala, and we sit down together.

Glenda slips on a black robe, ties a large white cross around her neck, and begins the service. "This is the largest gathering for a memorial in the Tenderloin in some time. I want to thank you all for being here. I know Paul meant a lot to you all." More than a hint of her Southern roots can be heard in Glenda's voice. "It's good that you are here. I know this isn't the first time most of us have mourned together. So many memorials in the Tenderloin. So much suffering." She pauses for a long moment, looks out into the group of sad faces, then opens up her Bible and begins to read, "Yea, though I walk through the Valley of Death...." When she finishes, she asks for memories or offerings from those gathered.

An older black woman gets up and sings in a good strong voice, "Come on up to Bright Glory, I'll be waiting up there for you." A few softer voices join in. Lots of street noise is coming through the open windows, competing with the song.

Two large black men go to the front of the room together. One starts to say something about Paul, but chokes up and can't talk. The other recalls a Neville Brothers' song about "Joe, who comes up in life, but doesn't belong everywhere." It reminds him of Paul. (Paul actually sang back-up vocals for the Neville Brothers in New Orleans in the 1970s.) The other man composes himself to say, "I'm not very religious, but I think God was inside Paul everywhere he went." The two men go back to their seats.

A fidgety white man, bald on top, with a long ponytail hanging down, wearing a white tee shirt, jeans, and sneakers, stands up by his seat and says, "Only the good die young."

Raymond, Paul's musical partner (they called themselves Aki, "My Brother" in Arabic), has been sitting in the front row, crying. He stands up and turns around to the audience and says, "Paul got me into singing, you know, in the BART station. It's not begging, you know. It's giving something and getting something. It felt good and people liked it. Everybody loved Paul. I loved Paul." Raymond is overcome with emotion and sits down, hunched over, head bobbing up and down. Deep sobs fill the room.

Glenda reads more scripture, shares a few comments about Paul. We all sing "Come on up to Bright Glory," and the service ends.

Handshakes and hugs follow. Cocktail sandwiches are brought in, put on the table next to the punch bowl, and we eat together, chatting softly. We all feel the loss of life and ponder what it means. Then we all go home. Death in The TL is a lot like anywhere else. It just comes sooner here, more easily, and more often.

A year before Paul died, Kevin, once the street performer, himself, went down into the BART station to listen and wrote about Aki[2]:

> Ray Evans and Paul Decuir are everything that is good about music and nothing that is bad about poverty.
>
> They are living, scruffy, street-singing soul.
>
> The melody is universal, the words timeless, the voices pristine. By now a crowd has knotted around the pair, toes tapping and heads nodding in the eternal daylight of the underground station. And before long, the clink of coins being tossed into Decuir's cap sets up a rhythm of its own. Below everyone's feet, the BART and Muni trains rumble in and out like some mechanical percussion section low in the background.
>
> Street music is as old as instrumentation itself, coming in a kaleidoscope of forms and gimmicks, and San Francisco is a world center of the craft. Some folks wear clown costumes and twist balloons on the sidewalk, some bang out Stratocaster chords on amplifiers. Decuir and Evans don't do gimmicks. They don't do costumes. They simply stand on the concrete in front of turnstiles when the foot traffic gets heavy, wearing their cleanest pants and shirts, and belt out gospel, rhythm and blues – a cappella, with nothing but their own hand claps to dress up the songs. Just pure, sweet throat.
>
> But in the way of so many such things that black men with no money and few prospects know so well, the threads always spool out and disappear. So this is what they do now, living on welfare in a clean little government-subsidized Tenderloin hotel called the Ritz: They sleep, they eat, they sing.
>
> And when they put their voices together, all the dreariness of a poor man crawling along in a world that doesn't really give a damn, or even notice, is forgotten. For just a moment, people pay attention.

Paul told Kevin, "No way could we just sit on the sidewalk and beg. We have to feel like we're earning what we get. And all these years we've been singing together, it keeps us out of real trouble. It's a way of keeping peace with ourselves."

Paul was not a beggar-man. He was not a "bum," or a "tramp," or a "hobo." He earned his way through life. He brought joy to the world.

And though he had cleaned up from drug addiction and matured out of scrapes with the law, he still died young, at the age of 42, of complications from diabetes. He told Kevin,[3] "Thank God I can sing. It's about the only thing that's really gone right in my life. No matter what I do, I'd like people to remember that."

* * *

Do people remember Paul Decuir? Do they remember what Kevin called his "pristine" voice? Does it still echo off the walls of the BART station or in the hearts of his friends at the Ritz Hotel? How many of the homeless or SRO dweller street people are remembered after their passing and for how long? How long are *any* of us remembered, and for what reasons, let alone those who die alone, often anonymously, on the streets of San Francisco?

Glenda remembers.

Even today, though her "light blond hair, touch of gray" is now white, her clear, intelligent blue eyes remain the same. And on too many occasions, she still dons the white collar for sad gatherings. And every Christmastime, in Civic Center Plaza, in front of City Hall, she calls us to remember the once almost dead, who have joined the ranks of the completely dead.

Interfaith Memorial for the Homeless Dead: December 21, 5:30 p.m.

Please join us and San Francisco Network Ministries on December 21, 5:30 p.m., in Civic Center Plaza for an interfaith memorial for our family members, friends, and community members who have passed away while homeless in 2011.

This is not a protest, but a memorial service. All are welcome.

If you have loved ones or acquaintances who have passed away while homeless in 2011, please send their names to Reverend Glenda Hope, so that we may read their names among those we memorialize.

Posted by San Francisco Coalition on Homelessness
STREET SHEET Alert

Illustration 12.2 Reading of the Names

"John Witkowski, Carlos De Jesus, Steven Nolner, Luis Hernandez-Olguin, Charles Morrison, David Ricci, Lorenzo Sandoval."

We've gathered, on several occasions with Glenda and other homeless advocates, to witness the reading of the names.[4] She has done this for years.

"Barry Holton, Steven Dougherty, Michael Smith, Jane Doe."

On December 21, 2011, the longest night of the year—and the anniversary of the Mayflower landing at Plymouth Rock; Apollo 8's liftoff from Kennedy Space Center; the bomb exploding on Pan Am Flight 103 over Lockerbie, Scotland; the birth of Jane Fonda; and the death of F. Scott Fitzgerald—a hundred names were read, many never to be mentioned again.[5]

"Peter Gianquinto, Carlos Martinez, Anthony Jackson, Gustavo Ochoa, Charles Hill, Elwyn Davis, Freddie Powell."

Cause of death, according to the Homeless Death Forms from the Department of Public Health,[6] included "Natural" "Accidental," "Suicide" (by firearm, hanging), "Homicide" (by firearm, vehicular), "IPV" (Intimate Partner Violence), but mostly "Drug Related."

Most of the dead were in their 40s, for whatever that's worth.

"Eric Anderson, Gilbertto Guiterrez, Terrance Adale, Patrick Koehler, Thomas Brewer."

Place of death included "Public sidewalk," "SFGH" (San Francisco General Hospital), drug or alcohol treatment programs, the 6th Street corridor, SoMa, the Mission, under freeway on-ramps, the streets of the Tenderloin.[7]

The names were read, a bell rung after each one, we prayed, we sang, we called for compassion and action.

It was December 21, the first day of winter, and the holiday season began. So did a new list of San Francisco's homeless dead. Next year, on December 21, their names will be read and they will be remembered for one more day by those who gather with Glenda. Then most will be forgotten, forever, by everyone.

Who were they, when they were still alive?

* * *

"Dr. Don, they're all so nice." My student, Chris Lum, articulated what so many other students have said of the homeless. "They're so appreciative." This may seem naïve or cynical, but it is neither. It is another *discovery*, brought about by real-life encounters.

Chris was born in San Francisco. His family's roots are in Chinatown, but they moved out to the Avenues, as have many Chinese families, spreading out, as San Francisco's population became one-third Asian, and growing. His family only goes back a couple of generations here (he showed his fellow students in my Cultural Anthropology class a picture of his grandmother's bound feet), but Chris is all-American. And he's a city-boy. But he never spent any time in the Tenderloin—his mom forbid it—except to pass through on The Muni or by car, before he enrolled in Inner City Studies classes. So he, like most of my students, was having a first-time, face-to-face, extended experience with homeless people, when he participated in one of his Promise of the Inner City assignments, PHC.

Usually, PHC is held in the large Bill Graham Auditorium, part of the Civic Center complex, near City Hall. PHC was initiated during the Newsom administration, as part of the Mayor's commitment to changing the way we deal with homelessness. On a typical day, 800 or so volunteers will gather on a Wednesday, every other month,[8] to help around 2000 homeless people access services: housing, groceries, meals, dental, HIV testing, California IDs, emailing home, phone calls back home, back and foot massage, podiatry, acupuncture, Veteran's benefits, needle exchange, food stamps, flu shots, eyeglasses, haircuts, employment opportunities, wheelchair repair, medical care with follow up services, TB tests, veterinary care, legal support, access to service programs, and much more. My students help serve meals in the cafeteria, hand out food bags, work the various stations, act as translators (Spanish, Arabic, Chinese), escorts, and greeters.

On the day that Chris worked PHC, it was at their Veterans Connect event, held at the VA Downtown Clinic on 3rd Street. Chris signed in the homeless vets (name, age, ethnicity, services desired) as they came in (San Francisco has 1500 homeless vets[9]). Since Veterans Connect involves fewer homeless participants on any given day, PHC recruits proportionally fewer volunteers, but they work just as hard. Sitting for hours at the sign-in desk is always an intense assignment, with little let up. Several times, I asked Chris if he wanted to move over to some other service, but he declined. "I'm good," he said. It was when the day was over, and we did our class debriefing, that Chris told us how "nice" and "appreciative" the homeless vets were. These sentiments are typical of my students who have participated in PHC, St. Anthony's and Glide's soup kitchens, week-long immersions, Faithful Fools Street Retreat, the Bi-Annual Homeless

Count, and just walking the streets. "They're nicer than people who aren't homeless," one student said. That's been our experience, even if it doesn't always seem that way.

* * *

"Hey, bish! Whadafuyado'n? Yalookytagefuckinraped? Tha'swha,' stubish!" The words were incomprehensible, mashed together, and loud.

"Dr. Don, I think she's talking to *me*," a worried young woman in the Exploring class said. "I think she's *yelling* at me." The student, Margie,[10] pulled back a little, putting me between her and the stranger.

We had just walked by a homeless group on Turk Street, heading over to The Shooting Gallery (a lowbrow art gallery on Larkin Street), but first we were stopping by Tenderloin Community School to look at the tile mural on its outside walls, created by children of the Tenderloin. The encampment was spread out on the sidewalk, maybe a half-dozen people, sleeping bags, bundles, and a lean-to made out of cardboard and shopping carts. The homeless people ignored us, except for the woman.

"Muddafuckcrazybish! Looky!" The words were slurred and ran together, but the more she talked, the more they made sense. Meaning began to emerge.

The woman was small, skinny as a rail. Her dark brown skin had a gray-ish pallor; her intense eyes were made even more so by a network of red lines that webbed across the white. Most of her teeth were gone, only a few crooked ones poked up in front. And her unkempt hair stuck out every which way. But she had a lot of energy and had no trouble keeping up with us. She hurried ahead, then turned to face us. "Waddafu? Lookydabelly. Bigass. Shiiit. Fuckin' strippah? Youstrippah? Gonnagedfuckinraped, tha'swah! Gangraped! Tha'swah, stubitch."

"I think she's *worried* about you," I told Margie.

"Worried? Why?"

"Because of what you have on."

Margie looked down at herself—short, sleeveless blouse, cut off at the midriff, exposing her belly, tight blue jeans—then up at me with a "What's wrong with this?" look on her face. This has come up before with other students, especially when we visit San Quentin State Prison. Before the tour, the Public Information Officer sends us a list of restrictions, among them a strict dress code:

Revealing clothing:

A.No transparent clothing.
B.No tank tops/sling shot tops.
C.No strapless, halter, spaghetti straps and/or bare midriff clothing.
D.Tights are acceptable alternative to hosiery for wear under dresses or skirts.
E.Skirts will be no more than 2 inches above the knee. Slits in the garment shall not expose more than mid-thigh.
F.Dress or sport shirts/blouses unbuttoned past the second button from the top of the shirt/blouse are not authorized.
G.No open toe shoes

Still, students are *shocked* when they are told they are dressed inappropriately and, to enter the prison, have to put on an unattractive, typically oversized for them, clean but smudged from use, white jumpsuit to cover up the offending garments and whatever skin is exposed. As with lifestyles and habits, fashion is normalized, independent of context, in this case, the streets of the Tenderloin.

"She's worried that you might get attacked if you walk around the Tenderloin wearing what you have on."

"This is what I *always* wear," Margie said. She took another look at herself. "OK, I get it." Margie, a very attractive star volleyball player, comes from a small, rural community a couple of hours north of San Francisco. She told me, when we started our walk down Turk Street, "My town doesn't even have sidewalks," let alone the sights that are commonplace in The TL. She was used to being looked at, but had never encountered anything like this skinny, pissed-off, little lady yelling at her now.

I edged up to the homeless woman. "OK," I said. "She knows better now."

She glared at me and said, " *You*knowbedda?"

I nodded and our homeless Good Samaritan went back to her sidewalk community.

* * *

January 27, 2011:
It was a dark, cold fog-shrouded night in San Francisco. The streetlights cast an eerie golden glow on the bundles curled up under bushes and people setting up their sleeping bags in Civic Center Plaza. Most of the city workers were long gone. So were the tourists and most other passersby. Only the homeless remained, and other Tenderloin folk on their

way home from chores or visiting or going to or from work. A few others hurried into the garage or down Hyde Street to catch a streetcar or BART train. The dealers, streetwalkers, and people going to bars or clubs were further up the hill or down toward Turk and Taylor.

The six of us walked along a long, lonely, concrete wall, the rear of an office building, with decorative alcoves set deep inside the façade. A bundle curled up inside one of them, a tiny woman wrapped in blankets, lying on a piece of cardboard, her personal items lined against the back wall, protected by her own body from larcenous intent.

"Don't count me!" she demanded, as we stopped to check her out.

"Should I count her?" Leslie whispered, as we continued on down the street.

"Yes," I said. "Yes, we should."

Every other (odd-numbered) year, a "Point-in-Time" homeless census is taken, intending to take a "snapshot" of "sheltered" and "unsheltered" homeless populations on a single night. Sometime, during the last ten days of January, all jurisdictions (meaning, virtually the entire country) receiving federal funding to provide housing and services for the homeless through the McKinney–Vento Homeless Assistance Grant are required to conduct the count. Unsheltered homeless persons include people who live in places not meant for human habitation, such as the streets, abandoned buildings, vehicles, or parks. Sheltered homeless persons are those staying in emergency shelters, transitional housing programs, or "safe havens." Safe havens provide private or semiprivate long-term housing for people with severe mental illness and are limited to serving no more than 25 people within a facility.

On the evening of January 27, 2011, I met four Inner City Studies students, Amanda, Leslie, Maria, and Milañ, at Celtic Coffee Company, and, together, we walked over to the corner of Grove Street and Carlton B. Goodlett Place, kitty-corner from Civic Center Plaza and across the street from City Hall, and went into the Department of Public Health building to be oriented, along with a couple of hundred other volunteers, to the homeless count, scheduled between 7:00 p.m. and midnight. It was an upbeat crowd, made more so by the enthusiasm of the department employees who walked us through the paperwork and census process. Specific written instructions included "Whom to count":

Counting requires subjective judgments as to who is homeless. The following should help you determine whom to count.

Automatically count:
- People sleeping outside.
- Vehicles with windows covered (see below)
- Tents, Makeshift structures, Boxes (see below for all of these)

Do NOT Automatically Count:
- People engaged in illegal activities (drug activities, prostitution)
- People leaving bars/other establishments
- People waiting for buses

Consider these factors when deciding whether to count. Not everyone engaged in these activities is homeless.
- Walking, sitting, or standing "with no purpose" (loitering)
- Panhandling (with or without a cup/sign) (This should be considered with other factors as not all panhandlers are homeless.)
- Carrying bags/backpacks/garbage bags/suitcases,/blankets/bedrolls.
- With shopping cart containing personal belongings
- In possession of recycling, especially large numbers of items.
- Disheveled
- Inebriated/passed out on sidewalk

Illustration 12.3   Homeless count instructions

The instructions also included when to include cars ("vehicularly housed"), tents, abandoned buildings, and to identify, as accurately as possible, gender (Male, Female, Transgendered, Unsure), single or family, and age (Youth, Adult, Unsure).

Census staff encouraged us not to be overly zealous in our counts. "Not everyone sitting on a bench is homeless. If they don't have any belongings with them, it's probably best not to count them."

Then routes, distributed throughout the city, covering every block, alley, lot, park, and underpass, were assigned to teams of volunteers, sometimes composed of strangers, though many went out into the streets in groups of friends or colleagues. My students and I stayed together. Our assigned area: McAllister to Van Ness to Market to Leavenworth. "Good!" We could have been sent anywhere in the city, but this was "our" neighborhood, the blocks around City Hall and Celtic Coffee Company.

"Hello, my name is Sy." The woman, introducing herself to us, appeared to be fiftyish, maybe a few years younger or older. She looked like someone who had been through hard times, but was OK now. "I work with the census project," she told us. "I'm gonna tagalong, keep you company on the walk. Answer any questions." I assumed she was assigned to us a street escort, to help us feel more comfortable. Keep us safe and out of trouble. But of the four students with me, three had taken several inner-city courses, and I was in my 16th year in the neighborhood. We felt pretty comfortable in The TL, but it was fine that she was joining us.

We all walked across the Grove–Goodlett intersection and entered Civic Center Park.

Shadows moved in bushes and we went over to take a look. Two men were spreading out their sleeping bags. Leslie held a clipboard with the tally sheet attached, and she marked down four Xs (two for "Males," two for "Adults"). Others were setting up in other corners of the park. More Xs. We made the rounds of the neighborhood. Men and a few women sat on the steps of the Library. They all looked pretty much the same, but we only counted those with sleeping bags or what looked like bags of food or other necessities of living on the streets. Those without any obvious evidence of being homeless, who were just sitting there, were not represented by Xs on Leslie's tally sheet. We thought that many who *looked* homeless, *were* homeless, but knew, and were told, that not all necessarily are. Often, it was a judgment call. They could be SRO residents, or drug dealers, or people wrapping up a day in Faithful Fools Street Retreat program, as Milañ had done the previous semester, and Becky Morrison a couple of years before. Maybe we knew too much, that many SRO residents, for example, hang out in the streets with homeless or formerly homeless friends, especially those in SRO hotels that lack lobbies or other community rooms and the street become their "living rooms." And many Care Not Cash recipients still push shopping carts around, collecting whatever, a carryover from before. But if they had a cart, we counted them. We weren't allowed to ask anyone about their status. Word had come down from Trent Rhorer, the head of the city's Human Services Agency, that "it would not be safe to have volunteers approach the people they are counting and in most cases it is obvious if someone is homeless."[11] Since Care Not Cash, it really isn't that obvious, and we worried that the warning about safety—while certainly understandable, especially considering the litigious society that we live in—reinforced the negative, but in our experience, most often incorrect, stereotype of the "violent" homeless person. But we did as we were told.

We peeked in a few vehicles that had the stuff of life piled inside, but no people. We marked Xs in the column for "Car" or "RV/Van." A couple of other vans had curtains covering the windows, so we couldn't see if anyone was inside: X, X: two vans. A group was scattered on the walkway in front of Bill Graham Auditorium. Some were in their sleeping bags, with other bags and shopping carts pushed off to the side. We counted all of them. Windowsills and nooks and crannies sheltered people with living provisions, and we counted them. Others sitting alone or in groups were "obviously" homeless, but maybe not, and without the accessories, we weren't sure. So, we just counted some.

"Hey! Hey, *you* guys!" A very large white man with long blond hair and a big, gravelly voice, rushed toward us. His hair was tied back in a ponytail and his beard looked like someone had glued some kind of prickly bush to his face. His clothes were stained and wrinkled. And he was coming right at us! "HEY!" he called again. The six of us turned to face him. I moved between him and the students, not sure what I was going to do, or could do, in the face of someone so much larger than I am.

In all the years I have been in the Tenderloin, I've only been man-handled twice: once by two men holding a sidewalk sale on Leavenworth Street, who picked me up when I slipped on wet leaves. My feet actually flew out from under me, my briefcase flew across the sidewalk, and I slammed down flat on my back. The two men laughed as they hauled me to my feet, brushed leaves off of my clothes, patted my back, and handed me my briefcase. "Crap, man," one said, as he grabbed the cuff on a leg of my pants and pulled up my foot to inspect the sole of my Birkenstock sandal. "Ya gotta get some retreads here, man! Or better yet, *real* shoes." And they laughed some more. So did I, but my back ached too much to get into the fun. On another occasion, at PHC, I was volunteering as an escort, bringing people to the various stations. My last "client" of the day was Gary, a totally stoned black man from New Orleans. He was very friendly. Too friendly. Gary hung all over me as we went from station to station. He wrapped his arms around me, put his head on my shoulder, pressed his body against mine, and pushed his face against my face as he whispered the story of his life and his opinions on everything in my ear. Then he'd jerk away, dragging me with him, and swerve over to say hello to friends, who obviously knew and liked him. One said, "Hey, Gary, how ya doin,' man?" Another said, "Lookin' good, Gary. Ha! Not really." And both he and Gary cracked up at that one. Gary pushed up against me, pressed his mouth against my ear, and whispered some more about being raised on a farm in Louisiana, eating lots of vegetables, "That's why I looks so good at fifty!" He did. "We was slaves, but the white man like us better than his own kids. Gave us more money when the crops come in. His kids hated that. 'Why give the niggers more? They just gonna piss it away!' He was a good man. Kids sucked!"

When I got home, I stripped down and threw all my clothes into the washing machine, showered and changed. When I went to pick up my glasses, keys, and cell phone, no phone. "Damn!" The last I saw it, it was in the pocket of my shirt-jacket, now in the wash. And that's where I found it. I packed it in rice, but that didn't help. Water and cell phones don't go together, something like Gary and me.

The big, white man, approaching our little group, raised my anxiety and that of my students, but when he got close, he yelled, "Hi! Count me!"

While most ignored us, or casually checked us out, the street people knew what was going on. A few, recognizing us in our reflective census takers' vests and seeing the clipboard, called out as we passed by, "Count me!" or "Don't count me!" as the big blond man was doing and the little lady in the alcove had.

The big man eagerly told us that clusters of homeless could be found tucked away in the bushes at Civic Center Park, alongside the wall of the Asian Art Museum, in front of the library, on the steps of the BART stations, and down on the train platforms. By then, we had already checked out most of the sites he recommended, but not the BART stations. We thanked him and headed over to BART. Leslie marked Xs on her tally sheets as we went down the stairs and walked on the underground platform.

As the students counted the homeless, I chatted with Sy. She told me that she is a recovered addict, "Twelve years clean. Walden House did it for me."

"Walden House?" I repeated. "Do you know Ana Bolton?" Ana Bolton was one of the two main subjects for my book, *City Baby and Star*. As an addict and gang leader, in and out of prison, Ana was "Star." When she decided to clean up her act, she spent some of her time at Walden House, but she said the style of rehab there didn't work for her. She found her sober self at the now closed Milestone drug treatment program for ex-cons.[12]

"I was in prison with Ana," Sy said. "I ran the streets with her, back then. I was turning forty-eight when I realized I was facing three-strikes if I went back. Twenty-five years to life. Didn't want to die in prison. Walden worked. I'm still friends with Ana."

"So am I," I said.

As we finished our walk through the Tenderloin, Maria, one of the four students, told the rest of us, "What's most impressed me is the quiet of the streets. So unlike the daytime, here. It's as if the people respect that this is the time and place for sleep. This is their bedroom. It felt ... *peaceful.*"

We went back to the Public Health building and turned in our results. Fifty-four homeless people in our zone: McAllister, to Van Ness, to Market, to Leavenworth. Twelve city blocks. "The highest count so far," a youngish blond woman at the check-in desk said. "I don't know if that's good news or bad." Fifty-four. Four and a half homeless people per block. There were many more, we were sure, but they didn't meet the criteria. No sleeping bags or boxes of food or shopping carts or other evidence of living on the streets, except that there they were, as the evening wore on, sitting alone or in small groups, when everyone else had gone home.

* * *

In 2011, the San Francisco Homeless Point-in-Time Count found the following[13]:

- The number of homeless individuals reported as "living" (but actually, just "counted") in San Francisco in 2011 was 6455, 59 less than in 2009, when 6514 were counted, but 207 more than the 6248 counted in 2005, and 78 more than the 6377 in 2007.
- A total of 3106 were "unsheltered homeless," including individuals counted on the streets.
- The number of people estimated to be living in the occupied cars, vans, RVs, encampments, and makeshift structures.
- A total of 2622 were "sheltered homeless," in emergency shelters (including domestic violence shelters), transitional housing facilities, resource centers, and stabilization units.
- Of the 6455 counted in 2011, 5728 met HUD's definition of homeless. In San Francisco, an additional 727 individuals were counted in institutional settings not recognized by HUD for the Point-in-Time count, such as residential rehabilitation facilities, hospitals, and jails.
- In the several weeks following the homeless count, more than 1000 surveys of homeless individuals were conducted, on the streets and in shelter facilities, to generate detailed profiles of homeless individuals, including information about population demographics, family status, causes of homelessness, length and recurrence of homelessness, usual nighttime accommodations, and access to homeless ser-

vices. The surveys were conducted by a trained team of paid current and former homeless workers, and unpaid community volunteers. Survey findings included:

- Fifty-five percent of the homeless persons were 31 to 50 years old.
- Seventy-three percent were living in San Francisco at the time they became homeless.
- Fifty-three percent had been homeless for more than one year.
- Seventy-five percent were receiving some form of government assistance.
- Sixty-eight percent of the homeless respondents were male, 29 percent were female, and 3 percent identified as transgender.
- Of the total survey respondents, 38.5 percent were black/African-American, 35 percent were white/Caucasian, 12 percent were Hispanic/Latino, 7 percent were other/multiethnic, 4.5 percent were Asian Pacific Islander, and 3 percent were Indian/Alaskan Native. (In the overall San Francisco population, 6 percent identified as black/African-American, 48 percent as white/Caucasian, 12 percent Hispanic/Latino, and 31 percent Asian.)
- The largest percentage of chronically homeless persons indicated they were white/Caucasian (42 percent).
- Fifty-three percent were experiencing homelessness for the first time.
- Fifty-five percent of survey respondents reported that they had one or more disabling conditions.
- Thirty-one percent of survey respondents reported that they were currently experiencing substance abuse issues.
- Twenty percent of survey respondents reported that their alcohol or drug use was the primary cause of their homelessness.
- Twenty-five percent of homeless respondents reported the loss of a job as the primary reason they became homeless.
- A total of 635 individuals in families were counted during the Point-in-Time count, compared to 549 in 2009.
- Eighty-five percent of individuals living in families were counted in shelters. The remaining 15 percent were counted on the street.
- Thirty-eight unaccompanied homeless children (under the age of 18) were counted.

* * *

During the next semester, in Exploring the Inner World of the Inner City, we reviewed the homeless count outcomes, and were particularly perplexed by the census results on homeless children, including "unaccompanied" and "individuals in families." In September of 2011, eight months after the census, the class met with Liz Perzanowski of Larkin Street Youth Center. Liz—who worked out of Larkin's Haight-Ashbury office and had been a street teacher for the class for several years—told us that her organization estimates that there are about 5700 homeless or marginally housed youth in San Francisco, and Larkin Street serves around 4000 homeless youth each year (including runaways, young people following bands passing through, self-identified "gypsies," and hard-core homeless). A couple of months later, Jill Tucker, a reporter for *The Chronicle*[14] (who has also been a street teacher for the class), wrote an article, "S. F. schools struggle with more homeless kids." In it, she reported, "In the city's public schools, there are 2,200 homeless children, some in shelters, others in cars, or on couches, or in long-term hotel rooms." Compare that with the homeless census. If two-thirds of the 635 homeless individuals counted in families were children, a reasonable assumption (homeless families usually consist "of a young mother with two children under the age of six"[15]), that would mean 423 of them were children. Add to that the 38 unaccompanied homeless children, and the total number of homeless kids counted in San Francisco on January 27, 2011, was 461. But the Unified School District reported a few months later that there were *2200* homeless students. And Liz's organization, the highly regarded Larkin Street Youth Center, serves 4000 homeless youth every year, and says 5700 young people living in San Francisco are homeless or marginally housed. And consider the following comment in the Bi-Annual Report[16]:

[S]ignificant progress ... has been made in getting individuals into needed treatment programs and transitioning individuals out of homelessness and into stable housing.

From January 2004 to February 2011, 7,225 single homeless adults were placed in permanent supportive housing through Care Not Cash Housing, Housing First, Direct Access to Housing, Shelter Plus Care, and the Local Operating Subsidy Program.

During this time span, another 5,376 homeless individuals left San Francisco to be reunited with friends or family members in other parts of the country through the City's Homeward Bound Program.

From January 2004 to February 2011, a total of 12,601 individuals exited homelessness through various initiatives.

In seven years, 12,601 people were moved off the homelessness rolls in San Francisco and 6455 remain. At least another 1739 homeless children (2200 in school, minus the 461 counted) are in the public schools, and there may be thousands more passing through or, otherwise, under the census' radar. And, given these problematic results, how many adults were missed? What *is* the actual scope of our homeless problem in San Francisco? What is it throughout the nation?[17]

The most recently available national data are from the January 2011 point-in-time count. The 2011 count data show that an estimated 636,017 people experienced homelessness in the United States on a given night. This translates to an incidence, or rate, of 21 homeless people per 10,000 people in the general population.
Analysis of the 2011 point-in-time count conducted for this report provides a more detailed portrait of the population of people who experience homelessness in the nation.... A majority of the homeless population is composed of individuals (63 percent or 399,836 people). The number of people in families with children makes up 37 percent of the overall population, a total of 236,181 people in 77,186 family households. Of the individuals, about one quarter of the population is chronically homeless (107,148 people).
A majority of homeless people lives in shelters or transitional housing units (392,316 people), but 38 percent of the population lives on the streets or in other places not meant for human habitation. Veterans comprise 11 percent of the homeless population (67,495 people). *Data on unaccompanied homeless youth are not included in the main text of this report, as a reliable national youth population count has not yet been completed* [italics added].

On the morning of the day that the homeless count was conducted in San Francisco, Katie Worth wrote, in *The San Francisco Examiner*, "Methods for counting San Francisco's homeless questioned,"[18]

The homeless count: Important measurement or asinine, arbitrary exercise? The debate rages on, even as hundreds of volunteers prepare to fan out across The City tonight to count people who appear to be homeless.
The count is intended to establish a snapshot of the homeless population on city streets, and it is one factor that federal grant providers consider when determining how much money to dole out to municipalities.
However, homeless advocates have long complained that the count's methods are so flawed that the result is inaccurate. During the count, volunteers are asked to canvass a particular neighborhood and count the number of homeless people they spot. However, they are not supposed to approach or speak to the people, so in some cases they might not be homeless.

"If you see a person and you decide through clairvoyance that they're homeless, then you count them," said Bob Offer-Westort, a civil-rights organizer for the Coalition on Homelessness.

But Trent Rhorer, the executive director of The City's Human Services Agency, defended the process.

"It's one method we have in measuring the level of homelessness in San Francisco," Rhorer said. "And when you deploy 350 people to cover every square block of The City, it's a pretty accurate way to count the people on the street."

He said it would not be safe to have volunteers approach the people they are counting and in most cases it is obvious if someone is homeless.

"And at 9 or 10 o'clock, when someone is sitting on the sidewalk, it might be pretty easy to determine whether they're homeless," Rhorer said.

But Paul Boden, the organizing director of the Western Regional Advocacy Project, said there are many more-scientific methods of counting people experiencing homelessness at a given time.

"If the government wanted a serious analysis of how many people in this country are experiencing homelessness, nobody would say the best way to do that is to have a bunch of volunteers go out for two hours on a January night and do a head count," Boden said. "It's ludicrous."

Paul Boden, an extremely articulate advocate for the homeless, who came to NDNU to participate on a panel on homelessness, was once homeless himself. A critic of the Homeward Bound program that provides bus tickets for homeless people to go to another community, he refers to it as "Greyhound Therapy." He and other advocates (e.g., Jennifer Friedenbach, our Kansas City panelist and regular street teacher) are *not* arguing that the homeless census is padding the count by including people who are not homeless, although Katie Worth's article seems to imply that, and government funding is, in part, based upon the outcome (San Francisco receives $18–20 million in federal support). What they are saying is the Point-in-Time census is including people who are not actually homeless, but is also *overlooking* many thousands more by using its volunteer-census-taker, one-night-in-January approach. Apparently, many citizens in San Francisco agree:

San Franciscans still rate homelessness as the city's top problem
Posted By: Heather Knight, sfgate.com, Mar 13, 2012[19]

In his seven years in office, Mayor Gavin Newsom moved 12,210[20] homeless people off the streets.

He created more outreach teams to help them, lowered their welfare checks in exchange for housing and created Project Homeless Connect for them to receive all kinds of services in one place.

So finally – finally! – residents see a change on the streets. Right? Uh, not so much.

A new Chamber of Commerce poll of 500 registered voters found that residents are still supremely frustrated by homelessness.

They were asked if homelessness has gotten better, worse or stayed the same over the past few years. Forty-six percent say it's gotten worse, 36 percent say it's the same and only 13 percent say it's better.

Pollsters also asked respondents to name the city's most pressing issue and allowed them to name more than one. Thirty-two percent mentioned homelessness, beating out jobs and the economy (26 percent), the city budget (21 percent), education (21 percent) and Muni (17 percent).

"It's just a strong indication of how entrenched this problem is," said Steve Falk, the chamber's president. "While the city has gone to great lengths to provide services and housing, the pipeline to homelessness is alive and well."

Jennifer Friedenbach, director of the Coalition on Homelessness, said the poll results are no surprise considering the recession's impact. Take the 6-month waiting list for families to get into shelter, which has grown from 75 families before the recession to 175 now.

Or the 50 percent increase in people seeking shelter at some resource centers. Or the 3,000 people who wait in line some days for food at St. Anthony's, she said.

"There are all these different indicators that look to me like things are getting much worse," Friedenbach said.

* * *

Are things getting much worse? In a 2003 paper, *Ending Homelessness: The Philanthropic Role*,[21] The National Foundation Group for Ending Homelessness found, at that time, that although an accurate count is elusive, because the "population is transient, turns over rapidly, and is difficult to locate," reliable estimates place the number of people experiencing homelessness, in 2003, at three to four million people every year, including more than 1.35 million children. They reported:

> Homelessness continues to increase in every region of the country. Principal causes include a dramatic decline in public investment in the creation of affordable housing, escalating housing costs in the face of stagnant or declining incomes, a rise in female-headed families living in poverty, and drastic reductions in public and private safety-net services that protect against homelessness. A focus on funding emergency shelters rather than systemic solutions allows the problem to persist.

Catastrophic personal events such as injury or illness, loss of employment, flight from domestic violence, substance abuse, and mental illness also contribute.

Experiences of extreme poverty and homelessness have devastating effects. Acute and chronic physical and mental illness dominate the lives of many homeless men and women. Women experience high rates of severe violence and abuse. Homeless children are sick more often, go hungry, have high rates of delayed development and mental illness, and have trouble attending school.

The Foundation, however was hopeful:

Along with the precipitous rise of homelessness in the U.S. has come a renewed sense that this problem can be solved. The federal government has dedicated more than $1 billion to fund local housing and services and has recently reactivated the Interagency Council on Homelessness. States and communities are crafting detailed plans to end homelessness rather than simply treat it. More than a decade of program and policy development has produced a range of tested and evaluated services to eliminate the effects of being homeless. A cross section of the community – government agencies, private foundations, businesses, nonprofit service providers, and concerned citizens – are now rallying together to realize the vision of ending homelessness in America.

That was 2003. In the year following the report, on June 30, 2004, Angela Alioto presented Mayor Gavin Newsom with her task force's Ten Year Plan on Ending Homelessness in San Francisco. Federal funding followed and Care Not Cash, PHC, Housing First, Direct Access to Housing Program, harm reduction, homeless prevention programs, a medical respite center, detox centers, and a behavioral health treatment system became San Francisco's formal response to the problem. And four years later, in 2008, Angela told the Greater Kansas City Chamber of Commerce, "There's been a 26 percent decrease in overall homelessness and a 40 percent decrease in street homelessness." When we did the Bi-Annual Homeless Count in 2011, San Francisco reported that 12,601 individuals had exited its homeless rolls since January 2004.

Still, San Franciscans rank homelessness as their number one problem, many question the reliability of the homeless count, and, at this writing, professionals in the field worry that the problem is about to get much worse.

The National Alliance to End Homelessness and The Homeless Research Institute issued *The State of Homelessness in America 2012*[22] in January of 2012. In it, the authors note that between 2009 and 2011, a time of economic downturn, homelessness decreased 1 percent. The decline, they speculate, "was likely due to a significant investment of federal resources to prevent homelessness and quickly re-house people who did become homeless. The Homelessness Prevention and Rapid Re-Housing Program (HPRP, funded through the American Recovery and Reinvestment Act of 2009) was a $1.5 billion federal effort to prevent a recession-related increase in homelessness." During the first year of operation, HPRP assisted nearly 700,000 at-risk and homeless people. The report noted that it appeared the government "was successful in achieving its goal of preventing a significant increase in homelessness." Still, it says, "there is much reason for concern."

Economic and demographic variables linked to homelessness persist. "Homelessness is a lagging indicator, and the effects of the poor economy on the problem are escalating and are expected to continue to do so over the next few years." Why? HPRP money has run out in many of the communities that had some success reducing homelessness, and the program ended completely in the fall of 2012. Debt and deficit reduction legislation will further shrink federal aid. The Report notes that "In the year since the data in this report was collected (January 2011), there have already been reports that the number of homeless people is increasing. So while holding the line on homelessness between 2009 and 2011 was a major accomplishment of federal investment and local innovation, the failure to sustain this early recipe for success threatens to undermine progress now and in the future."

Since the future of any society rests upon its youth, we have reason to be concerned. A study (January 2007) by the National Scientific Council Center on the Developing Child at Harvard University, *The Science of Early Childhood Development: Closing the Gap Between What We Know and What We Do*,[23] stated:

The future of any society depends on its ability to foster the health and well-being of the next generation. Stated simply, today's children will become tomorrow's citizens, workers, and parents. When we invest wisely in children and families, the next generation will pay that back through a lifetime of productivity and responsible citizenship. When we fail to provide children with what they need to build a strong foundation for healthy and productive lives, we put our future prosperity and security at risk.

Are we investing wisely in children and families? Homeless families? Homeless children? In the tiny Marshall Islands, there is little to distinguish family from community. As noted earlier, the embassy in Washington portrays the Marshallese society *as* family:

> The concept of family and community thus remain inextricably intertwined in Marshallese society. People still consider grandparents, aunts, uncles, cousins and far-flung relatives among their closest family. The strong family ties contribute to close-knit communities rooted in the values of caring, kindness and respect.

The reader will recall Milañ telling me about the Marshallese sense of community, when she first saw all the homeless people in the Tenderloin and said, "There are no homeless back home.... We have family."

Is the American community's commitment to family revealed when we read:

Homeless Students Top 1 Million, U.S. Says, Leaving Advocates 'Horrified'
Saki Knafo and Joy Resmovits
Huffingtonpost.com
Posted: 06/28/2012 6:34 pm
.... reported that, for the first time, the number of homeless students in America topped one million by the end of the 2010-2011 school year. These kids live in shelters and on the streets, and increasingly in hotels and on the couches of friends and relatives.... The government report said 1,065,794 homeless kids were enrolled in schools in the 2010-2011 school year, an increase of 13 percent from the previous year and 57 percent since the start of the recession in 2007.
"The number is horrifyingly high but it probably is half of what the number really could be if the kids could be counted," said [Diane] Nilan [a homeless advocate]. The count doesn't include homeless infants, children not enrolled in school, and homeless students that schools simply failed to identify.

The article goes on to report that only 52 percent of the homeless students who took standardized tests were deemed to be proficient in reading, and only 51 percent passed math tests. It noted that if children don't have a permanent place to stay, they have to change schools frequently, falling behind academically and socially.

* * *

In the Promise of the Inner City class, during the first two meetings of spring semester 2013, as we prepared to participate in the next Biannual Homeless Count on January 24, we reviewed the previous classes' work and the articles and reports that followed. We noted that, beginning in the 1970s, and then taking a leap in the early1980s, we, as a nation, experienced a wave of homelessness, unprecedented since the Great Depression of the 1930s. During the last few years, we were able to "hold the line" on its expansion, and actually reduce the number of homeless people by 1 percent, according to comparative analyses of the 2009 and 2011 Point-in-Time counts, but much of that success—and it wasn't much—was due to stimulus money that ran out in the fall of 2012. Was another outbreak of homelessness about to erupt? Another wave about to wash over us? "What can *we* do to make a difference?" I ask my students. "Is there any hope at all?"

In 2011, San Francisco's Point-in-Time count was 6455. In 2013, it was 6436. In 2015, 6686.

Notes

1. Fagan, Kevin, "Street Singer Popular With Downtown BART Riders Succumbs to Diabetes," *SF Chronicle*, June 30, 1999.
2. Fagan, Kevin, "Finding Faith in Their Songs / Street performers' harmonies belie lives of poverty, discord," *SF Chronicle*, February 24, 1999.
3. Fagan, Kevin, "Street Singer Popular With Downtown BART Riders Succumbs to Diabetes," *SF Chronicle*, June 30, 1999.
4. The names of homeless dead here were taken from "District 5 Diary," http://district5diary.blogspot.com/2012/07/27-homeless-deaths-in-2010.html
5. See http://www.huffingtonpost.com/2011/12/23/national-homeless-persons-memorial-day_n_1166908.html for article and images.
6. See "District 5 Diary," http://district5diary.blogspot.com/2012/07/27-homeless-deaths-in-2010.html
7. See "District 5 Diary," http://district5diary.blogspot.com/2012/07/27-homeless-deaths-in-2010.html
8. In October, 2012, PHC started "Everyday Connect," see http://blog.sfgate.com/cityinsider/2012/10/29/daily-project-homeless-connect-gets-underway/
9. http://www.swords-to-plowshares.org/

10. Not her real name.
11. http://www.sfexaminer.com/local/2011/01/cities-depend-homeless-count-federal-funding-process-questioned#ixzz2CKE4BgXY
12. See "A Hard Straight" PBS film on what works (Milestone) and what doesn't at http://www.pbs.org/independentlens/hardstraight/revolving_door.html.
13. See United States Interagency Council on Homelessness, "2011 San Francisco Homeless Count Report," http://www.usich.gov/
14. Tucker, Jill, "S.F. schools struggle with more homeless kids," *SF Chronicle*, December 4, 2011.
15. *Ending Homelessness: The Philanthropic Role.* The National Foundation Advisory Group for Ending Homelessness, 2003. www.nfg.org.
16. http://www.usich.gov/media_center/news/2011_san_francisco_homeless_count_report_released/
17. "SOH 2012: Chapter One-Homelessness Counts" Report, January 17, 2012, National Alliance to End Homelessness: http://www.endhomelessness.org/library/entry/soh-2012-chapter-one-homelessness-counts
18. Worth, Katie, "Methods for counting San Francisco's homeless questioned," *San Francisco Examiner*, January 26, 2011.
19. Knight, Heather, "Homeless dad featured in The Chronicle finds new jobs, plenty of hope," *SF Chronicle*, April 28, 2013.
20. As noted earlier, The City's official count of moving people out of homelessness is 12,601.
21. *Ending Homelessness: The Philanthropic Role.* The National Foundation Advisory Group for Ending Homelessness, 2003. www.nfg.org.
22. *The State of Homelessness in America 2012*, National Alliance to End Homelessness and The Homeless Research Institute, January 2012, http://msnbcmedia.msn.com/i/MSNBC/Sections/NEWS/z-pdf-archive/homeless.pdf
23. National Scientific Council Center on the Developing Child at Harvard University, www.developingchild.net

CHAPTER 13

The Secret Garden

TENDERLOIN NATIONAL FOREST

© The Author(s) 2016

D. Stannard-Friel, *Street Teaching in the Tenderloin*,

DOI 10.1057/978-1-137-56437-5_13

The place was a wilderness of autumn gold and purple and violet blue and flaming scarlet and on every side were sheaves of late lilies standing together – lilies which were white or white and ruby. He remembered well when the first of them had been planted that just at this season of the year their late glories should reveal themselves. Late roses climbed and hung and clustered and the sunshine deepening the hue of the yellowing trees made one feel that one stood in an embowered temple of gold. The newcomer stood silent just as the children had done when they came into its grayness. He looked round and round.

"I thought it would be dead," he said.

"Mary thought so at first," said Colin. "But it came alive."

Frances Hodgson Burnett,
The Secret Garden

* * *

No one remembered that its real name was "Cohen Place." Everyone just called it "Shit Alley." Feces, used syringes, and used-up people littered the pavement; desperate streetwalkers took desperate johns there; and contractors, working in more affluent neighborhoods nearby, dumped their junk there.

Then a majestic, 15′ tall, metal gate went up, closing off unfettered access. A garden of colorful flowers and lush bushes was planted. Cobblestone walks were laid, a kiln constructed, a fountain, and beautiful art adorned the walls of the three tall buildings that contained the alley. The wooden fence that ran along one side was covered with exotic murals and paintings of neighborhood people. Sculptures were placed in an island of grass and plants. Lights were strung overhead and a photo shed built, inviting visitors to take their own pictures and tell their own stories. A tall, slender, young redwood tree sprung from the ground. Then another one. A sign went up with the alley's new name: "Tenderloin National Forest."[1]

* * *

"Shhh." The mom gently shook each child. "We have to go." It was the middle of the night, long past the time they should have left. Months, maybe years past. Grandfather had chastised them, "Go! Go!" Other family members had already left the country. But with so many children, how could they leave? Little by little, everything they had worked so hard for, everything that they had built together as a family, was taken away. The war was over, and so was their life in Vietnam. Eight children. So many, how could they get away? It was dangerous leaving. It was dangerous staying, especially if—when—the communist government found out that the father had served in the South Vietnamese Army. As ethnic Chinese, called "Hoa" in Vietnam, they were already being persecuted. There was nothing left to keep them here, anyway. Quietly, they gathered up the children and slipped off into the night. It was time to start a new life.

They began their escape by "vacationing" in the countryside. It was 1978, three years after the fall of Saigon. Their livelihood, a wholesale food business, had been confiscated by the new regime. Two generations of hard work wiped clean.

Midnight. A truck took them down to the river where a small boat waited, sloshing about in the troubled water. A storm was brewing. They climbed on board. It was at this moment that they joined the legion of "boat people" who had been fleeing since the end of the war, but just now, in this year, were beginning to flood other Southeast Asian countries in unprecedented numbers.[2] Of the two million people who fled Vietnam after the war, 800,000 were boat people. It is estimated that one-third of them died at sea from drowning, starvation, disease, or were murdered by pirates. Others were raped, robbed, or taken and trafficked as slaves or prostitutes. These numbers were not known by those contemplating escape, but the stories, some real, some rumors, were circulating. This was not an easy decision to make.

For two days, they traveled downriver. Other refugees came on board. How many could this small boat hold? Fifty? Seventy? That was too many. Still, they came on board. A 163 in a boat three yards wide, nine yards long. The storm hit and battered them. They squeezed together for warmth and security. Frightened people told stories of their lives in Vietnam, before, during, and after the war, and what they had heard of those who already had left. Some were horrible stories, terrifying stories. A woman on board went into labor. Then there were a 164.

The storm chased the little boat as it entered the sea. For a month, waves battered and washed over it. The passengers clung together, parents and older children wrapped their arms around the littlest ones, who cried, and vomited, and held on for dear life.

The crew worried that there was too much weight on board. "Excess" items were thrown away, including everyone's shoes. The twins cried; they loved their sandals. The mom promised she would buy them new ones. All any one of them had brought to begin with were three outfits of clothing and some jewelry that could be used as barter in emergencies. Then the pirates arrived and took what they could find, including the mother's wedding ring.

Finally, the sun came out. Everyone was so happy. A ship with a big white cross on it led them to an island. At last! The little boat couldn't dock in the surf, so the passengers swam ashore. None of the eight children could swim. So, with one child at a time clinging to their backs, the parents swam ashore, back and forth until all were safe on an island that was uninhabited, with no drinking water.

Malaysian officials arrived and told them they needed to go back home. The government wanted nothing to do with Vietnamese refugees, afraid that their carefully managed Muslim society would be overwhelmed by pork-eating ethnic Chinese, which made up a large segment of the boat people, including the family with eight children. "They treat us worse than animals," the mother cried. "Go now!" the authorities demanded. But instead, the desperate boat people scuttled their boat. Going home was not an option. Now, there was nowhere to go and no way to get there. Boats arrived to take them all to a new refugee camp on Bidong Island. Back and forth, the parents swam to the boats, one child at a time.

In August of 1978, Bidong Island was officially opened as a refugee camp for boat people fleeing Vietnam, with an expected capacity of 4400 residents. Within months of the family's arrival, the population swelled to 18,000. Before they left, there would be 40,000, crowded into an area of about one square kilometer, less than two-thirds of a square mile, becoming, it was said, among the most densely populated places on earth: Pulau Bidong Refugee Camp, aka "Hell Isle."[3]

For three months they lived under a sheet of plastic. Rain was intermittent but a constant part of life there. When the sun did come out, so did the bugs in the sand, and the family would run into the sea to find relief. With help and supplies from other refugees, they built a makeshift hut, one among thousands on the island.

The community organized a system of distributing clean water and food. People used to running farms and small businesses established a bartering economy. The dad, taking his wedding band that he hid from the pirates, swam out to boats that came to trade with the refugees. He swapped the ring for a box of water apples, hoping to exchange them for more goods on the island and build on his precious investment as he had in Vietnam. But his kids and many other children on the island recognized this delicious, juicy, bright red fruit, also known as "the rose apple" for its beauty, as a delicious treat from home in tropical Vietnam, and they loved the apples, so he let them eat them all.

In an attempt to gather food, the dad fell and broke his foot. It was set by a volunteer doctor, one of a growing number of medical professionals provided by the international aide community. But with limited medical supplies and virtually no technology, working without proper equipment, the doctor didn't set bone correctly. The dad's mobility was significantly impaired. Mother now had nine people to care for.

After ten months on the island, the family was flown to Oakland, California, and a new life in America. Finally! The land of golden opportunity. Freedom! They were picked up at the airport and taken across the Bay Bridge to live in San Francisco, with the mom's brother in the Tenderloin.

* * *

I met Nancy Ong, number three of the eight children, in 1996, at BAWCC on Leavenworth Street, right around the corner from the brother's two-bedroom apartment that her family had moved into. The ten of them, eight kids and two parents, had joined the brother's family of seven, and Nancy's "baby uncle" who was living with them. Eighteen people in two bedrooms, a living room, a kitchen, and a bathroom. This sort of arrangement, usually with fewer bedrooms, would become commonplace in The TL as Southeast Asian refugee families were relocated there. They changed the nature of the community, as children, for the first time, became a prominent part of the neighborhood. Nancy was 11 when she arrived in America. When I met her, she was 28 and office manager for the Center. In the years since, she and Midge Wilson, the Executive Director of BAWCC, have been street teachers for Tenderloin U.

"I came here when I was eleven," she tells the Promise class in 2014. "I'm an old lady now." She laughs. Hardly. Tiny, pretty, with dark hair and eyes, a smile on her face most of the time, and an easy to come by laugh, she looks and acts a decade younger than she is.

"How are your kids?" I ask.

"All good!" she answers. Four girls, all born since I met her.

She tells the students her family's story of fleeing Vietnam and coming to America. "When we arrived here, eighteen of us lived in my uncle's two-bedroom apartment. My family slept on the floor for two months until we were able to get beds. Eight kids, two blankets, one for the girls, one for the boys." She chuckles at the memory. Hard at the time, it all turned out well. "We got help from the community. Section 8 housing in Bernal Heights. Eventually, I bought a house in the Excelsior District, and we all moved in." She was only 25 years old.

In the years since I first met Nancy, I have watched her and her family grow and succeed. I first met the mom at the ground breaking of Tenderloin Community Elementary School (a school that was built because of the persistent efforts, over ten years, of the women of BAWCC), shortly after I met Nancy. I had tea with her parents at their house in the Excelsior District, an ethnically diverse, historically working-class neighborhood on the southwestern side of San Francisco. A few of their other children were there, too. I was an honored guest. "In the Asian community," the father explained, "there are the children, above them parents, then the teacher." I was placed at the head of the dining room table and offered Kung Fu tea and afternoon snacks. At the time, I thought that Kung Fu tea was the hot drink they were serving me, but have since learned it is a Chinese ceremony of the ritualized preparation and presentation of tea. "Kung Fu" refers to not just a martial arts form, but also hard work and dedication. This certainly symbolized the lives of Donald Ong and Sue Ann Tang, Nancy's parents who fled Vietnam with their eight small children.

Shortly after the Ong family moved to the Tenderloin, the brother moved on, leaving them with the apartment on Ellis Street. They lived there for two years, as they learned to speak English, got their kids enrolled in school, and took what jobs they could, which at first meant being a stay-at-home dad for Donald, who was still suffering the poor repair of his broken foot. Sue Ann studied long hours to learn the language of her new country, got a job at a bilingual school until the grant that supported her position ran out, and then went to work in a "sewing factory" in Chinatown, pushing her employer to give her more work that she could take home to earn more money. She was so happy that public education was free in America, and made sure her children got everything they could out of it, but the whole family would work at night on pieces that Sue Ann brought home from the sewing factory. Eventually, she started her own sewing business. Donald's foot was looked at by doctors in his adopted country and the bone reset. He could now walk. And get a job! And he did, as a maintenance worker at Fisherman's Wharf. He also practiced Chinese medicine, a profession he learned as a young man growing up in China, before fleeing the Communist's revolution to Vietnam, then fleeing from them again to America. He introduced me to a client, a woman in a shop on Fisherman's Wharf, who spoke highly of his skill as a traditional medicine practitioner. It was hard, but life was good. Donald and Sue Ann never recovered economically, but all of their children succeeded. In the tradition of their culture, in the tradition of Kung Fu, the parents made sure the kids did well in school and life. When they went to college, the parents would visit them at campus on weekends. I mentioned this to my students when Nancy was talking to my class.

"Wasn't that hard?" one of my students asked, incredulous that the parents would sometimes sleep on the dorm room floor.

"It was normal for us," Nancy laughed, amused at the student's response. Nancy has her own American-born kids now, but is, herself, a woman of two cultures.

All the Ong children graduated from college. They went to work in business, engineering, computer science. Nancy is the only one to work in social service. She started at BAWCC in a part-time summer job in 1984, after she graduated from high school (she was only 15 years old, but her immigration papers had her as two years older, so she was placed two years ahead of her actual age-related grade), and has worked there ever since.

Nancy still lives in the Excelsior District house. The parents eventually moved in with another daughter, but Nancy and her brood live there now. When she married Dr. Calvin Gong, Nancy asked me about the origin of my last name, Stannard-Friel. "Stannard was mine, Friel was my wife's. We hyphenated them when we got married in Golden Gate Park in 1974," I told her. A hippie wedding.

"I like that," she said. "Maybe I'll do that. Nancy Ong-Gong. Onggg-Gonggg! Nancy Onggggg-Gongggg!" She cracked up. "I don't think so." In the tradition of her culture, she is still Nancy Ong, mother of the four Gong girls, American girls, all doing very well.

What would the eight Ong children's lives, and their children's lives, be like if Donald and Sue Ann had not secreted their family onto that boat in 1978 and taken that dangerous journey? They found refuge in the Tenderloin and cultivated a family of love and dedication to hard work and each other. They planted seeds and nurtured them. And like flowers in a garden, they came alive.

* * *

It's a beautiful day in San Francisco. Leavenworth Street is jumping. People are standing in line outside of the AIDS/detox clinic on the corner of Golden Gate, clustered alongside Mayflower Market at Turk, and dealing dope in front of Bahrah's Market and Deli across the street ("known as a good place to grab an Arizona Iced Tea and some smack"[4]). We're headed, again, to BAWCC at 318 Leavenworth, the tiny storefront office, invisible to most who walk and all who drive by, like so many of the nurturing, effective social service agencies in the Tenderloin. BAWCC has been ground zero for an amazing amount of creative ideas, public policy proposals, political action, and concrete outcomes since 1981, led almost all of that time by Midge Wilson, Nancy's boss. Because of the Center, The TL has five mini-playgrounds, Tenderloin Children's Recreation Center, and Tenderloin Community Elementary School, with an on-site family center run by BAWCC that includes a state-of-the-art dental clinic, computer center, counseling rooms, rooftop learning garden, beautiful library, and a welcoming family room.[5]

Every week, BAWCC works with nearly 600 children and women. Services and programs include a food pantry; a free clothes closet; an Angel Child Program that coordinates gift-giving for more than 350 children at holiday time; a Tenderloin Scholarship Program; a Parent–Child Program (with City College), teaching child development classes to mothers with preschoolers, women often isolated in SROs or tiny apartments, who become friends with, and supporters of, each other; the Tenderloin Youth Sports Initiative (the program Midge started with John Wooden, that she brought us into in 2002, and we have participated in with our annual sports clinic ever since) for over 500 children, including an ice skating program in partnership with the skating school at Yerba Buena Ice Skating Center. On their website,[6] BAWCC reports, "One young skater, Dinh Tran, has won more than 30 gold medals in Bay Area and national ice skating competitions. He is now working on his double axel, and has his eye on the Olympics. Coaches at the skating center have said they would not be at all surprised if Dinh made it all the way!" The Center also produces a Resource Directory and conducts neighborhood surveys, one that led to the initiative that resulted in Tenderloin Community Elementary School. All this, and more, from the little office on Leavenworth Street—with a "living room" area, where clients can rest and talk, a small conference room for community partners to explore neighborhood needs and ways to advocate for the poor, and the clothes closet—staffed by three women and a network of volunteers.

As the class settles on the coach, various chairs, and the floor, Midge's friendly golden retriever sniffs around to say hello, before settling down on the rug. Nancy tells us a quick version of her story coming to America, living in the Tenderloin, growing up in the city, and raising her four children there, before rushing off to pick them up from school and deliver them to after-school activities (Chinese school, ice skating, golf lessons). Midge tells us about the history, mission, and accomplishments of the Center.

In the previous class meeting, I had distributed a handout to the students, BAWCC's breakdown of the 2000 Census. The US government does not specifically report on the number of children living in the Tenderloin neighborhood. So, for several years, BAWCC did. Nancy and a UC Berkeley student intern would go out into the streets to knock on every door, ring every bell in the neighborhood. Their count of kids under 18 years of age was consistently around 4000. In the 2000 census, the US government census showed 3025, but most would agree that the "official" count was an undercount. Not only is Nancy a known member of the community who knows the community, she speaks five languages and dialects, giving her access to people who might not otherwise trust or respond to government representatives. But the 2000 census had very useful information on ethnicity and ages of residents in identified "census blocks."[7] BAWCC took the Census Bureau's findings for each census block in the Post to Market, Van Ness to Powell neighborhood, added them up, and came up with this demographic profile:

Tenderloin Census 2000
Race and Age

Total Population

White	10,594 (36.33%)
Black/African-American	2,898 (9.94%)
Asian	9,004 (31.02%)
Native Hawaiian/Pacific Is.	117 (0.04%)
Indian/Alaska Native	230 (0.78%)
Hispanic/Latino	4,796 (16.45%)
Some other race	113 (0.39%)
2 or more	1,403 (4.81%)
Total population:	29,155 (100.0%)

18-Years and Over

White	10,315 (39.48%)
Black/African-American	2,745 (10.51%)
Asian	7,582 (29.02%)
Native Hawaiian/Pacific Is.	98 (0.38%)
American Indian/Alaska Native	223 (0.85%)
Hispanic/Latino	3,854 (14.75%)
Some other race	103 (0.39%)
2 or more	1,209 (4.63%)
Total population:	26,129 (100.0%)

Under 18-Years

White	279 (9.22%)
Black/African-American	153 (5.06%)
Asian	1,422 (46.99%)
Native Hawaiian/Pacific Is.	19 (0.63%)
American Indian/Alaska Native	7 (0.23%)
Hispanic/Latino	942 (31.13%)
Some other race	10 (0.33%)
2 or more	194 (6.41%)
Total population:	3,026 (100.0%)

Illustration 13.1 Tenderloin Census

Before our first class meeting in the Tenderloin, I had asked the students to estimate the rank order by size of racial groups in the neighborhood. I've asked the same question to other classes and visiting groups new to The TL. Most guess that African-American is the largest population, followed by Hispanic, then white, then Asian. BAWCC's analysis revealed that, in the adult population, the largest group is white, followed by Asian, then Hispanic/Latino, then African-American at less than 11 percent. But among children, the breakdown is Asian, Hispanic/Latino, then white, and African-American.

"What's that tell you?" I asked the class.

"That the white and black are mostly single adults, and Asian and Hispanic are families?"

"That's right."

It was the end of the war in Vietnam that spurred the growth of Southeast Asian families in the Tenderloin, and the cost of living in San Francisco that has kept many of them there, as did village, family, common language, and cultural ties (ethnic grocery stores, holiday celebrations, social organizations). The same dynamics have attracted Hispanic families, especially in recent years, with the hipster/hi-tech worker gentrification of the Mission District that has pushed rents into the stratosphere and resulted in rent-controlled housing being converted into high-priced, owner-occupied units. With the arrival of refugees from Southeast Asia, especially Vietnam and Cambodia, came social services to meet their needs. Many were started by the refugees, themselves. Services for the Hispanic population have long been established in the Mission, and, for the most part, remain there. That may change as the current radical transformation of the Mission District continues. But existing services, even those organized to serve a particular ethnic group, have opened their doors to the growing number of "others" in the neighborhood: Yemeni, fleeing the battlegrounds and poverty of their homeland, people from Eastern Europe, Latin American refugees, African refugees, and domestic refugees fleeing poverty or family violence or rejection, often because of their sexual orientation, who wind up in the Tenderloin.

VYDC and IHDC's TAG, two of Tenderloin U's longtime community partners, were developed to serve families fleeing the aftermath of the war in Southeast Asia. For years, their clientele was almost exclusively Cambodian, Thai, Vietnamese, and Lao. The Boys and Girls Club, Tenderloin Children's Playground, Boeddeker Park, and TASP have all hosted Tenderloin U classes and partnered with us in service-learning projects. Most of the children, and many on the staff, were Asian when we first arrived. Today, to walk into the storefront office of VYDC, or the basement operation of IHDC (before it closed), or any of the other programs, is to walk into a multicultural, multiethnic, multiracial mix of children from all over the world. Southeast Asian kids still predominate, and the brown skin and high cheekbones of many of the Latino children are increasingly apparent. Black and white kids are still part of the scene. But little girls with hijabs run around the playgrounds and their older sisters attend our College Night in the Tenderloin. Moms in burkas gather in circles, speaking Arabic, at the Halloween in the Tenderloin Festival, while their children play the games in the Tenderloin Children's Playground gym, eat beef hot dogs, provided by SFPD, or jump in the bounce house outside. Sometimes the mothers join their children in the face-painting line to have one of my students paint the Yemeni flag on their face.

"Dr. Don, what's the Yemen flag look like?" a Streetwise student asked the first time that request was made. Usually, kids ask for butterflies, or flowers, or rainbows, or scary or clown faces, geometric designs.

"I don't have the slightest idea."

"No problem," the student said. "I'll google it on my phone."

A lot's changed since I rode with the cops on Leavenworth Street, 20 years ago. The whole world's changed.

* * *

Every year, after meeting for two weeks on campus, the Promise of the Inner City begins its community-based classes in Portsmouth Square in Chinatown, where the promise of the city that came to be known as San Francisco began. What is now a multilevel underground garage with a park on top was the original town plaza for Yerba Buena, the Mexican settlement that became San Francisco when Captain John Montgomery of the USS *Portsmouth* seized the square and raised the American flag there. The founding of the first public school in California is remembered on a plaque near the northwest corner where the school once stood. Civic buildings, saloons, bordellos, shops, gambling halls surrounded and occupied the plaza in the early years. The discovery of gold at Sutter's Mill was announced here in 1848, setting off the California Gold Rush in 1849, resulting in the 1850 admission of California as the 31st state, which was officially recognized, right here, with a 13-gun salute.

In spite of racist persecution, the Chinese community formed around Portsmouth Square, convinced the Caucasian city fathers that being allowed to remain (they were being told they had to leave after the 1906 earthquake) would be an economic tourist boom for San Francisco. The neighborhood became the largest Chinese community outside of Asia, and an economic success story. Every spring semester, the Promise class walks through the park on top of the garage, past dozens of Chinese people, many of them elderly, sitting or standing in small clusters, animatedly playing Go, or xiangqi (Chinese chess), or Chinese card games. Groups of women solemnly practice Tai Chi in the middle of the square. Children climb the jungle gym or swing on swings or dig in the sandbox in the playground near where a replica of The Goddess of Freedom statue stands, commemorating the failed democratic movement in Tiananmen Square in China. Laughter and shouts of delight punctuate the noise coming up from traffic on Kearney Street in this, the birthplace of San Francisco.

The Promise class stands on the bridge connecting the plaza to the Chinese Cultural Center in the Hilton Hotel on the other side of Kearney Street. We look at the tall buildings to the immediate east, where Yerba Buena Cove used to bring bay water all the way up to Montgomery Street, a block away, the main drag of today's Financial District, an entire neighborhood built on landfill that eliminated the cove, a worrisome development in earthquake country. Old ship parts, sometimes entire hulls, and other maritime artifacts are often discovered when a new office building's foundation is dug. A few blocks off to the northeast was the notorious Barbary Coast, San Francisco's original red-light district, serving the onslaught of thousands of mostly young men seeking their fortunes in gold in the Sierra foothills. A local nineteenth-century historian described the lawless district this way[8]:

> The Barbary Coast is the haunt of the low and the vile of every kind. The petty thief, the house burglar, the tramp, the whoremonger, lewd women, cutthroats, murderers, all are found here. Dance-halls and concert-saloons, where blear-eyed men and faded women drink vile liquor, smoke offensive tobacco, engage in vulgar conduct, sing obscene songs and say and do everything to heap upon themselves more degradation, are numerous. Low gambling houses, thronged with riot-loving rowdies, in all stages of intoxication, are there. Opium dens, where heathen Chinese and God-forsaken men and women are sprawled in miscellaneous confusion, disgustingly drowsy or completely overcome, are there. Licentiousness, debauchery, pollution, loathsome disease, insanity from dissipation, misery, poverty, wealth, profanity, blasphemy, and death, are there. And Hell, yawning to receive the putrid mass, is there also.

And so began the promise of San Francisco. California.
I turn and point toward the tops of buildings on a hill west of Portsmouth Square. "That's Nob Hill," I say. "On the south side is what came to be known as the 'Uptown Tenderloin,' then, and still, an entertainment district, with vice operations that were more upscale than those found in the Barbary Coast. Over the many years since, the Barbary Coast disappeared and now is a neighborhood of restaurants, professional offices, and shops. 'Uptown' was eventually dropped from the Tenderloin's name, as it became considerably less 'upscale.' That's where we'll spend the rest of the semester." I refer the students to the syllabus and remind them that, next Wednesday, we meet at the coffeehouse and will walk together to VYDC on Ellis Street.

* * *

July 21, 1981. Two young Asian men are engaged in conversation in front of Atherstone Apartments at 545 O'Farrell Street. One pulls out a gun, shoots the other in the head, and runs away toward Leavenworth Street. The wounded man screams, staggers toward Jones Street, and falls to the ground. Lam Trong Duong, founder of VYDC, is dead.

* * *

Every spring semester, after our meeting in Portsmouth Square, I bring the Promise students into the Tenderloin to meet the staff and young people of VYDC, as a way of introducing them to the positive, nurturing, dedicated organizations that work to serve the community. The syllabus reads:

The Promise of the Inner City is an exploration of reasons to celebrate life in the inner city. It includes an examination of the inner city as fertile ground for personal and social development. Learning outcomes include understanding the positive impact of government offices, private organizations, social services, community policing, the art community, and social activism on the lives of the people of the inner city, and, by extension, on all of our lives. The student will learn how the inner city may be viewed as a model and catalyst for broad-based social change. This will involve learning methods, opportunities, and skills used in service to the community – such as democratic leadership, community organizing, and cross-cultural communication – and developing empathy, sensitivity, and the appreciation of others, abilities and attitudes that are significant in building meaningful lives anywhere.

VYDC, the first Vietnamese youth center in America, was founded in 1978 by Lam Trong Duong. Originally housed in a single room in Glide Memorial Church, Lam Duong, coordinating his efforts with various Asian youth-serving organizations in Chinatown and other inner-city agencies, worked to meet the needs of newly arriving refugee Vietnamese youth who faced the challenges of acculturation, assimilation, limited parental involvement with school, the language barrier, gaining public assistance, housing and work, and isolation from mainstream society. Many of the 3,000,000 refugees fleeing the aftermath of the war in Southeast Asia—which, from 1887 to 1954, had been called "French Indochina," a grouping of French colonial territories—were unaccompanied young men and boys, overwhelmed by anxiety, depression, and PTSD. Unprepared for life in America, they were susceptible to criminal street life in our inner-city neighborhoods.

Lam Duong was not a typical refugee from Vietnam. The son of a lieutenant colonel in the South Vietnamese Army, he came to America even before the Vietnam (American) War ended. He studied philosophy and mathematics at Oberlin College in Ohio, noted for its liberal values, including being the first institution of higher learning in America to regularly admit women and African-Americans to a previously all-white male student body. Joining American peers (he was the only Vietnamese student at Oberlin), Lam Duong became active in the antiwar and civil rights movements of the era. After graduating, he moved to San Francisco to work with Vietnamese refugees who were flooding into the country after the fall of Saigon. He settled in the Tenderloin, where many of the poorest of his countrymen, people who had lost everything, like the Ong family, or had little to begin with, were being relocated. He took a special interest in the *boi doi*, "dust of life," boys and young men without families, who had escaped on the boats on their own or had been separated from loved ones along the way.

In the Tenderloin, he organized young Vietnamese to tutor others, produce cultural events, and strengthen ties to their Asian roots. He became involved in a "Pro-Vietnam" movement, a term used by antiwar Vietnamese refugees to distinguish themselves from pro-Communists. But he also published a progressive, Vietnamese-language newspaper, called *Cai Dinh Lang*, that, in addition to his articles about refugee housing and civil rights, reprinted stories from Hanoi, supporting the new government in Vietnam and its leader, Ho Chi Minh.

Ho Chi Minh was a French-educated, Communist revolutionary, who began his fight for the liberation of Vietnam during World War II. France justified its 67-year-long colonial occupation as a "necessary" measure to protect Catholic missionaries and their efforts to impose Christian values on the Vietnamese. It was also convenient to economically exploit the country and its people as Europeans had been doing in Africa, India, South America, and other places for centuries. During World War II, when the invading Japanese occupied his country, Ho Chi Minh began his revolution. When Japan was defeated in 1945, the French reoccupied the country, and Ho Chi Minh's fight continued.

In 1954, the Geneva Conference was established to deal with ending the Korean conflict and other Cold War issues. With the imminent defeat of the French by the Việt Minh (Ho Chi Minh and his Communist brethren), the Conference issued an accord to dismantle the colonial administration, establish an interim government, and arrange a pathway for Vietnamese independence. The Geneva Accord "temporarily" separated the country into two zones: the North, to be governed by the Việt Minh, and the South, by the State of Vietnam, headed by former emperor Bảo Đại. It was proposed that free elections be held by July 1956 to unify the country. This was "acknowledged," but not agreed to by the State of Vietnam and the USA. It was reluctantly signed by Ho Chi Minh, under pressure from China and the Soviet Union. The elections never took place. This failure of reunification led to what came to be known as the Vietnam (or American) War. In North Vietnam, this meant Communist control, backed by China and the Soviet Union. In South Vietnam, this led to a concentration of power in a series of corrupt, military governments, held together by the USA.[9]

In America, the zeitgeist was shifting from waging war to waging peace. The Baby Boom Generation was growing into young adulthood. The largest cohort ever born was a transition generation that bridged the Industrial Age (machines, standardization, and mass production) and the Age of Information and Communication (electronics, diversity, and accelerated change). Their collective consciousness was being shifted by new technologies that produced and encouraged a loosening of the ties that bind us, called for new ways of thinking and being (a paradigm shift), impacting all of our most fundamental institutions: family (separating sex from marriage), education (women's studies, black studies, ethnic studies), economy (service and computer-based), religion (for many, individual "spirituality" replaced organized religion), politics (massive

protests), and language ("Far out!"). A large segment of the new generation pushed the limits of this shift even further, with its music, dancing,
meditations, mushrooms, weed, LSD, and other kinds of mind-altering,
"consciousness-raising," experiences. And with it came their own culture:
its norms ("Don't lay your trip on others"), values ("Peace and love"),
and symbols (long hair, tie-dye, bell-bottoms, the peace sign). And they
believed that they could change the world. One of the first things they
were going to do was put an end to that "goddamn war in Vietnam."

Muhammad Ali refused to be drafted, saying, "No Viet Cong ever called
me nigger." Young men burned their draft cards. Peace marches drew
thousands. Rallies were held to denounce the war. Returning American
fighters founded Vietnam Veterans Against the War. One of them, John
Kerry, later a US Senator and Secretary of State, testified to the US Senate
Committee on Foreign Relations,[10]

> We found ... that all too often American men were dying in those rice pad-
> dies for want of support from their allies. We saw first hand how monies
> from American taxes were used for a corrupt dictatorial regime. We saw
> that many people in this country had a one-sided idea of who was kept free
> by the flag, and blacks provided the highest percentage of casualties. We
> saw Vietnam ravaged equally by American bombs and search and destroy
> missions, as well as by Viet Cong terrorism – and yet we listened while this
> country tried to blame all of the havoc on the Viet Cong.

Actress Jane Fonda visited North Vietnam in 1972. She was photographed sitting on top of an antiaircraft battery, earning her the nick-
name "Hanoi Jane." Bob Dylan, Joan Baez, Pete Seeger, County Joe
MacDonald, John Lennon, Bruce Springsteen, and Jim Morrison and
the Doors sang protest songs. Demonstrators shouted, "One, two, three,
four, we don't want your fucking war!" and "Hey, hey, LBJ, how many
kids did you kill today?" Buttons with less confrontational messages read,
"Make love, not war!" and "Draft beer, not boys!"

It was in this context, in this country, that Lam Duong wrote his articles and reprinted stories from Hanoi in his newspaper, *Cai Dinh Lang*.

Most of the displaced refugees, especially the boat people who had
risked their lives and those of their loved ones fleeing Vietnam, hated the
new regime in the homeland. For many of these refugees, the Pro-Vietnam
members were traitors, Communist sympathizers, or worse, Communists
themselves. Anti-Communists, including many former members of the
Vietnamese military, organized "Freedom Fighter" groups, vowing to bring

the war back to Vietnam. To them, Vietnamese war protesters here were not just political opponents, but enemy combatants.[11] Lam Duong was so identified. On July 21,1981, the day he was murdered on O'Farrell Street, AP received a communiqué from the Anti-Communist Viet Organization (ACVO), claiming that its "Shock Squad" had assassinated Lam Trong Duong, "a Vietnamese Communist infiltrating the US since 1971."[12]

Was Lam Duong murdered for his political views? Probably. Or was he killed for other reasons? No one, except those responsible, knows for sure. SFPD investigated ACVO and other suspected individuals and organizations, but never did solve the crime. VYDC, initially labeled a Communist front by some of the militants, continued to operate and evolved to become one of San Francisco's premier youth-serving organizations. VYDC describes its current status this way[13]:

VYDC has ... grown from a one-room office offering translation services, English as a Second Language and vocational classes, to a locally and nationally-recognized multi-service center serving all youth, of all backgrounds, throughout San Francisco.

The mission of VYDC is to empower underserved Asian-Pacific Islander and urban youth with the knowledge and confidence to define their future and reach their full potential. We do this by developing leadership skills, supporting academics, providing job opportunities, and strengthening relationships with family and community.

The seed that Lam Duong planted in the Tenderloin blossomed into a vibrant organization that has been serving the needs of thousands of young people since 1978. And for more than a decade, VYDC has been a community partner of Tenderloin U.

* * *

The Promise of the Inner City class walks by the men hanging around outside the VYDC office on Eddy Street. Usually drunk or stoned, they are an animated group, but keep pretty much to themselves and have never been a bother to us, but some of the teenage VYDC girls complain that they have been harassed as they walk by. We enter the door leading into the storefront operation. The 16 of us (15 undergraduate students and me) stir up the already lively gathering of mostly young Southeast Asian staff and Center members. The room is brightly painted, decorated with paintings of the homelands and photographs of youth who are a part of VYDC in one way or another.

We're greeted by Yen Dinh, a refugee from Vietnam (I first met Yen in 1996, with David Tran, then a program director at VYDC, when I was first learning about the neighborhood). Yen grew up in the Tenderloin. With her MSW degree, she could get a better-paying job, but loves working here. We follow her down the aisle, between two rows of desks, a worktable, a couch, and a few scattered chairs. Kids on either side are busy working or socializing, but most look up and smile as we walk by. Some of these VYDC youth have been here when other Inner City classes came by, and many have come to College Night or the Halloween in the Tenderloin Festival. It was a nice welcoming for us, especially for those Promise students who are having their first experience in the Tenderloin, after our initial community-based meeting of the semester the previous week at Portsmouth Square in Chinatown. The walk here, today, was a long walk through The TL, so seeing the smiling, young, enthusiastic faces here is a relief for the Tenderloin U rookies.

Yen introduces the students to Judy Young, VYDC's Executive Director. Judy's mother fled Laos with her children to Thailand, when Judy was only a year old. Laos, a landlocked country surrounded by Vietnam, Cambodia, Thailand, Burma, and China, is another sad story of French and Japanese occupations and the Vietnam (American) War. Waging a secret war against the Pathet Lao communist insurgency fighting the monarchy, the USA dropped "more than two million tons of ordnance on Laos during 580,000 bombing missions – equal to a planeload of bombs every eight minutes, twenty-four hours a day, for nine years – making Laos the most heavily bombed country per capita in history."[14] Innocent villagers fled their homes. Hundreds of thousands of civilians, including Judy's family, left the country. As with Cambodia and Vietnam, Laos came under communist rule after the war, and is now considered one of the most corrupt governments in the world.[15]

Judy's family waited in Thailand until the father could escape and join them. That took six years. Judy was seven when the family reunited in a refugee camp, came to America, and settled in the Tenderloin.

Judy joined in VYDC's activities as a teenager, before graduating from SF State, coming back to the Center as a staff member, and working her way up the organizational ladder. Even after getting married and starting a family, she lived in the Tenderloin until 2002, when she and her husband bought a house in the Bayview District.

Yen, Judy, and the Promise class are chatting outside Judy's office, when Phoeut Tak joins us. Phoeut ("Put"), a Cambodian-American, was born, raised, and still lives in the Tenderloin. To me, she looks much younger than her 28 years. She is short and feminine, but with an appealing edge of street savvy about her. Phoeut is an accomplished member of the VYDC leadership team, and has been active in, among many other things, bringing teens to College Night and the "A Christmas Carol" performance.

I met Phoeut a few years ago, but have known her younger brother, Mikey, for about a decade, as a participant in many of our programs and events since he was in his early teens. In addition to our ongoing Tenderloin U projects, Mikey was in the audience when U Sam Oeur read his poetry at IHDC and participated in a several Youth Philanthropy workshops, when we partnered with DonorsChoose to teach teenagers from IHDC, VYDC, the Boys and Girls Club, the playground, and other programs about philanthropy. The workshops went like this: DonorsChoose gave groups of 15–25 teens up to $3000. The teens used the money to support public school teachers' projects that are posted, as proposals, on the DonorsChoose website. Workshop participants had to decide, as a group, which to fund. The problem was, there are a lot of very good proposals and, although given a generous amount to distribute, limited funds relative to requests. So passionate debate, negotiation, and strategizing fill the room with enthusiastic chatter as individuals and small teams urge support for one project or another. Participants sometimes decide to partially support many projects, rather than fully support just a few, or mix the awards with full and partial funding.

It's not always just TL kids that attend the workshops. On one occasion, we held an all-day conference/workshop on the NDNU campus in Belmont, bringing together high school students from the Tenderloin, more affluent communities down the peninsula, and East Palo Alto, a poor community that lost its access to business tax revenues when neighboring cities greedily annexed commercial areas surrounding the small, historically black community that in 1992 earned the undesirable distinction of being "The murder capital of America."

On another occasion, a young woman from a well-to-do Silicon Valley high school, on a CBL, three-day stay-over in the Tenderloin with her classmates, argued in support of a project that was designed to help autistic school children. "Why give it to them?" a fellow student asked, not as a challenge, but because there were so many other good causes in the schoolteachers' proposals on the DonorsChoose website. The girl ran off a surprisingly long and informed list of reasons why, and concluded with this convincing appeal, "My brother has autism," she said, her voice rising to a near wail, "but my father doesn't *believe* in it. But it's *real!*" The project got fully funded.

Phoeut leads us down the stairs to the basement work, activity, and conference rooms. Youth, mostly Asian, but also a few black, white, Hispanic, and Middle Eastern, sit at rows of computers. Staff members work at desks on the far side of the large room. A few wave, but Phoeut takes us off in the other direction to an area lined with rows of folding chairs. Blank sheets of butcher paper are taped to the wall in the front of the "classroom."

"This is Alex Abalos and Thear Chum," Phoeut says. The two 20-something-year-old men, standing at the front of the room, wait for us to settle down. Alex I know from previous visits. Among other responsibilities here, he has taught kids computer technology, including how to make documentary videos. Thear is new to me. They introduce themselves—Alex, a Filipino, has professional musical ambitions; Thear, born and raised in Stockton, California, a city with a large Cambodian refugee population, including his own family, is a recent UC Berkeley grad and plans on pursuing his MSW degree. The two men introduce VYDC's programs.

Alex and Thear give a brief history of the Center, explain that over the years VYDC has built a community of "encouragement and empowerment" for thousands of Southeast Asian youth and other disadvantaged kids. The primary mission is to provide assistance, education, and opportunity for immigrant adolescents, American-born kids from immigrant families, and other urban youth to develop themselves and their communities. Annually, VYDC serves over 650 young people between the ages of 12 and 24.

Alex lifts the blank butcher paper to show more sheets of butcher paper underneath, with VYDC programs listed on them in thick, black ink:

AFTER SCHOOL ENRICHMENT:

Academic Support

Computer Technology Classes

Cultural, Social and Recreational

Activities

HEALTH AND WELLNESS:

Asian Youth Prevention Services (AYPS)

Case Management

Life Skills

LEADERSHIP DEVELOPMENT:

Empowering Southeast Asian Youth

(ESAY)

Tobacco Free Project

YOUTH EMPLOYMENT SERVICE:

Mayor's Youth Employment and

Education Program (MYEEP)

San Francisco Young Adults Working

(SFYAW)

Illustration 13.2   VYDC Programs list

Over the years, I've seen the remarkable success of VYDC's programs. Adolescents enthusiastically engaged in academic achievement programs, conducting projects designed to make the Tenderloin a healthier place, and participating in confidence-building experiences. And I have been in the audience during informed and articulate presentations, performances, and productions.

It was one of their productions that first led me to VYDC.

I was hanging around IHDC, talking to Sam Soun and some other teen workers. Sam asked if I had seen the video, "a.k.a. Don Bonus." I hadn't, and he told me where I could get a copy, "VYDC."

"a.k.a. Don Bonus: The life of a Cambodian refugee in USA"[16] tells the story of Solky ("Don Bonus") Ny, Sam Soun's cousin, one of many living in the Tenderloin, navigating his senior year at Balboa High School, while struggling, with his family, to survive life in the projects. At home, his windows are smashed by neighborhood youth; his sister's house is broken into and everything, including all the furniture and appliances, is stolen; the family is threatened; his brother is arrested for attacking a fellow student with a knife (the brother had suffered constant harassment and threats). The family is eventually relocated to the Tenderloin, then to Section 8 housing out in the Avenues, which seems like Paradise to Don and his family.

The documentary was a collaboration with VYDC and filmmaker Spencer Nakasako, who taught VYDC teens video production and guided Don through a year of self-filming. Using a shoulder-mounted video camera (this is before cell phones), Don captured his life in class, talking to teachers and guidance counselors, hanging out with friends in The TL, partying, being with family during holiday celebrations, being sad over family relations, musing in the bathtub, discovering the results of the home burglary, visiting his brother at Youth Guidance Center, graduating from high school, and much more.

The video won a National Emmy Award and was shown at the Berlin International Film Festival.

After filming "a.k.a. Don Bonus" in 1995, the year I came back to the Tenderloin, Spencer filmed "Kelly Loves Tony" (1998) and "Refugee" (2002), the story of Mike Siv returning to the country his mother fled from, to visit his father, who did not, and David Mack and Sophal (Paul) Meas, Cambodian-Americans who were making their first visit to the land of their ancestors. David and Paul had previously enrolled in Tenderloin

U classes. David, street savvy, maybe too street savvy, was the one who, when stabbed in the stomach, decided it was time to change his life. He was not a very engaged student in my class when it came to academics. He participated enthusiastically in discussion and made important contributions, but term papers and reflection essays were not his thing. Later, he became a charismatic street teacher for other classes, but he was hard to understand. "He's speaking Ebonics!" Keesha, one of my campus-based students said, when David talked to the Promise class that facilitated the Kansas City panel discussion and tour. David looked confused by her comment. He was just talking.

Paul, ever sincere, brought money to Cambodia from his mom to help a sister, who he never met, left behind when his family fled, build a house. And he gave away almost all of his own money to relatives there. He took his studies with me very seriously, is now a dad living in The TL, and coaching basketball at the YMCA. Mike never took my classes, but did talk to one at VYDC as a street teacher. Recently, he went back to Cambodia to film his own documentary, one of several he has done over the years.

* * *

The Tenderloin is ground zero for street crime, homelessness, the mentally ill, the prostituted, the drug addicted, and other victims of social problems that we, as a society, just aren't willing to take on in meaningful and productive ways. Instead, we place unprepared young refugees in environments that we know produce negative outcomes; we abandon the mentally ill to the streets; we blame the homeless for being homeless, discounting the socioeconomic forces that produce the problem in the first place; we put trafficked tweens in juvenile detention, then, after living the life from 12 to 18, we declare them to be criminal adults. We create our own problems. Then we blame the victim. Fortunately, at least for the children of the Tenderloin, there's the Yellow Brick Road.

* * *

The Yellow Brick Road works its way around the corner of Golden Gate Avenue, across the street from St. Anthony's kitchen, and climbs up Jones Street, past a cluster of men in dark blue jumpsuits, preparing for a day of street cleaning, needle pickup, and graffiti removal, and under the shuffling feet of men and women passing money and drugs to each other at a spot so well known that their business is inquired about on Yelp: "jason of the funky persuasion says: when's the best time to cop OC at turk and jones?"

"What is it?" I asked one of Boys and Girls Club members, of the yellow "brick" rectangles painted in the middle of the sidewalk to look like a path. "Safe passage for kids," he said.[17]

"What is it?" my students always ask. "Safe passage for kids," I say. The pathway running down Leavenworth Street, branching off at Eddy and Turk, looping its way around the corner of Golden Gate Avenue, traveling up Jones Street hill, turning left at Ellis, and reaching its final destination, Tenderloin Children's Playground, is an outcome of a collaboration between neighborhood groups, led by Dina Hilliard. On their website,[18] Tenderloin Safe Passage reports:

> With an estimated 4,000 children living in only a half square mile, the Tenderloin neighborhood is home to the densest concentration of children and families in San Francisco. However, when these children leave their homes they face a neighborhood with the highest concentration of sex offenders in California, open drug dealing, and the constant threat of violence. The Tenderloin Safe Passage Program grew in response to street safety concerns expressed by Tenderloin families.

Dina Hilliard, then Executive Director of North of Market/Tenderloin Community Benefit District (NOM/TCBD), before she founded and assumed leadership of the new service program, Tenderloin Safe Passage, explained the evolution of the Yellow Brick Road to my Promise class, and her own evolution in The TL. Raised in the Midwest, she graduated from Central Bible College in Missouri, and took a job sight (more accurately, "site") unseen, teaching at City Academy, a small Christian school in San Francisco. Her dad drove her across the country, the car loaded with everything she needed to start her new life in the beautiful "City by the Bay." When they arrived, he took her right to the school, located on Jones Street in the Tenderloin, a quarter block from the walkway through Boeddeker Park, still known, then, as "running the gauntlet." A man was shooting up in the doorway to the school.

"OK, look," her dad said, "we can just turn around right now and they'll never know. They'll just think you never showed up."

"But, I wasn't scared," Dina told the class. "I was curious." She got out of her dad's car, said her goodbyes, taught at the school for seven years, went on to work for neighborhood service organizations, and became an important member of the Tenderloin community.

I met Dina when she enrolled as a neighborhood resident in my Promise class, but had to withdraw when she assumed the Assistant Director position at NOM/TCBD. A community benefit district (CBD) is an NPO funded through property assessment, established by a vote of local property owners, to improve public space. With NOM/TCBD, this includes such services as sidewalk cleaning, beautification, needle pickup, neighborhood greening, street fairs, improving lighting, graffiti removal, and other activities that make the neighborhood safer and more desirable to live and work in. In addition to greening and cleaning, TCBD has sponsored concerts at the Cadillac Hotel and in Boeddeker Park, community health and safety fairs, the Asian Heritage Street Festival, and the Safe Passage Street Program, aka "The Yellow Brick Road."[19]

The Yellow Brick Road is actually a very long mural, painted on the sidewalk, a winding path that links many of the neighborhood youth programs. Other murals sponsored by NOM/TCBD include "Windows into the Tenderloin," on two sides of a building at Golden Gate and Jones, that depicts the neighborhoods' past, present, and utopian future; "Humming with Life," a musical garden with humming birds on Hyde; and "Fear Head," a three-headed monster that feeds on fearful emotions in the neighborhood, on Golden Gate Avenue.[20]

It is interesting that it's the historically poorer neighborhoods that celebrate their uniqueness with mural art (many of San Francisco's can be seen at sfmural.com).[21] The Mission District is well known for its murals throughout the neighborhood, but especially on 24th Street and its tributary, Balmy Alley, emphasizing the community's Latin American, especially Mexican, heritage, the people's indigenous roots, and the civil rights movement in the USA. The Women's Building on 18th Street houses programs that advocate self-determination, gender equality, and social justice, and symbolizes its commitments on its exterior, which is covered with large images of women of the world. Down near 16th Street, across from the Mission police station, is Clarion Alley, devoted to a more hipster, but still, mostly, political rendition of street art.[22] To go down Haight Street is to take a walk-through the neighborhood's psychedelic past, with images of mushrooms and rainbows, rock stars and kaleidoscope explosions. And in The TL, murals celebrate the community, its unique history, and its children. "The Gift You Take is Equal to the Gift You Make" is on Leavenworth near Golden Gate; its yellows and purples and greens and blues catch our attention every time a class walks up the hill to visit a street teacher. The Precita Eyes website,[23] a program in the Mission that sponsors street art throughout the city, describes it this way:

> "The Gift You Take is Equal to the Gift You Make" celebrates the gifts that the community brings and receives in the Tenderloin neighborhood including diversity, varied backgrounds, and rich cultural heritages and experiences. The "SS New Tenderloin" breaches the turbulent ocean and arrives from distant lands, bringing the various people who will make the neighborhood their home. As the children leave the ship, they join others, and grab the rope [a common Tenderloin practice, to guide groups of children through the neighborhood] to traverse the streets. They head for "National Family Night Out", a scene of fun, art and entertainment for all. As they cross the space, they approach neighborhood landmarks such as the Hibernia Bank, and the Cadillac Hotel with its portrait of community leaders, Kathy and Leroy Looper.

"Windows into the Tenderloin" by Mona Caron, one of the murals sponsored by NOM/TCBD, wraps around the corner of Golden Gate and Jones. The artist has this to say about her work[24]:

> The mural has several "windows" that show various views of the neighborhood, each with intricate descriptions of the street scene there, and different references to history, local legends, and a collaboratively envisioned future dreamscape of the community.
> Countless little details in this mural were added in direct response to spontaneous interactions with the local population while painting. Among other things, they include just under 300 little figures based on real people

of the neighborhood: not civic notables and heroes, but anyone there who wanted to be a part of it. This mural is therefore a time-capsule documenting this neighborhood's street life during a time that narrowly preceded a period of accelerated change in this City.

Across the street from "Windows" is the Boys and Girls Club— Tenderloin Clubhouse, one of our longtime community partners. Phanna Phay worked there for a long time and was a regular street teacher for our classes, before getting married, starting a family, and moving on to work at The Exploratorium on the Embarcadero, San Francisco's famous hands-on museum of "science, art, and human perception." Sammy Soun worked at the club, receiving accolades, including a national award for his work on child nutrition, but left recently when his class schedule at Skyline College clashed with his work schedule. Now he works for MYEEP (the Mayor's Youth Employment and Education Program) at VYDC. Another longtime Boys and Girls Club street teacher is Kay Weber, the Art Director. He had his kids contribute to Mona's "Windows" mural by decorating ceramic, hand-size "seeds" for the utopian panel of what might come from what is now. A group of my students molded blank seeds for the project, because Kay worried that some of his kids were too young to make the forms. Kay spoke to my classes at the Boys and Girls Club over several years, we observed children working in the art studio, and I knew him to be a dedicated, hardworking, and talented art teacher, living in the apartment building that also houses the Boys and Girls Club in the heart of the Tenderloin, before I discovered what a remarkably talented artist he is, that he had an MFA from the University of Hamburg, has shown at prominent galleries in America and Europe, and was recognized by the State of California for "inspiring and mentoring underprivileged children to develop their creativity and self-esteem."

One day, when I was visiting on my own, he asked if I would like to see a piece he made that had just come back from the Oakland Museum of California's "Day of the Dead" exhibit.

"Sure," I said, and to myself, *Oakland Museum?* I was surprised, not yet knowing of his incredible creativity and accomplishments.

He took me into the art studio and there, on the wall, was a wild woman.

4′ × 8′, made out of a single sheet of white paper, I didn't realize at
first that the "black" was empty space, showing the color of the backboard
it was attached to. He had cut out the image, "Hel, Goddess of Death,"
with a manicuring scissor and an X-Acto knife. Skeletons danced around

the perimeter of the cutting, the volcano Pele was erupting, a Viking warship sailed across the sea, souls emerged from cauldrons, delicate symbols surrounded and made up body parts of the mermaid Goddess, with withering snakes for hair and Māori face tattoos, hovering over flames of the underground.

"Kay, that's incredible! What does it mean?"

"I made it a year after my mother's death. It was a way I mourned her and connected with the cycle of life and death. It was inspired by her."[25]

We both stood there staring at the Goddess. His mother must have been quite a woman.

* * *

You are invited to a reception for

Seeds of Hope

The Art of Kay Weber
and
the Children of the Tenderloin.

Thursday November 1, 2007
All Saints Day/Day of the Dead

Exhibit in Gellert Library 5:00 p.m.
Reception in Wiegand Art Gallery 6:00 p.m.
Notre Dame de Namur University
1500 Ralston Avenue
Belmont, CA 94002

Come, celebrate the future! See the bounty of the autumn harvest, the art and crafts of the children of the Tenderloin, as they honor the lives and deaths of their ancestors in Asia, Africa, Europe, the Americas and all those places where the ancient bones of loved ones lie buried, bringing forth new life And come honor the good work of Tenderloin playground and program directors, who plant seeds of hope in young hearts and minds. Produced by NDNU's Sr. Dorothy Stang Center for Social Justice and Community Engagement, in partnership with the NDNU Department of Art, Boys and Girls Club of SF-Tenderloin Clubhouse, Tenderloin Children's Playground, Indochinese Housing Development Corporation, and Tenderloin After-School Program.

Exhibit will be in Gellert Library from October 30 – December 31, 2007.
Contact Dr. Don Stannard-Friel, 650-508-3770 for information.

Illustration 13.3   Seeds of Hope flyer

* * *

On February 12, 2005, 74-year-old Sister Dorothy Stang, a member of the Sisters of Notre Dame de Namur (SND), the founding order of NDNU, and a 1964 graduate of then CND, was assassinated in Brazil for her decades-long work protecting the indigenous people, poor farmers, and rain forest of the Amazon. Her death, similar to many hundreds of murders in Brazil in the recent years before her death, was unique in that the wealthy instigators of the crime were convicted and actually went to prison. It is also unique that the murder prompted worldwide outrage and honors. Martin Sheen commissioned a painting of Dorothy, and wrote a prayer for her; Greenpeace held a memorial protest in front of the presidential palace in the Brazilian capital; *National Geographic* wrote about her in its January 2007 issue; and Tarcísio Feitosa da Silva, a recipient of the 2006 Goldman Environmental Prize, created a Dorothy Stang Memorial mosaic; Sister Roseanne Murphy, SND, wrote *The Martyr of the Amazon*; Binka Le Breton wrote *The Greatest Gift: the Courageous Life and Martyrdom of Sister Dorothy Stang*; a documentary, "They Killed Sister Dorothy," by Daniel Junge, narrated by Martin Sheen, won the Audience and Competition Awards at the South by Southwest (SXSW) Film Festival; an opera, "The Angel of the Amazon," was composed by Evan Mack; PBS and CNN did special reports on her life and death; and a feature-length film is underway. So is a call for her canonization as a martyr.

In 2007, I was appointed Director of our new Sr. Dorothy Stang Center for Social Justice and Community Engagement. We held special social justice-oriented events and offered programs related to community engagement for NDNU faculty, staff, students, and the greater community; invited Dorothy's brother to campus, to honor her and her family; and held a fund-raising luncheon, hosted by the actor, Marin Sheen, who was so involved in protesting her death to the world because his own family had been helped through difficult times by the SNDs when he was growing up. Of all the powerful and significant honors and accolades following her death, among the most moving and meaningful, were words expressed at her vigil the night before her funeral at St. Lucy's Church in Anapú. In this gathering of people who work the land, it was proclaimed, "Dorothy is not buried, she is planted!" Throughout the world, ever since, these words have been repeated, as people celebrated and mourned her life, work, and death.

"Dorothy is not buried, she is planted!" I said, opening the art exhibit, "Seeds of Hope: The Art of Kay Weber and the Children of the Tenderloin," on campus. The children made sugar skulls, paintings, drawings, statues, spirit catchers, and street altars, commemorating All Saints' Day/Day of the Dead. Some did their own miniature version of Kay's "Hel: Goddess of Death." Standing majestically in front of all the other works of art was the Goddess herself, mounted on a new wooden stand, built and painted red by the maintenance guys at NDNU just for her. The show was supposed to last for two months, but the Goddess stood in the library for a year. So did some of the kids' work, but not the sugar skulls. They were taken down when the librarians discovered that they had been invaded by ants. Lots of ants, inside little works of art that were seeds of hope.

* * *

Inner-city neighborhoods, like the Tenderloin, have always been fertile ground for artists of one kind or another. The (relatively) cheap rent, cheap and ethnically diverse restaurants, and stimulating street scene have drawn writers, performers, and artists to The TL since its beginnings. Dashiell Hammett lived and wrote his detective stories here. William Vollmann wandered these streets, researching *Whores for Gloria*,[26] a novel about the bar life and street prostitutes working the Hyde and Larkin Street corridors. The Grateful Dead practiced their music here, as did Creedence Clearwater Revival and Jefferson Airplane (Jefferson Starship). Billie Holiday sang her songs here. Miles Davis played his horn here. So did Dizzy Gillespie. Pearl Ubungen taught dance at Children's Playground, choreographed shows in her studio at St. Boniface Church's old community building, and performed "Take Me to the Tenderloin, Now!" in Cohen Alley, as it was transitioning from Shit Alley to Tenderloin National Forest. Artist and art collector Justin Giarla, a Tenderloin U street teacher since 2005, opened his Shooting Gallery, an art gallery, on Larkin Street. His brief bio is on the gallery's website[27]:

Shooting Gallery opened its doors in 2003 to the historic Tenderloin district of San Francisco; one known for its diverse culture and history. Owner and curator, Justin Giarla, founded the space to offer a welcoming environment for viewing the art he loves. Taking up collecting art at the age of 23, Giarla has since amassed over 500 pieces in his own collection. Growing up in Southern California gave Giarla an affinity with pop art, street art, and outsider art. Giarla has long since recognized the necessity to provide lowbrow artists with a platform, which is exactly what Shooting Gallery has done for a full decade. In addition to the exhibition of leading shows in pop surrealism, figurative realism, and color abstraction, Shooting Gallery also participates in art fairs around the world and hosts annual fundraisers for local nonprofits. Since opening Shooting Gallery, Giarla has gone on to start his own publishing company, and as of February, 2013, has expanded White Walls and Shooting Gallery into a 5,000 sq ft state of the art gallery space, featuring two new project spaces.

That's all true, but not his whole Tenderloin story.

I first became aware of Justin when I read about him in 2004 in *The Chronicle*. He had been arrested for dealing dope out of the Shooting Gallery. "How ironic," I remember thinking. A year or so later, a story came out about a filmmaker renting the gallery to shoot a porn movie. "I've got to meet this guy, Justin," I said to myself. I called him up, went down to the Tenderloin, met him, and asked if he would talk to my class. "Be happy to," he said. And he has, every year, ever since.

* * *

March 12, 2012. The Promise class is sitting on the floor of 941 Geary Street, a big, old warehouse that Justin recently leased and remodeled for a new art gallery. We met him at the Shooting Gallery on Larkin Street, across from New Century Theater, a strip joint and after-hours night-club. He walked us down Myrtle Street, the alley that runs alongside the Shooting Gallery, past murals on the building's wall, painted, in part, by residents living in the halfway house on the floors above the art gallery, and brought us through the back door of his new gallery called, simply, 941 Geary. We entered a cavernous room, with walls of brick and natural wood ceiling and support beams. Large paintings of exotic-looking women, draped in robes colored with intricate patterns, dominated by rich reds, hung from the wall. A notice describing the show read[28]:

> *New Works by Hush* continues the artist's unique style, recognizable through its focus on geisha-like women set within backgrounds filled with an expressionist's freedom of layering and color. The serene balance of traditional Eastern art is combined with a messier passion, influenced by Western traditions of action painting and graffiti, culminating in a harmony that feels surprisingly natural. The artist's mark-making bears the distinct aesthetic of tagging, bringing the rough texture of street art into each piece.

Justin is wearing a loose-fitting white tee shirt and jeans; tattoos cover both his muscular arms; his thick, brown hair is combed straight back; he sports a buzz cut mustache and goatee, and sideburns; and he's looking out through rectangular nerd glasses. He has an easy smile, which he shares with the students, as he plops down on the floor in front of them.

I introduce him: "This is Justin Giarla, founder of the Shooting Gallery, White Walls Gallery, and now this new gallery," I say, gesturing at the man sitting on the floor. "He's a major player in the Tenderloin art scene and beyond. He's got a story of what all this is," I wave my hand around the room, "and how it came to be. He definitely represents the promise of the inner city. Justin?"

"Hello everyone," he says. "Thanks, Don. How long we been doin' this?"

"Seven years. Since 2005. This is the eighth time."

"Wow! Yeah, well, cool, lots happened in that time. Where to start?"

And Justin tells the Promise class his story.

Justin was a skateboarding, dope-toking, wild child, growing up in Southern California. He skipped most of his high school classes, but went to school most days anyway, to study and do ceramics, art, and photography. Somehow, he managed to graduate. ("There were fewer requirements then, and I think they were happy to see me go.") Two weeks later, his dad dropped him off in Tahoe. He was 18 years old. "Tahoe had my three favorite things," he told us, "drugs, skateboarding, and art."

He stayed in Tahoe for three years, mostly partying, using every drug imaginable, until he broke a rib snowboarding. That must have been a wake-up call. He joined AA, got clean and sober, and moved to San Francisco. He was 21.

"I got a job in San Francisco, working in a restaurant, did my skateboarding and art, and stayed sober. Then, I got a job in a nightclub as a bar back, and started to make some real money in tips."

"What's a bar back?" a student asked.

"The bar back helps the bartender. They get ice, wash glasses, cut lines, hold the mirror up to the bartender's nose while they're working … bar back shit."

That got a chuckle out of the class.

"With that, my ten-year career in bars began. I'd get my own little art shows here and there, worked my way up in the nightclub business, bartender, eventually general manager. I worked at four different nightclubs, learned how to deal with people, manage people, get people to show up for an event. I was shot at, broke up fights, learned CPR. I was around people constantly, people who were constantly high, constantly drunk. And I was clean and sober the whole time, managing small clubs, big clubs, events with 5000 people. Nothing fazes me now. It gave me confidence. By 30, 31, I was burned out, working 8:00 p.m. to 8:00 a.m. Last year and a half, I started doing drugs again.

"I had taken a vacation in Europe. On a train, my friend offered me a beer and I figured, 'What the hell.' And it starts again. The last year I worked in nightclubs, we'd work until 8:00 a.m., bartenders, security, then we'd get shitfaced, *at 8:00 a.m. in the morning*, go home, sleep, go back to work at 8:00 p.m., and start all over again. I was making $90,000 a year, but I just walked away. I had it. I didn't want to be one of those nightclub 40-year-olds who look 10, 20 years older than they are, hanging around nightclubs, being 'cool.' But all I knew was art, skateboarding, getting high, and nightclubs.

"It was December 2002. I was at a Christmas party, all drunk and high. I think, 'I'm going to start an art gallery!' I didn't know anything about running an art gallery, but I knew how to run a business, market a business, advertise an event, get people to come. Manage people. In February, I signed a lease for 839 Larkin Street. But I didn't have enough money to start up, so I sold drugs and continued to sell drugs, pay the rent, postage stamps, bills. First month I made $2000, with $6000 expenses. First year didn't make money. Kept it going on drug sales. But in March 2004, four undercover cops came in. Had been watching me for months. Arrested me. Found a loaded Glock, $7000, crystal meth, a pound of cocaine. 'You're going to prison!' I was definitely shitting in my pants."

Justin's family and friends bailed him out of jail and he hired the best lawyer he could find. He tried to keep the arrest quiet, but the lawyer told him that wasn't going to happen. His arrest had made *The Chronicle*. "The headline read 'The Art of Selling Drugs,'" he told the class. That's when I first read about him. "The next few months were hell!" he said. "Some lowbrow artists gave me a high five. Others pulled out. Others didn't care, one way or the other." After a convoluted process of court dates being postponed, a switch of judges, more publicity about the porno movie being shot in the gallery ("Justin, what were you thinking?" his lawyer chastised him. "You have to keep a low profile!"), and his involvement in stopping a man from beating a woman outside a bar he was working in while the legal process unfolded, an experience that turned out to be helpful to his own case when the judge learned that he had stopped the attack, called the police, and testified in court. His crimes were reduced to misdemeanors and he received an eight-month house arrest sentence.

"A total fucking nightmare ended. I'll never go down that path again!" he told us. "A miracle, that's how I feel about it. I had the best fucking lawyer in San Francisco!" Justin could work eight hours a day while on house arrest, but had to be home the rest of the time. "So between the eight hours at the gallery and working at home, I worked on the gallery 24/7. I was obsessed. This is what I *had* to do!" And he had to do it legitimately.

"In 2005, I expanded into the space next door to open White Walls Gallery, specializing in street art, lowbrow art."

"What's lowbrow art?" Alexis asks.

"Lowbrow art is hotrod art, comic art, tattoo art, skateboard art. Street art. When street art crosses the threshold of the gallery, it's 'contemporary art.' 'Lowbrow art.'"

For Justin, there is no real separation between the gallery and the street. When he first opened the Shooting Gallery, he had to move crack-heads out of the doorway all the time. That was too much. "But when street guys came in to see a show, they were respectful. They came in and enjoyed the show. Told me what they liked and didn't like, 'Hey, Justin. This is my favorite show.' Or, 'it isn't.' They took it seriously. Art can bring all kinds of people together. Like a nightclub, anybody can come. In a nightclub, it's all about the music. In an art gallery, it's all about the art. It's for everyone. I try and treat everyone with respect, no matter who they are."

Justin also felt he had to give back, especially after his "miracle" happened. He volunteered at Hospitality House, a program for the homeless that offers, among other services, free use of art supplies and studio space. He opened up White Walls Gallery for the annual Hospitality House Art Auction fund-raiser.

One of his earliest artists was Shepard Fairey in 2004. That was before Fairey's iconic Obama "HOPE" poster fame. Still, the show almost sold out. "We made $22,000. He was stoked and so was I. In 2006, we did another Fairey show. We made $170,000. Half goes to the gallery owner. I bought a house. I never thought I'd own a house! In 2008, with the Obama publicity, we took in $1.2 million. Totally insane! If you love something, if you care about something, if you work hard, you can make it happen. My stepdad can't read. My mom spent all they made on clothes. We got kicked out of our house and lived in a motel. Still, I learned I can do anything if you work hard and really want to do it. Luck helps."

In 2009, the recession began to hit his business, hard. "Every bill was paid late. Everybody was cool, they knew they'd get paid, but I was working my ass off, hoping that lightning would hit." That something good would come along to change his luck.

Lightning struck again. Its name was Eine.

Justin had set up a show with Ben Eine, a British graffiti artist, a then not-so-well-known artist, except in the street art world. After booking the show, but before it opened, British Prime Minister David Cameron presented President Obama with a gift of Eine's "Twenty First Century City." It turns out that Eine is a favorite of the Prime Minister's wife, Samantha. Ben Eine gained instant widespread fame and his show at 941 Geary was a smashing success. Justin and Eine split $300,000 from the show. The artist wanted to buy an apartment in San Francisco with his share of the proceeds, but Justin told him, "You can't buy an apartment in San Francisco for that kind of money." But they could, and did, use the money as a down payment on an old, but beautiful, brick former garage on Geary Street, and turn it into the newest location for White Walls and Shooting Gallery.

Justin told my students, "Anything you want, anything you are passionate about, willing to work hard for, willing to sacrifice for, you can make happen. Miracles really don't just happen. You have to play the game to win the lotto. Just don't sell drugs."

Seven months after the Promise class's visit to White Walls/Shooting Gallery, *Complex* magazine, a cutting-edge, award-winning, New York-based media platform for youth culture, especially Millennials, with 120 million unique users per month, published a list of great art galleries. In an article titled "The World's 100 Best Art Galleries,"[29] Layla Bermeo wrote,

With art fairs booming all over the globe, we know more about international contemporary art than ever before. Young artists and the galleries who love them are still taking notes from earlier generations of Conceptualists and Minimalists, but engaging with new media, style, and dialogue coming out of burgeoning scenes in places like Istanbul, Oslo, and São Paulo. Today, "art world" actually refers to nearly the whole world, and as part of this global awareness we see famous names of the 20th-century sharing wall space with brand new talent. Galleries that specialize in street art are commanding as much attention as blue-chip spaces, and "the next big thing" could literally turn up anywhere. So where can you go to see the newest of the new, and the best of the best?

Where *can* you go? Try number twenty-nine on the list of 100 Best Art Galleries in the World. White Walls Gallery.

The article continues, "A big gallery with big ideas, White Walls taps into the urban art scene, elevating street-based art to fine art. Their artists draw inspiration from everything from comic books to surrealist painting, creating diverse shows that keep us wondering what will come next." And so the garden grows.

* * *

My first days back in the Tenderloin were actually nights, walking the streets and riding with the cops. All of my—and most other people's—preconceived notions of the Tenderloin were reinforced by the night-time street life I encountered: Big D and the Fish Stick Gang on Crack Corner, Southeast Asian gamblers in the coffee shop on Hyde, street-walkers in Tendernob and all the way down the slope of the hill, drug deals all over, crazy people, homeless people, scary people. Then I went to a police community meeting and met Ana Bolton, "Star," the woman I would write about in *City Baby and Star.* She was running Adopt-A-Block at the time, a community-organizing agency, whose mission was to "Take back the Tenderloin, building by building, block by block." She was working with volunteers to clean up the neighborhood and trying to find out how to meet the needs of people living in The TL. I saw another side of the community. She was also on the board of Promise, an organization working to help women leave prostitution, and she introduced me to Rev. Glenda Hope, founder of Promise and Executive Director of San Francisco Network Ministries. Glenda was well known for developing programs that would serve the needs of the poor, then spin them off for others to run, while she would start up another program. I had previously met with Glenda's husband, Scott Hope, through an old friend, Jacque Spencer-Davis, then of BAWCC. I had briefly met Scott before, when he was a philosophy professor at San Francisco State and I was a lecturer in sociology there. At his San Francisco Network Ministries office, he introduced me to the concept of "containment zone," when he described the dynamics of the Tenderloin that he and his wife had been working in for so long. Scott died not long after our reintroduction, but Glenda has become a longtime street teacher for Tenderloin U and offers the conference room in the beautiful apartment building she and Scott built for poor refugee families on Ellis Street for our classes.

Through Ana and Glenda, I began connecting with other service providers and attending other community meetings. At one, I met Jim Thompson, who was running San Francisco Community on Patrol (COP) and managing two hotels for the aged and disabled. He invited me to walk the streets with him at 6:00 a.m., when he would check out the early morning street scene and fax the police his report on goings-on that weren't supposed to be going on. Then we'd head over to Aunt Charlie's Bar on Turk Street, a long-established gay bar and neighborhood hangout, with its two locally famous transgender bartenders, Delores and Delicious, for morning coffee and conversation. It was Jim who introduced me to Halloween in the Tenderloin in 1998. I joined him and a group of old-timers from his hotels, a homeless guy who lived behind the McDonald's on Van Ness, then Sergeant "Big Red" Garrity from SFPD, a Hasting's College of Law student, and other neighborhood volunteers who were organizing one of two Halloween celebrations at the playground that year. The staff of Tenderloin Children's Playground had been holding its own, separate Halloween celebration on the Fridays before Halloween for years. Halloween in 1998 fell on a Saturday, and in 1999, it would be on Sunday, and Jim's group was planning the festival on the evening of the holiday, itself. As a result, Halloween events were being held on two different nights, independent of each other, at the same location. I had been hanging around the playground, getting to know Diana Chin, Kay Rodrigues, and other staff members there, and as I connected with both groups, I realized that there was some tension, and suggested they merge into one festival. Diana, graciously (because, as senior playground director, the site was her turf, and she and her staff had been running the holiday celebration, even in the basement and patio of St. Boniface Church, before the Ellis Street playground was built), joined the next COP meeting, and beginning in 2000, there has been a single, grand celebration ever since. A few years later, Jim retired to Costa Rica. I integrated the event into Streetwise Sociology, and we became core community partners with Diana and Kay and the other playground directors in the Halloween in the Tenderloin Festival, signing up 50 neighborhood safe sites for trick-or-treating (taking over a COP project) and recruiting 70 or so volunteers, most from NDNU and neighborhood youth groups, and disc jockeys, at first friends of students, then from KMEL radio station. Recently, we were joined by street crossing monitors from Dina Hilliard's Tenderloin Safe Passage program. We raise funds, make posters and staff badges, solicit donations of prizes, pumpkins, and candy, and rely on SFPD to obtain

300 hot dogs, drinks, and chips for Tenderloin goblins and witches, mon-
sters and princesses, and superheroes and villains, from all over the world,
who come to play games, win prizes, bounce in the bounce house, get
their faces painted, carve pumpkins, do art projects, compete in "donuts
on a string," push their faces into whipped cream and pumpkin pies in the
pie-eating contest, and play musical chairs.

At the suggestion of Nancy Ong, we developed the College Night
in the Tenderloin program in 1999. Since 2000, we have facilitated
the NDNU theater department's musical, "Scenes from A Christmas
Carol" at the Seneca Hotel, later moved to Boeddeker Park, then to the
Children's Playground, and, recently, back to the Seneca. Midge Wilson
encouraged us to do the sports clinics beginning in 2002. DonorsChoose
gave us the idea and resources to organize philanthropy workshops. PHC
brought us together with thousands of homeless people, narrowing the
physical and emotional distance between "them" and "us," as did St.
Anthony's, the Glide kitchen, and the Bi-Annual homeless count. We
engaged the compassionate, creative, and thoughtful energy of North of
Market Planning Coalition (NOMPC), Lower-Eddy Street Task Force,
Leavenworth Corridor Task Force, The Outreach Workers Coalition,
Vietnamese Family Services Agency, COP, SAGE, the Boys and Girls Club,
Tenderloin Children's Playground, VYDC, IHDC, TNDC, TASP, THC,
SFPD-Tenderloin Station, The Salvation Army, The YMCA, Coalition on
Homelessness, Hamilton Family Center, Boeddeker Park, the Sheriff's
Department, the Shooting Gallery/White Walls Gallery, the Luggage
Store Art Gallery/509 Culture Club, San Francisco Network Ministries,
Larkin Street Youth Center, Faithful Fools, City government, De Marillac
Academy, and merchants and residents and other community organiza-
tions and individuals. These are the people who make a difference; they
are the neighborhood gardeners. The Tenderloin is the Secret Garden.

Notes

1. Tenderloin National Forest was a project of Darryl Smith and Laurie Lazer,
cofounders, directors, and curators of The Luggage Store, an art gallery on
Market Street, and 509 Culture Club, a small gallery right next to TNF on
Ellis. Since 1991, they have created and sponsored an incredible variety of
art-related projects and programs that have deeply benefitted the neighborhood without gentrifying it.

2. See http://www.americanforeignrelations.com/O-W/The-Vietnam-War-and-Its-Impact-Refugees-and-boat-people.html for a discussion about the emergence of the boat people.
3. See https://www.youtube.com/watch?v=7F_xNVu_vww and https://www.youtube.com/watch?v=sJsfc9PS6ds for videos and discussion about Pulau Bidong Refugee Camp.
4. Dalton, Andrew, "Tenderloin Deli To End Heroin Sales, Pay City $30K, *SFist*, July 17, 2012: http://sfist.com/2012/07/17/tenderloin_deli_will_end_late-night.php
5. See http://www.bawcc.org/about_bawcc/
6. http://www.bawcc.org/youth_sports/
7. "Generally small in area. In a city, a census block looks like a city block bounded on all sides by streets. Census blocks in suburban and rural areas may be large, irregular, and bounded by a variety of features, such as roads, streams, and transmission lines. In remote areas, census blocks may encompass hundreds of square miles." Blogs: census.gov/2011/07/20/what-are-census-blocks/
8. Lloyd, Benjamin Estelle, Lights and Shades of San Francisco (1876) in Herbert Asbury, The Barbary Coast, An Informal of the San Francisco Underworld, New York: Thundermouth Press, p. 100.
9. See http://alphahistory.com/vietnam/geneva-accords-of-1954/
10. "Vietnam Veterans Against the War Statement by John Kerry to the Senate Committee of Foreign Relations," http://www2.iath.virginia.edu/sixties/HTML_docs/Resources/Primary/Manifestos/VVAW_Kerry_Senate.html
11. See Coburn, Judith, "Terror in Saigontown, U.S.A.," *Mother Jones*, February/March 1983
12. Coburn, Judith, "Terror in Saigontown, U.S.A.," *Mother Jones*, February/March 1983.
13. http://mycbo.org/mycbo/profile/vydc-esay/
14. "Secret War in Laos," Legacies of War, http://legaciesofwar.org/about-laos/secret-war-laos/
15. See Transparency International's "Corruption Perceptions Index," http://www.transparency.org
16. "a.k.a. Don Bonus," in Spencer Nakasako Trilogy, directed by Spencer Nakasako, produced by Aram Sui Wai Collier and Emunah Yuka Edinburgh, Associate Producers Mike Siv and Judy Chea, in collaboration with VVDC Youth DVD Crew, 2002.
17. See YouTube video on Yellow Brick Road at www.youtube.com/watch?v=N0Z666O2aIg
18. http://tenderloinsafepassage.org

19. See //www.youtube.com/watch?v=N0Z666O2aIg for a YouTube video on the Yellow Brick Road.
20. See http://www.tlcbd.org/programs-services/
21. See http://www.sfmuralarts.com for a display of SF neighborhood murals.
22. See http://www.streetartsf.com/tag/clarion-alley/ for visual of Clarion Alley.
23. http://www.precitaeyes.org
24. See:http://monacaron.com/murals/windows-tenderloin#sthash.6Wdccs52. dpuf
25. See Kay's website for the inspiration and explanation of the symbols in the Goddess paper cutting at http://www.kayweberartstudio.macmate.me/ KayWeberArtStudio/Papercutting/Pages/Hel,Goddess_of_Death.html
26. Vollmann, William T., *Whores for Gloria*, New York: Penguin Books, 1994.
27. http://www.shootinggallerysf.com
28. See Past Shows + Exhibitions : 941 Geary Gallery, SF, www.941geary. com/shows/
29. http://www.complex.com/style/2012/10/worlds-100-best-art-galleries/

CHAPTER 14

Trendy Loin

TWITTERLOIN

© The Author(s) 2017
D. Stannard-Friel, *Street Teaching in the Tenderloin*,
DOI 10.1057/978-1-137-56437-5_14

"it's no use going back to yesterday, because I was a different person then."

Alice in
Alice's Adventures in Wonderland,
by Lewis Carroll

"Hello, Dr. Stannard-Friel." It was a woman calling me on my office phone at NDNU. A writer from a New York woman's magazine. "I understand you are an expert on San Francisco's Tenderloin District."

"I know the Tenderloin."

"Well, we're doing an article on the neighborhood. On how it's becoming absolutely trendy." The writer mentioned a "chic woman's apparel store" that I never heard of (so much for my "expertise"), and Bourbon and Branch, a "speakeasy" on Jones. That I did know.

"Absolutely trendy?" I said back to her. "That's not gonna happen." But I might've been wrong about that.

* * *

Brad Paul was the first to tell us about zoning laws that were passed in the 1980s, designed to protect the Tenderloin from gentrification. He was speaking to the Promise class in the old Salvation Army chapel, before Joan B. Kroc, widow of the founder of the McDonald's Hamburger empire, left the national organization $1.5 *billion*, and the Tenderloin hotel, offices, chapel, and decommissioned homeless center in the basement, that we stayed in for a week in 2001, was torn down and replaced by the beautiful, new Salvation Army Kroc Community Center. Brad had been Deputy Mayor for Housing under Art Agnos, the mayor made famous by the homeless encampment in front of City Hall that came to be known as "Camp Agnos." After Agnos lost his reelection bid, Brad moved on to other significant community leadership positions, but always stayed active in fighting for the welfare of the Tenderloin poor.

Brad graduated from Williams College in Massachusetts and headed west in the 1970s. He settled for a while in the Cadillac Hotel on Leavenworth and Eddy, the same building that has housed BAWCC— with no rent raises—for more than three decades. Leroy Looper and his wife Kathy bought the hotel in 1977 and turned it into the first nonprofit SRO hotel in California providing affordable housing and support services, pioneering and becoming a national model for supportive housing. A former heroin addict and alcoholic, Leroy had previously opened Reality House West out on Guerrero Street in the Mission (after founding a similar program in New York City), and before that a drug treatment program in the Fillmore that police routinely raided and arrested addicts, waiting for treatment, for drug possession. He met with the chief of police, arranged an accommodation, and a career so illustrious unfolded—cofounding the Tenderloin AIDS Clinic with Rev. Glenda Hope; Chateau Agape board-and-care home for the mentally ill; YouthBuild USA, helping underprivileged kids build homes and learn job skills; "Concerts at the Cadillac," a free musical series at the hotel, designed to "uplift and inspire," that included artists ranging from Motown to the San Francisco Symphony, and much more—that he became known as the "Father of the Tenderloin."

He died with his boots on.

Leroy finished a speech at his college reunion, talking about his programs and how he appreciated his education at Antioch College West (Leroy received his bachelor's and master's degrees from there in 1980 and 1981, and an honorary doctorate from St. Michael's College in Vermont in 1993), sat down, and passed out. Four days later, on September 11, 2011, at the age of 86, Leroy Looper was dead from heart failure. His legacy lives on, but trouble (depending on your point of view) may (or may not) be brewing on the horizon.

For years, neighborhood improvement in the Tenderloin did not seem to encourage gentrification. In 1980, Richard Livingston—former director of the pioneer runaway and homeless youth program Huckleberry House (founded during the Summer of Love in lower Haight to house "flower children" descending on the neighborhood. Police raided Huckleberry shortly after it opened and arrested the staff for "contributing to the delinquency of a minor." Willie Brown, then Assemblyman, later Mayor, was hired and managed to get the charges dropped), currently the managing director of the innovative Exit Theater in the Tenderloin—was working for Leroy at Reality House West and the Cadillac. A longtime community activist, Richard obtained federal funding to organize a group of community service providers and VISTA volunteers, calling them the NOMPC.[1] This occurred at a time that three major hotel chains, the Hilton, Ramada, and Holiday Inn, were proposing to build luxury tourist hotels in the neighborhood. Many in the Tenderloin were shocked to learn that their "residential" neighborhood was zoned the same as downtown in general, permitting commercial and tourist high-rise development. The Tenderloin was (and is) recognized as highly desirable real estate, especially if you get rid of the community of people who survive there. With good weather; a block from the cable car tracks and Union Square, which is surrounded by high-end retail stores and the upscale St. Francis Hotel (rebuilt after the 1906 earthquake) and the boutique1920s Sir Francis Drake Hotel (with its "secret" Prohibition Room, reflecting the era of its origins); bordering Market Street, the main throughway through downtown, with its BART stations bringing people into the City from down the Peninsula and across the bay; near the Financial District and tourist attractions; and City Hall and other civic buildings within its Powell to Van Ness, Post to Market Street borders, why not move the people, demolish old buildings, and extend downtown all the way to Van Ness? What a great plan!

Except that NOMPC took exception to the plan. So did hundreds of residents who attended Planning Commission meetings, and thousands who endorsed a rezoning plan that was produced by NOMPC and submitted to San Francisco's Planning Department. The fear was that other high-rise buildings and businesses would displace the people living and working in the neighborhood, and rents would rise substantially, forcing thousands of residents to leave, including recently arrived refugees from Southeast Asia, the elderly poor, disabled, and other low-income individuals and families.

The three hotels were built. None actually displaced residents, but the zoning in place threatened a radical transformation of The TL. However, now community activists were ready to act.

Leroy Looper, Rev. Cecil Williams of Glide Memorial Church, NOMPC, and other community leaders and organizations, while losing the fight against the hotels, had won groundbreaking "mitigation measures": the hotels contributing to the purchase and renovation of low-cost housing, funding for service projects, and agreements to make good faith efforts to hire locals.[2] They were motivated, confident, and organized as never before. The battle was lost, but the war had just begun.

An effort to replace low-income housing with a "Union Square West" was defeated by the Tenderloin coalition. Brad Paul, then the Executive Director of NOMPC (and much later our street teacher in the Salvation Army chapel and at other locations on other occasions), and others lobbied the director of the Planning Commission and eventually achieved their primary goals: downzoning much of the Tenderloin, prohibiting new tourist hotels and commercial development above the second floor, and maintaining the Tenderloin's mostly eight-story heights, with some areas allowing up to 13 stories. The result was, according to Randy Shaw, Executive Director of THC, "the Tenderloin's transformation from an undefined area of disenfranchised, low-income people to a self-identified community of resident activists capable of protecting their future."[3] The rezoning plan was signed into law by then Mayor Dianne Feinstein on March 28, 1985. A decade later, I returned to the Tenderloin, attended community meetings, including NOMPC's that included Brad Paul, Glenda Hope, Leroy Looper, Richard Livingston, and others who led the campaign to recognize The TL as a residential neighborhood, and was extremely impressed by what they accomplished and who they were.

Today, Leroy is dead; Glenda recently "retired" (I put that in quotes because, while she stepped down from leading San Francisco Network Ministries, she is still active in SafeHouse "for homeless, prostituted women who want to escape the violence, brutality and trauma of life on the street"[4]); Brad is Senior Program Officer at the Evelyn and Walter Haas, Jr. Fund, and still active in TL politics; Rev. Cecil Williams keeps "retiring" from Glide, but never leaves. His current title is "Co-founder and Minister of Liberation." And the neighborhood is still alive with service providers and residents active in preserving *and* improving the neighborhood. Good people worked hard to make The TL a better place since the 1985 rezoning law passed, but it held on to its reputation as a very *untrendy* neighborhood–until now.

* * *

A few years ago, *San Francisco Chronicle* columnist C.W. Nevius, in an article called "Tenderloin gets Trendy, apparently on its way up," wrote[5]:

> "People try to say it is kind of Nob Hill. But no, actually it is the Tenderloin," said Jordan Langer, a partner and general manager of Jones, a dinner and custom cocktail spot with a huge rooftop deck on Jones Street, just off Geary.
>
> Jones, which opened in February, is almost too cool for the Tenderloin. Mixed drinks are $10, there's an extensive list of wines – none of them Thunderbird – and the place has such an insider vibe that there's only a small sign next to the entrance. But last Saturday, Langer says, they had more than 1,000 customers, including the dinner and drinks crowd, with 800 for cocktails after 10 p.m.

* * *

A lot has happened since the late 1980s when Diana Chin, dedicated, innovative, hardworking playground director, was working out of the basement in St. Boniface Church. Sam Soun was a little kid playing there and in the concrete patio just outside its doors, more of an open pit than a play yard, but Diana and the other playground directors did what they could with very limited resources, and Sam grew up, not without a bump or two along the way, to be a talented, educated, compassionate, youth counselor, much like his mentor, Diana.

In 1995, Midge Wilson of BAWCC, Brother Kelly Cullen of TNDC, and other neighborhood activists succeeded in their ten-year effort getting Tenderloin Playground and Recreation Center built, home base for many of our Tenderloin U programs and events, and Diana, her crew, and neighborhood kids moved in. The motivation for the new playground was the failure of Boeddeker Park as a children's playground, in spite of many attempts to take back the park, and periodic announcements that it had been "reclaimed,"[6] once in response to a neighborhood petition sent to the Recreation and Parks Department that said the park had become a place "where open alcohol consumption and intoxication are more frequent sights than children playing, where drug dealing and abuse are blatant, and where visitors are exposed to violence as well as trash, urine and used drug needles."[7] But reclamation failed as drug dealers returned and the homeless and mentally ill came back to one of the few places they could sit and rest during daytime hours when the shelters were closed to them or their SRO rooms were too confining to sit in all day long. But in December of 2014, Boeddeker *was* reclaimed after a $9.3 million makeover. Everything—every blade of grass; the basketball court; the play structures; the old, concrete building with its few, narrow, high-placed windows; "The Gauntlet" walkway, where drugs were sold, mentally ill people suffered; where I re-met my former student, now police officer Irene Huey Michaud; and where Diana and her kids, on their way to one of our *A Christmas Carol* performances in the old Boeddeker building, squealed and jumped into the air like popcorn popping in response to the rats scurrying out of garbage cans filled with leftovers from the food giveaway earlier in the day—was replaced, except for a few metal sculptures that represented the people of the neighborhood and the community in general.

Today, Boeddeker is beautiful, filled with children playing on the outside courts and play structures, digging in its flower garden, or gathering inside the glass-walled building—letting light shine in and reminding the street community hanging out on the other side of the fence that children are in here doing homework, or art or community projects, or attending classes on culinary arts or life skills. Adults from the neighborhood gather in the community room for morning coffee, Tai Chi, or to play mah-jongg. On Saturdays Zumba classes happen on the lawn. Stairs have been replaced by sloped walkways so disabled adults with canes or in wheelchairs can move through the park unhindered. The Boys and Girls Club received $250,000 to develop programs and monitor the site, Shih-Yu-Lang Central YMCA organizes activities there, and Tenderloin Safe Passage was awarded $150,000 to locate there and develop strategies to help insure that kids get to and from the park safely.

Midge and the women of BAWCC worked with the City to develop the neighborhood miniparks and Tenderloin Community Elementary School, VYDC moved to newly refurbished offices and expanded its operations, NOM/TCBD commissioned the Yellow Brick Road, and IHDC's TAG program received a grant to show movies in its backyard. *The Chronicle*'s Meredith May wrote about the "Tenderlointreon" program[8]:

> Tucked behind a tenement apartment in the Tenderloin, a hidden outdoor movie theater is bringing free cinema to San Francisco children whose parents can't afford today's ticket prices.
> "Tenderlointreon" is projected onto the side of a coin laundry from the courtyard behind the nonprofit Indochinese Housing Community Afterschool Program.

The Tenderloin Sidewalk Improvement Program (TSIP) began steam cleaning the sidewalks. The City brought in portable toilets, mounted on trailers, to three locations in the Tenderloin (more are planned). With toilet paper, seat covers, soap, paper towels, and air fresheners, with needle disposal boxes nearby, they are staffed by attendants who make sure the toilets are clean, occupied only for a reasonable amount of time, and that no drug use or sex takes place inside (managed in part, by making sure that only one person goes in at a time). The program was inspired by children from De Marillac Academy, the little Catholic school in the neighborhood, who read poems to city officials about growing up in the Tenderloin. Many of the children said they had to be very careful to avoid stepping on syringes and human feces. "Code Brown" they would shout. "You had to be cautious and you had to be looking at the floor to make sure you didn't step on poop," student Karina Bonilla, 14, said. "But not anymore!"[9]

Portable showers were introduced by the Lava Mae program (*lavame* means "wash me" in Spanish). Two old city buses (with more on the way), painted bright blue to attract attention, were outfitted with two showers and toilets. The need was obvious. Only seven shelter facilities in San

Francisco offered showers in a city with 6686 people counted in the 2015 Point-in-Time homeless count, up from 6436 in 2013, and many more who were missed in the biannual census. Lava Mae's mission is to "Deliver dignity one shower at a time."[10]

Glenda Hope's San Francisco Network Ministries, working with Asian Neighborhood Design, built the beautiful apartment building for poor families on Ellis Street, across the street from the playground. Randy Shaw's THC developed over 1600 permanent supportive housing units for the very poor, formerly homeless, and mentally ill by master-leasing existing SROs and other low-income housing buildings; TNDC built or acquired 31 buildings in the Tenderloin and surrounding neighborhoods, providing safe and affordable housing for 3400 poor people. Mercy Housing developed housing for over a thousand people with special needs or families in the Tenderloin and 6th Street corridor, including constructing 90 units for seniors in the eight stories of airspace they purchased above the new two-story St. Anthony's building on Golden Gate and Jones (in the area zoned for up to 13 stories). Glide Community Housing, Chinatown Community Development Center, Community Housing Partnership, and others added to the housing stock for low- or no-income people in the Tenderloin. Many of the new buildings were multi-bedroom, attractive units, with supportive and truly engaged staff.

In 1986, Chip Conley (then 26 years old) bought an old crack motel at 601 Eddy and turned it into the Phoenix Hotel. Informally, it became known as the "Rock 'n' Roll Hotel," where singers, bands, actors, and other celebrities rented rooms and partied. Johnny Rotten stayed there, so did M.C. Hammer, Red Hot Chili Peppers, Anthrax, Robert Plant, Joan Jett, David Bowie, Courtney Love, Johnny Depp, Keanu Reeves, and John F. Kennedy, Jr. The Phoenix became[11]

the spot for bands, booze, and bacchanalia.... One Yelper relates a typical story from this time: "It's 4:15 a.m., I'm full of booze and mushrooms, there's a mound of coke on the dresser and a fresh 30 pack on the ground. We decide to go skinny-dipping. Don't remember much after that. I think we were in the same room where David Bowie and Mick Jagger had sex. Yeah, the Phoenix knows how to party...." Every inch of the bar and poolside was full from 11 a.m. till closing time. Big-name DJs would play and between 2,000 to 3,000 people would be getting their heat on. We're talking every type of drug ingested, nitrous balloons behind the bar, and people having sex *at* the bar, even while ordering their drinks.

But the Phoenix evolved as its owner matured as CEO of the award-winning, 35 properties, Joie De Vivre hotel chain. The Phoenix became the epicenter for hip corporate parties and Internet start-up launches in San Francisco. Young entrepreneurs gathered there to network, do business, *and* party. That's when I first visited the Phoenix.

It was at TNDC's annual "Celebrity Pool Toss," a fund-raising party that attracts Bay Area socialites, corporate leaders, politicians, and others willing to pay to see celebrities thrown into the Phoenix swimming pool (the site of the wild wet parties of old), fully clothed. To date, the Pool Toss party has raised more than $4,000,000 for TNDC's youth and family programs. In addition to an entrance donation ($125 in 2015), bidders compete to win the honor of contributing the most money to see a well-known person jump into the pool. Over the years, most of the "tossees," as they are called, have been noted locals: Captain Susan Manheimer, head of the Tenderloin Police Station; Fr. Louie Vitale, pastor of St. Boniface Church; Fire Chief Joanne Hayes-White; Margo St. James, founder of COYOTE; and Chip Conley, owner of the Phoenix. Police chiefs, the sheriff, members of the Board of Supervisors, business executives, the heads of service agencies, the DA, socialites, and professional athletes have all jumped into the pool to support TNDC's program. So did more famous people like Robin Williams, Cheech Martin, and Darryl the Wonder Dog. The first year I attended, author Danielle Steel gave $3000 to see Gavin Newsom, then recently appointed County Supervisor (later Mayor and Lieutenant Governor) and his business partner, Billy Getty, scion of the billionaire Getty family, take the plunge. Two years later, I watched as Mayor Willie Brown's campaign manager, Jack Davis (well known for his outrageous publicity stunts), tried to get Willie to be a tossee, but the mayor refused. Willie (as he is commonly referred to in San Francisco. Even his current about-town column in *The Chronicle* is called "Willie's World"), once dubbed "The Best Dressed Man in California" by *Esquire* magazine for a wardrobe that included $6000 Brioni suits, was not about to be submerged, so Davis snatched the mayor's hat from his head and auctioned that off as a tossee. Willie looked exasperated until the winning bid for the $450 Borsalino fedora reached $10,000. The hat went into the water to thunderous applause.

The police department's Tenderloin Task Force, housed in the basement of the old Hibernia Bank on McAllister Street, became the permanent Tenderloin Police Station on Eddy Street in 2000. In 2004, a two-block stretch of Larkin Street, between Eddy and O'Farrell, became officially designated "Little Saigon," hoping to boost the neighborhood's reputation as a Vietnamese cultural and commercial center, as Chinatown and Japantown are for their communities, and draw locals and tourists to its stores and restaurants. Victor, the Middle Eastern owner of Wild Awakenings, sold the coffeehouse to the Irishman Joe in 2008, who spruced the place up, hung the Irish and Rainbow flags next to each other on the entrance wall, and changed the name to Celtic Coffee Company. After same-sex marriage was legalized in California, Joe married, moved to Southern California to become a physical education teacher, and sold the business in 2014 to a Chinese family, Doris (the mom, a former professional singer), Cary, (the dad, a computer engineer), and Isaac (the son, being groomed to run the business). The family did a makeover of the coffeehouse, painting the walls, redoing the floors, replacing the tables and chairs, changing the music to a softer style, and hanging new works of art, but early on made a small change that symbolized changing times in the Tenderloin. The sign on the bathroom door, warning that drug use inside would result in a call to the police, was taken down.

* * *

Promise of the Inner City class is walking Mid-Market today, that section of the city's main drag between 5th Street and Van Ness Avenue that is going through a transformation with significant implications for the Tenderloin. We are studying changing times in the neighborhood. The walk from the coffeehouse to Market Street takes us by the old Hibernia Bank. Though seriously damaged, it was one of the few buildings east of Van Ness to survive the 1906 earthquake. Abandoned by the bankers in 1985, the Police Department's Tenderloin Task Force was housed in the still seismically unsafe basement of this beautiful building ("Who made *that* decision?" asked one incredulous cop) from 1991 to 2000. During that time, when I was doing research for what emerged as *City Baby and Star*, I stood outside, sometimes for more than an hour, waiting at the alley gate for my ride-along police escort. I listened to people shout their complaints about being victimized into the voice box connecting the outside sidewalk to an on-duty officer inside, or watched cops bring those arrested into the building or out to a paddy wagon. There were no cells inside, only a metal bench that the arrested would be handcuffed to, waiting to be transported to the county jail. Then, in 2000, the permanent police station was established in a renovated auto body shop on Eddy Street and the bank was abandoned, again. Now, plywood walls and scaffolding surround the building as the corner of McAllister, Market, and Jones, as Mid-Market goes through a radical transformation.

Beginning in 2009, when the country began to recover from the Great Recession, San Francisco was already experiencing a remarkable recovery. Not as hard hit as much of the country, it emerged from the economic crisis, perhaps stronger than ever, if you only count accumulated wealth and not how it is spread around. The *New York Times* reported on the "recovery," and its impact on the Tenderloin, this way[12]:

> In 2000, according to Ted Egan, the city's chief economist, median household income in the Tenderloin was just $12,163. A nearby census district, leading to the Financial District, had a median household income of $71,985. In 2013, the Tenderloin's median household income was $12,210, while the Financial District's was $115,233. Adjusting for inflation, income in the Tenderloin fell about 30 percent, while income in the wealthier area increased 14 percent.

The TL, however, was not untouched by the economic recovery. Philz, a coffeehouse popular with hipsters in the Mission (and elsewhere, as the one-time grocer found that his hand-poured, one-cup-at-a-time coffee preparation drew customers in gentrifying neighborhoods), opened a new location on Golden Gate and Larkin. Jebena, an upscale coffee and tea place, opened on Polk Street (it stayed at the location even after a man was chased into the coffeehouse, robbed, and murdered). Hooker's Sweet Treats, that opened on lower Hyde in 2010, received this review from Northern California Hostels[13]:

> Since opening last year, the local reaction to Hooker's couldn't be sweeter. Their sea-salted dark chocolate caramel won a 2010 Best of SF award from SF Weekly: "[These] just might be the most searingly adult confections to emerge from San Francisco." The caramel praline made 7x7's list of the 12 Best Cookies in San Francisco, and Bay Area Bites raves "You haven't tried a rich, buttery, complex salted caramel until you've tried one of his treats."

Bourbon and Branch, the "speakeasy" popular among Millennials and downtown professionals, opened on the corner of O'Farrell and Jones. Brick Restaurant, opening on Sutter and Larkin, announced that it was striving "to bring a combination of exceptional food and casual night-life to San Francisco's Tenderloin district. Guests can expect high quality, Modern American cuisine, gracious service, and a lively crowd. Rotating art and our modern-rustic design create comfortable and energizing surroundings. Whether in our exhibition kitchen, at our communal table, or in one of our private rooms, the innovative, internationally influenced food will delight locals and travelers alike."[14] The Hemlock Tavern presents "a nightly cavalcade of top-shelf up & coming local, national and international touring bands in our back room performance space."[15] Lush Lounge, offering watermelon martinis to upscale customers, is where The Polk Gulch Saloon used to serve transgender patrons and drag queens. Rye, "a perennial favorite of drink connoisseurs, features a diverse liquor menu with a fine selection of whiskey and the afore-mentioned rye, as well as specialty cocktails such as their basil gimlet and pisco sour. The atmosphere is subtle and low-key, a great place to meet friends after work or to read a novel on a grey, rainy night."[16] The Ambassador, Mr. Lew's Win Win Bar & Grand Sazerac Emporium, and Bambuddha Lounge in the Phoenix Hotel all beckon the young and the moneyed.

In an article titled "Suds, Scents and Soup in San Francisco's Tenderloin" (August 5, 2014), *The New York Times* referred its readers to four new Tenderloin venues[17]:

MIKKELLER BAR Beer lovers have crowded this year-old outpost of the legendary Copenhagen "gypsy" brewer, on the hunt for rare European and American brews and pub grub like house-made sausages. 34 Mason Street;
TURTLE TOWER One year ago, one of San Francisco's most popular pho restaurants moved to new, larger digs whose lemon yellow walls are hung with photos of old Hanoi. 645 Larkin Street
HANDSOME OXFORD
Stepping into Handsome Oxford is like entering a closet-size time machine packed with gently used, mostly pre-1970s American-made men's work wear and casual clothing. You'll find wool Pendletons, college sweatshirts, a Levi's western shirt with pearlescent snap buttons and more, all of it amid décor that runs to old bottles of false teeth adhesive, galvanized metal milk cans, and a hodgepodge of other junk shop finds.
646 Hyde Street;
IN FIORE Vintage apothecary vessels and an old mercury glass urn adorn this tiny perfumery, where custom black walnut cabinets hold artfully packaged and mostly house-blended solid perfumes, body oils and complexion and body treatments. The shop makes many of its own essential oils and infusions from raw floral materials like jasmine from India and rose from Bulgaria. *868 Post Street*

Airbnb has taken notice,[18] "Fidgety loiterers frequent the streets of the Tenderloin, a fickle San Francisco neighborhood not necessarily suited to certain palates. Raw to the core, the Tenderloin is an abrasively honest neighborhood in the heart of the city. Cheap hole-in-the-wall eateries and paling historic buildings provide the backdrop to this neighborhood's cast of sidewalk occupants. Recognizing the Tenderloin for its rich diversity and architectural potential, San Franciscans are working to redefine their dubious heartland," as have other real estate interests. Rent SF Now included the following in its list of available apartments:

Welcome To 666 O Farrell[19]
Live in a well-maintained architectural gem at 666 O'Farrell, centrally located in the trendy Tenderloin district, right near Union Square, Civic Center, and sophisticated Nob Hill. This stately Edwardian dates back to the glamorous 1920s, and its exquisite construction and ornate details continue to impress today. Our exceptional studios and one- and two-bedroom apartments are loaded with modern amenities and plenty of homey touches, providing a cozy respite from the bustling city.

Historically known for its rainbow of culture and diversity, the Tenderloin is fast becoming a popular destination for its vibrant nightlife, live music, art galleries, consignment stores, and boutiques. Its streets are flush with cozy ethnic corner restaurants, neighborhood bars, coffee shops, and new hotspots serving hip fare like hand-poured coffee, praline shortbread cookies, or Cajun gumbo. Our central location places residents within steps from world-class theater, elegant hotels, and fine shopping in Union Square. The easy access to public transportation allows you to access every corner of the city at a moments' notice. Live in the center of it all!

666 O'Farrell offers a sensational opportunity to live large in one of San Francisco's most vibrant and trending neighborhoods. Call us today for an appointment!

And in another posting:

Welcome To 725 Ellis[20]
Live in the heart of San Francisco at 725 Ellis, where our well maintained property offers beautifully appointed studios and one-bedroom apartments in San Francisco's trendy Tenderloin neighborhood. Here, you'll find a warm retreat from the city's bustling energy.

Bordering Union Square, Civic Center, and sophisticated Nob Hill, 725 Ellis is a collaboration of polished and hip. Historically gritty and culturally diverse, the Tenderloin is fast becoming a popular destination for its vibrant nightlife, live music, art galleries, consignment stores, and boutiques. Its streets are flush with long-standing ethnic restaurants, neighborhood bars, and coffee shops, as well as new hotspots serving hip fare and craft cocktails. Our central location places residents within steps from world-class theater, elegant hotels, and fine shopping in Union Square. Easy access to a number of transit lines makes 725 Ellis a prime location to explore San Francisco and the Bay Area.

And perhaps the ultimate indication of changing times in The TL:

A Turning Point For The Trendyloin?[21]
February 9, 2015
Having been on and off the market for over five years, the full-floor penthouse unit atop the Art Deco Hamilton building at 631 O'Farrell Street, in the heart of the "Trendyloin," is in contract to be sold.

The asking price? $3,950,000.

In 1985, when the zoning laws passed seemed to prohibit gentrification, no one thought anyone but the poor would ever want to live in The TL, let alone in an SRO, but with the emergence of "Silicon Valley North" on Mid-Market Street, SROs are becoming a popular living situation for recently arrived, well-paid Millennials. In the SoMa, for example, between 6th and 7th Streets ("Tenderloin South"), an older SRO was promoted as a "tech co-op"[22]:

Rooms at The Negev on Folsom Street have been advertised on Craigslist. One post titled, "$1500 Awesome Co-Op Folsom Street – young professionals" started with the description: "We are like minded group of people, all of us are in our 20's, we are active, into sports, and looking to constantly learn something new (everything from programming to new meditation methods)." The listing said the roommates included an engineer at Google, an associate program manager at Google, a front-end Web developer at Edmodo, among others.

In the Tenderloin, two eight-story buildings, containing 250-square-foot market-rate studios with private bathrooms and limited cooking facilities, were recommended for approval by the Planning Department. Neighbors objected, claiming that the new buildings are "tech dorms" for the thousands of techies moving into the neighborhood and nearby SoMa. "Is this something we want in the Tenderloin? ... We know who this is for – young techies who eat breakfast, lunch and dinner at work and just need a place to sleep at night."[23] The monthly rents are expected to be at least $2000 a month or $24,000 a year, about twice what the Tenderloin's median household annual income was reported to be by the city's chief economist in 2000. Parking lots and alleys throughout the Tenderloin are being looked at by developers, hoping to "fill" them in with new tech dorms and other housing.

What happened to cause this wave of change? Most would say, "The Twitter tax break."

*　*　*

The Promise class's walk down Market Street is a walk through the past, into the future. Beautiful, old, many of them until recently neglected, buildings line the street, while huge construction cranes (called, only half-jokingly, the city's new mascot) loom ahead, symbolizing the rapidly changing neighborhood.

In San Francisco, this most recent wave of gentrification began in the Mission District, with the city embracing an interpretation of the New Urbanism movement (whose characteristics include diversity in use and population; increased density, with residences, entertainment, shops, and services within a ten-minute walk; and a pedestrian-friendly design that allows greater use of bicycles, skateboards, scooters, walking, and public transit as daily transportation).[24] This combined with increased interest by Millennials and retiring Baby Boomers to live in the city, with all of its excitement and amenities (instead of high-density suburban hubs that characterized much of the early days of the movement). The Mission was a vibrant, affordable, largely Hispanic community that, with the end of the Great Recession, drew young, well-paid tech workers from Silicon Valley. Their workplaces were 35 miles away, but the neighborhood had easy access to the freeways heading south. Google, Apple, Yahoo, and other high-tech companies—discovering that the suburban lifestyle that became so attractive after World War II and remained so for decades was not appealing to new generation workers—offered what became commonly known as "Google buses," large, private, attractive, "cool" (often painted black with pinstripe-like designs, tinted windows, outside racks for bicycles, and an open-door policy for pet dogs) to transport employees from their urban apartments to workplaces in suburban Santa Clara County. One result was rapid gentrification of the Mission, with soaring home and business rents, evictions, new market-rate housing at a much higher market rate, and a new look to the neighborhood with upscale restaurants, clubs, and shops. New wealth moved in and many existing residents, many of them Spanish speaking, were pushed out.

The Mission is often a community engagement site for Tenderloin U classes. I like to begin the semester with a walk from Muddy Waters Coffeehouse (our main Mission District meeting place at 16thand Valencia), down Valencia Street to 24th Street, and back to 16th by way of Mission Street, exploring the side streets and alleys along the way. What used to be one community is now two. Mission Street, the neighborhood's main drag, is still largely "old town," with taco bars, pawnshops, tattoo parlors, cheap hotels, pizza joints, Mexican grocery stores, a Dollar Store, Thrift Town, mom 'n' pop clothing stores, smoke shops, and a MetroPCS store. Valencia Street, just a block away and running parallel to Mission Street, is "new town," with businesses catering to the new arrivals: a farmer's market, an herb store, Buffalo Exchange, home furnishing stores, coffee bars, parklets (little patio-like extension of the sidewalk, occupying several parking spaces, that offer comfortable seating for café customers and passersby), art galleries, and the Good Vibrations store (selling sex toys and other erotic products for women). On Valencia, we walk by a new restaurant near 18th Street that includes sidewalk tables set up with white tablecloths, cloth napkins, and silverware. On Mission Street, we walk by a taqueria, with cardboard plates, paper napkins, and plastic forks and spoons.[25]

The next class meeting begins at Sugarlump Coffee Lounge (a hipster hangout) on 24th Street; 24th Street cuts across Mission and Valencia Streets, its blocks to the east of Valencia historically offering Latino businesses: bakeries, restaurants, grocery stores, clothing stores, art galleries (e.g., Galería de la Raza), and shops selling religious figures or Mexican and Indian jewelry or both. The outside (and sometimes inside) walls on many of the buildings are covered with colorful murals, with Balmy Street, the alley between 24th and 25th, an outside urban art gallery. To the west, especially on the other side of Dolores Street (where the original Spanish Mission, established in 1776, still stands near 16th Street) are mostly upscale shops, restaurants, and a Whole Foods Market. This is Noe Valley, long ago a gentrified neighborhood. Between the two neighborhoods is Dolores Heights, where Facebook founder Mark Zuckerberg and his wife invested $10 million in the purchase and renovation of a new home on 21st Street, three blocks from the heart of the Mission District.

But it is the Mission, not Noe or Dolores Heights, that drew the new wave of well-to-do Millennials, changing the nature of the community and driving out many established business and residents. Even Hispanic 24th Street is changing as bookstores and shops that catered to San Francisco's more hip lifestyles (e.g., Modern Times Book Collective, Alley Cat Books, Wise Sons Jewish Deli, and Sidewalk Juice, "bringing a healthy alternative to the neighborhood," offering a "Free 3 Day Juice Cleanse Guide," and such menu items as "Green Energy Juice," a combination of spinach, parsley, kale, celery, cucumber, apple, lemon, ginger) were priced out of their Valencia Street corridor digs and moved to less expensive (for now) shops on 24th, whose own rising rents are pushing older Latino businesses. All this was first wave, post-Great Recession gentrification that was seeing median housing costs and business space rentals rise dramatically not only in the Mission, but citywide. From 2011 to 2015, the combined median sales price for homes and condominiums in San Francisco increased 81 percent.[26]

In the Tenderloin, gentrification was creeping in, but for better or worse, depending on your point of view, the culture stayed pretty much the same, until the "Twitter tax break" came along and all hell broke loose.

* * *

The Promise class continues its walk down Market Street. It's a beautiful spring day. Street people mix with shoppers and young people going to and from work or headed to local hangouts. New stores, restaurants, and other business are popping up all over. We walk by the bright red, recently redone, Strand Theater, San Francisco's beloved American Conservatory Theater's new presence on Market Street. Built in 1917 as the 1200-seat Jewel Theater, the building went through many transformations over the years. When it closed in 2003, it was a porno theater that also specialized in crack cocaine and prostitution.

When I first thumbed into San Francisco and lived at the Lyric Hotel in the Tenderloin, Mid-Market was still a vibrant hub of San Francisco commerce and entertainment. Then it went through decades of decline. Mark Ellinger, a Tenderloin U street teacher and former homeless, bipolar, heroin addict, now a noted photo-historian of the Central City area, describes what happened in his upfromthedeep.com website[27]:

Following the 1906 cataclysm, the stretch of Market Street between Powell and Polk developed as a lively theater and shopping district that by night was a sea of flickering chase lights and glowing neon tubes that seemed to stretch to the horizon on marquees announcing theater and cinema fare, and on towering blade signs like gigantic, fiery chart pins identifying each theater and department store along the broad and bustling thoroughfare; a protean street of dreams, alive with the pulse of the City.

When in 1963 the San Francisco Redevelopment Agency demolished the celebrated Fox Theater, a San Francisco landmark designed by Thomas Lamb on the corner of Polk and Market, it was replaced by high-rise apartments and commercial space covering the entire block of Market Street between Polk and Larkin, named Fox Plaza in memory of the theater. In 1964 BART began construction of its subway system, which for a decade turned downtown Market Street into a massive, gaping trench.

The destruction of the Fox was a death knell signaling the end of an era. The district lost much of its glamor when, under the 1967 Market Street Beautification Act, all of Market Street's brightly-lit marquees and most of its neon blade signs were removed. When traffic was diverted away from the mid-Market area by BART construction, the district's fate was sealed and it sank into a decline from which it has never recovered. Stores and theaters that had thrived for decades struggled on for a while and then closed forever. Mid-Market became a constantly changing landscape of liquor stores, fast food outlets, porn shops, check-cashing companies and gaudy storefronts, few of which have survived more than a few years. The downturn in quality and character of mid-Market commerce and a profusion of unused buildings and boarded-up storefronts have obscured the district's glorious past and left in its stead an oppressive hollowness and blight. Transience and decay have become ingrained, attracting derelicts, outcasts, and petty criminals from far and wide. One consequence of these changes, largely overlooked, has been a harsh decline in the quality of life for the area's many long-time residents.

This was the Mid-Market strip I knew for years. Beginning in 1995, when I came back to the Tenderloin, I wandered the street at night to see what its nightlife was like. It was as if I was on another planet. Streetlights cast an eerie orange glow that washed over everything and everyone. Homeless people set up camp in groups. Individuals tucked themselves into doorways or just snuggled into the cracks where sidewalks meet building walls. Dealers dealt. Hookers hooked. Mentally ill people wandering the strip looked ghoulish in the strange light that added an alien look to already distraught faces. I was, for the most part, ignored, which I appreciated. I walked Mid-Market in the daytime with my students, but even the added flow of daytime workers, shoppers, and lost tourists didn't diminish the suffering that was on display. Then, in 2012, the neighbor-hood began its own up-from-the-deep experience.

In 2011, Twitter, the online social networking company, was planning to move out of its operation in the SoMa. It was going through a rapid expansion, from a few hundred to a few thousand employees, and claimed it couldn't afford to stay in San Francisco with the city's payroll tax and lev-ies on stock-based compensation. In response, the brand-new mayor, Ed Lee, a longtime city bureaucrat appointed by the Board of Supervisors to finish Gavin Newsom's term as mayor when Gavin was elected California's Lieutenant Governor, worked with other politicians to come up with what has become known as "The Twitter tax break," an effort to keep Twitter in town, specifically relocating to the Mid-Market area, and attract more tech companies to the same designated zone.

The Twitter tax break is an exemption for businesses located in a defined Mid-Market area from the 1.5 percent city payroll tax and levies on stock-based compensation for new (but not continuing) employees for six years. It was a controversial move, bringing protests from the city's progressives and labor unions, who argued that the city was giving up revenue that could benefit city employees, would raise rents for neighborhood residents and businesses, and displace the very poor. All that has happened, but the city claimed that net tax revenues would increase over time, that tax revenues would have been lost anyway, as Twitter and other companies moved out of the city, that the Mid-Market neighborhood would emerge from its decrepit state, and that everyone would benefit.[28]

Seventeen technology companies, and more on the way, moved to Mid-Market, including Twitter, Zendesk, Yammer, Spotify, and online retailer One Kings Lane. Other companies moved into the area, even though they didn't qualify for the tax incentives, including Uber Technologies, Square, and Dolby. And the neighborhood culture changed. "'The youth-ful energy that comes with a project like this – or any place where you're going to put 7,000 employees on a city block that's been essentially vacant for a decade – will create an energy for the area that we haven't seen here,' said Tom McDonnell, VP of Leasing for Shorenstein [real estate com-pany]"[29] Oz Erickson, chairman of San Francisco-based Emerald Fund, which is building a high-rise apartment tower with 400 market-rate units just outside the "benefit zone," said,[30] "The Twitter tax break was a stroke of genius that catalyzed the whole neighborhood. This used to be a scary, dangerous place."

In addition to renovating old buildings in the neighborhood, businesses constructing new buildings in San Francisco are required to invest 1 percent of the construction costs in "POPOS," privately owned public open spaces, that are publicly accessible spaces—plazas, terraces, atriums, or small parks—that are provided and maintained by private developers, or donate an equivalent amount to a Public Art Trust Fund, administered by the San Francisco Arts Commission. Just before our Promise class walk, I read in *The Chronicle* about two new installations,[31]

> Look up and they will see that there are granite monoliths with ledges to sit on. One ledge has the word "Promised" etched into it in gold, the other has the word "Land," and the person who put those words there is sitting against the "Land," facing west toward "Promised."
>
> "I'm not so much about the promise, I'm more about the land," says artist Topher Delaney, whose public installation "Promised Land" will have its grand opening Sunday. A free festival, with taiko drumming and a klezmer quintet, will start at noon and run for four hours, which is about as long as it takes to figure out all the elements at work here.
>
> "It's a very complex space with layers of maps," says Delaney, who works in diverse media and notched this plaza out of the footprint of an apartment tower called NEMA. "There are multiple framings."
>
> These privately owned public open spaces, called POPOS, are clustered at the east end of Mid-Market Street. Delaney's "Promised Land," and Brian Goggin's 13 twinkling glass pianos overhanging the sidewalk one block away, are the first to decorate the new residential towers that are sprouting like spring flowers on Mid-Market.

On the Wednesday after the grand opening, the Promise class visited the "Promised Land." We walked the map of the Bay Area embedded in the ground. We sat on the ledges and gazed at the monoliths. It was very interesting, sleek, attractive, and symbolic of the new culture emerging. We went over to see Brian Goggin's "twinkling glass pianos overhanging the sidewalk." Goggin is well known and admired in the Tenderloin and 6th Street corridor for his "Defenestration" project, installed on the abandoned Hugo Hotel in 1997 for what was supposed to be one year, but stayed for 17, when the building was torn down to be replaced by new low-income housing being built my Mercy Housing.[32]

Goggin covered the exterior of the building with tables, chairs, lamps, grandfather clocks, a refrigerator, and couches, seemingly climbing out of the windows. Their insect-like legs, fastened to the walls and windowsills, seemed to be crawling over the surfaces and hanging off the roof.

"Defenestration," the word literally means "to throw out of a window," symbolizes, in this context, the 6th Street community, society's throwaways. On his website, Goggin explains,[33]

Reflecting the harsh experience of many members of the community, the furniture is of the streets, cast-off and unappreciated. The simple, unpretentious beauty and humanity of these downtrodden objects is reawakened through the action of the piece. The act of "throwing out" becomes an uplifting gesture of release, inviting reflection on the spirit of the people we live with, the objects we encounter, and the places in which we live.

Three blocks and a world away, Goggin's Mid-Market work, "Caruso's Dream," is located in the rapidly gentrifying neighborhood. Abstract "pianos," made out of glass and salvaged factory windows, hang from the side of Ava 55 Ninth, a new 17-story apartment building. More subtle in its presentation than the scurrying furniture on the Hugo Hotel, the glass and steel sculpting emerges to the viewer as a cluster of pianos being tossed into the sky, which was, at least in the artists' imagination (it was cocreated by Dorka Keelin), the inspiration for the piece. Enrico Caruso was performing in San Francisco and staying at the Palace Hotel on the day of the city's Great Earthquake on April 18, 1906. Of his experience, Caruso wrote,[34] "I wake up about 5 o'clock, feeling my bed rocking as though I am in a ship on the ocean.... I get up and go to the window, raise the shade and look out. And what I see makes me tremble with fear. I see the buildings toppling over, big pieces of masonry falling, and from the street below I hear the cries and screams of men and women and children." That was just before the Palace Hotel collapsed. Caruso got out alive, but never returned to San Francisco again.

With a recording of the opera star's singing voice emerging from one of the pianos, pedestrians walking by hear and see Caruso's Dream.

Brimming with entropic energies of a force of nature, this arrangement of materials on the side of a building evokes a precarious equilibrium of objects in space....

The pianos glimmer and shimmer during the day, as rays of natural light refract through the glass pianos and create brilliant prismatic patterns on the building and the sidewalk. From dusk until dawn warm light emanate from the pianos, harmonically flickering to the majesty of Enrico Caruso's operatic recordings. It is as if Enrico Caruso and his fellow performers appear as illuminated essences moving inside the pianos passing from one to another inside the composition, as actors move across a stage.

If Defenestration reflects "the harsh experience of many members of the community, the furniture is of the streets, cast-off and unappreciated," what does Caruso's Dream? How does the symbolic expression of people being tossed out the window compare with the symbolism of opera in the streets? Is the new art better than the old? For whom is it better, and why?

The new Mid-Market works aren't Tenderloin art. They are of and for the new community. They are urbane, sophisticated, and refined, not the colorful, sensuous art of the Tenderloin. They are beautiful and interesting, but lack the gritty soulfulness of the Tenderloin. They reflect the new culture emerging, a new way of life. Do they also reflect the death knell of the Tenderloin? Will the whole neighborhood become what some say Mid-Market already is, Twitterloin?

Maybe, maybe not.

* * *

Text message, Thursday October 15, 2015, 1:09 pm:

Hi dr don. I heard there was a shooting on market and 8th. do you think its still safe to go to our class in the tenderloin?

The next day, Friday October 16, 2015, a *San Francisco Chronicle* headline reads:

**Man dead after fight
with S.F. officers**
Mid-Market shooting
stuns lunchtime crowd

NOTES

1. Shaw, Randy, *The Tenderloin: Sex, Crime, and Resistance in the Heart of San Francisco*, San Francisco: Urban Reality Press, 2015.
2. See Randy Shaw, *The Tenderloin: Sex, Crime, and Resistance in the Heart of San Francisco*, San Francisco: Urban Reality Press, 2015.
3. Shaw, Randy, *The Tenderloin: Sex, Crime, and Resistance in the Heart of San Francisco*, San Francisco: Urban Reality Press, 2015, p. 193.
4. http://www.sfsafehouse.org/mission/mission-statement
5. Nevius, C.W., "Tenderloin gets trendy, apparently on the way up," *SF Chronicle*, July 2, 2011.

6. Martin, Glen, "Neighbors Reclaim Park in Style," *SF Chronicle*, June 20, 1996.
7. Sullivan, Kathleen, "Cleaning up Tenderloin park, Petition seeks to rid Boeddeker of squalor, violence," *SF Examiner*, September 28, 1995.
8. May, Meredith "'Tenderlointreon' a hit with young film fans," *SF Chronicle*, May 1, 2009.
9. CBS SF Bay Area Newsletter, "Six Months Later, San Francisco's Tenderloin Cleaner Thanks To Portable Toilets For Homeless," April 8, 2015. http://sanfrancisco.cbslocal.com/2015/04/08/san-francisco-tenderloin-toilets-bathrooms-homeless/
10. http://www.lavamae.org/#!lavamae-about-us/c20r9
11. Anspaugh, Heidi, "Staying Rock 'n' Roll," The Bold Italic: http://www.thebolditalic.com/articles/1049-staying-rock-n-roll
12. Hardyaug, Quentin, "Blending Tech Workers and Locals in San Francisco's Troubled Mid-Market, *NY Times*, August 16, 2015.
13. Posted by Mary, "Meet the Neighbors: Hooker's Sweet Treats," Northern California Hostels News, June 23, 2011, http://www.norcalhostels.org//news/
14. http://www.brickrestaurant.com
15. http://www.hemlocktavern.com/club-info/
16. Roberts, Nancy, "Trendy Nightlife in San Francisco's Tenderloin" Ask Miss A, Charity Meets Style, June 15, 2011:http://askmissa.com/2011/06/15/trendy-nightlife-in-san-franciscos-tenderloin/#sthash.4wnePzEn.dpufhttp
17. Hall, Christopher, "Suds, Scents and Soup in San Francisco's Tenderloin," *The New York Times*, August 5, 2014.
18. https://www.airbnb.com/locations/san-francisco/tenderloin:
19. http://www.666ofarrell.com
20. http://www.725ellis.com
21. http://www.socketsite.com/archives/2015/02/turning-point-trendyloin.html
22. Kwong, Jessica, "Former tenants sue after SRO housing made into group apartments," *The Examiner*, September 13, 2014.
23. Hoodline, "*Neighbors Organize Against Tenderloin Group Housing Proposal,*"http://hoodline.com/2015/04/tenderloin-residents-property-owners-organize-against-group-housing-proposal
24. See principals of New Urbanism at http://www.newurbanism.org/newurbanism/principles.html
25. For a visual illustration of the culture conflict that has arisen, see YouTube video "Mission Playground is Not For Sale," about a confrontation at a Valencia Street park between Dropbox employees, who had reserved the soccer field through a new Recreation and Park app, and neighborhood

kid who had played there their entire lives and knew nothing about reserving their field.

26. Knight, Heather, "Mayor Lee's 5 years changed face of SF," *San Francisco Chronicle*, October 11, 2015.
27. Mark Ellinger, upfromthedeep.com
28. See online video, "'5 Blocks': A Cinematic Look At The Transformation of Market Street."
29. Kurwa, Nishat, "City Divided Over Tech's Clout in San Francisco," Huffington Post, March 15, 2013.
30. Vekshin, Alison, and Dan Levy. "Twitter Tax Break is Target in San Francisco Income War," Bloomberg Business, April 2, 2014.
31. Whiting, Sam, "Promise fulfilled: Required public art springs up on Mid-Market," *SF Chronicle*, Wednesday, February 11, 2015.
32. See http://www.metaphorm.org/works/defenestration/ for photographs of Goggin's Defenestration and Caruso's Dream projects.
33. See http://www.metaphorm.org/works/defenestration/ for photographs of Goggin's Defenestration project.
34. See http://www.history.com/this-day-in-history/enrico-caruso-survives-the-san-francisco-earthquake

CHAPTER 15

The Soul of the City

SRO

© The Author(s) 2017
D. Stannard-Friel, *Street Teaching in the Tenderloin*,
DOI 10.1057/978-1-137-56437-5_15

Twelve-year-old Nam Thai walked through the village plaza on her way to school, trying not to look at the dead people piled up there for everyone to see. It was a warning: "Do not try to flee!" The bodies had washed ashore near Nam's village on the southern tip of Vietnam that jutted into the South China Sea. From here, escapees hoped to make a quick, direct journey to Thailand and freedom. But not all made it. Many did not. Pirates and Nature made sure of that.

A street teacher's story

* * *

Sofia Lozano Pallares was a new transfer student from Mexico City when she enrolled in Streetwise Sociology. A 23-year-old Presidential Scholar at NDNU, a prestigious scholarship for a few incoming students who have already demonstrated leadership and involvement in community service and are committed to continuing those efforts at Notre Dame de Namur, wrote this about her time in the inner city.

> The experience of working in the Tenderloin was a rather intense experience for two fundamental reasons. The first one is very obvious. We were physically engaged with the projects and the people. We drove to San Francisco and interacted in the city with real people in real time. The second reason is a consequence of the first one. Although we were in the TL only once a week, the TL was with me every day. By that I mean the level of engagement became intellectual, but also emotional and spiritual.
>
> The Tenderloin became a point of reference to understand many concepts, such as deviance, resilience, and social justice, and how I fit in the picture. But the experience went beyond an intellectual exercise. It felt almost like the end of a long transformation. For a long time I had the theoretical knowledge to understand and analyze poverty and social injustices. But this time I felt directly involved and capable.... This time, my theory was meeting the practice and the conjunction of the two was very powerful.

Intellectual, emotional, and spiritual, what better qualities could a learning experience have? Sofia brought to her time in the Tenderloin some obvious credentials that allowed her to place her experiences in a rather sophisticated context. At 23, she was certainly young, but had spent enough time on the planet to have a lived-experience perspective. She has a history of community service, so much that she was awarded the Presidential Scholarship. She comes from Mexico City, with 21,000,000 inhabitants[1] in its metropolitan area, where 40 percent of the people live below the poverty line, so she is no stranger to urban issues and many of the social problems she found in San Francisco's inner city. In her personal life, she had gone through her parents' divorce; an existential crisis when she was 19 that led to her immersion in a poor, young, immigrant community in Montreal; the prolonged illness and early death of her father when she was 20 years old; and, perhaps most significant, being born into a family with a complex history of poverty and wealth, abandonment and strong family ties, and professional careers in business and public service.

Sofia's life and personal qualities had prepared her for a deep learning experience in the Tenderloin, but what was it that made these experiences intellectual, emotional, and spiritual? What do these aspects of being human mean in the context of her time studying in the inner city?

The first, intellectual, is what many perceive what American higher education is all about, maybe all that it is or should be: to develop the necessary knowledge and skills to be a contributing member of society and gain access to a professional career. ("Dr. Don," asks my new advisee, after changing her major from nursing, "my parents want to know what I can *do* with a degree in sociology?") The second, emotional, underlies almost everything we do. Emotions motivate us to take action. (The Promise class, walking down McAllister Street, sees a woman sprawled on the sidewalk, not an unusual sighting, but a worried student says, "Dr. Don, I don't think she's breathing." We call 911 and wait for the police to arrive.) The intellectual and emotional are intertwined aspects of our mental capacities. One informs (intellectual), the other motivates (emotional). Combined, they lay a foundation for discovering individual and collective *purpose*. ("Dr. Don, I think I'm going to be a social worker.") The third, spiritual, is concerned with *transformation* and *meaning*. Not just a sense of accomplishment, but a reason for *being*. Spirit is future oriented, and involves becoming a better person and making the world a better place.[2]

What is it about the Tenderloin that stimulated these powerful learning qualities in Sofia? What is it that has moved so many students over the years to come back, sometimes long after graduating, and walk the streets with me, volunteer at the Halloween festival, donate to our activities, write to me about their memories in the Tenderloin or to tell me how their time there influenced their decisions in life or changed the way they think?

Sometimes, it takes a little while to sink in.

* * *

"Hi, Dr. Don?" Anna Ricardo[3] called me on the phone. She graduated the year before. "I'm applying for the Education Credential Program. Will you write me a letter of recommendation?"

"Of course I will."

Anna, a good student, took several classes with me. In Deviant Behavior, she toured San Quentin Prison, entered cell blocks, and inspected a lifer's cell while he greeted and chatted with the students at the cell door. She talked to guards and inmates, and stood at the railing around the green, metal death chamber while Lt. Vernell Crittendon, Public Information Officer and prison historian, explained its construction and talked about who died inside, how, and why. She participated in our Witness Program, standing with schoolmates outside the prison gates at midnight, joining hundreds of others as an execution took place inside, in the green, metal death chamber that we had peered into on the tour, staring at the modified dentist's chair, with wings added to strap the condemned person's arms to, exposing veins for the lethal injection, a death chamber in which someone would die that night, strapped to that chair, as we stood outside the prison gates.

In Analyzing Social Settings, Anna studied the mom 'n' pop businesses struggling to survive along 24th Street in San Francisco's Latino Mission District, and examined the vivid murals that appear there on walls and garage doors on virtually every block and alley, depicting the ravaged and lost world of the Aztecs, the oppression of the indigenous people of Latin America, the farmworkers' struggles, racism of every kind, and ultimate salvation through protest, revolution, Jesus Christ, and Our Lady of Guadalupe.[4]

In Streetwise Sociology, she helped organize Halloween in the Tenderloin for 300 neighborhood kids, and participated in other CBL events. She did it all. But she never really did agree with the fundamental premise of the classes, that societies *produce* their own social problems and that solutions that engage underlying cause require *social* action and *social* change.

She, as do most people, held the individual responsible.

"Dr. Don, I've been working at Hillcrest for the past year," she said, the juvenile detention center in Belmont, just up the street from Notre Dame. "These kids have real issues. They come from very difficult backgrounds. Hard lives. They need help *before* they get to Hillcrest. I want to become an elementary school teacher, get into *prevention*."

It was a year after graduation, after working with kids in trouble, some on the path to San Quentin, maybe to the green death chamber, that it all came together. Lives are *shaped* and can be *reshaped* by social circumstances: home, school, peers, community. Anna was moved by her relationships with the children, arrived at a new understanding of human behavior, and was clear on a course of action.

* * *

What is it about the Tenderloin that is so engaging, so meaningful, that it moves students to want to make a difference, to learn about the causes and consequences of how our society treats some of our most vulnerable citizens? Not just the dark side, the suffering and deviance that is apparent every time we walk the inner-city streets, but the bright side, too, the promise of better lives that we find as we learn from street teachers who have dedicated their lives to healing others or work to bring about social change to prevent the suffering that the Tenderloin contains. Often, street teachers are from the streets themselves, or have gone through difficult times, terrible times, and survived, then dedicate themselves to making a difference. By sharing what happened and what they do now, they allow us into some important aspect of their most private lives, and inspire us to become better than we are.

* * *

Twelve-year-old Nam Thai walked through the village plaza on her way to school, trying not to look at the dead people piled up there for everyone to see. It was a warning: "Do not try to flee!" The bodies had washed ashore near Nam's village on the southern tip of Vietnam that jutted into the South China Sea. From here, escapees hoped to make a quick, direct journey to Thailand and freedom. But not all made it. Many did not. Pirates and Nature made sure of that. The dead in the plaza, men, women, and children, were some of the boat people who did not find the kind of freedom they had hoped for.

Nam's family was planning its own escape. Her mother had concealed others still trying to leave Vietnam in the early 1980s, and the Communist authorities were doing all they could to stop them. The mom was caught and jailed because of her efforts, but was recognized by one of the head jailers as a comrade. When the two were idealistic teenagers, furious at the injustices perpetuated on their people by the French colonists and the repressive military governments of the Republic of South Vietnam, they left with other young people to join forces in the North, but Nam's mom, only 16 years old, missed her family and turned back. Now, years later, in prison for helping others escape the outcome of the revolution she had hoped to join in her youth, she was remembered by her friend of long ago and sent home.

Nam's dad did not plan to join the family in the escape. He had abandoned them all for a new love. So, it was up to the mother, alone, to bring their six children to a refugee camp in Thailand. On several occasions, she gathered them and tried to flee, but there were just too many of them to slip off, sight unseen. The only way, the mother decided, was to break the family into two, the older children—13, 12, and 11 years old—going off on their own; the younger ones would follow with her. Nam, her older sister, Phuong, and younger brother, Truong, prepared to leave. All in the family prayed that they would not end up on the pile in the plaza.

Nam, her two siblings, and 20 others squeezed onto the tiny boat and entered the sea. It seemed simple enough. There was nothing in the way between the tip of Vietnam and Thailand, except open water and the pirates.

"When the pirates boarded the boat," Nam told me years later—as I sat in her kitchen in San Jose, while her ten-year-old son and nephew wandered in and out, asking me if I was really a professor, did I like my students, was I a Republican or Democrat, and what was my IQ—"they separated the men from the women, boys from girls. I felt like I had no bones in my body. I couldn't walk. My legs couldn't hold me." But a ship of the United Nations High Commissioner for Refugees appeared and the pirates left before savaging Nam and her family.

I met Nam in 1996 in the Tenderloin. She was 25 years old. Nancy Ong told me, "You have to meet Nam. She has a story to tell." Nam was volunteering at the Vietnamese Family Services Center (VFSC) that she was in the process of cofounding with fellow refugee, The Ha. The Center was offering ESL classes and courses that helped Vietnamese parents bridge their traditional child-rearing methods with American parenting expectations. It wasn't easy. Roles and identity in the Vietnamese family are very different than they are in America, and the parents thought they were losing control and respect, especially as their children increasingly became a part of the new culture.

Nam introduced me to volunteers at VFSC. One was a lawyer in Vietnam, who in turn introduced me to her husband, a former Vietnamese Army officer, who was sent to a "reeducation camp" after the war, actually a prison camp where former military officers, South Vietnamese government workers, employees of American businesses, and others seen as loyal to the old regime were "rehabilitated." Of the more than a million who were imprisoned, many for years, 165,000 are thought to have died.[5] The lawyer's husband was one of the "lucky" ones.

When I went to visit the aging soldier, he met me at the door. He wore an American dress Army jacket, an officer's hat, blue jeans, and tennis shoes. His wife translated. Her husband's affect was flat, he seemed depressed, and, without the language of his new country or practical work skills, other than killing the enemy, his life seemed hopeless. He was hopeful for his nearly grown son, but was worried about the future of his Down syndrome daughter, who I could hear moving about in another room in the tiny apartment.

I attended a graduation ceremony at the Center and talked to a woman who was among the earliest to leave Vietnam. As a member of the more moneyed class, she flew out right after the fall of Saigon, with leaves of gold hidden in her garments. I learned later that many refugees, even boat people, tried to convert whatever they had to gold leaf to begin new lives in America, or Australia, or wherever they might wind up. Many lost their gold, and often their lives, to the pirates in the South China Sea.

On several occasions, Nam talked to my classes at CND (now NDNU). She told her story to my Human Services class, which was joined, for the evening, by a graduate International Business class. Another time, The Ha joined her to speak to my Sociology of the Family class. And in the Tenderloin, although it was campus-based, I took the Human Services class on a walking tour. "Look for unique symbols of community dynamics," I told my students. "Like this one," I said, pointing to a bullet hole in the wall at Leavenworth and Eddy, Crack Corner, that I had seen police investigators study a few days before. "Or that one," I point across the street to a storefront with a sign in the window, "Vietnamese Family Services Agency," then located at 250 Leavenworth Street, right across the street from where Donal and the Fish Stick Gang hung out. Nam and Center volunteers met with students and faculty from team-taught Language, Culture, and Image, my first full-semester, CBL class. All this was more than 20 years after the end of the Vietnam (American) War, but, although we had some Vietnamese students at the college, few American students really knew the plight of the refugees or had ever even met someone from Vietnam, outside of a restaurant.

Nam told the classes, as she had earlier told me, her story of fleeing on the boat to Taiwan in 1983, living in the Phanat Nikhom refugee camp for a year and a half, relocating to the Philippine Refugee Processing Center in Morong, Bataan, receiving a "Certificate of Completion" for a 14-week program in "English as a Second Language and Cultural Orientation," being flown to Seattle, then on to Buffalo, New York, a community about as foreign to the Vietnamese culture and climate as one can imagine. She lived with a series of foster families, the first ending with the divorce of the foster parents. She left the second when the family expected her to conform to their religious beliefs, which didn't match her own. The third was with her best friend's family, who took her in and are still "family," today. She graduated from high school in 1991, and the State University of New York in Fredonia in 1995, with a degree in sociology and a minor in social work. She joined AmeriCorps and became a community organizer in Washington, DC. Her AmeriCorps placement was with Young Women's Project (YWP), a "multi-cultural organization that builds the leadership and power of young women so that they can shape DC policies and institutions so they can expand the rights and opportunities of DC youth. YWP programs guide youth through a process of personal transformation so they can become leaders in their peer groups, families, and communities who are able to analyze problems, identify solutions, and advocate for change."[6]

Nam learned her lessons well. In 1996, the little girl who, 12 years before and 8915 miles away, averted her eyes when she walked by the pile of dead bodies in the village plaza, got on a plane in Buffalo to reunite with her family who had emigrated to San Jose. Then she moved to San Francisco to work at Cameron House in Chinatown as a community organizer.

* * *

It's October 2015. I'm sitting in Nam's kitchen, renewing my relationship with her and trying to answer her son and nephew's questions until she shoos them away. It's been nearly two decades since I've seen her, but she hasn't changed much at all. Her dark hair is not as long as I remember it. She is tinier than I pictured in my mind, around 4'10". She still has that great smile and looks much younger than her 44 years. The energy and passion that I remember her using so effectively when she was young is still there. We talk about her life growing up and what's happened since. She reminds me of a letter I wrote in support of her application to San Francisco State's MSW program. For years after graduating from State, she worked as a community social worker, until her family (her husband, from Mexico, teenaged daughter, and the ten-year-old son) needed more of her time and energy, so she got an LCSW (Licensed Clinical Social Worker) credential and became a therapist. "Better time management." She feels good about being a psychiatric social worker, but she also misses the challenges of contributing more directly to social change. Nam takes a three-ring binder from a stack of books and papers she set aside for me to see and says, "Do you want to see your letter?"

"Sure," I say.

She opens up the binder and we look at it together.
The book is a collection of memorabilia from her life as an immigrant
social activist: certificates from the refugee camps she spent two years in; a
photograph of her as a 14-year-old getting ready to leave the Philippines;
a news clipping of her arrival in Buffalo, with a photograph of her, her two
siblings, and their new foster parents; and another at 23, graduating from
college. There are programs from conferences and community events she
presented at ("Immigrants Pride Day Festival," that she was outreach
coordinator for when she was working as a community organizer for The
Northern California Coalition for Immigrant Rights; "Serve the People
Conference on Asian-American Community Activism"; and "Symposium
on Immigrant Families"); articles she has written ("The Bay Area
Vietnamese Community: An Organizers Perspective," in the newsletter for
the Northern Coalition for Immigrant Rights; "Dianne Feinstein's Wake
Up Call," in the Political Ecology Group Newsletter, about an early morning gathering in front of the senator's exclusive Presidio Heights home in
San Francisco, to let the "undecided" senator know "loud and clear – that
we are demanding she reject the entire package of anti-immigrant legislation," and a *Chronicle* article on the protest, showing a sleepy Senator
Feinstein at 7:00 a.m., wearing a sweatshirt, addressing the crowd), and
a letter to the editor of *Asian Week* ("Scapegoating Immigrants"). There
are articles about her; short stories by her, one comparing rainy days
in Vietnam and America, the other about meeting her estranged father
in Canada; and a "Culturally Specific Curriculum Outline: Vietnamese
Group," for Asian Pacific Islanders Parent Education/Support Program.
At the very end of the binder is the letter I wrote for her, on November
25, 1997, which includes the comment, "In the community, Nam is well
known for her work with the Coalition for Immigrant Rights and the
Vietnamese Family Services Center, which she co-founded. At numerous
events that I have attended – at street fairs, community meetings, gatherings of activists, and other neighborhood events – Nam was a principal
organizer and, often, a featured speaker. She has exceptional interpersonal
skills, is always very well prepared, and speaks with conviction, but is open
to and very respectful of the perspectives of others."
Nam was one of my first street teachers in the Tenderloin, educating
my students and me about the experience of Vietnamese refugees coming to America and living in the Tenderloin, opening up our hearts and
minds to the horrible burdens that so many people on the streets of the
Tenderloin carry. Lessons that, hopefully, would stay with us as we walk

by Vietnamese and Cambodians and all the others in the Tenderloin, and encourage us to remember that every one of them has a story to tell. Eighteen years since I last saw her, I am sitting at Nam's kitchen table, recalling a personal journey that began with a little girl averting her eyes from dead people, tossed onto a pile in her village plaza.

* * *

CBL can be a transformative experience. The combination of sharing an intense learning experience with a group of fellow students; becoming immersed in difficult, entrenched social problems; developing relationships with community people through service, research, or just hanging out with them; reflecting with your cohort on the experience; and learning from street teachers, class discussion, and the literature about social roots of the issues at hand can produce a fundamental reorientation of the way one thinks about "deviant" and "normal" behavior, human nature, and life in general. I have seen and heard about such transformations from many other teachers who use community-engagement pedagogy. As a Campus Compact-Carnegie Foundation Fellow in Political Engagement, I spent two years communicating with, presenting at conferences with, and learning from other Fellows from such diverse disciplines as agriculture, architecture, communications, computer science, education, engineering, English, modern languages and literature, history, political science, psychology, sociology, and Spanish. Each had his or her own approach to CBL. One took students to post-Katrina New Orleans. Another worked on helping to design a museum for indigenous people. One had her students ride the bus late at night and interview homeless people trying to stay safe and dry. Another used her class to encourage the joy of reading to underprivileged children in an elementary school. I used several inner-city neighborhoods in San Francisco to learn about causes of and solutions to social problems, but from the very beginning, I was drawn to the Tenderloin because of its soulful nature.

* * *

The history of the Tenderloin as jazz scene has left an indelible mark on the neighborhood. Jazz greats who played here, such as Billie Holiday, who was arrested at The Linden Hotel on Taylor Street for possession of opium (she had been framed and was acquitted), appear on murals. Billie's rendition of "Strange Fruit," sung at the end of all of her club performances, a deeply emotional song about the lynching of black men in the South, moved all who heard her. These emotional feelings that Billie, and Miles Davis and Thelonious Monk and other black musicians, evoked in the neighborhood through music and song still linger. Jerry Garcia and the Grateful Dead practiced here at the Hyde Street Studio. Their "Casey Jones (High on Cocaine)" song is remembered right across the street by users who hang out in front of Faithful Fools Street Ministry and along the fence at the edge of the parking lot that used to be the site of The Black Hawk, the world-famous jazz club. Jazz clubs and other music venues still dot the neighborhood. Glide Memorial Church is packed on Sundays with people from the streets, outlying neighborhoods, and out-of-towners coming here to hear the powerful sermons on social justice and redemption and listen to the GLIDE Ensemble and Change Band. The church's website proclaims,[7]

> Every Sunday, the drums pulse and the brass rise and fall as the GLIDE Ensemble and Change Band take center stage with their signature open-ing song, "Pass Me Not Oh Gentle Savior." Calling all who have ears to hear, they beckon San Francisco (and indeed, the world) to the corner of Ellis and Taylor for a transcendent spiritual experience that heals and saves lives. Touching thousands of people every year, the GLIDE Ensemble and Change Band draws together those with disparate spiritual paths and life circumstances to sing of liberation, truth telling, love, and hope.

It is, everyone would agree, a soulful experience.

What is soul? Soul has been variously described as the spiritual part of human beings, the seat of our feelings or sentiments. It is noble, it is warm, earthy, deep, the source of courage. It is our emotional nature, our moral force. According to Thomas Moore, psychotherapist, former monk, and author of many books, including *Care of the Soul: A Guide for Cultivating Depth and Sacredness in Everyday Life,*[8] soul is the essence of who we are, and by extension, the essence of human community. For Moore, soul is distinct from spirit. While spirit transcends the human experience, it is uplifting and oriented to the future, soul is immersed in the human experi-ence, it lives in the here and now.

The sounds of sirens, traffic, people shouting across the street to each other, and music blaring; seeing someone lying on the sidewalk, being loaded into an ambulance, getting into a street fight; walking through swarms of drug sales and homeless encampments; passing by sidewalk "garage" sales, massage parlors, strip joints, porno shops, and peo-ple selling sex: all this brings us to the here and now. Watching groups of very young children walk these streets holding hands or gripping a rope anchored front and back by their teachers, seeing them play in the mini-playgrounds that BAWCC was instrumental in having built, looking through the glass walls at the new Boeddeker Park in which Asian ladies do Tai Chi or play mah-jongg, studying colorful and dramatic neighborhood murals, watching police make an arrest, smelling the cooking odors coming from ethnic restaurants of many kinds, hearing languages from all over the world, and receiving kind comments like "Have a nice day" or simply "Hello," that homeless people often toss our way, engaging many of the charismatic characters who make up the street society[9]; listening to street teachers tell stories of their own or other people's struggles; learning that good people are doing good work all over the neighborhood, and helping service providers do that work are all emotional experiences that stir the soul. And all this can happen in one afternoon, in one class session in Tenderloin U. No one is daydreaming. No one is bored. Everyone is alert and moved by their experience. We are in the here and now, walking in the soul of the city. It was Thomas Moore who wrote, "Soul enters life from below, through the cracks, finding an opening into life at the points where smooth functioning breaks down.... [S]oul power may emerge from failure, depression, and loss. The general rule is that soul appears in the gaps and holes of experience.... in those places where we feel most inferior."

Sadness is a soulful sensation. So is loss. To attend the funeral of a young Tenderloin victim of suicide or homicide, to hear the monk chant or the priest pray, to smell the incense and the candles burning, to stand before a statue of the Buddha or Christ on the cross, to see flickering candlelight and sunbeams filtered through the stained glass windows of St. Boniface Church, to look at the distraught faces of mourners, not just in The TL, but in Cunningham Chapel on campus, for students who have died unnatural deaths, Christian Foster, who represented the university so well at College Night in the Tenderloin, shot in the back three times, or another young, charismatic student who never took my classes, but helped raise funds for Halloween in the Tenderloin, collected pumpkins, and volunteered at the Festival, who came to my office and told me about addictions that he had had, that he used to buy black-tar heroin on the corner of Ellis and Hyde, right across the street from the playground, but had kicked the habit, only to be found dead in his bed, an overdose victim. To stand in the back of St. Boniface during a heavy rain, listening to pounding raindrops and the sacred sounds of sleep, to hear U Sam Oeur sing his poem in Cambodian, and repeat the words in English, words that tell the terrible story of the murder of his newborn twin girls: these, too, are soulful experiences.

There are other inner-city neighborhoods in San Francisco, the Haight, the Mission, Hunters Point, and pockets of poverty and its consequences in other parts of the city, but none has the concentration and mix of people, problems, and promise that is, literally, *contained* in The TL. In years to come, students who have taken Tenderloin U classes may not remember the names of theorists or all of the statistics and theories we discussed, but many will *think* differently and remember the Nam Thais, the Nancy Ongs, the Midge Wilsons, the Souns, the Phanna Phays, the Tom Heaths, the Diana Chins, the "Big Red" Garritys, the Judy Youngs, the Kay Rodrigueses, and all the other people we encountered that students may, otherwise, never have had a chance to know, hear their stories, and learn from. These were emotional experiences, and emotional memories remain embedded in our own souls, forever.

NOTES

1. Sofia says 35,000,000 when you count all the people living in the "Parachutas" (slums or shantytowns). This up to 14,000,000-person undercount compares with San Francisco's reported undercount of an estimated 100,000 in a city of 776,000 in the 2000 census. Most of the missing, it has been argued (source), live in the Tenderloin and other poor neighborhoods.
2. See Moore, Thomas, *Care of the Soul: A Guide for Cultivating Depth and Sacredness in Everyday Life*, New York: HarperCollins, 1992.
3. Not her real name.
4. Online images of Mission murals, see http://www.sfmuralarts.com/neighborhood/mission/2.html
5. Do, Anh, Tran Phan, and Eugene Garcia, "Camp Z-30-D: The Survivors," *Orange County Register.* April 29, 2001.
6. http://youngwomensproject.org
7. http://glide.org/ensemble
8. Moore, Thomas, *Care of the Soul: A Guide for Cultivating Depth and Sacredness in Everyday Life*, New York: HarperCollins, 1992.
9. See DVD "Love Me Tenderloin," directed by Henri Quenette, coproduced by Denny Packard and Henri Quenette, 2004 for an introduction to "Indian Joe" and others.

CHAPTER 16

Compassion as Pedagogy

To understand is to forgive

© The Author(s) 2017
D. Stannard-Friel, *Street Teaching in the Tenderloin*,
DOI 10.1057/978-1-137-56437-5_16

"I used to walk through the Tenderloin like this." She held up her open hands on either side of her face, mimicking blinders. "Just walking by people. Then, I got depressed, really depressed. It was very bad. I couldn't do anything. I couldn't function. Couldn't work. I withdrew. Meds really helped. When I came back to the Tenderloin, I saw things differently. Very much so. I could relate to their [the street people's] experience. I could relate to their suffering, being overwhelmed by emotions. It happened to *me*!"

Longtime Tenderloin service provider

* * *

Compassion: "Literally means 'to suffer together'… the feeling that arises when you are confronted with another's suffering and feel motivated to relieve that suffering."[1]

Pedagogy: The "process of accompanying learners; caring for and about them; and bringing learning into life."[2]

This definition of "pedagogy" is not a traditional one, nor is it one that I have articulated to others, or even to myself, over the many years that I have been teaching, but it is the one that, in reflection, I have been *using* in the Tenderloin for 20 years. I came across this particular explanation online, while writing this book, at infed.org, a not-for-profit site by the YMCA George Williams College, London. In an article called "What is Pedagogy," Mark K. Smith, a specialist in informal education, social pedagogy, and community learning, explains,

A common way of approaching pedagogy is as the art and science (and maybe even craft) of teaching. As we will see, viewing pedagogy in this way both fails to honour the historical experience, and to connect crucial areas of theory and practice. Here we suggest that a good way of exploring pedagogy is as the process of accompanying learners; caring for and about them; and bringing learning into life.

Drawing on the work of Paulo Freire, Smith explains, teachers often try to drill learning into students, making "deposits of knowledge."[3] This can "descend into treating learners like objects, things to be acted upon rather than people to be related to. In contrast, to call ourselves 'educators' we need to look to acting *with* people rather on them."

Education is a deliberate process, Smith says, of *drawing out* learning, of *encouraging* and giving time to discovery. Referring to John Dewey, a major architect of progressive education and what came to be community-engagement learning, education is a social process "of living and not a preparation for future living."[4] It is a process based on values and commitments, such as respect for others and the truth, and the search for "possibility." Education is born "of the hope and desire that all may share in life and 'be more.'" Citing Ron Miller, an early contributor to holistic education, he writes, "We find identity, meaning, and purpose in life through connections to the community, to the natural world, and to spiritual values such as compassion and peace."[5] Education, according to Smith, "is concerned not just with knowing about things, but also with changing ourselves and the world we live in." This, he says, "involves a committed and action-oriented form of education."

These are the values, commitments, and pedagogy of Tenderloin U. Underlying it all is the goal of instilling *empathy* in the mind and soul of the student for those who have fallen by the wayside, been *pushed* to the edge of society by the culture, including its economy. This involves, as was said earlier, helping the student relate intellectually *and* emotionally to the lives of the people of the inner city—as a way of enhancing compassion and understanding (of the self as well as the other). By appreciating the *social* and *shared* nature of the human experience, individuals can be empowered to engage in meaningful social and personal change.

* * *

"Hello?"

"Hello, Dr. Rubin?"

"Yes?"

I'm calling Lillian Rubin, sociologist, psychotherapist, and best-selling author.

"Dr. Rubin, my name is Don Stannard-Friel. I'm a professor at Notre Dame de Namur University in Belmont, but I teach community-based classes in the Tenderloin. This semester we're using your book, *The Transcendent Child*. I'd like to talk to you about, maybe, speaking to the class in the Tenderloin."

I explained to her the nature of the program and the learning objectives of the class.

"You teach *in* the Tenderloin?"

"Yes."

"Where?"

"All over. The day I'd like you to talk, April 21, we'll be meeting at St. Boniface Church, on Golden Gate Avenue, near Jones."

"I live on Jones. Not in the Tenderloin." There was a pause on the phone. "Let me check." A few minutes of silence, except for the sounds of shuffling in the background, then, "OK. Call me a week or so before."

"Fine, thank you very much."

On April 21, Lillian Rubin met us at Wild Awakenings. I didn't know it when I called her, but she was 81 years old at the time. She was dressed stylishly, but didn't stand out too much in the neighborhood, except that she was a very attractive woman who looked much younger than her years. I called the week before and offered to pick her up at home or she could meet us at St. Boniface, but she wanted to meet at the coffeehouse to "see what that's all about, but you can drive me home." We walked up Leavenworth Street, 15 students, Lillian Rubin, and I, and turned onto Golden Gate Avenue. The church gates were already chained closed, the Sacred Sleep program was over for the day, but we were meeting in the rectory conference room. The receptionist buzzed us in and Fr. Louie Vitale, the pastor and our frequent street teacher, came out of a back room to greet us. Fr. Louie, as everyone calls him, is a Franciscan priest-activist, who cofounded the Sacred Sleep program, officially called the Gubbio Project. The St. Boniface webpage tells the story of its founding.

> The Gubbio Project is named for an Italian town where, according to legend, St. Francis negotiated a peace agreement between frightened townsfolk and a hungry wolf. Francis brokered a deal between the two parties in conflict by recognizing that with communication they could find common ground. In the Tenderloin, working poor people live next to desperately poor people and sometimes misunderstandings and conflicts occur. The Gubbio Project is a creative response to this situation – helping housed parishioners and visitors of the church connect with their unhoused neighbors. The Gubbio Project believes that by creating opportunities for these two groups to interact and care for each other's needs, the Tenderloin neighborhood will be strengthened.

Fr. Louie was 73 at the time, and he and Lillian hit it off.
"Would you like to see inside the church?" he offered.
"Yes, I would. Thank you."
We all went down a hallway and into the church, with its majestic organ, stained glass windows, beautiful woodwork, plush red rug, flickering candles, and multiple, mini-ethno-specific altars (Vietnamese, Latino, Filipino). The students had been there the week before to hear Louie talk about "Individual and Organizational Development in the Inner City," but because the class begins after the Sacred Sleep program ends for the day, neither the students nor Lillian got to see its impactful outcome, because the church was empty, though, later, some of the students volunteered to

serve there on the university's "Call to Action Day." Louie walked Lillian through the church, explained the program and the community to her, told her the history of the Franciscans in the neighborhood, and then led us all to the conference room and said his goodbyes.

Lillian was very engaging and friendly, but professional in her manner. She explained the theory behind her book and what motivated her to write it. "My father died when I was five years old and my mother was mentally ill. My brother was troubled and, we think, took his own life in a one-car accident, crashing it into a tree."

Her Ukrainian Jewish parents had fled pogroms after World War I and settled in Philadelphia. After her husband died, Lillian's mother moved the family to New York and did piecework in the garment industry. Lillian discovered the insecurity and shame of living in poverty and the difficulty of having a cruel, mentally ill mother. In *The Transcendent Child: Tales of Triumph Over the Past*,[6] she describes her mother force-feeding her vegetables until she swallowed them, choked, or vomited. The mother clearly favored her son and told her daughter on many occasions, "Girls shouldn't be born."

It was in *The Transcendent Child* that Lillian explored why some people are crushed by such early life experiences, and others, like herself, thrived. "I wanted to know," she told us in the rectory of St. Boniface Church, "why my brother committed suicide, while I, an unwanted child in a very difficult family, am a happy, accomplished person." What intrigued her was how she was able to overcome a childhood where, she writes, "death, poverty and a mother's nearly psychotic rage determined daily life…. Why did he [her brother] get stuck in our frightful past? How did I escape?"[7] To answer, she studied the lives of eight people who were able to transcend their own difficult pasts. Her research question,[8] "What are the personal qualities and social conditions that make it possible for some people to flourish when they have grown up in 'bad' families?" Her answers were summarized in class, but more fully explained in *The Transcendent Child*: "Certainly, the tangled strands of DNA that determine our genetic predispositions make a difference in the way we respond to the world around us," she wrote.[9] "Particular psychological proclivities, class background, subcultural differences, personal experiences, and the way they are internalized all make a difference in the making of an adult – an idea that, once expressed, we intuitively recognize as true, yet one that has been neglected by both mental health professionals and popular culture," who, she says, focus on early childhood experience as *determining* the future of the child.

Such psychological explanation is not enough to explain why some are able to take new paths. She argues,[10] "it's one of the great failings of psychological theory that it doesn't adequately take account of the impact of the larger social milieu – whether economic, cultural, or political – on human development."

People who transcend their pasts, Rubin writes,[11] find other adults who provide support as mentors, role models, or friends, offering hope for a new way of life. "Sometimes these are long-lasting relationships; often they are not. It makes no difference. Their importance lies in their *meaning* to the persons involved and in the fact that there is someone to hold out a hand in time of need, someone also who can help fill the empty space inside."

"A sense of mission – a commitment to something larger than self and personal interest – is prominent in most of the stories" that she writes about in her book. "At the most obvious level, such a mission provides purpose and meaning in people's lives.... The mission is related to the gratitude that expresses itself in a sense of indebtedness that impels them to try to pay back what they call their 'good fortune.'" They want to use their pasts to help others. "In doing so, they not only give meaning to their suffering but help to heal themselves."

Lillian Rubin talking to the Promise class in the rectory of St. Boniface Church was a powerful learning experience for everyone in the room. That she was speaking not only as a scholar, but as a survivor, one who has been so successful in life in spite of her extremely difficult childhood, a childhood that she transcended, inspired us all.

The lesson that Lillian taught us is similar to one explored in Deviant Behavior, the class where we visited San Quentin State Prison and organized the Witness Program, and in some of the earlier Promise of the Inner City classes. Bonnie Benard, MSW, an author and award-winning researcher for her work as a prime architect of "resiliency theory," writes about children overcoming extremely negative life experiences. In "The Foundations of the Resiliency Framework," she explains,[12]

resiliency research refers to a body of international cross-cultural, lifespan developmental studies that followed children born into seriously high-risk conditions such as families where parents were mentally ill, alcoholic, abusive, or criminal, or in communities that were poverty-stricken or war-torn. The astounding finding from these long term studies was that at least 50% – and often closer to 70% – of youth growing up in these high-risk conditions did develop social competence despite exposure to severe stress and did overcome the odds to lead successful lives. Furthermore, these studies not only identified the characteristics of these "resilient" youth, several documented the characteristics of the environments – of the families, schools, and communities – that facilitated the manifestation of resilience.

What are those "characteristics of the environments…that facilitated the manifestation of resilience"? In "Fostering Resiliency in Kids: Protective Factors in the Family, School, and Community,"[13] a paper that has been credited with introducing resiliency theory and its application to the fields of prevention and education, she explains,

> A resilient child has been described as one who is socially competent, self-efficacious, and an effective problem-solver who is able to negotiate through a web of adversity. Longitudinal studies of resilient children indicate that the following protective factors, present in the family, school, and community, serve as a buffer against those variables that put the child at risk of unhealthy behavior such as violence:
>
> • a positive, caring relationship with an adult.
> • high expectations for behavior and abilities; and
> • opportunities for meaningful participation and involvement.

People who make a difference—that Lillian referred to as "adults who provide support as mentors, role models, or friends, offering hope for a new way of life"—according to Benard, are the adults who not only care for the child and expect her or him to behave in socially appropriate ways, but also believe *in* the child, have appreciation and high expectations for his or her abilities and talents, and help provide opportunities for meaningful involvement in society.

* * *

From: Sam Soun   Sent: Wed 3/3/2010 9:07 AM
To: Don Stannard-Friel
Subject: Hello Dr. Don…. It's Sam…

Dear Dr. Don,

Thank you for your email. It is always a pleasure to hear from you. It sounds like you have been busy occupied with work and writing another book. I hope everything works out as you plan. Knowing you, the book will have a wonderful turnout. Best wishes to you. Anyhow, Tatum and I are doing well. She has one more grad-school year until accomplishing her Ph.D. in counseling psychology. I'm very proud of her as she is excited as well. As for me, I don't know what and where I'll be when I'm done with college. Going to grad-school is an option, but that decision will depend on the relocating site that Tatum and I will decide on. She has to look for an internship site, and when she's done we are planning to take it from there. You know me, my life goes wherever the wind blows; taking life as it approaches making one decision at a time. I used to view my life as a card-game where I'm dealt a bad hand. And for some odd reason, i had always correlated that concept to a natural process that was done by a higher supernatural object or being/s. But I finally realize. Society is consisted of human doings, we place meanings and values into ideas, policies, patterns and systematic institutions to govern human life. Everything we do, the choices we make, what we value are influenced and revolves around this ideology. Humans create society, but in turn, society creates us. Now, I understand that the cards that I was dealt with was a social process consisted of human doings rather than natural. Therefore, if someone gives me something that I don't like, I realize that I can actually throw it away. My point is, I never thought that I could leave my struggles and the Tenderloin due to some powerful force/s, however, I now realize that I can. I can throw away a bad hand and pick up a new one, but I still had/have to negotiate with the dealer (I still have to conform to society). What can I do if I want to exist successfully with/in society without having to always conform to it? Any ideas Dr. Don? I have been asking myself this question. Maybe the question is inane, but I'm a bit baffled. I just want to live life more free with less contingencies.

Best,
Sam

* * *

Five months later. It's Thursday, August 12, 2010. I'm meeting Sam in the neighborhood at IHDC. We walk up Leavenworth Street to Thai Noodle restaurant on the corner at Geary to celebrate his graduation from the university. It's a popular place. Most of the customers today, and most days, are Asian. Must say something good about the authenticity of the food. We're led to a booth by a waitress. I order Pad Thai, Sam a beef stew dish with thick noodles. He starts off the conversation, "Thanks for being my mentor, Dr. Don." In each of the four classes he took with me, before heading off to University of Oregon, Sam was a star pupil. His academic skills were not what they would become in Oregon, where he could take courses at its Teaching and Learning Center, catching up in some areas that he fell behind in when he dropped out of sixth grade. But, his natural intellectual skills and academic curiosity, sharpened by his education in the streets and working for service programs, writing grants, organizing programs and events, and being Oral History Assistant for IHDC's book, *Stories of Survival*, prepared him to absorb the lessons of Tenderloin U and be an in-class street teacher at the same time.

"My two guides," he says, "are resilience theory and Margaret Wheatley's 'out of chaos comes order.'"

We had talked in class about resilience theory and Wheatley's book *Leadership and the New Science: Learning about Organizations from an Orderly Universe.*[14] Wheatley received her EdD from Harvard and, among many awards, was recognized as one of the American Society for Training and Development's "living legends" and received its highest honor, "Distinguished Contribution to Workplace Learning and Performance." She has been a business professor, author, public speaker, and consultant specializing in systems theory and organizations as self-organizing entities. I became aware of her when I was teaching Human Service courses at NDNU. Hers was a contribution to a "new paradigm" book genre that was emerging as the Internet and computer technologies were fundamentally reordering many aspects of our culture and the way we think, as the Age of Information and Communication was imbedding itself in global society. She believes in an organic process of organizational leadership. This is how she presents her perspective on her website[15]:

> If we are to contribute to this unendingly complex world and the complicated, exhausting lives we now live, we need to develop much greater insight and understanding before we choose our actions.
>
> Seeing with new eyes gives us the capacity to solve problems instead of creating more of them. As the American newsman Eric Sevaried remarked, "the cause of problems is solutions." This is increasingly more evident as we watch programs and policies not only fail, but create unintended consequences that cause greater harm. Only if we take the time and discipline to see with new eyes will we be able to discern more clearly and choose more wisely. And as our clarity and wisdom grows, we develop the confidence and strength necessary to persevere in the work that is ours to do.

Some of her fundamental points, as I presented them in class, are:

Margaret Wheatley
Leadership and the New Science

I.   Order can emerge out of chaos:
      • Order develops naturally from within.
      • Chaos creates new systems of order; new perspectives.

II.   Information informs us and forms us:
      • Information has been guarded (in the old paradigm)
      • Information is essential to growth.
      • Something we can not see or experience is forming us.

III. Relationships are all there is:
      • We (like particles) are potential that forms significance in
      relationship to others.

IV.   Vision is an invisible field:
      • Vision emerges from interactions, good thinking, and good
      hearts on the team.

Illustration 16.1   Margaret Wheatley h.o.

"I think of my life as 'beautiful chaos,'" Sam says. We talk about his
recent college graduation, his history of dropping out of sixth grade,
and the struggles he had growing up in the Tenderloin. He was contemplating not going to his college commencement ceremony. He told me
that his only graduation before was from grammar school, fifth grade.
His mother came to the celebration with her head bandaged, "from
being split open and stitched together," after a beating by Sam's father.
"People at the graduation, even some of her own relatives, laughed at
her," Sam told me. "I was embarrassed. I think I was thinking about that
when I decided that I didn't want to go, but then I thought this would
be a way to make up for it. For people laughing at her. For me being
embarrassed."
"Make up for it by walking in the university commencement?"
"Yeah."
"She'd be proud of you." (His mother died before he went to the
university.)
"I hope so. I think so."

I ask Sam about his brother, Tee, in prison for manslaughter. We talk about the old Cain and Abel question: How is it that one brother does so well and the other gets into trouble? Sammy, the number three brother, and Laura, the youngest of the siblings, are also doing well. Why not Tee? "I used to run around and do stuff, get into trouble, but I never got caught," Sam tells me. "I got arrested five or six times for fighting, not for dealing or anything. I just didn't want to do that anymore. So I channeled my anger into weight lifting, that's when I got into working out. I was working three jobs, five to nine in a restaurant, ten to two in another restaurant. And in the afternoons to four o'clock at IHDC. I went to City College, but I didn't go to classes. Not until yours. That and IHDC is where I got my praise. Tee would fight and he would get rewarded for that from his group. That's where he got his praise. That's where he put his anger."

* * *

I met Sam, Sammy, and Laura, one at a time, in 1997 and 1998, at IHDC, and our lives have been intertwined ever since. They all attended the Halloween in the Tenderloin Festivals, Laura and Sammy still do, each with their own child now, and, for many years they all attended College Night in the Tenderloin, including our very first one in 1999, and Campus Visit Day. Theirs has been a case study of transcendence and resilience theories, and a demonstration of how order can emerge out of chaos. Tee and I met off and on over the years, but we never made much of a connection. We were both involved in other things and our paths rarely crossed. I did meet his then baby son and the child's mom in front of the playground on one of the rare occasions that he came by. He was a lot like the other Souns, good-looking, charismatic, and charming. But his was a different path.

Manslaughter verdict in parking-space slaying[16]

Jaxon Van Derbeken, Chronicle Staff Writer
Friday, January 23, 2009

(01-22) 17:26 PST SAN FRANCISCO --
A 27-year-old San Francisco man has been convicted of manslaughter for stabbing a man to death over a parking space on Geary Boulevard, authorities said Thursday.

Sarith Soun was charged in the Sept. 16, 2006, stabbing death of 19-year-old Boris Albinder of Pacifica, who was attacked outside a club at Geary and Third Avenue after he tried to park in a spot that a friend had attempted to save for him.

Sarith Soun. That would be Tee.

* * *

The Soun family story begins in Cambodia, sometime during the reign of the Khmer Rouge. What happened in the early years is murky in the minds of the children. Mom and Dad didn't talk much about it, except that three or four of their daughters died from starvation and illness. Only the oldest survived. And everyone on the father's side of the family was murdered.

He was a carpenter, she of a more affluent family, but they married. Maybe that wasn't such a good idea. With their one remaining girl, they fled Cambodia, crossing over the border into Thailand, where the three boys—Samnang, Sarith, and Sambath—were born in the Khao-I-Dang refugee camp.

Sambath, the youngest, was just a baby when they were taken to the Philippines to be processed for transport to the USA. A photograph shows him in a stroller by a sign outside the processing center. "People think I was born there," Sammy (Sambath) tells me three decades later, "but I was born in Khao-I-Dang, just like my brothers."[17] It would take four years of living in the camps before the Soun family would be sent off to their new home in America, the Tenderloin.

It did not go well for the children. Maybe even worse for the parents.

None of the kids, except Laura, knows exactly when they were born. No birth certificates were issued and birthdays weren't celebrated, so it didn't really matter in the refugee camps. Laura was born in San Francisco at General Hospital. The birth was recorded and a certificate issued on July 26, 1985. The given name on it is the name of the doctor that delivered her. An American name. "I wasn't happy with that growing up," Laura told me. "All the others had Cambodian names. I wanted a Cambodian name, until I looked up 'Laura.' It means 'Lady of Victory.' I like that." The boys use Laura's birthdate, the only one officially recorded, to gauge their own: Sam (Samnang) was told two different birthdates by his mom. He thinks one came from her picking an auspicious date in America to tell the immigration people, January 1, 1979, New Year's Day, but it might have really been September 23, another date he was told. Sammy was told he was born September 26, 1983, which he figures is about right, nearly two years older than his sister. Tee's (Sarith) is between his two brothers. With the older sister and parents, that made seven people living in a studio apartment at 270 Turk Street. The closet housed a bunk bed. Everyone scattered at night to sleep in nooks and crannies of the tiny apartment. The eldest, the sister, left home as soon as she could.

The Soun mother was in a wheelchair at the time of Sam's birth, and sickly ever since. Sam described her to me as "physically ill" his whole life, and his dad as "mentally ill." His siblings, in their own words, would concur. Sam said, "My dad used drugs, alcohol, and violence, until he left us when I was 15. He never worked. My mother worked until midnight. He drank and got drunk and would beat her up when she got home." Sam would call the cops, the dad would be arrested, and Sam would clean up the blood. But it got to the point that the cops didn't want to make an arrest, unless he really pressed them to do so. "If we take in your dad," he was told, "and your mom is in the hospital, you'll all wind up in foster care."

All the kids agree that, besides the mom, Sam was the most consistent victim of the father's rage. He would kick Sam when he was only three and four years old, jealous of the mother's love for their son. When Sam was older, he won the family's first Christmas tree at the rec center. It had no ornaments, but it was a Christmas tree. Dad threw it out the window.

Laura says it was hard sharing the Turk Street studio with so many other people, and growing up in the Tenderloin. She's tried to erase a lot of what happened from her mind, but that's hard to do. Especially when what happened is unforgettable. "When I was young, there was always abuse. Dad was always hitting my mom. He never hit me, but Sam. Sam got hit the most of the kids."

Laura remembers: "Once Dad came home, hit my mom with a thick cutting board. The boys were in and out, staying with friends a lot of the time. I was alone with my mom when Dad came home and hit her with a toy metal airplane. I was seven, eight years old. I dragged her upstairs to my friend's on the fourth floor and called the ambulance. I remember Mom saving up and buying a radio. Dad threw it out the window.

"He moved out when I was ten years old. Moved to Oakland. We moved to a studio at 237 Leavenworth Street."

"237 Leavenworth?" I ask, "Did you know Donal? Big D?"

"Big D ran the block."

"I know Big D," I told her. "Used to hang out with him." Laura thought that was *very* funny.

She asked if Donal was dead.

"I don't know. I heard he is. I know some of his buddies are. He moved to LA and I lost track of him, but I heard he's dead."

Laura went on with her story, "Leavenworth was very alive in a bad way. Lots of personalities. I remember leaving the apartment to buy some food and there was a shooting. I remember thinking, 'What are you going to do? I have to get food for my mom. Gotta obey my mom.' So, I went and got the food."

She continued, "I remember going to the corner store to buy balloons for my mom's boyfriend."

"Balloons? Why balloons?" I asked.

"He was selling drugs. Black stuff. I think it was heroin. He'd put the heroin in the balloons."

When I was writing *City Baby and Star*, City Baby told me about selling crack cocaine in balloons. "If the cops arrest you, you swallow the balloon, pass it through, and fish it out of the toilet bowl. Then smoke the crack inside. It's called 'shit rock.'"

When the boys were young, they hung around the rec center, which was then in the basement of St. Boniface Church. Diana Chin and Kay Rodrigues were playground directors and it was a safe haven for a lot of the kids in The TL. Sammy never really hung out with Big D and the guys on Leavenworth Street. They were too old for him at the time. But Tee and Sam, at 14 and 16, were on the edge of that generation, the older 1.5ers who didn't have a good command of English, were unfamiliar with the mores and customs of their American peers, lacked work skills, and felt alienated from American society. Sammy told me, "Fresh from Cambodia, they just understood street life, drugs." The streets were a dead end for young men who were a lot like Phanna's brother, Chet, who sought "freedom" by hanging himself.

Sam had dropped out of sixth grade, going only, on occasion, for the minimal days required when a letter was sent home saying he had to attend or the mother's welfare checks would be discontinued. When his mom was beaten, and taken away by ambulance, he would run away to avoid being teased by friends. Sam just wanted a normal family, a normal life.

He left home for good when he was 14.

No home, no education, and no money, he slept on benches in Boeddeker Park, stayed at friends' houses, when he could, waited all night outside the St. Boniface basement doors until Diana or Kay came to work.

Laura, Tee, and Sammy were still staying with their mom on Leavenworth Street, until she got depressed, came down with psoriasis, and was admitted to the hospital. Laura told me, "The boys were pretty tight. On the streets a lot, together. I'm the only daughter, so I go to hospital to be with my mom. Since she can't work, she can't pay the rent, so we get kicked out of 237 and went to live with grandparents in a house on Paris Street [in the city's outlying Excelsior District]. It was my mom's family, but we weren't wanted, the poor members of the family, on welfare and food stamps." There were three related families living there. The boys were in and out with their cousins, drinking all the time. Laura stayed home and watched her mom. "I hated it. Wanted to be a teen. I didn't even know how to be a girl, be clean. Overweight. I wore baggy clothes like the boys. Ran away to The TL, my comfort zone. Felt safer here than in any suburb."

She was 15, with her mom in the hospital, when the doctor told her that her mother only had a few months to live. "I was massaging her legs, when, for the first time, you know what, ever, she said, 'I love you guys.' First time ever. I started freaking out. Then she yelled at me, 'Take me home.' We took her home. Granddad came in the middle of the night, 'Your mom just died.' Dad showed up. 'Why is he here?' But I think he really loved my mom. Sat with her throughout the funeral.

"After the funeral, my grandfather says, 'You've got to go.' The boys too crazy. We wind up on the street, busting an all-nighter. Staying with friends. 111 Jones. Can't stay every day, cause you gotta sign in and out. Can only stay a couple of nights. Sam gave me money and I got welfare; uncle minded it, but I never saw any of it. I didn't go to school, couldn't even think. I tried going back, loved history and stuff, but Galileo [High School] was too much. 2000 kids. Do I even exist?

"Mr. Phelps asked questions. Current events. I knew the answers. Nobody else did. But I dropped out. On the streets. Sam said, 'You have to go to your sister's in San Jose. So I did. But she's alcoholic, abusive. Was traumatized herself in Cambodia. Different guys coming in all the time. I was smoking weed all the time. And I ran away to The TL.

"Sam and Vee [her cousin] were hanging out at City Impact [Christian church, school, and community service program]. My friends hung out there, too. I went by the church, asked 'Can I have a Bible?' I was raised

Buddhist, but I asked for a Bible. Sam saw me in The TL. 'Get out of here! Why are you here?' I said. 'This is my home, Sam.'

"I smoked weed all the time to get out of the physical realities. I was thirsty for life, for truth. Jehovah Witnesses, I would ask for their brochures. Cut out pictures of Jesus. I was mad at God, but I was attracted. Sam was working at IHDC then. Going to church. But he said, 'You can't do this. The crowd, your crowd, love them, but you gotta leave them.'

"I went to Continuation High, Ella Hutch in the Fillmore. A Christian teacher prayed over me. Kay prayed over me. You know she's into that. I wanted to be like these people. Going to church, VYDC, IHDC, the rec center. Kay and Diana. 'I want what you guys have. I want to experience you in a real way.'

"Then I had a dream, people chasing me. Pulling me down. Dream of my whole life. Someone stood up for me, a masculine figure. A bigger presence. 'You just keep going. I am here for you.' I was 18 years old then. Stopped smoking weed. Told Sam, 'I just want to live my life for God.' Moved into the church. I just wanted to trust God. I have to learn forgiveness. Be humble. Mop the floor and thank God.

"I visited Dad in Oakland, lying in bed with a caretaker. She showed me a mountain of Olde English '800' beer cans. 'They're all his.' I held his hand. He said, 'I loved your mom.' I believed him.

"I learned a lot at City Impact. Public speaking. I had a different [training] job every three months. I was assistant to Dina for three months [Dina Hilliard, who went on to run the Benefit District and Tenderloin Safe Passage]. When she resigned, I replaced her. It was a self-taught curriculum and I went to workshops. Dina was a great role model. And I had loved working with the kids at the rec center, helping Kay and Diana. Went back to City College, took child development classes.

"At first, I had a hard time with church. People had friends. I hated that. I wanted that. People would say, 'I love you.' Do I believe that? Can I believe that?"

* * *

Laura and I are sitting in the community room in Boeddeker Park. She is 30 years old now. I am finishing an interview with her for this book. She is still working at City Impact, where she is a highly regarded, beloved teacher. She wraps up the interview, saying, "I never thought I'd marry. Never thought anyone would love me. So crazy in the head. All that I went through. I hid my conflicts. Never thought I'd have a baby. Now I have my own family."

Laura and I hug. Her husband Joshua, working for the Boys and Girls Club at the new Boeddeker, comes over to say hello. I say my goodbyes and head up to see Sammy, who is working up at Tenderloin Children's Playground, to hear his version of the Soun story.

He's in the gym. Too much noise to talk, so he suggests we step outside. It's an unusually cold day in San Francisco, but I figure we can give it a shot. He tells me much the same story that Laura had, and Sam before that, and I watched unfold over the years. Living in The TL, moving to the grandparents, dropping out of high school. "My mom was sick. It was that time of life that I was losing a lot of people [he went to all the funerals I did, and then some]. My older brother moved out. My dad had moved out. That was a good thing. There was good times with my parents, and there was bad times, but they were never good when they were together.

"My mom died on January 27, 2001. From that day forward the family was really conflicted. In the summer, trouble. Not gang life, street life, this and that, you know, controlling drugs, you know, selling drugs. I jumped into that. Making money, but I wanted to join the Army. I'm always running away. People always wanted to mug us, rob us. I was very young. I didn't have a place to live. Living with friends. Sometimes their family didn't want you there, friend didn't want you there.

"Didn't feel comfortable without a home, on the streets. When you in a position that you have to defend yourself it's not just, hey that's cool man, and walk away. You solve it by violence. Sam was working, doing good. Cops warn him that they're onto me. Cut it out! I'm 18 years old, 120 pounds, and I get busted. Had no business being on the streets. Busted, jailed. Where are my friends? Where's some money for my [jail] account?

"I was sent to Mentor Court. No felony charge and no jail if I attend classes and take pee tests. That was OK. I never really used drugs. I finished the program. Tee and me was hanging out, always together. Still no place to live, jumping from house to house. Sometimes different houses. See each other in the morning. Tom Heath rents me a room for $100 a month.

"Tom was always there for me. For us. He was a banker, but volunteered at TASP [Tenderloin After-School Program], and did Midge [Wilson]'s Walk-A-Thon. We met there when I was 12. Been friends ever since. He bought me and my friends Giants tickets, got us food and clothes. Me and Rin, when we were 12, 13, would stop by the bank and ask for lunch money. They'd all be in suits and ties, and us in baggy shit, but it was alright with Tom. He was really close to my family, wants to see people happy. He's caring and considerate. Tom will always be family.

"When I was 20, I got really sick. Skinny and sick. A real bad pain in my stomach. I woke up in the night and told Tom maybe he should call an ambulance, but he took me right to the hospital. Appendicitis. It was so bad, they thought they'd have to put a bag on me, but a doctor came in and said, 'No! No! No! It's just an abscess.'

"After a while, I went to live with Sam, who was working with Tom at IHDC then. Tom got him a studio apartment at Eddy Street. I went to work for Boys and Girls Club [where he became a superstar, working with middle school kids and developing the national award-winning nutrition program]. When Sam went off to school [University of Oregon], I took over the studio. When my girlfriend got pregnant, I let Phanna use the apartment, then Laura. I came back when my girlfriend and I broke up, and I'm there now with my daughter and nephew, Jacob [Tee's son].

"I went back to college. I had earned my high school equivalency, and had tried City College before, but didn't do very well. Didn't go to classes. But having my daughter changed me, grounded me. Learned I like math, solving problems, problem challenges. A lot of my work has been being a problem-solver. I guess that's the mentality I have. Make things better. That's what I do in the community. Want to do something better in the world, better food, better water resources. I found that I like chemistry, math. I wanted to get a better job and needed a college degree to advance. I tried to enroll in an LVN private program, but it was a rip-off. $38,000 for 15 months. 'You'll make so much money,' they told me. But it was a rip-off. I figured that I could go to community college for $5000 and get my AA. CCSF was too big. But Skyline [down the Peninsula] was not. First semester, 4.0. Did I really deserve this? I asked the teachers to let me know. My art teacher, basic drawing and all that, 'You've exceed the work of a lot of these students, Sammy. Exceeded it!' The American History teacher, 'You're an excellent student, helped your fellow student, and on top of that, you know what you're doing. You do need to work on your vocabulary,' cause, you know, I have to write an essay, 'but you know history.' I was so proud of myself I *was* disappointed semester two: 3.87. But third semester, 4.0. Becoming a father grounded me.

"So many things connect. Jacob needed help with his homework, I can help him. Math problems. I learned it at school. Middle School Director at Boys and Girls Club, I can help them: chemistry, algebra. That's what I feel proud of. I could model: go to school, never too old to learn. A cycle of encouragement. 'I can do it, you can do it.'

"I have two part-time jobs, Rec and Park and MYEEP [the Mayor's Youth Employment and Education Program] with JCYC [Japanese Culture Youth Center] at VYDC, go to school at night, come home to parent two kids [with his new girlfriend], and be a good boyfriend. I want to buy a house, invest in my daughter and Jacob. Want to be mentally and physically there for Tee when he gets out of prison, financially too.

"At 40, if I reach that age, I want to explore the East Coast, get away from all this."

* * *

For Sam, the oldest of the four who remained in the Tenderloin, the existential questions are: What happened? Who am I? Throughout all the horror of his childhood, Diana Chin, the playground director, was always there for him, starting when he was four years old. Even after he left the Tenderloin, she visited him at college and went to his graduation. So did Tom. Sam said she is his godmother, and Tom Heath, his godfather. When he was working for BAWWC at Tenderloin Community School, he met Tatum, a refugee from Vietnam, who was doing an internship there before going off to Oregon for her PhD. He followed her and received his bachelor's degree in sociology. "Tatum broke me out of a cage," he told me. "Tatum is my savior." She provided stability and got him out of The TL, out of San Francisco. They live in Sacramento where he is working with special-needs kids, and she is doing her postdoc hours. They have a daughter, named Harper Sophat Soun. Sophat was his mother's name.

"Diana was always there, every day, even in dark times. Tom was the guardian angel for the family. Tom cares. IHDC, VYDC, Bay Area Women's and Children's Center, without these people to help me become more effective, wise, available, I would still be struggling."

Among many awards, while growing up in the Tenderloin, Sam received the Youth Recognition Award for Leadership and Community Service for Dist. 6 (Tenderloin and South of Market) and a Certificate of Recognition for Community Service and Dedication by the San Francisco Board of Supervisors and Mayor's Office.

Still, he does have some regrets:

"Regret number one: Not being there for my mom. I should have been there for her. I try and honor her by being good to women I dated, naming my daughter after her. I didn't have the means to take Mom to Disneyland, which she would have liked to do, didn't have the money to buy her a house. But I can honor her with the way I live my life.

"Regret number two: Not understanding my father's struggles and pain. Not being able to understand what my dad went through. Lost his whole family in Cambodia, lost his four daughters, not enough to feed the family, placed in Tenderloin. When he died, I was in college, heard he died. I felt no pain, don't know what happened to him, didn't care. I was getting back at him. But now I understand, I forgive him. Dad lost all his family, triggered his negative behavior."

* * *

And then there is Tee. What happened to Tee? He is in prison for man-slaughter, for killing a young man over a parking place that the victim's friend was standing in, saving, while the victim made a U-turn. Tee and his crew wanted the parking place, so they nudged the victim's friend aside with their car, and a fistfight broke out. And Tee pulled out a knife.

Tee was well known for his artistic abilities, drawing tattoos, and fighting prowess. Sam told me Tee could have been a successful professional boxer. But he had struggles that the others didn't have. Learning disabilities resulted in his being placed in special ed. As a kid, he was traumatized when he was hit by a car. Although I found him to be friendly the few times I met him, I was told by his siblings that he had problems socializing and low self-esteem. But his good looks and toughness got him his recognition. While his siblings were able to find caring adults in Tenderloin community programs, his recognition came from the streets. And the streets became his community.

* * *

I've heard the question, "What happened to Tee? The other kids are doing so well, why not Tee?" That's not a fair question. The real question is, "What happened to Sam, Sammy, and Laura, that they were able to escape consequences of a very difficult childhood?"

They were all born into a family that had been traumatized by the slaughter in Khmer Rouge Cambodia. Three of them began life in a refugee camp, the fourth in the Tenderloin, where they all grew up. Why the Tenderloin? What was our government thinking when it placed unprepared families, suffering severe PTSD, in such a stressful, menacing, foreign environment? The father brutalized the family. Helpless children watched their mother being regularly beaten, were beaten themselves, saw items precious to them tossed out the window, were forced to live on the streets, turned out by their extended family when their mother died, and on and on and on. And three out of four turned out better than OK.

Bonnie Benard has already been quoted as reporting on studies of "children born into seriously high-risk conditions such as families where parents were mentally ill, alcoholic, abusive, or criminal, or in communities that were poverty-stricken or war-torn." The Souns were all of the above: "The astounding finding from these long term studies was that at least 50% – and often closer to 70% – of youth growing up in these high-risk conditions did develop social competence despite exposure to severe stress and did overcome the odds to lead successful lives."

How is that possible? Because, as Lillian Rubin told us at St. Boniface Church, as she found in her own childhood, people who transcend their pasts find adults who provide support as mentors, role models, or friends, offering hope for a new way of life. "Sometimes these are long-lasting relationships," she said, "often they are not. It makes no difference. Their importance lies in their *meaning* to the persons involved and in the fact that there is someone to hold out a hand in time of need, someone also who can help fill the empty space inside."

For Sam, it was Midge, Diana, Tess, Tom, and Tatum, and the opportunities that they provided. For Sammy, it was Tom and the Boys and Girls Club. For Laura, it was her siblings and City Impact. For Tee, it was the streets.

Benard's "Protective Factors": a positive, caring relationship with an adult, high expectations for behavior and abilities, and opportunities for meaningful participation and involvement were fulfilled for three of the siblings by service providers in the Tenderloin. For the fourth, the caring adults were fellow youths abandoned by society, who had high expectations that he would be a great street fighter, and provided opportunities for him to do so. And he killed a boy, and went to prison, where he is now.

The significant question is not "Why did Tee do what he did?" That we all understand, or at least we should. The big question is, with all the evidence that supports our collective ability to create order out of chaos, why do we, as a society, not do more?

* * *

The three Soun siblings who survived their lives in the Tenderloin and are now doing well, developed, what Rubin calls, a sense of mission, a commitment to something larger than self and personal interest, that provided purpose and meaning in their lives. She says the mission is inspired by the gratitude they feel for their "good fortune." This impels them to give back, to use their pasts to help others, to be compassionate. "In doing so," Rubin writes, "they not only give meaning to their suffering but help to heal themselves."

Stories of transcendence and resilience are found throughout our tenderloins in America and the world. But they are not just tenderloin stories. They can be found in every community, and on every campus, too.

SUPERIOR COURT OF CALIFORNIA, COUNTY OF SANTA CLARA

STREET ADDRESS: 191 N. FIRST STREET
MAILING ADDRESS: SAME
CITY AND ZIP CODE: SAN JOSE, CA 95113

IN THE MATTER OF (NAME)
Ashley Novosad

DECLARATION OF EMANCIPATION OF MINOR AFTER HEARING   CASE NUMBER
1. The proceeding came on for hearing as follows: xxxxxxx
   Date: 10/17/06   Time: 9:30 AM   Department: 15
   Judge: xxxx x xxxxx
   Present in court: Petitioner
2. THE COURT FINDS THAT:
   Notice of hearing was given as prescribed by the court.
3. THE PETITION IS GRANTED. THE PETITIONER IS DECLARED TO BE EMANCIPATED FOR THE
PURPOSES SET FORTH IN FAMILY CODE SECTION 7050 ET SEQ

Illustration 16.2   Ashley emancipation doc.

* * *

Ashley Novosad was my student. I first met her in Sports, Service and Society, the community-based learning class that organizes a sport clinic in the Tenderloin. Ashley had been, but was not at the time, a volleyball and soccer player, and she was serious about the value of sport in developing the person. In the course of her studies with me, it became apparent that she was also very serious about engaging the youth of the inner city. She wanted to make a difference in their lives. I found out the reason when we visited San Francisco County Jail. Phelicia Jones and I were facilitating a "Meeting of the Minds" discussion between students in my Deviant Behavior class and 50 inmates. We were sitting in a circle, talking about our life experiences, when Ashley shared her personal story. After the class and over the years, she told me more about her life's journey.

Ashley Novosad was born in Idaho. Her mother and father were not in a relationship. Her father, of Mexican descent, was working in the Idaho potato fields. Her mother, 20 years old at the time of Ashley's birth, was living at home with her parents. She had been adopted and her ancestry was unknown. She was still pregnant when the father moved to California with his girlfriend. Ashley was given up for adoption, but the mom had second thoughts and went back and brought her baby home. Two years later, Ashley's half brother was born.

The second pregnancy, Ashley was told, triggered postpartum depression and schizophrenia in the mom. The young mother took her two children and moved around Idaho, Wyoming, Utah, and other neighboring states. When she returned home, Ashley's grandfather called Child Protection Service. The mom's relationship with her medication had been an on and off thing, and it was decided that she was an unfit mother. Ashley was four years old, and she and her brother were placed in a foster home, then separated, and moved to new foster homes. "It was weird," Ashley told me of the second placement. "I could look out my window and see my grandparents' house right across the field. I wondered, 'Why wasn't I living with them?'"

Ashley has vague memories of that time of her life, going to food banks, using food stamps, attending a Head Start Program. Then, at seven, she was back with her mother, living in the grandparents' basement.

Ashley told me, "My mother started hearing voices, 'Kill Ashley!' She ran to her car and drove off to Utah, called her mother, told her what was happening, and that she had no plan of coming home." But the Grandmother had no plan to raise another child. She called Ashley's father in California, and Ashley was headed west to the Bay Area.

The dad had married his girlfriend and they had a two-and-a-half-year-old son. His wife knew nothing of any previous children, and it did not sit well with her. Things were apparently not going well at home to begin with, and soon after Ashley's arrival, the wife took her son and moved to Southern California, where she was from.

"My dad had a good job, working at a Sunnyvale golf course, but he didn't get along with his boss. So he quit, and started his own landscaping business. He was doing well, until the recession hit in 2001. He went out of business." A former coworker was selling drugs and suggested that the dad do so also. Apparently, the dad thought this was a good idea. "I remember him selling weed, coke, crystal, ecstasy. The shed out back he had huge bags of weed, drugs in bedroom drawers. People in and out.

He took me on trips to Vegas where he was doing business." It must have been stressful. "He started having migraines. I remember driving him to the hospital when I was 11 years old. I learned to drive at the golf course. He told me I had to drive because he couldn't afford an ambulance, $800.

"My dad met a girl at the supermarket. She got pregnant with my dad's third child, each born to a different mother. My little sister." This was Ashley's third half sibling, a half brother from her mom, and a half brother and half sister from her dad. Before the birth, Ashley remembers her stepmother being nice, but after, "She turned against me. She was *not* nice. Jealous and angry. When I was 13, I was watching TV with my little sister. I had given her this lollipop. When she came out of the bedroom, she said to me, 'I don't want you here you here you blah, blah, blah,' calling me everything in the book. She grabbed the lollipop out of my sider's hand and threw it at me. I stood up and said, 'Why are you doing this' and she punches me. We were about the same size and went at it. My sister is crying, it was kind of a blur, I think I kind of blanked out, and my father came in and broke it up. I went to my room and I could hear her say, 'You need to choose me or her.' She was mean to everyone. I climbed out the window and went to my aunt's house next door, who wanted to 'go kick her ass.'" The dad came in and told Ashley, "I told her to leave." She packed up and left the next day. "Then things really started going downhill. My dad would start doing crystal, smoking in front of me, offering it to me. I didn't want it. Tried other things, but wasn't into it. I was going to parties, working, sports, getting into leadership. At home, people were going in and out: prostitutes, dealers, friends' older siblings doing dope, mafia-types arriving with women.

"When I went to parties, my dad would say, 'Here's some party favors,' gave me coke, weed, ecstasy to take to the parities. I never liked them, never got into it. My dad was doing hard stuff, getting paranoid. Pounding on my bedroom door, come into my room, go through everything. 'Where is he?' Three thirty, four in morning. I have school next day, seven, seven thirty. Dad was supposed to pick me up at ten thirty at night from work. Wouldn't show up. My coworker, she was older, 21 or so, would take me home. She lived with her parents in a big house, invited me to stay there. So I told my dad I was moving out. He was stoned. Didn't care. I stayed with her for a month and a half or so, but she got jealous when I visited my family during the holidays. 'I thought you didn't want to be with them?'

"Two cousins, actually half sisters, one from Chicago, the other from Alabama, came to stay: 21 and 17. I was 15. They moved in with our aunt and uncle. Eight in a two-bedroom apartment. My uncle helped us all get our own studio apartment. We were all working, but my cousins lost their jobs. I wound up paying the whole $800 rent. Meanwhile, my dad gets caught selling to minors and goes to state prison. It's all crazy.

"A friend told me about emanciapation. LACY. Legal Advocates for Children and Youth. You had to be 14, on your own, have a good reason, can support yourself. I was 15. I brought in my statement, transcripts, and had to prepare to inform my parents. They said they would help me prepare my story. I tried to notify my parents, but my mom was living all over. My dad was out of prison, living in a van, selling drugs. I was told I could apply for a fee waiver, $3000, but run the risk of not being seen as able to support myself. But $3000? I got the waiver.

"On October 17 I went to the hearing with a LACY lawyer. The judge says he already approved the emanciapation, but said, 'Is there no one who can adopt you?' and 'Don't get pregnant!' The LACY lawyer was really embarrassed by that, 'I'm so sorry.' She was really great, and it was OK. The judge said, 'I don't want to hear anything bad about you,' and I was emancipated. I was considered adult under law, but no one seemed to know what that meant. I couldn't get credit, couldn't get a license without an adult's signature. My boyfriend's dad signed for me. After, I helped with funding for LACY, telling my story to doctors, lawyers. Giving back to them."

In high school, Ashley was an athlete, playing volleyball and soccer. She was in the leadership program and served as copresident of the school's student government. In her first two years, she had suffered academically, but had pulled her grades up since. Still, she was worried that her just over 3.0 GPA would be a problem getting into college. The school knew her situation at home. She felt particularly supported by the vice principal and the teacher who met with her leadership class first thing in the morning. But they didn't know that she had moved out of the district and was commuting 30 miles, from her apartment in Hayward to the school in Sunnyvale. At commute time, schooltime, that's a terrible trip. Ashley was often late for the leadership class that she, as copresident, was supposed to help lead. Gilt-ridden, she went to the vice principal, "I have something to tell you." "*Don't tell me you're pregnant!*" he almost gasped. "No, no." She explained her lateness, that she lived out-of-district. Relieved, he replied, "Not a problem."

Ashley did graduate from high school and got into every State University that she applied to, with near full scholarships. But the size of the public schools intimidated her, and her school counselor told her about a small, private Catholic school on the Peninsula. She checked it out. NDNU. That's where I met her.

Sometime after leaving high school, Ashley went back and asked her leadership teacher, "What do you remember?" of her time there. The teacher replied, "You were surviving." But she was also thriving.

In 2007, she received the prestigious Fremont Foundation Award for those who have overcome many obstacles, yet are on a path to great accomplishments.

In 2012, I had the honor of presenting the NDNU Community Engagement Award in Psychology to a graduating senior. The student's mom was in attendance. She was staying in her van in the university parking lot, the only way she could afford to attend the ceremonies. Her daughter sat with her in the large room, packed with graduates and their families. It was my turn to speak:

This year's awardee has been deeply involved in community engagement on and off campus. She has been a GEN 1 Mentor (she, herself, is a first generation college student). She is an Orientation Team Member and serves on the Orientation Board. The National Orientation Directors Association awarded her with one of only two Outstanding Student Leader Awards for the region consisting of colleges and universities in California, Arizona, Nevada, and Hawaii. She was a Resident Assistant and this year is Senior RA. She was a Call-to-Action Day Leader, volunteered at Thanksgiving in Golden Gate Park for the homeless, did community service in the Tenderloin, participated in the Free Hug Campaign, volunteered at Samaritan House, providing food for the homeless, was a Sausalito Carnival volunteer, a Belmont Community Center volunteer, a Walden House West (drug rehab program) Camp Leader, a Shelter Network volunteer, a volunteer at the San Mateo Head Start Program, a volunteer for Belmont's Parks and Recreation, helped raise money for the American Youth Soccer Organization's Turkey Bowl, and this summer, she will be volunteering at Collective Roots (a food justice program) in Redwood City.

Her path through life has not been an easy one. Her family faced many challenges, she lived in foster care, and emancipated herself when she was fifteen. Still, she was an athlete, student leader, and community volunteer in high school, and received recognition from the Fremont Foundation for her accomplishments.

She will receive her bachelor's degree in psychology in three days, and has been accepted by the Peace Corps, leaving Feb. 2013 to do health education in Latin America.

Of herself, she has said, "Most people who get to know me would say that I am beyond my years, and I do feel that way. All that I have experienced has aged me mentally." In the opinion of this professor, that translates to: wiser than her years. And the world will benefit. She says, "As for the future, I hope to be able to help as many people as I can, in whatever field I go into." In recognition of those who cared about her, and encouraged her, she says her mission in life is to do good work for others

I give you this year's Community Engagement Awardee in Psychology: Ashley Novosad.

I look across the room. Ashley rises, hugs her mother, and walks across the floor to receive her award.

* * *

August 18, 2015. I'm waiting at the train station at Fourth and Townsend to pick up Ashley, coming up from the Peninsula on Caltrain. We're heading over to Crossroads Café, Delancey Street Foundation's coffeehouse, to catch up and celebrate her two years in Paraguay with the Peace Corps. I see a crowd appear at the station exit. Out of it emerges Ashley, smiling, as is often the case. She waves, I pop open my door, and she climbs in, "Hi, Dr. Don." It's been three years since I've seen her, and she's been on a great adventure. She looks great and more relaxed than I remember. We drive over to Crossroads, just a few blocks away, settle in, and Ashley begins the story of this latest chapter of her life.

"I loved Paraguay," she tells me. "A different lifestyle and it can get frustrating. Things don't get done in a timely manner. People move slower. I didn't know I needed that. I was stressed out when I got there. At first, I felt unproductive. People just sit. They don't even have to talk. Just being present with each other. They don't feel like they have to fill the silence with something. It's so nice. I'm trying to keep that, trying to bring that home. I didn't even know I was so stressed out. I did do a lot and I loved my community." I knew that she had been doing well. Not long after she arrived in South America, she sent me an email.

Saludos from Paraguay!
Jeez Paraguay is wonderful! I feel extremely fortunate to have the opportunity to be here and share all of this with my community. Projects are starting to develop, and I truly feel part of this community.

As we began our lunch at Crossroads, part of the Delancey Street drug treatment program, I explained to her how everyone working here was underdoing their own transformation. "Every one of them is in recovery from some very heavy-duty stuff." Then I asked, "Well, how was the Peace Corps?"

"Amazing!"

Even before our meeting at Crossroads, I had followed her activities on Facebook, so I knew the overall picture as her life was unfolding in Paraguay, but as she talked, I was even more impressed with how much this young woman, who had gone through so much just trying to grow up, had achieved.

Ashley began her Peace Corps commitment in Guarambaré, a small agricultural town, 45 minutes south of Asunción, Paraguay's capital city. She lived with a host family for ten weeks and engaged in language, culture, and technical skills training; CORE studies (education, youth development, health, community economic development, agriculture, and environment); health, safety, and security sessions; and field-based activities. Only then was she officially sworn in as a Peace Corps Volunteer and assigned to her permanent placement, Unión, San Pedro.

Her primary job there was to develop sexual health education workshops for elementary and high school students and their parents. In this rural, Catholic community, she offered condom demonstrations, discredited condom myths, and showed how to practice correct condom usage. "I'm not shy about talking about that stuff," she told me over lunch in San Francisco. During her service, she presented 12 HIV/AIDS, STIs, and teen pregnancy prevention workshops to over 400 participants. "It was fun for them and fun for me." Working with three other Peace Corps Volunteers, she trained three community adults and six high school youth, taking them to workshops on how to do these kinds of presentations and how to do this kind of work, and helped plan out what they might do in the future. She applied for grants for condoms, asked for donations from NGOs that were working on prevention for fun little prizes, like tee shirts and notebooks, and offered four workshops for over a 190 high school students on human rights, gender and self-development, self-esteem, prevention of domestic abuse, and career planning. She also coordinated two successful Girls Leading Our World (GLOW) Camps designed to empower young female participants to affect real change in their own lives and their communities. And she created a continuation manual that was given to all Camp GLOW participants and volunteers to take back to their communities.

Ashley became a teacher, but she also was a learner. Ashley's host family were activists. At 66, the wife, and at 70, the husband, were respected members of the community. He was a carpenter; she ran a small shop out of their home. Ashley says, "They were so humble and so involved with everything that had to do with their community. Asunción was dumping garbage next to their community and people were getting sick. All the flies. They started a big campaign. The wife was the president of all this. They stood in front of the trucks, blocked the garbage trucks, got on the news. They're old people, but so active and so involved.

"People would come by selling soap. Even though she was selling soap in her shop, she bought the soap to help them. They did fund-raisers for people who were sick and she would cook all night to help them.

"They were so loving, so nice. They were like my mom and dad in Paraguay. I call them 'Mom' and 'Dad.' If I marry, I am going to fly them out."

* * *

As with the three Souns, Ashley has discovered a sense of mission in life. She is committed to something greater than herself. She has discovered meaning and purpose. Inspired by her vice principal, leadership teacher, the legal team at LACY, faculty, staff, and fellow students at NDNU, Tenderloin street teachers, social service providers and clients that she volunteered with, and the people of Paraguay, she felt gratitude for her "good fortune," impelling her to give back, to use her past to appreciate and understand the struggles that others face, to be compassionate, to contribute, and, in so doing, give meaning to her own childhood suffering and continue the process of healing herself.

* * *

The grown-up Souns have forgiven their father. They each told me of the pain that he suffered living in Cambodia under the Khmer Rouge, losing his daughters and all of his family, living in the refugee camps, being relocated to the Tenderloin where he had nothing to offer. He had no sense of purpose or meaning in his own life. They understood what he went through and how that can corrupt the individual, affecting the way one thinks and behaves.

Ashley came to understand that her mother, burdened with depression and schizophrenia, deserved to be forgiven. When I talked to her last, trying to understand her dad was not her task at hand. He had called her, but she didn't return the call. There was really nothing productive that she could see in renewing their relationship at this time of her life. Too much had happened over the years, too much water under the bridge. I got the impression that forgiveness was not in the near future.

* * *

I married into a family of blue-collar philosophers. My wife and I were out to dinner with one of them, my brother-in-law Tom and his wife, Kitty, when the subject of "compassion" came up. Tom said, "To understand is to forgive. That's compassion." I hadn't heard that before. I went home and googled it. There is a lot of discussion on the Internet about its origins. It's been attributed to Spinoza, the Buddha, the Swiss author Madame de Staël, and others.[18] In an article on *Huffington Post*, psychologist Pavel Somov says that the[19] "'To understand is to forgive' formula is more than just perspective-taking, more than just seeing the event from other person's perspective. In order to forgive, you also have to understand why what happened *had* to happen. You have to understand the *psychological determinism* of the particular 'why' that led to whatever happened."

Somov goes on to explain that to understand "why," one has to understand "motive." He says there is one "core motive"—the pursuit of wellbeing. "Some pursue their wellbeing by going to work, others—by boosting your lawnmower for a quick re-sale on the way to buy drugs. Motivationally, there is no difference." It is the pursuit of "wellbeing."

He goes on, "to forgive, you have to see beyond the behavior, you have to be willing to hear the whole story and to unravel the psychological determinism of the other person's actions to see the inevitability of what happened, the intricate interplay of nature and nurture that wove into any given fact. And only then you will be able to see the event from their point of view, i.e. you will be able to identify with them and, thus, forgive."

To understand why people wind up homeless, prostituted, dealing and using drugs, living in SROs, in our prisons, on death row, or being part of sidewalk society, we have to see beyond the behavior and know the whole story, why what happened, happened. We have to put ourselves in their shoes. In an ideal world, this leads us to formulate *compassionate* methods and strategies to relate to these people, respond to their circumstances, and prevent such occurrences from happening in the future. To understand may not always lead to forgiveness, but it should encourage a meaningful course of action to, at least, ensure *society's* wellbeing. It is not always an easy path to walk on.

"To understand is to forgive" may apply to Ashley's mother, depressed and schizophrenic. It may apply to the Soun father, and all that he went through and all he lost. But how does it apply to the kidnapping, rape, and murder of 18-year-old Loretta Ann Bourque and murder of her boyfriend, 17-year-old David LeBlanc, by Elmo Patrick Sonnier and his brother Eddie on November 5, 1977?

In early March of 2002, Sr. Helen Prejean, author of *Dead Man Walking*, a book based in part of the murder of Loretta and David and the execution of their killer, came to NDNU, one of several visits over the years, to talk about the writing of the book and her work to end the death penalty in the USA. On the evening of her talk, Sr. Helen dined with a group of us in the ballroom of Ralston Hall, the mansion that is the historic center of our campus. Students who were present had been enrolled in inner-city classes, toured San Quentin, been inside the death chamber, and stood outside the prison gates while condemned inmates were executed inside. One student's brother was on death row in Guam for a crime his sister was convinced he did not commit.

Sr. Helen expressed her appreciation for their willingness to so deeply engage the community. She gave us a brief overview of her upcoming talk, about who wound up on death row and who did not, that innocent people were sometimes executed, and that the death penalty was inherently immoral. She also told us about the father of one of the two victims. In Ralston Hall, and in her book, Sr. Helen recalled Lloyd LeBlanc being brought to the site of the murder to identify his boy's body. The father— seeing his son lying face down in the dirt, "with his two little eyes sticking out like bullets," and wearing the new blue velour shirt that his mother had just bought him—knelt down beside his son and said the Lord's Prayer. "And when he came to the words: 'Forgive us our trespasses as we forgive those who trespass against us,' he had not halted or equivocated, and he said, 'Whoever did this, I forgive them.' But he acknowledges that it's a struggle overcoming the feelings of bitterness and revenge that well up."[20]

I am a father, and I can't even begin to bring myself to put myself in Lloyd LeBlanc's shoes, let alone Elmo Patrick or Eddie Sonnier's, nor can I imagine forgiving anyone who may trespass against my family in such a manner (I can barely write these words). But as a sociologist, I do know that to understand why people wind up on death row (Tookie Williams), in our prisons (our street teachers in San Quentin), and on our streets (the hundreds of people we have walked by or served in some way, often engaging in conversation, in the Tenderloin), we have to see beyond the behavior and know the whole story, why what happened, happened, and to begin to formulate *compassionate* methods and strategies to respond to and prevent such occurrences from happening in the future. To understand may not always lead to forgiveness, as anger and unbearable grief may get in the way, but at least on a societal level, it should lead to a meaningful course of action.

At NDNU, the community was inspired by the passion, words, and work of Sr. Helen Prejean. The Catholic Church is opposed to the death penalty, and the university mission calls for social justice. We felt it was our obligation to do something to support the ministry of Sr. Helen. Shortly after her visit, we received a letter from her, inviting us to pilot a play based on her book, which would eventually be produced at colleges and universities throughout the nation. We organized a task force to develop an Institute of Peace and Justice, to be housed in the School of Arts and Humanities. We had a conference on the death penalty, with participants from various groups and individuals opposed to it, including a man who had been exonerated after spending years on death row. We networked with Community Works, an educational and theater organization whose mission is "to strengthen lives and our community by responding to survivors of domestic violence and sexual assault, and high-need youth and their families, through support services and advocacy." Community Works worked with the San Francisco Sheriff Department's Soapstone Theater to produce a play on campus on the subject of "restorative justice," a practice that strives to repair the harm caused by criminal behavior by including all stakeholders, the criminal, the victim, and the community, and, in so doing, help transform people, relationships, and communities. The Community Works/Soapstone production was on domestic violence, and included convicted abusers and victims as actors, including a member of Families of Murder Victims, and a woman I had met in the Tenderloin early in my days there, whose father, a pimp, had severely abused her. "I remember him throwing me against the wall, then making me clean up the blood," she told me, as we sat in Wild Awakenings Coffeehouse.

In late October and early November of 2003, the Department of Theater and Dance and the NDNU community presented six well-attended performances of the play *Dead Man Walking*.

I don't know if the play moved anyone to forgive the Sonnier brothers, but the performance, combined with the other experiences that began with Sr. Helen's visit, evoked a high level of thought and discussion about our criminal justice system and when, if ever, is it OK to take another human's life.

* * *

A recent report on another murder did evoke the "To understand is to forgive" message, when I introduced a news article to my Deviant Behavior class before our annual trip to San Quentin. It was about "Joseph H," who killed his father. Shot him in the head while the dad lay sleeping. He received a 40-year sentence for the murder. Joseph was ten years old.

In the *Chronicle* article, "Confession of boy, 10, raises doubts over grasp of Miranda rights," Bob Egelko writes,[21]

> The Riverside youth found his father's gun and shot him in the head as he lay sleeping on a sofa.... The father was a leader of a neo-Nazi group called the National Socialist Movement and was also a drug addict who frequently beat Joseph, according to a state appeals court ruling in the case. When police arrived, the court said, Joseph told them his father had beaten him and his mother the day before.
>
> The court said Joseph had been exposed to drugs in his mother's womb, was abused by both parents, had below-average intelligence, suffered from attention-deficit hyperactivity disorder, and was prone to violent outbursts against fellow students and teachers.

Egelko's article is not about a ten-year-old boy's ability to distinguish right from wrong. And it's not about extenuating circumstances. It's about the California Supreme Court's ruling that he was old enough to understand his Miranda rights (the right to remain silent, to speak to an attorney, and anything you say can be used against you), before confessing to the crime. Joseph had already been found "responsible" for the homicide (the equivalent of a second-degree murder conviction for an adult) by a juvenile court judge, whose ruling was upheld by the state's Fourth District Court of Appeal. Under state law, he will be freed when he turns 23. So he'll *only* have to serve 13 years in juvenile detention. It seemed to me and the students in the class that justice had not been done. What value is there in stigmatizing a ten-year-old and incarcerating him for the prime developmental years of his life? He obviously suffered all his life and needs compassionate care. There was no "To understand is to forgive" outcome here.

* * *

In the beginning of this chapter, two definitions fundamental to Tenderloin U were given. The first, "Compassion": "Literally means 'to suffer together'.... the feeling that arises when you are confronted with another's suffering and feel motivated to relieve that suffering."[22]The second, "Pedagogy": The "process of accompanying learners; caring for and about them; and bringing learning into life."[23]

The people of the Tenderloin who are suffering have personal stories that help explain their situations, as do the students who learn from them. The goals of Tenderloin U include opening students' minds to the stories that they see and engage in the community (bringing learning into life) and motivating them to help relieve that suffering (and their own and those close to them) through compassionate action. This second goal is not only encouraged through the pedagogies of service-learning and meeting with street teachers who work with or are from disadvantaged groups, but also encouraged by studying and being inspired by promising courses of action that are already underway. These are some *new paradigm* (new cognitive frameworks, new ways of thinking) lessons we explore in Inner City Studies.

HARM REDUCTION

Harm reduction has been shown to be extremely effective. For example, by accepting people "where they are," and providing them with clean needles and safe sex kits, the transmission of AIDS and hepatitis has been significantly reduced, and overall wellbeing improved.

HOUSING

Another harm reduction approach, providing the homeless with permanent housing without requiring that they first be clean and sober, stabilizes their lives, increases the likelihood of healthier lifestyles, and reduces costs from $60,000 per homeless person per year (for emergency medical costs, criminal justice system costs, and cost of other services) to around $20,000 when given permanent housing.[24] One obstacle to housing the homeless is that there is an extreme shortage of housing of all kinds in San Francisco, a city surrounded on three sides by water, with few places to grow but up. The 2015 San Francisco Homeless Count reported that,[25]

> The number of individuals counted in the 2015 general street count and shelter count was 6,686. Compared to 2013, this was an increase of 250 individuals. The supplemental youth count found an additional 853 unaccompanied children and transitional-age-youth, a decrease of 61 individuals from 2013. When the youth count and general count are combined,

the total number of unsheltered and sheltered persons in San Francisco on January 29, 2015, was 7,539. This combined count shows a 2% increase (189 individuals) in homelessness since 2013.

A ten-year trend of comparable Point-in-Time data from general count efforts (excluding the targeted youth count) identified a 7% increase in the number of persons experiencing homelessness in San Francisco between 2005 and 2015.

For obvious reasons, the number one complaint in the city is still homelessness, but the old methods of harassing and moving the homeless along have not only proven to be unpopular, but they don't improve the situation.

NAVIGATION CENTER

While San Francisco is struggling to increase its stock of "affordable housing," it is also expanding efforts to permanently house the homeless. In the meantime, it has created a "Navigation Center" in the old continuation high, "1950," near 16th and Mission, that the Tenderloin girls hanging around the 200 block of Leavenworth told me they attended years ago, a school that was set up for dropouts, teenage moms, at-risk kids, and teens with discipline problems. It's been closed for years. The building is now a one-stop homeless aid center, providing dormitory-style living, shower and bathroom facilities, laundry facilities, counseling offices, and a dining room open 24/7, where entire existing encampments of homeless can be moved, bringing along their tents, carts, dogs, and lovers, and stay all day until the city finds them permanent housing, hopefully within a short period of time.[26] The Center has only 75 beds, and there is only one Navigation Center, but the city envisions more.

WAR ON DRUGS

The War on Drugs is over. Congress ended it. A bipartisan effort in both chambers brought it to a close when it was determined that it only made matters worse. A recent AP article reported,[27]

> Congress is moving swiftly on a sweeping overhaul of U.S. sentencing laws that has the rare backing of ... Republicans, Democrats and President Obama.

The House Judiciary Committee on Wednesday approved legislation that would allow judges discretion to give lesser sentences than federal mandatory minimums, reducing prison time for some nonviolent drug offenders.

The aim of the bipartisan bills, the product of years of negotiations, is to reduce overcrowding in the nation's prisons, save taxpayer dollars and give some nonviolent offenders a second chance while keeping the most dangerous criminals in prison.

Disparate voices – from the American Civil Liberties Union to the conservative Koch Industries – have agreed the current system is broken. Since 1980, the federal prison population has exploded, in part because of mandatory minimum sentences for nonviolent drug offenders.

PRISON REALIGNMENT

In California, Governor Jerry Brown initiated "prison realignment." With voter backing, the program is designed to move inmates out of state prisons, releasing them altogether or sending them to county jails, near their homes.[28]

Since the Legislature approved Gov. Jerry Brown's realignment plan in 2011, the number of inmates has declined by 40,000 in the state prison system and 18,000 overall, even including those who are now in local jails, said the Public Policy Institute of California. Part of that decline was due to passage of two voter initiatives, exempting some nonviolent felons from life terms under the state's three-strikes law in 2012 and reducing sentences for some drug and property crimes in 2014, the report said.

Despite predictions by law enforcement groups that realignment would endanger the public, rates of violent crime and property crime have fallen since 2011 and are at "historic lows" in California, the report said.

The sole exception was auto theft, which has increased since 2011 and is about 17 percent higher than it would have been without realignment, the study said. But it said the findings – that crime is down overall, even though 18,000 ex-convicts are on the streets rather than behind bars – suggests that locking up more people is not a cost-effective way to fight crime.

Mass Incarceration

In addition to the decision to end the War on Drugs at the federal level, and prison realignment on the state level, San Francisco's Board of Supervisors made a local contribution to ending mass incarceration with a controversial decision in the closing days of 2015.

The main jail at 850 Bryant Street is a disaster waiting to happen. Built in the late 1950s, the Hall of Justice is seismically unsafe. Mayor Ed Lee requested $215 million from the Board to replace the old building, and the State of California offered $80 million to subsidize the costs. But in a unanimous decision, the supervisors turned down the request. None of them challenged the claim that the building is unsafe and that inmates should not be housed there, but they did challenge the use of incarceration as the proper response to dealing with people who break the law. Board of Supervisors president, London Breed (who has been a Tenderloin U street teacher) had this to say,[29] "[The building] needs to come down, but more than a building we need to tear down the system of mass incarceration it represents.… I am not going to support another stand-alone jail to continue to lock up African-Americans and Latinos in this city."

Opponents of a new jail, including the DA, argue that the city should invest in diversion programs that decrease the jail population, and that inmates in the Hall of Justice should be moved to one of the city's three other jails. London Breed told us, when the Promise class met with her at City Hall, that her own brother was incarcerated at 850 Bryant for drug and robbery convictions, and said that the city has to develop better ways to treat people, instead of just locking them up.

* * *

We live in the Age of Information and Communication. It's an age of innovation and rapid transformation. New ways of life and new ways of thinking are emerging faster than ever before in the history of humankind. In 1970, as the Age was just emerging, Alvin Toffler called this "Future Shock,"[30] the human response to over stimulation, when its beginnings were first overtly presenting themselves, "the roaring current of change, a current so powerful today, that it overturns institutions, shifts our values and shrivels our roots." The only constant in this changing society is change itself.

In 1963, when I was living at the Lyric Hotel, gay men were being arrested in Tenderloin and SoMa nightclubs for dancing together. In 2015 same-sex marriage was guaranteed by the US Supreme Court.

In 1964, when I moved over to the edge of Chinatown, African-American teenager Tracy Sims led sit-ins at the venerable Palace Hotel on Market Street (founded by William Ralston, himself) and the Cadillac dealership on Van Ness, protesting hiring discrimination against blacks. On January 20, 2009, Barack Obama became the first black president of the USA.

In 1966, I was back in the Tenderloin when disrespected transgender customers at the Compton Cafeteria at Turk and Taylor rioted. In 2014, *Time* magazine had *Orange Is the New Black* star Laverne Cox on its cover with the heading, "The Transgender Tipping Point: America's New Civil Rights Frontier."

When I was staying at the Henry Hotel on 6th Street, my first night in San Francisco, the mayor, the police chief, the fire chief, the DA, the public defender, and the president of the Board of Supervisors were all white males.

In 2015, the mayor was a Chinese-American male (raised in public housing in Seattle), the police chief was a white male, the fire chief was a white female, the DA was a Latino male (born in Cuba, his family immigrated to the USA in 1967), the public defender was Japanese-American (his family was interned during World War II), and the president of the Board of Supervisors was a black female (raised in public housing in the district she now represents).

Change happens. People make it happen. We are inspired by others and, in turn, inspire others. For 20 years and counting, my students and I have been moved by the people of the Tenderloin to be more informed, more compassionate, and more inclined to be engaged with the issues of the inner city and the greater society. The Höküaos, the Milañs, the Beckys, the Sofias, the Ashleys, and hundreds more went on to do good work, important work, as did Nancy Ong, Nam Thai, the three Soun siblings, Phanna Phay, and so many others who came to America under very trying circumstances or were born here and raised in the Tenderloin. Transcendence/resilience theory has become an important part of the Tenderloin U program, not just as a way of understanding how some people are able to emerge from significant life challenges, but as a model for engagement, a blueprint for action: become that caring adult in the lives of others, have high expectations of them, and help them and the rest of us discover opportunities for meaningful, purposeful lives. It all begins with a jump down the rabbit hole.

Notes

1. http://greatergood.berkeley.edu/topic/compassion/definition
2. Smith, M.K., "What is pedagogy?" The encyclopaedia of informal education, 2012, http://infed.org/mobi/what-is-pedagogy/
3. Freire, P., *Pedagogy of the Oppressed*. Harmondsworth, UK: Penguin, 1972.
4. Dewey, J., *Experience and Education*, New York: Collier Books, 1963 [First published in 1938].
5. Miller, R. (2005). *Holistic Education: A Response to the Crisis of Our Time.* Paper was presented at the Institute for Values Education in Istanbul, Turkey, in November, 2005. http://www.pathsoflearning.net/articles_Holistic_Ed_Response.php.
6. Rubin, Lillian, *The Transcendent Child: Tales of Triumph Over the Past*, New York: Harper Collins, 1997.
7. Rubin, Lillian, *The Transcendent Child: Tales of Triumph Over the Past*, New York: Harper Collins, 1997, p. 1.
8. Rubin, Lillian, *The Transcendent Child: Tales of Triumph Over the Past*, New York: Harper Collins, 1997, p. 4.
9. Rubin, Lillian, *The Transcendent Child: Tales of Triumph Over the Past*, New York: Harper Collins, 1997, pp. 2–3.
10. Rubin, Lillian, *The Transcendent Child: Tales of Triumph Over the Past*, New York: Harper Collins, 1997, pp. 9–10.
11. Rubin, Lillian, *The Transcendent Child: Tales of Triumph Over the Past*, New York: Harper Collins, 1997, pp. 8.
12. Benard, Bonnie, "The Foundations of the Resiliency Framework," *Resiliency in Action*, https://www.resiliency.com/free-articles-resources/the-foundations-of-the-resiliency-framework/
13. Benard, Bonnie, *Fostering Resiliency in Kids: Protective Factors in the Family, School, and Community*, Portland, OR: Northwest Regional Educational Laboratory, 1991.
14. Wheatley, Margaret, *Leadership and the New Science: Learning about Organizations from an Orderly Universe*, San Francisco: Berrett-Koehler Publishers, 1994.
15. http://margaretwheatley.com
16. Van Derveken, Jaxon, "Manslaughter verdict in parking-space slaying," *SF Chronicle*, January 23, 2009.

17. See http://www.websitesrcg.com/border/camps/Khao-I-Dang.html for a visual and narrative exploration of Khao-I-Dang refugee camp, where the Soun boys were born.
18. For discussions about "To understand is to forgive," see https://zenrevolution.wordpress.com/2012/04/18/to-understand-everything-is-to-forgive-everything/;http://fakebuddhaquotes.com/to-understand-everything-is-to-forgive-everything/; http://www.iwise.com/18AH0
19. Somov, PhD, Pavel, "Compassion: To Understand Is To Forgive, *Huffington Post*, January 24, 2010.
20. Prejean, Helen, *Dead Man Walking*, New York: Vintage, 1993, p. 244.
21. Egelko, Bob "Confession of boy, 10, raises doubts over grasp of Miranda rights," *San Francisco Chronicle*, October 25, 2015.
22. http://greatergood.berkeley.edu/topic/compassion/definition
23. Smith, M.K., "What is pedagogy?" *The encyclopaedia of informal education*. 2012: http://infed.org/mobi/what-is-pedagogy/
24. Our street teacher, Kevin Fagan, news reporter, author of the award-winning series "Shame of the City," emailed me that "the thumbnail cost comparison is $60,000 a year to leave a homeless person on the street (through ambulance calls, etc.), or $20,000 a year to house him/her in supportive housing."
25. http://sfgov.org/lhcb/event/2015-san-francisco-point-time-homeless-count
26. To see a video of a homeless camp that organizers say could be served well by the Navigation Center, go to: http://tinyurl.com/kqoc46a
27. Jalonick, Mary Clare "House panel approves bill to overhaul sentencing laws," Associated Press, November 18, 2015.
28. Egelko, Bob, "Crime down, costs up since prison realignment, study finds," *SF Chronicle*, September 29, 2015.
29. Green, Emily, "No new S.F. jail after supervisors refuse funding," *SF Chronicle*, December 16, 2015.
30. Toffler, Alvin, *Future Shock*, New York: Random House, 1971.

APPENDIX I

EXPLORING THE HISTORY AND CULTURE
OF THE TENDERLOIN

* * *

I think that the most comprehensive and accessible accounting of the history, culture, and changing nature of the Tenderloin, Mid-Market Street, and the 6th Street corridor ("Central City") is to be found in Mark Ellinger's upfromthedeep.com website. Mark's life in San Francisco began as a nineteen-year-old art student at San Francisco Art Institute over in North Beach in the late-1960s, later he taught there and at the Academy of Art. He got into the technical side of filming as an engineer and technician, and became a partner in a recording studio over in the Mission in the 70s and 80s, before suffering, what he describes on his website as, a "cataclysmic manic-depressive breakdown that left me shell-shocked, severely depressed, and prone to bouts of Acute Stress Disorder." He spent the next ten years trying to recover, a period during which he lost all his friends, family, and everything he owned. He became a homeless heroin addict, and tried to kill himself.

Following hospitalization from the suicide attempt, and another hospitalization and surgery for bacterial infections brought on by his lifestyle, he gradually found his way back. He was able to move into a 6th Street SRO, "someplace cheap, safe, and quiet." Always a journal writer, in 2002 he salvaged a cheap digital camera and began writing about and photographing life around him. Since then, he has been sought after by news

© The Author(s) 2017   373
D. Stannard-Friel, *Street Teaching in the Tenderloin*,
DOI 10.1057/978-1-137-56437-5

reporters, civic leaders, not-for-profits, and others seeking his expertise and visual presentations. He has also been a street teacher for Tenderloin U and visited the campus to watch an Analyzing Social Settings class presentation, called "The Trail of Tears," on the 6th Street-Taylor Street corridor, at the annual NDNU Social Science Research Conference. Of his life, Mark writes,

> I have only memories of my life from childhood till 2001. Absent corroboration, such memories over time become tenuous and elusive. Aside from surgical disfigurements and emotional scars, it is as though I dreamed it all; a lifetime lived by someone else, inhabited only by phantoms. For what did I live those fifty-one years? Perhaps there are many reasons, or in the end there may be no reason at all, but for my life to have meaning, I must seek understanding. Thus, elucidating history is for me a very personal matter. Within the larger context of San Francisco history are fragments of my own past, wherefore my new life is immutably melded with the heart of the City.

Mark has recovered from his heroin addiction, but still struggles with emotional, psychological, and physical scars. He lives in subsidized housing and periodically hocks his precious photographic equipment to get by. But he continues to write and, when his camera is out of hock, photograph the world around him. He is a remarkable photo-journalist-historian of the history and culture of Central City.

* * *

Unlike its archetypes, The Bowery and the mid-town entertainment district (the original "tenderloin") in New York City, San Francisco's most inner city neighborhood has not been the focus of a great deal of literary or academic attention over the years, in spite of its colorful history and interesting culture. Dashiell Hammett did use the neighborhood (*his* neighborhood, where he once lived and worked as a Pinkerton detective and author) in his writings, most notably *The Maltese Falcon*: Alfred A. Knopf, 1929; and Billie Holiday recalls it in her *Lady Sings the Blues*: Doubleday, 1956, as a place where she was arrested for opium possession (she had been framed and was acquitted). William Vollmann explored the neighborhood, especially the prostituted community in the Larkin Street corridor, for his novel *Whores for Gloria*: Penguin, 1994. Jack Kerouac, in *On the Road*: Viking, 1957, and Jack London, in his short story, "South of the Slot," *Saturday Evening Post*, May 1909, wrote about what was once "Skid Road," now often referred to as "Tenderloin South," the inner-SoMa district, especially the 6th Street corridor, not technically the Tenderloin, according to official neighborhood boundaries, but geographically and culturally connected, and a part of our Tenderloin U "campus." Curt Gentry's *The Madams Of San Francisco: An Irreverent History of the City by the Golden Gate*: Doubleday, 1964, includes the Tenderloin in his examination of infamous San Francisco brothels, and, more recently, Larry Wonderling, in *San Francisco Tenderloin: heroes, demons, angels & other true* stories: Cape Foundation Publications, 2001, Gary Kamiya, *Cool Gray City of Love*, Bloombury USA, 2013, Philippe Bourgois and Jeff Schonberg, in *Righteous Dopefiend*: University of California Press, 2009, and Josh Sides, in *Erotic City: Sexual Revolutions and the Making of Modern San Francisco*: Oxford University Press, 2009.

Tom Carter, Marjorie Beggs, and Others, edited by Geoff Link, *Death in the Tenderloin: A slice of life from the heart of the Tenderloin*, San Francisco: Study Center Press, 2012, is a collection of obituaries of homeless people in Central City and reflections on the neighborhood. My own *City Baby and Star: Addiction, Transcendence, and the Tenderloin*: University Press of America, 2005, describes the neighborhood and the experiences of two female drug addicts there, one who emerged as a community leader, the other was chased out of town by her husband's lover. And very recently, Randy Shaw, executive director of Tenderloin Housing Clinic, wrote in his aptly named book, *The Tenderloin: Sex, Crime and Resistance in the Heart of San Francisco*: Urban Reality Press, 2015, about the history, evolution, and, especially, politics of the neighborhood (which he has been deeply involved in for thirty-five years).

Books that focus on the children of the Tenderloin include *Children of the Tenderloin*, by Vibha Lal Vasi, with photographs by Nita Winter, San Francisco: Bay Area Women's and Children's Center, and *I Have Something to Say About This Big Trouble*, children's stories collected by Rev. Cecil Williams and Janice Mirikitani, with a forward by Maya Angelou, San Francisco: Glide Word Press, 1989. See also, *Voices of Our Own: Mothers, Daughters, and Elders of the Tenderloin Tell Their Stories*, San Francisco: Published by Nancy Deutsch, 2001, and *In Our Village: San Francisco's Tenderloin Through the Eyes of Its Youth*, edited by Barbara Cervone, Next Generation Press, Providence, Rhode Island 2015.

Of particular interest to the reader may be video productions about the neighborhood. "Love Me Tenderloin" (a play on Elvis Presley's song, "Love Me Tender"),[1] a film by Henri Quenette (Indiegogo), shows the harsh conditions of the neighborhood, while, at the same time, takes the viewer into what the producers call "the 'heart' of San Francisco, the last refuge for elderly, disabled and low-income working people striving to stay in the city. At the same time," they say, "we're talking to people about how much love there is among the residents of this neighborhood and the people who work there in order to improve the life of the Tenderloin residents. "Love Me Tenderloin" follows the everyday life of four people living there: Bridchette, Arnold, Woody and Indian Joe.

"Drugs Inc." by the National Geographic Channel,[2] tells the story of the people and process of distributing the world's illegal drugs, with a segment on "San Francisco Meth Zombies." Ground Zero for street sales in San Francisco is shown, Leavenworth and Turk Streets, kitty-corner from where Big D and the Fish Stick gang hung out, right on the route of The Yellow Brick Road, and our pathway to BAWCC, SFPD, and many other street teacher destinations.

The Emmy Award winning documentary "Screaming Queens: The riot at Compton's Cafeteria," (a production of Victor Silverman and Susan Stryker, in association with ITVS and KQED) tells the story of Tenderloin "street queens" and "the first known act of collective violent resistance to the social oppression of queer people in the United States" in 1966, including recent interviews of participants.

For a long time, Vietnamese Youth Development Center and filmmaker Spencer Nakasako collaborated to produce videos on the lived experiences of Southeast Asian youth who lived in the Tenderloin. "a.k.a., Don Bonus," the Emmy award winning film shows the senior year of a Cambodian youth struggling, with his family, to become a part of American society. "Kelly Loves Tony," is about a young Mien (an ethnic group that migrated from China to Southeast Asia over several centuries) couple in Oakland, she a straight A student, planning to go to college, he trying to leave the gang life behind; and "Refugee" the story of Mike Siv returning to Cambodia, bringing along David Mack and Sophal (Paul) Meas, Tenderloin residents and Tenderloin U students, going, for the first time, to the land of their ancestors.

Finally, on YouTube, there are many videos that people have lovingly or discontentedly posted over the years, supporting or denigrating The TL.

APPENDIX II

LIST OF STREET TEACHERS

- Jim Thompson, Tenderloin Community on Patrol; Manager, Aspen Apartments
- Diana Chin, Tenderloin Children's Playground
- Angela Alioto, Chair, Mayor's Task Force on Homelessness; former President, Board of Supervisors Vietnamese Youth Development Center
- Michael Marcum, Under Sheriff, SF Sheriff's Department
- Lillian B. Rubin, author, *The Transcendent Child*
- Judy Young, Executive Director, Vietnamese Youth Development Center
- Yen Dinh, Vietnamese Youth Development Center
- Phoeut Tak, Vietnamese Youth Development Center
- Catharine Karrels, Principal, De Marillac Academy
- Paul Terry, SF Renaissance Entrepreneurship Center
- Jen Arens, The Salvation Army
- Tami Suzuki, San Francisco Public Library
- Ana Bolton, California Prison Focus and Adopt-A-Block
- Angelina Barisone Cahalan, St. Anthony's Foundation
- John Fitzgerald. St. Anthony Foundation
- Rev. Glenda Hope, San Francisco Network Ministries
- Capt. David Shinn, SFPD – Tenderloin Station
- Chris Daly, San Francisco Board of Supervisors

© The Author(s) 2017
D. Stannard-Friel, *Street Teaching in the Tenderloin*,
DOI 10.1057/978-1-137-56437-5

- Midge Wilson, Bay Area Women's and Children's Center
- Dan Yee, Tenderloin Children's Playground
- Don Mallioux, Tenderloin Children's Playground
- Fr. Louie Vitale, Pastor, St. Boniface Church
- Cade Burkhammer, Artist
- Elaine Buckholtz, Artist, Luggage Store Art Gallery
- Garland Hall, Artist, Seneca Hotel
- Jason Brown, S F Network Ministries
- Tom Heath, Indochinese Housing Development Corporation
- Fang Wen Liao and her family, residents, IHDC
- Nancy Ong, Bay Area Women's and Children's Center
- Nam Thai, Vietnamese Family Services Center
- Kay Rodrigues, Tenderloin Children's Playground.
- Brother Kelly Cullen, Tenderloin Neighborhood Development Corporation
- Brad Paul, Evelyn and Walter Haas, Jr. Fund, former Deputy Mayor for Housing
- Darryl Smith, Director of 509 Culture Club and the Luggage Store Art Galleries
- Jane Kim, San Francisco Board of Supervisors
- Katy Tang, San Francisco Board of Supervisors
- Justin Giarla, Director of The Shooting Gallery
- Connie Handlin, Larkin Street Youth Center
- Dana Blecker, Larkin Street Youth Center
- London Breed, President, San Francisco Board of Supervisors
- Jaedon, Lavender Youth Recreation and Information Center (LYRIC House).
- N'Tanya Lee, Coleman Advocates for Children and Youth
- Lt. Larry Minasian, SFPD-Tenderloin Station
- Kevin Fagan, San Francisco Chronicle
- Sam Marcum, San Francisco Food Bank
- Kris Johnson, Glide Memorial Church
- Kate Robinson, Tenderloin Safe Passage
- George Jurand, SF Sheriff's Department
- Phelicia Jones, Hope Preservation/SF Sheriff's Department
- Joel Lopez, San Francisco LGBT Community Center
- Sharon Woo, Assistant District Attorney (Narcotics), San Francisco
- Sister Carmen Barsody, Faithful Fools
- Bart Casimir, Cecil Williams House

- Anne Williams, Mermaids Tattoos
- Denis, Faithful Fools
- Kat, Faithful Fools
- "Fred," SRO Collective
- Barry Stenger, St. Anthony's Foundation
- Don Falk, Tenderloin Neighborhood Development Corporation
- Julie Dougherty, Tenderloin Neighborhood Development Corporation
- Jennifer Friedenbach, San Francisco Coalition on Homelessness.
- Jory John 826 Valencia: The Pirate Store
- Ken Sommers, Tenderloin Neighborhood Development Corporation
- Jill Tucker, SF Chronicle
- C.W. Nevius, SF Chronicle
- Sgt. Gaetano Caltagirone, SFPD
- John, the bicycle cop, SFPD Chinatown
- Buddhist nun in Chinatown
- Mario and Bob, Coalition on Homelessness
- The women of SAGE
- David Mack, VYDC
- Alex Abalos, VYDC
- Kay Weber, Boys and Girls Club
- Adrian Maldonado, Community/Union Organizer, Delancey Street Foundation
- Capt. John Goldberg, SFPD
- Robert McDaniel, Beoddeker Park
- Penny Schoener, California Prison Focus
- Jamie Kong, DonorsChoose/YouthChoose
- Donal, King of Leavenworth Street
- Lt. Vernell Crittendon, San Quentin Prison
- Lt. Samuel Robinson, San Quentin Prison
- Sgt. Gabriel Walters, San Quentin Prison
- Chief Susan Manheimer, San Mateo P.D. (formerly, Captain SFPD-Tenderloin)
- Dina Hilliard, NOM/TLBD, Tenderloin Safe Passage
- Capt. Joe "Big Red" Garrity, SFPD-Tenderloin Station
- Irene Huey Michaud, SFPD-Tenderloin Station
- Tech Tran, VYDC
- Tiffany Torrevillas, Senior Planner, SF Human Services Agency
- Dan Kelly, Director of Planning, SF Human Services Agency

- Phanna Phay, Boys and Girls' Club, Tenderloin Clubhouse
- Laura Soun, City Impact
- Sam Soun, Indochinese Housing Development Corporation
- Sammy Soun, Boys and Girls' Club, Tenderloin Clubhouse
- Ivan Corado, Boys and Girls' Club, Mission Clubhouse
- Donald, homeless volunteer for Halloween in the Tenderloin
- Leroy Moore, Co-founder and Community Relations Director, Sins Invalid
- Patty Berne, Co-founder and Director, Sins Invalid
- Hugh D'Andrade, Artist
- Sam Dennison, Faithful Fools
- Mary Ganz, Faithful Fools
- Susan Curry, Tenderloin Children's Playground
- Capt. Teresa Ewins, SFPD-Tenderloin Station
- Dean Oshida, Indochinese Housing Development Corporation
- Annie Corbett, Corbett Group Homes and the R.I.S.E. Program
- Necole, Corbett Group Homes and the R.I.S.E. Program
- Yvette Robinson, Tenderloin Neighborhood Development Corporation
- Wai La, Indochinese Housing Development Corporation
- Blair Czarecki, Indochinese Housing Development Corporation
- Glenn Havlan, Tenderloin Children's Playground
- The Larkin Street Youth Center teams, Haight Ashbury office.
- Brent Miller, Center for New Music
- Numerous, nameless others who stopped to talk to us, or responded to our questions, as we walked the neighborhood or engaged them at Project Homeless Connect, County Jail, San Quentin Prison, SRO hotels, or other environments in which they lived, worked, played, received services, or did their time. These "spontaneous street teachers" were a significant part of our learning experience.
- There were other arranged street teachers whose names were left off this list because of the passing of time or their contributions were after it was compiled. Their contributions were also deeply appreciated.

Appendix III

Recommended Readings in Community Engagement

* * *

The broadening appeal of community engagement is demonstrated by a growing demand for books explaining its history, benefits, and uses throughout the academic world, from kindergarten through graduate studies. Most of the rich and varied professional literature on direct learning has been aimed at describing the emergence of the pedagogy, advancing the knowledge and skills of academic leaders and practitioners in the field, or to facilitate students' work in service-learning classes. Among the most notable examples are Stanton, Giles, and Cruz's, *Service-Learning: A Movement's Pioneers Reflect on Its Origins, Practice, and Future*: Jossey-Bass, 1999. Written by three highly regarded, longtime scholar-practitioners, it puts the movement in historical, philosophical, and practical perspective for serious students of community engagement. Colby, et al, in *Educating for Democracy: Preparing Undergraduates for Responsible Political Engagement*: Jossey-Bass, 2007, explains and encourages effective pedagogical strategies, including direct learning, for supporting students' understanding and involvement in democratic political processes. And, *Creating Our Identities in Service-Learning and Community Engagement*: Information Age Publishing, edited by Moely, Billig, and Holland, 2009, presents and discusses more recent aspects of program development, student outcomes, community benefits, and future directions of service learning and community engagement.

© The Author(s) 2017   381
D. Stannard-Friel, *Street Teaching in the Tenderloin*,
DOI 10.1057/978-1-137-56437-5

Illustrations of strategies for, and implementation experiences in, community engagement, written primarily for practitioners, can be found in Paula Mathieu's, *Tactics of Hope: The Public Turn in English Composition*: Boynton/Cook, 2005, which examines "public-academic partnerships" in composition studies; Sally Cahill Tannenbaum's (ed.), *Research, Advocacy, and Political Engagement: Multidisciplinary Perspectives Through Service Learning*: Stylus, 2008, that offers a number of innovative service learning approaches that introduce students to political engagement; and *Democratic Dilemmas of Teaching Service-Learning*: Stylus, 2011, by Christine M. Cress, David M. Donahue, and Associates, which examines the political nature of teaching, in general, and service-learning, in particular, using practitioners' case studies of implementation "dilemmas."

Community Engagement 2.0?: Dialogues on the Future of the Civic in the Disrupted University, edited by Scott L. Crabill and Dan Butin, Palgrave Macmillan, 2014, articulates theories and practices of community engagement in context of the changing nature of traditional "place-based institutions" and the impact of online learning; *Turning Teaching Inside Out, A Pedagogy of Transformation for Community-Based Education*, edited by Simone Weil Davis, and Barbara Sherr Roswell, Palgrave Macmillan, 2013, an exploration of the Inside-Out Prison Exchange Program, that offers classes inside prisons, bringing together inmates and college students as peers; *Deepening Community Engagement in Higher Education*, edited By Ariane Hoy and Mathew Johnson, Palgrave Macmillan, 2013, is a collection of writings that report on the highly regarded work of institutions that reflect qualities recognized by such leaders in the movement as the Carnegie Classification and the Bonner Leadership programs; and *The Engaged Campus: Certificates, Minors, and Majors as the New Community Engagement*, *edited by Dan W. Butin and Scott Seider*, Palgrave Macmillan, 2012, offers ethnographic studies, exploring critical issues and best practices for developing community-based, academic programs in higher education.

NOTES

1. https://www.indiegogo.com/projects/love-me-tenderloin#/
2. www.nationalgeographic.com/channel

ACKNOWLEDGEMENTS

Tenderloin U is network of relationships, organized around the author's Inner City Studies classes. All of the street teachers listed in Appendix II made significant contributions to the classes and this book. Some, not listed as individuals, connected only once, sometimes spontaneously on the streets, but most were scheduled beforehand as representatives of a particular organization or service or way of life. Their contributions are recorded in the pages of this book, but some require special recognition for their longtime involvement and frequent availability. This would include the women of BAWCC and SAGE, service providers from Tenderloin Children's Playground, Boeddeker Park, the Boys and Girls Club, VYDC, IHDC, and TASP. The officers of SFPD and the staffs at TNDC, THC, COP, NOM/TLBD, Faithful Fools, St. Anthony's, Glide, SF Coalition on Homelessness, the Sheriff's Department, Larkin Street Youth Center, San Francisco Network Ministries, White Walls/Shooting Gallery, SF Chronicle, San Quentin State Prison, members of the San Francisco Board of Supervisors, and individuals from Delancey Street Foundation and HOPE Preservation, Inc.

I am also indebted to the owners and staff of Wild Awakenings/Celtic Coffee Company for allowing us to use the coffeehouse as our meeting-up place in the Tenderloin, twice a week, almost every week during the academic year, for two decades, and Farley's Coffeehouse, my "office" on Potrero Hill, for allowing me to sit and write there for hours on end. I am particularly appreciative of Tenderloin residents who opened up their homes so my stu-

© The Author(s) 2017   383
D. Stannard-Friel, *Street Teaching in the Tenderloin*,
DOI 10.1057/978-1-137-56437-5

dents could see how they managed to make such good use of very limited living situations, and the young people of the Tenderloin, who met with my students, attended my classes, participated in our events, and shared their lives. All these people, and many more, made Tenderloin U possible, and gave my students and me lessons in life that we will treasure and benefit from forever.

I also deeply appreciate the NDNU community who supported me by giving me the time and resources to do the work in the Tenderloin, and by volunteering at events and raising and contributing funds and donations of toys, and prizes, and pumpkins. I am, in particular, indebted to the students who enrolled in my classes and gave their all to projects and studies in the Tenderloin and other inner city neighborhoods and often shared stories of their own lives that enriched us all.

And then there is my family, who supported me, walked the streets with me, made suggestions, and volunteered at our events, but most of all, loved me through some of the most challenging and satisfying experiences of my life. I am particularly indebted to Kathy, my wife, who, as always, was there for me day and night, year after year. She worried about me, listened to me, encouraged me, and made comments and suggestions that made my time in the Tenderloin and the writing of this book far more meaningful and valuable than it otherwise would have been. Without her loving support, none of this would have happened.

* * *

I am also indebted to those who wrote articles and took photos that help deepen the reader's appreciation of the issues and stories that I write about, and for those who gave me permission to use those news articles, photographs, poems, emails, personal statements, reflections, and other materials that helped bring these pages to life. Credits for written materials are given in the Endnotes and Bibliography. Permission for photographs were given by San Francisco Chronicle/Polaris for photos by Jeff Chiu: "IHDC" (05339933) and Brant Ward, "San Quentin" (05340439), "Sacred Sleep" (05326223) and "Goin' Down the Rabbit Hole" (05326222). Permission for other photographs were given by U Sam Oeur, "U Sam Oeur: Poet/Survivor;" Tom Heath, "Cemetery Reunion;" Nick Wilcox, "Laura Wilcox: March 5, 1981 – January 10, 2001;" Kate Robinson, Tenderloin Safe Passage, "Yellow Brick Road; Marjorie Beggs, San Francisco Study Center, "Rev. Glenda Hope: Street Minister," Darryl Smith, Luggage Store/509 Cultural Center, "Tenderloin National

Forest;" Kay Weber, "Hel: Goddess of Death;" and Michael Friel for photos of the author and "Twitterloin." Michael, photographer for my earlier book on the Tenderloin, *City Baby and Star: Addiction, Transcendence and the Tenderloin,* was also my consultant on *Street Teaching,* helping me to choose and improve the quality of many of the images.

BIBLIOGRAPHY

BOOKS

Ashbury, Herbert, *The Barbary Coast: An Informal History of the San Francisco Underworld*, New York: Thunder's Mouth Press, 2002

Bell, Megara, *The Fallen Woman in Fiction and Legislation*, Boston: University of Massachusetts at Boston

Benard, Bonnie, *Fostering Resiliency in Kids: Protective Factors in the Family, School, and Community*, Portland, Oregon: Western Center for Drug-Free Schools and Communities, 1991

Bourgois, Philippe and Jeff Schonberg, *Righteous Dopefiend*, Berkeley: University of California Press, 2009

Carroll, Lewis, *Alice's Adventures in Wonderland*, New York: New American Library (Signet Classic Printing), 2000

Carter, Tom, Marjorie Beggs and Others, ed. Geoff Link, San Francisco: Study Center Press, 2012

Castenada, Carlos, *The Teachings of Don Juan: A Yaqui Way of Knowledge*, New York: Ballantine Books, 1968

Davey, Joseph Dillon, *The New Social Contract: America's Journey from Welfare State to Police State*, Westport, CT: Praeger, 1995

Deutsch, Nancy, *Voices of Our Own: Mothers, Daughters, and Elders of the Tenderloin Tell Their Stories*, San Francisco: Published by Nancy Deutsch, 2001

Dewey, J., *Experience and Education*, New York: Collier Books, 1963

Erickson, Kai, *Wayward Puritan: A Study in the Sociology of Deviance*, Upper Saddle River, New Jersey: Prentice Hall, 2004

Fisher, Trevor, *Prostitution and the Victorians*, London: Palgrave Macmillan, 1997

© The Author(s) 2017   387
D. Stannard-Friel, *Street Teaching in the Tenderloin*,
DOI 10.1057/978-1-137-56437-5

Freire, P., *Pedagogy of the Oppressed*. Harmondsworth, UK: Penguin, 1972
Gentry, Curt, *The Madams of San Francisco: An Irreverent History of the City by the Golden Gate*, New York: Doubleday, 1964
Hammett, Dashiell, *The Maltese Falcon*, New York: Alfred A. Knopf, 1929
Heath, Tom, et al., *Stories of Survival: Three Generations of Southeast Asian Americans Share Their Lives*, San Francisco: Indochinese Housing Development Corporation, 2001
Holiday, Billie, *Lady Sings the Blues*, New York: Doubleday, 1956
Kamiya, Gary, *Cool Gray City of Love*, New York: Bloombury USA, 2013
Kerouac, Jack, *On the Road*, New York: Viking, 1957
Kesey, Ken, *One Flew Over the Cuckoo's Nest*, New York: Penguin, 2003
Laing, RD, *The Politics of Experience and The Bird of Paradise*, New York: Penguin, 1970
Lloyd, Rachel, *Girls Like Us*, New York: HarperCollins Publishers, 2011
Lal Vasi, Vibha, with photographs by Nita Winter, *Children of the Tenderloin*, San Francisco: Bay Area Women's and Children's Center, 1987
Moore, Thomas, *Care of the Soul: A Guide for Cultivating Depth and Sacredness in Everyday Life*, New York: HarperCollins Publishers, 1992
Moulden, Julia, *We are the New Radicals*, Columbus, OH, McGraw Hill Education, 2008
Oeur, U Sam, translated by Ken McCullough, *Sacred Vows*, Minneapolis: Coffee House Press.1998
Rubin, Lillian, *The Transcendent Child: Tales of Triumph Over the Past*, New York: Harper Collins, 1997
Shaw, Randy, *The Tenderloin: Sex, Crime, and Resistance in the Heart of San Francisco*, San Francisco: Urban Reality Press, 2015
Sides, Josh, *Erotic City: Sexual Revolutions and the Making of Modern San Francisco*, New York: Oxford University Press, 2009
Stannard-Friel, Don, *City Baby and Star: Addiction, Transcendence, and the Tenderloin*, Lanham, Maryland: University Press of America, 2005
Stannard-Friel, Don, *Harassment Therapy: A Case Study of Psychiatric Violence*, Boston: G.K. Hall & Co./Schenkman Publishing Co., 1981
Stevenson, Bryan, *Just Mercy: A Story of Justice and Redemption*, New York: Spiegel and Grau, 2015
Szasz, M.D., Thomas S., *The Myth of Mental Illness: Foundations of a Theory of Personal Conduct*, New York: Harper Perennial, 2010
Szasz, M.D., Thomas S., *Psychiatric Justice: How the Psychiatric Profession and the Legal Establishment Unwittingly Conspire to Deny Citizens their Constitutional Right to Trial*, New York: The Macmillan Company, 1965
Toffler, Alvin, *Future Shock*, New York: Bantam Books, 1970
Torrey, M.D., E. Fuller, *Out of the Shadows: Confronting America's Mental Illness Crisis*, New York: John Wiley & Sons, 1997

Vollmann, William T., *Whores for Gloria*, New York: Penguin Books, 1994
Wheatley, Margaret, *Leadership and the New Science: Learning about Organizations from an Orderly Universe*, San Francisco: Barrett-Koehler Publishers, 1994
Williams, Rev. Cecil, and Janice Mirikitani, with a forward by Maya Angelou, *I Have Something to Say About This Big Trouble*, San Francisco: Glide Word Press, 1989
Williams, Stanley Tookie, *Blue Rage, Black Redemption, A Memoir*, Pleasant Hill, CA: Damamli Publishing, 2004
Wonderling, Larry, *San Francisco Tenderloin: Heroes, Demons, Angels & Other True Stories*, San Francisco: Cape Foundation Publications, 2001

ARTICLES

Anderson, Glenda, "Clearlake Man, Cleared in One Slaying, Convicted of Murder in Another," *The Press Democrat*, March 11, 2010
Anderson, Glenda, "Clearlake Robbers Shot from Behind," *The Press Democrat*, January 12, 2006
Anderson, Glenda, "Two Bay Area Men Killed, Third Arrested in Clearlake Home Invasion," *The Press Democrat*, December 8, 2005
Anspaugh, Heidi, "Staying Rock 'n' Roll," The Bold Italic: http://www.thebold-italic.com/articles/1049-staying-rock-n-roll
Bennetts, Leslie, "The Growing Demand for Prostitution," *Newsweek*, July 18, 2011
Benard, Bonnie, *Fostering Resiliency in Kids: Protective Factors in the Family, School, and Community*, Portland, OR: Northwest Regional Educational Laboratory, 1991
Cambodian female, age 18, "My Struggle, Too," Heath, Tom, et al, *Stories of Survival: Three Generations of Southeast Asian Americans Share Their Lives*, San Francisco: Indochinese Housing Development Corporation, 2001
Cambodian female, age 35, "A Daughter's Story," Heath, Tom et al, *Stories of Survival: Three Generations of Southeast Asian Americans Share Their Lives*, San Francisco: Indochinese Housing Development Corporation, 2001
Cambodian female, age 32, "Lucky Escape," Heath, Tom, et al, *Stories of Survival: Three Generations of Southeast Asian Americans Share Their Lives*, San Francisco: Indochinese Housing Development Corporation, 2001
CBS 5 Crime Watch, "Change of Venue Approved In Lake Co. Murder Trial," November 16, 2007, http://cbs5.com/local
CBS SF Bay Area Newsletter, "Six Months Later, San Francisco's Tenderloin Cleaner Thanks To Portable Toilets For Homeless," April 8, 2015, http://sanfrancisco.cbslocal.com
Clifford, James O., "School for 'John's' a Reality Check on Prostitution," *Los Angeles Times*, March 2, 1997

Coburn, Judith, "Terror in Saigontown, U.S.A.," *Mother Jones*, February/March 1983

Cothran, George, "Matrix's Happy Face New Statistics Contradict Jordan's Spin on Homeless Crackdown," *SF Weekly* News, March 22 1995

Dalton, Andrew, "Tenderloin Deli To End Heroin Sales, Pay City $30K, *SFist*, July 17, 2012

Do, Anh, Tran Phan, and Eugene Garcia, "Camp Z-30-D: The Survivors," *Orange Country Register.* April 29, 2001

Duggan, Tara, "Tu Lan: Cleaned Up but Still as Good as Ever," *SF Chronicle*, December 24, 2013

Egelko, Bob "Confession of Boy, 10, Raises Doubts Over Grasp of Miranda Rights," *San Francisco Chronicle*, October 25, 2015

Egelko, Bob, "Crime Down, Costs Up Since Prison Realignment, Study Finds," *SF Chronicle*, September 29, 2015

Fagan, Kevin, "Chance to Solve Homeless Crisis/New Mayor Arrives as Warring Factions Agree on Solution," *SF Chronicle*, February 1, 2004

Fagan, Kevin, "Eyewitness: Prisoner Did Not Die Meekly, Quietly," *SF Chronicle*, Wednesday, December 14, 2005

Fagan, Kevin, "Finding Faith in Their Songs / Street performers' Harmonies Belie Lives of Poverty, Discord," *SF Chronicle*, February 24, 1999

Fagan, Kevin, "SHAME OF THE CITY, Homeless 'Mascots' Find Niche in Tony Neighborhoods," Wednesday, December 3, 2003

Fagan, Kevin, "Street Singer Popular With Downtown BART Riders Succumbs to Diabetes", *SF Chronicle*, June 30, 1999

Farley, Melissa. *Prostitution: Factsheet on Human Rights Violations.* Prostitution Research and Education. 2 November 2006, http://www.prostitutionre-search.com

Ford, Matt, "America's Largest Mental Hospital is a Jail," *The Atlantic*, June 8, 2015

Friedenbach, Jennifer, "'Laura's Law a Looming Disaster for Mentally Ill," *SF Examiner*, June 6, 2014

Fugitive Watch, "21-Year Old Man Suffers Life-Threatening Injuries In Tenderloin Shootinghttp"://www.fugitive.com/2012/09/06/21-year-old-man-suffers-life-threatening-injuries-in-tenderloin-shooting/

Garchik, Leah, "Breakfast with Studs," *SF Chronicle*, Friday, October 31, 2003

Gorman, Steve, "California's Death Row Faces No-Vacancy Situation," *Rueters*, Mar 30, 2015

Gould, Jens Erik,/Fullerton, "Should Involuntary Treatment for the Mentally Ill Be the Law?" *Time Magazine*, October 27, 2011

Green, Emily, "No New S.F. Jail After Supervisors Refuse Funding," *SF Chronicle*, December 16, 2015

Hall, Christopher, "Suds, Scents and Soup in San Francisco's Tenderloin," *The New York Times*, August 5, 2014

Hardyaug, Quentin, "Blending Tech Workers and Locals in San Francisco's Troubled Mid-Market, *NY Times*, August 16, 2015

Hing, Bill Ong, "Detention to Deportation - Rethinking the Removal of Cambodian Refugees." *UC Davis Law Review*, Vol. 38, 2005

Hoodline, "*Neighbors Organize Against Tenderloin Group Housing Proposal,*" http://hoodline.com/2015/04/tenderloin-residents-property-owners-organize-against-group-housing-proposal

Jalonick, Mary Clare, "House Panel Approves Bill to Overhaul Sentencing Laws," *Associated Press*, November 18, 2015

Koopman, John, "Husband and Wife - Partners Both on the Beat and at Home," *SF Chronicle*, October 14, 2007

Knight, Heather, "Homeless Dad Featured in The Chronicle Finds New Jobs, Plenty of Hope," *SF Chronicle*, April 28, 2013

Knight, Heather, "Mayor Lee's 5 Years Changed Face of SF," *San Francisco Chronicle*, October 11, 2015

KTVU.com, 'SF Bernal Heights Birthday Party Brawl Leaves 2 Dead: Triple Shooting Rattles Quiet SF Neighborhood, Posted: 8:18 pm PDT May 14, 2011, Updated: 2:32 pm PDT May 16, 2011

KTVU.com, "Triple Shooting Rattles Quiet SF Neighborhood," Posted: 8:18 pm PDT May 14, 2011

Kurwa, Nishat, "City Divided Over Tech's Clout in San Francisco," *Huffington Post*, March 15, 2013.

Kwong, Jessica, "Former Tenants Sue After SRO Housing Made into Group Apartments," *The Examiner*, September 13, 2014

Lagos, Marisa, "Laura's Law Passes Easily in S.F. Supervisors' Vote Easy Passage Belies the Years of Debate on Implementation of State Measure," *SF Chronicle*, July 9, 2014

Larson, Elisabeth, "Edmonds, Norton Held on $1 Million Bail for Tuesday Homicide," *Lake County News*, September 22, 2009

Larson, Elizabeth, "Hughes Sentenced to State Prison; Appeal Expected," *Lake County News*, September 8, 2008

Lelchuk, Ilene "BAYVIEW-HUNTERS POINT / S.F.'s Invisible Majority / Area With Highest Density of Children is Most Underserved," *SF Chronicle*, May 31, 2006

Jack London, "South of the Slot," *Saturday Evening Post*, May 1909

Lucchesi, Paolo, "Tu Lan Shut Down by Health Department," *San Francisco Chronicle*, July 31, 2012.

Martin, Adam, "Police Resist Sexual Predator's S.F. Placement," *San Francisco Examiner*, Jan 13, 2007

May, Meredith, "Norma Hotaling Dies - Fought Prostitution," *SF Chronicle*, December 20, 2008

May, Meredith, "'Tenderlointreon' a Hit with Young Film Fans," *SF Chronicle*, May 1, 2009

Martin, Glen, "Neighbors Reclaim Park in Style," *SF Chronicle*, June 20, 1996

Moore, Derek J., "Hughes' Attorney Turns Tables on Edmonds, Defense Calls Witnesses Who Say Alleged Victim Is Really Violent Drug Dealer," *The Press Democrat*, Wednesday, June 25, 2008

Nevius, C.W., "Tenderloin Gets Trendy, Apparently on the Way Up," *SF Chronicle*, July 2, 2011

Nevius, C. W., "Tenderloin Police Captain Will Be Missed," *SF Chronicle*, May 11, 2013

Nevius, C.W., "Tenderloin Top Cop Reluctantly Accepts Promotion," C.W. Nevius, *SF Chronicle*, May 7, 2013

Padgett, Juliaglenn, "Author: Politics Responsible for Mass Incarceration," *San Quentin News*,

Phay, Chet, "What is Freedom?" Tom Heath, et al, *Stories of Survival: Three Generations of Southeast Asian Americans Share Their Lives*, San Francisco: Indochinese Housing Development Corporation, 2001

Phay, Phanna, "Freedom," *Stories of Survival: Three Generations of Southeast Asian Americans Share Their Lives*, San Francisco: Indochinese Housing Development Corporation, 2001

Phay, Phanna, "Life Ain't Free," *Stories of Survival: Three Generations of Southeast Asian Americans Share Their Lives*, San Francisco: Indochinese Housing Development Corporation, 2001

Rifkin, Rich, "At long last, Laura's Law is being implemented," *The Davis Enterprise*, May 13, 2015

Rinker, Brian, "Viral Vice Article On Tenderloin Drug Use Elicits Criticism, Personal Narrative," *Golden Gate Xpress*, March 9, 2013

Roberts, Nancy, "Trendy Nightlife in San Francisco's Tenderloin" Ask Miss A, Charity Meets Style, June 15, 2011:http://askmissa.com/2011/06/15/trendy-nightlife-in-san-franciscos-tenderloin/#sthash.4wnePzEn.dpufhttp

Salter, Stephanie, "New Team Spirit in the Tenderloin," *SF Chronicle*, June 29, 2003

Smith, M. K., "What is Pedagogy?' *The Encyclopaedia of Informal Education*, 2012, http://infed.org/mobi/what-is-pedagogy/

Somov, Ph.D., Pavel, "Compassion: To Understand Is To Forgive, *Huffington Post*, January 24, 2010

Sullivan, Kathleen, "Cleaning up Tenderloin park, Petition seeks to rid Boeddeker of squalor, violence," *SF Examiner*, September 28, 1995

Sward, Susan, and Jaxon Van Derbeken, "Internal Investigator Who Ruffled the SFPD / Cop Transferred Off Probe of Fracas Is Known as Straight-Talking, Duty-Bound Workaholic," *SF Chronicle*, January 19, 2003

Tanner, Lindsay, Associated Press, "Personality Disorders Affecting Young Adults," *U-T San Diego*, December 2, 2005

Torassa, Ulysses, "Method of Treatment for Drug Addiction / S.F. models 'harm reduction' theory" *SF Chronicle*, January 15, 2001

Tucker, Jill, "Hillary Clinton Turns to S.F. Doctor to Help Kids", *SF Chronicle*, June 23, 2013

Tucker, Jill, "S.F. Schools Struggle with More Homeless Kids," *SF Chronicle*, December 4, 2011

Tucker, Jill, "Teenager Shot and Killed in Own Home," *SF Chronicle Staff Writer*, June 14, 2010

Van Derbeken, Jaxon, "S.F. Man, 18, Charged in Teen's Slaying," *SF Chronicle*, July 20, 2010

Vekshin, Alison, and Dan Levy. "Twitter Tax Break is Target in San Francisco Income War," *Bloomberg Business*. April 2, 2014

White, Bobby, "San Francisco's Red-Light Denizens Fight to Stay Seedy," *The Wall Street Journal*, October 24, 2006

Whiting, Sam, "Promise Fulfilled: Required Public Art Springs Up on Mid-Market," *SF Chronicle*, Wednesday, February 11, 2015

Williams, Rita, "A CASE OF MURDER?" KTVU.com Special Report On Clearlake Murder Case, July 8, 2008

Worth, Katie, "Methods for Counting San Francisco's Homeless Questioned," *San Francisco Examiner*, January 26, 2011

Yollin, Patricia, "Bayview Success Story's Tragic End / Heroic Track Star Shot Dead After Failing School, Turning to Crime," *SFGate.com*, January 18, 2006

Yollin, Patricia, "Families Agonize Over Bizarre Murder Case / Hearing on Killings of Troubled Ex-hero, Friend Wrapping Up," *SFGate.com*, February 07, 2006

Zhu, Julie Chen, "A Chinese Massage Parlor: An Inside Look at an Oriental Massage Parlor in San Francisco," http://www.logoi.com/logi_notes.html

50-year-old Cambodian male, "My Country, My Children," *Stories of Survival: Three Generations of Southeast Asian Americans Share Their Lives*, San Francisco, Indochinese Housing Development Corporation, 2001

Reports

"Afghanistan Opium Survey 2008," United Nations Office on Drugs and Crime, August 2008

"Ending Homelessness: The Philanthropic Role," The National Foundation Advisory Group for Ending Homelessness, 2003

"The Forgotten: A Critical Analysis of Homeless Policy in San Francisco," San Francisco Coalition on Homelessness, May 2005

"*International Narcotics Control Strategy Report,*" U.S. Department of State. Bureau for International Narcotics and Law Enforcement Affairs. March 2002

"*National Drug Threat Assessment 2010,*" U.S. Department of Justice. Drug Enforcement Administration. December 2009

"*National Drug Threat Assessment 2010,*" U.S. Department of Justice. National Drug Intelligence Center. February 2010

"The San Francisco Task Force on Prostitution Final Report, March 1996

"*SOH 2012: Chapter One-Homelessness Counts Report*," National Alliance to End Homelessness, January 17, 2012

"*The State of Homelessness in America 2012,*" National Alliance to End Homelessness and The Homeless Research Institute, January 2012

"*2011 San Francisco Homeless Count Report,*" United States Interagency Council on Homelessness, August 2, 2011

VIDEOS

Spencer Nakasako's Trilogy:
    "a.k.a. Don Bonus," directed by Spencer Nakasako, 1995
    "Kelly Loves Tony," directed by Spencer Nakasako, 1998
    "Refugee," directed by Spencer Nakasako, 2002
Produced by Aram Sui Wai Collier and Emunah Yuka Edinburgh, Associate Producers Mike Siv and Judy Chea, in collaboration with VVDC Youth DVD Crew, 2002
"Drugs Inc." by Wall to Wall for National Geographic Channel, 2013
"Love Me Tenderloin," directed by Henri Quenette, coproduced by Denny Packard and Henri Quenette, 2004
"Screaming Queens: The riot at Compton's Cafeteria," produced by Victor Silverman and Susan Stryker, in association with ITVS and KQED, 2005
"Very Young Girls," directed by David Schisgall, Nina Alvarez, produced by Nina Alvarez, 2007

WEBSITES

Embassy of the Republic of the Marshall Islands, http://www.rmiembassyus.org
Mark Ellinger, upfromthedeep.com

Index[1]

[1] Note: Page numbers followed by 'n' refer footnotes.

© The Author(s) 2017
D. Stannard-Friel, *Street Teaching in the Tenderloin*,
DOI 10.1057/978-1-137-56437-5

0 1341 1717548 6

CPSIA information can be obtained
at www.ICGtesting.com
Printed in the USA
LVHW07*1438170518
577553LV00022B/301/P

9 781137 564368